THINKING THROUGH THE ESSAY

SECOND EDITION

THINKING THROUGH THE ESSAY

SECOND EDITION

Judith Barker-Sandbrook
Scarborough Board of Education
Scarborough, Ontario

Neil Graham
Scarborough Board of Education
Scarborough, Ontario

McGraw-Hill Ryerson Limited

Toronto   Montreal   New York   Auckland   Bogotá   Caracas
Lisbon   London   Madrid   Mexico   Milan   New Delhi
Paris   San Juan   Singapore   Sydney   Tokyo

Thinking Through the Essay
Second Edition

Copyright © McGraw-Hill Ryerson Limited, 1993, 1986. All rights
reserved. No part of this publication may be reproduced or
transmitted in any form or by any means, or stored in a data base or
retrieval system, without the prior written permission of McGraw-
Hill Ryerson Limited.

ISBN 0-07-551416-8

1 2 3 4 5 6 7 8 9 10   BG   2 1 0 9 8 7 6 5 4 3

Printed and bound in Canada

Care has been taken to trace ownership of copyright material
contained in this text. The publishers will gladly accept any
information that will enable them to rectify any reference or credit
in subsequent editions.

Canadian Cataloguing in Publication Data

Barker-Sandbrook, Judith
    Thinking through the essay

2nd ed.
Includes bibliographical references.
ISBN 0-07-551416-8

1. English language — Rhetoric.   2. Exposition
(Rhetoric).   3. Essays.   I. Graham, Neil.
II.   Title.

PE1471.B36   1993   808'.0427   C93-093761-9

The authors of this text have used inclusive, nonsexist language. The essays
have been reprinted using their original wording.

Publisher: Janice Matthews
Associate Editor: Nancy Christoffer
Senior Supervising Editor: Carol Altilia
Permissions Editor: Jacqueline Donovan
Copy Editor: Edie Franks
Typesetter: Compeer Typographic Services Limited
Cover and Text Design: John Zehethofer

This book was manufactured in Canada using acid-free and recycled paper.

Contents

Acknowledgements

Judith Barker-Sandbrook would like to thank Mac Gunter, Nora Campbell, Gabe Kampf, and Frank Calnan of Sir Oliver Mowat C.I., Scarborough, Ontario, for their assistance in the preparation of the manuscript. Thanks also go to Samantha, Richard, and Baxter for their help and patience.

Neil Graham expresses his thanks to Patricia Graham, teacher-librarian at Dr. Norman Bethune Collegiate, Scarborough, Ontario, for her assistance in locating material and to Michael Stubitsch, Program Department, Scarborough Board of Education, for his ongoing suggestions.

A number of people kindly reviewed the manuscript of the second edition of *Thinking Through the Essay*. The authors are grateful to the following persons for their instructive comments and suggestions: Marilyn Eisenstat, Beverley Miller, Hugh Penton, Peter Smith, and Jon Terpening. Thanks also to the many students who offered their perspectives on the manuscript, particularly the following reviewers: Peter Attia, Sam Blythe, Brenda Chow, Natasha Derewsha, Nick Holyome, Kris Janssen, Michelle Patterson, and Silip Sadana.

A special word of thanks is extended to Nancy Christoffer of McGraw-Hill Ryerson for her assistance in helping to shape and integrate the various elements of the text, and to Janice Matthews, Carol Altilia, Jacqueline Donovan, and Crystal Shortt of McGraw-Hill Ryerson for their encouragement, suggestions, and contributions.

A Note to Students

This text has been developed in collaboration with students like yourself and focusses on your specific needs as a student preparing for postsecondary work. We hope you will find the results both enjoyable and useful.

You are invited to refine your critical thinking and language skills and to exercise independence and initiative as you read the essays and complete the suggested activities. In consultation with your teacher and teacher-librarian, you may devise your own applications which will help you to achieve your personal and academic goals.

The essay collection represents the types of reading you will encounter at the postsecondary level. The essays have a high rating from students for their ability to stimulate independent thought, promote class discussion, and provide a model for good writing. The selected essays include a number of student-written essays, and tips for writing the specific essay form.

The text has been organized into two parts. Part A, Essays for Language and Literature, contains 11 units: an introduction to thought and language and ten other units covering the major reading and writing forms you will meet in the postsecondary world. Each unit contains:

- a Key Work modelling the essay form
- Associated Readings which enrich your understanding of the form and/or content of the Key Work

You and your teacher may wish to begin with several selections from the introductory unit, "Core Essays: The Link Between Thought and Language," and then explore other units according to individual needs and class interests. "Getting Started" (p. 1) and "Guide to Themes and Topics" (p. 333) suggest other avenues of exploration. We suggest that you read "Transitions" (p. 314) early in the course. In this interview with students and a Student Services Counsellor you will find practical tips on setting goals and focussing your efforts during this important school year.

You will notice that within each unit a broad choice of suggested activities is grouped under six headings:

- Before Reading — focusses your thoughts on an essay's content and form.
- Exploring the Essay — encourages close reading and analysis.
- Extensive Study — helps you to apply or respond to ideas in the Key Work, to synthesize, evaluate, assess, and draw comparisons and contrasts.
- The Writing Folder — focusses your attention on refining your writing process.
- Independent Study — directs you to develop a project related to ideas raised in one or more essays.
- Timed Reading and Writing — includes time constraints such as those imposed by tests and examinations.

Finally, you will find that Part B, Tips for Students, provides practical how-to advice on refining your writing process, conducting an independent study project, preparing a seminar, and writing examinations. Also included are suggested supplementary resources.

Part A

Essays for Language and Literature

GETTING STARTED

Before you begin working with the essays in this text, we suggest you peruse these introductory pages. They will guide you in reading and responding to the essays and will help you prepare for the work in this text and in your course as a whole.

Responding to the Content: Appreciation and Personal Response

When we read, we interpret, judge, and appreciate meaning in the context of our own personal experience. That is why we begin each unit in this text with questions that ask you to reflect on what you already know about what you will be reading. Questions then follow that ask you to interpret, evaluate, extend, and finally to apply ideas from your reading in personally relevant ways through independent study and exploration.

To ensure you get as much as possible from each essay you read, you should keep the following questions in mind.

- What is my overall reaction to the essay? e.g., delight, surprise, dismay, confusion, annoyance, fascination, anger, amusement, etc.
- What essential meaning do I get from the essay? Is there any point or part of it I would like to ask the author to elaborate on or clarify?
- What would I change if I had written the essay?

Responding to Conventions of the Form

As you know, essays come in a variety of forms, each with its own conventions. For example, the conventions of the literary essay are quite different from those of the report. On the other hand, some forms of essays are closely linked and share conventions, for example, the narrative essay and the classical essay. With modern journalism, you will note that writers experiment with new forms and develop new conventions.

With the exception of the first unit in this text, each unit begins by specifying the conventions of the essay form that is its focus. Before proceeding, you may wish to review the specific terminology used to describe the conventions of form.

Purpose	WHY has the author written the essay?
Audience	FOR WHOM is the essay written?
Tone	What is the writer's ATTITUDE to the subject?
Voice	Is the writer's own PERSONALITY evident?
Response	What intellectual and/or emotional AUDIENCE RESPONSE is intended?
Language	LEVEL — Is the language formal, colloquial, or a blend? CHARACTERISTICS — Is the language strongly denotative or connotative? Are there strong images?
Structure	What structural elements (paragraphing, thesis placement, graphs) are employed? Is there a clear introduction, body, and conclusion?

Responding Creatively to the Essay

As you work through the essays in this book, you may wish to create some of your own activities to share your learning. To begin, you might adapt the following suggestions for individual, partner, and whole-class presentations:

1. Capture a writer's style or voice in music, light, or movement.
2. Represent an essay's structure in a tableaux or freeze-frame.
3. Dramatize your response to an issue.
4. Recreate a key conflict from a narrative essay, profile, or diary.
5. Present a live story-telling session that presents an essay's controversies or conflicts.
6. Begin a presentation with a one-minute representation of the essay's central focus; e.g., a puppet show, mime, or in-role.

7. Review for a test by dramatizing "key moments" or issues from a group of essays.
8. Deliver a dramatic reading of a speech or an essay.
9. With a partner, debate conflicting issues, perhaps as an in-role presentation.
10. Present an essay's ideas or style on videotape.

1. Core Essays: The Link Between Thought and Language

KEY WORK:

> "Northrop Frye Talks About the Role of the Humanities" —
> *Columns*, Marvi Ricker

ASSOCIATED READINGS:

> "Politics and the English Language" — George Orwell
> "Knowing How to Think" — Royal Bank Letter
> "English as Second Language, English as First Love" —
> Stephen Baker
> "Guilty verdict in the murder of the language" — George
> Gamester
> "Revision or What Have I Actually Said?" — Jacques Barzun
> "The Writer at Work" — Brenda Chow (student essay)

Have you ever thought about the importance of language in our lives? Have you ever wondered what would happen if we were unable to communicate our most basic thoughts and needs? Or if we couldn't share a fascinating idea or a strong feeling? As someone has said, "language provides the handles with which we grasp the world."

The Key Work and the Associated Readings about language and thought provide the major focus for *Thinking Through the Essay:* that clear thinking and effective language are at the heart of successful communication. In the Key Work, Northrop Frye discusses the importance of thinking and language and explores their interrelation. The two Associated Readings, "Politics and the English Language" and "Knowing How to Think," also focus on the connection between thought and language and offer practical tips on successful communication. The other Associated Readings provide different perspectives on the link between thought and language: George Gamester takes a humorous look at the abuse of language and thought, Stephen Baker praises the versatility of English as a medium of communication, and Jacques Barzun describes the importance of revision as a means of clarifying thought. Finally, Brenda Chow reflects on the writing process from a student's perspective.

BEFORE READING

1. In small groups answer the question: "What is thinking?" Compare group responses and develop a class definition.
2. Discuss with a partner whether it is possible to think without language.
3. Should thinking be taught as a subject in school? If it were, what kind of activities might go on in the classroom?

Northrop Frye Talks About the Role of the Humanities

COLUMNS, MARVI RICKER, EDITOR

COLUMNS

What is the role of the humanities in today's technological world?

DR. FRYE

The humanities came into existence around the time of the Renaissance to distinguish the study of human matters from the things that were concerned with theology on the one hand and nature on the other. The things concerned with nature became the source of modern science, but that still left the study of mankind itself. Mankind is the only organism that has been able to study itself as a thing, as something in the world. And while part of that study belongs to the sciences, the central part of it, the construction of the imaginative models of experience, belongs to the humanities.

The humanities are primarily verbal disciplines. At the centre are language and literature, the disinterested study of words. Around them is philosophy, the verbal organization of ideas, and history which is essentially the actualizing of memory. Man without memory becomes senile, and this is just as true of a civilization as it is of an individual. The literary imagination, of course, creates a world of possibilities, and these possibilities are alternative ways of seeing things. Briefly, it is the business of the humanities to nurture the capacity to articulate. Articulateness builds the human community. The surest way to destroy freedom is to destroy the capacity to articulate freely.

COLUMNS

Would you say, then, that a training in the arts is a better preparation for our technological society than a training in science?

DR. FRYE

We tend to regard the arts and sciences as being very different from one another, and this is true up to a point. The sciences are primarily concerned with the world as it is, and the arts are primarily concerned with the world man wants to live in. What is not readily recognized is the fact that both require the same mental processes. Reason and a sense of fact are as important to the novelist as they are to the chemist. Genius and creative imagination play the same role in mathematics that they do in poetry. Laws and principles exist just as much in the verbal disciplines as they do in the sciences. And precision, clarity, and the ability to reason are just as much the concern of the student of the humanities as they are of the student of science.

The humanities graduate is not condemned simply to teach what he has been taught. In fact, he is much less likely to be the victim of technological unemployment than someone who has learned only specific skills. The businessman who hires someone totally inarticulate soon finds out that such a person is no more use to him than someone who falls asleep on the job. But the humanities graduate who has developed good verbal skills, whose mind has been framed to be flexible and adjustable, will find many options open to him.

COLUMNS

How do we develop good verbal skills?

DR. FRYE

The acquisition of verbal skill is a continuous process. The informal, and much larger part of it, comes from casual conversations, social contacts of all kinds, contacts with the media, with advertising and with the printed word. The formal part starts in school and continues through university. When we examine just this formal part we find that it is beset with difficulties and misconceptions.

How well you can read or write is largely a matter of practice. The habit of practice, of progress through repeated, sometimes mechanically repeated effort, is something that used to be inculcated through the formal classical training in Latin and Greek. It was a training which imposed a kind of mental discipline that is apparently impossible in the modern school. And an added advantage of the classical training was that it introduced you to languages that had certain kinds of structure. Linguists today are busy telling us that English is not constructed the way Latin was; nevertheless, if you approach English on something like a Latin model you get a sense of the structure of language. I don't think I could ever have become a writer if I had not been exposed to the teaching of grammar in elementary school of a kind that often is just not given now. Grammar taught me language as a structure. I even learned the elementary categories of philosophy from grammar, things like the concrete, the abstract, the particular and the universal.

I think that a student often leaves high school today without any sense of language as a structure. He may also have the idea that reading and writing are elementary skills that he mastered in childhood, never having grasped the fact that there are differences in levels of reading and writing as there are in mathematics between short division and integral calculus. Yet, in spite of his limited verbal skills, he firmly believes that he can think, that he has ideas, and that if he is just given the opportunity to express them he will be all right. Of course, when you look at what he's written you find it doesn't make any sense. When you tell him this he is devastated.

Part of his confusion here stems from the fact that we use the word "think" in so many bad, punning ways. Remember James Thurber's Walter Mitty who was always dreaming great dreams of glory. When his wife asked him what he was doing he would say, "Has it ever occurred to you that I might be thinking?" But, of course, he wasn't thinking at all. Because we use it for everything our minds do, worrying, remembering, day-dreaming, we imagine that thinking is something that can be achieved without any training. But again it's a matter of practice. How well we can think depends on how much of it we have already done. Most students need to be taught, very carefully and patiently, that there is no such thing as an inarticulate idea waiting to have the right words wrapped around it. They have to learn that ideas do not exist until they have been incorporated into words.

COLUMNS

Your comments suggest there are very few articulate people. Why?

DR. FRYE

The operation of thinking is the practice of articulating ideas until they are in the right words. And we can't think at random either. We can only add one more idea to the body of something we have already thought about. Most of us spend very little time doing this, and that is why there are so few people whom we regard as having any power to articulate at all. When such a person appears in public life, like Mr. Trudeau, we tend to regard him as possessing a gigantic intellect.

A society like ours doesn't have very much interest in literacy. It is compulsory to read and write because society must have docile and obedient citizens. We are taught to read so that we can obey the traffic signs and to cypher so that we can make out our income tax, but development of verbal competency is very much left to the individual.

And when we look at our day-to-day existence we can see that there are strong currents at work against the development of powers of articulateness. Young adolescents today often betray a curious sense of shame about speaking articulately, of framing a sentence with a period at the end of it. Part of the reason for this is the powerful anti-intellectual drive which is constantly present in our society. Articulate speech marks you out as an individual, and in some settings this can be rather dangerous because people are often suspicious and frightened of articulateness. So if you say as little as possible and use only stereotyped, ready-made phrases you can hide yourself in the mass.

Then there are various epidemics sweeping over society which use unintelligibility as a weapon to preserve the present power structure. By making things as unintelligible as possible, to as many people as possible, you can hold the present power structure together. Understanding and articulateness lead to its destruction. This is the kind of thing that George Orwell was talking about, not just in *Nineteen Eighty-Four*, but in all his work on language. The kernel of everything reactionary and tyrannical in society is the impoverishment of the means of verbal communication.

The vast majority of things that we hear today are prejudices and cliches, simply verbal formulas that have no thought behind them but are put up as a pretence of thinking. It is not until we realize these things conceal meaning, rather than reveal it, that we can begin to develop our own powers of articulateness.

The teaching of humanities is, therefore, a militant job. Teachers are faced not simply with a mass of misconceptions and unexamined assumptions. They must engage in a fight to help the student confront and reject the verbal formulas and stock responses, to convert passive acceptance into active, constructive power. It is a fight against illiteracy and for the maturation of the mental processes, for the development of skills which once acquired will never become obsolete.

EXPLORING THE KEY WORK: THE LINK BETWEEN THOUGHT AND LANGUAGE

1. a. Outline the similarities and differences Frye sees between the sciences and the humanities.
   b. Explain why Frye favours all students being taught the humanities.
   c. To what extent do you agree with his position?

2. a. Summarize Frye's response to the question, "How do we develop good verbal skills?"
   b. Explain what Frye sees as a weakness in today's high school graduate.
   c. To what extent do you agree with Frye's observations?

3. a. How does Frye describe the "operation of thinking"?
   b. Compare your prereading response to "What is thinking?" with Frye's description. Account for any differences.

4. State and react to Frye's concerns about the potential consequences for a society that "doesn't have very much interest in literacy."

5. In groups assess the extent to which you agree with Frye's contention that: "the vast majority of things that we hear today are prejudices and cliches, simply verbal formulas that have no thought behind them but are put up as a pretence of thinking." Refer to "the things we hear today" in such areas as advertising politics, sports, technology, and everyday conversation.

   [You may wish to refer to the Associated Reading "Guilty verdict in the murder of the language" (p. 37) and to "Bizbuzz" (p. 291).]

EXTENSIVE STUDY

1. Read "Politics and the English Language" by George Orwell (p. 12).
   As Frye indicated, Orwell's thesis is that just as our thinking can corrupt the language we use, so too can the kind of language we use corrupt our thinking. In the first half of the essay he examines the first situation, and in the last half he examines the latter, beginning "But if thought corrupts language, language can also corrupt thought."
   a. According to Orwell, in what ways can thought corrupt language?
   b. Use his six rules for clear thinking to rate your ability to think clearly.
   c. According to Orwell, in what ways can language corrupt thought?
   d. Use his six rules for effective language to rate your ability to employ language effectively.

2. In small groups role-play a political party "question and answer period" that demonstrates Orwell's contention that political language often obscures meaning. You might use a current newspaper or magazine to locate controversial issues. Try to mimic the political jargon you have heard on television or read in print. You may wish to brainstorm a list of these words and expressions before you begin.

3. Read "Knowing How to Think" (p. 24) which provides guides to more logical thinking.
   a. Identify these guides and explain their usefulness.
   b. In what way might these guides lead to a "happier and healthier life"?
   c. To what extent do you think it is possible to put these guides into practice?

4. a. Read "Politics and the English Language" (p. 12) and "English as Second Language, English as First Love" (p. 32), and compare Orwell's and Baker's perspectives on the state of the English language.
   b. Describe your thoughts on the state of the English language from your perspective as a speaker of English as a first or second language.

5. Read "The Writer at Work" (p. 40) by Brenda Chow and evaluate the essay according to Orwell's rules of thought and language. You might wish to compare evaluations with other students.

THE WRITING FOLDER

1. How would Orwell assess your writing style? Exchange one of the polished pieces in your writing folder with a partner. Use Orwell's rules for thought and language to evaluate the piece. In the persona of George Orwell, make observations on successful aspects of the writing and on areas for improvement.

2. Use Frye's and Orwell's discussion of the link between thought and language to develop a case against their use of gender-biased language in their essays.

3. Write an imaginative response to the key ideas in one or more of the essays. For example, you might write an interview with one of the authors in this unit with you in the role of a talk show host.

INDEPENDENT STUDY

1. Read *Doublespeak: How Government, Business, Advertisers, and Others Use Language to Deceive You* by William Lutz and *Amusing Ourselves to Death* by Neil Postman.

   Examine the impact of government, business, and the mass media on thought and language. Your study should culminate in an oral presentation and a written essay or report.

2. Read George Orwell's 1984 and one of Anthony Burgess's *A Clockwork Orange* or Aldous Huxley's *Brave New World* which examine the future of language and thought. Write a comparative study of the thought-language issue as it is developed in the two novels and present your findings to the class.

3. Throughout history writers have experimented with the links between thought and language in their attempt to better shape meaning. In consultation with your teacher and teacher-librarian, select one of the following genres and examine how one or more writers in that genre have experimented with language and meaning.

   Poetry — Consider writers such as T.S. Eliot, e.e. cummings, Leonard Cohen, Robert Frost (see "The Way to the Poem," p. 85), Eve Merriam, Carl Sandburg, Ezra Pound, Susan Musgrave, Dylan Thomas, John Lennon and Paul McCartney, Paul Simon, Bill Bishop, Emily Dickinson, and Sylvia Plath.

   Drama — Consider writers such as Harold Pinter, Luigi Pirandello, Thornton Wilder, Edward Albee, Albert Camus, and Samuel Beckett.

Fiction — Consider writers such as John Fowles, Virginia Woolf, Ernest Hemingway, J.D. Salinger, Anthony Burgess, Alice Walker, Herman Hesse, Margaret Atwood, Doris Lessing, William Faulkner, Kurt Vonnegut, and Evelyn Waugh.

TIMED READING AND WRITING

Your teacher will determine the time limit and length of written work when it is assigned.

1. Write a response to Orwell's claim that when composing hurriedly it is natural to fall into a pretentious style. Use your own experience to support your position. For example, do you think and write differently on examinations and tests than you do when composing for your writing folder?

2. a. Read "Revision or What Have I Actually Said?" (p. 38) and summarize it in three or four sentences.

   b. Analyze your revision habits in terms of this article. Describe how you could use the advice to improve your revision skills.

Politics and the English Language

GEORGE ORWELL

Most people who bother with the matter at all would admit that the English language is in a bad way, but it is generally assumed that we cannot by conscious action do anything about it. Our civilization is decadent, and our language — so the arguments runs — must inevitably share in the general collapse. It follows that any struggle against the abuse of language is a sentimental archaism, like preferring candles to electric light or hansom cabs to aeroplanes. Underneath this lies the half-conscious belief that language is a natural growth and not an instrument which we shape for our own purposes.

Now, it is clear that the decline of a language must ultimately have *political and economic causes*: it is not due simply to the bad influences of this or that individual writer. But an effect can become a cause, reinforcing the original cause and producing the same effect in an intensified form, and so on indefinitely. A man may take to drink because he feels himself to be a failure, and then fail all the more completely because he drinks. It is rather the same thing that is happening to the English language. It becomes ugly and inaccurate because our thoughts are foolish, but the slovenliness of our language makes it easier for us to have foolish thoughts. The point is that the process is reversible. Modern English, especially written English, is full of bad habits which spread by imitation and which can be avoided if one is willing to take the necessary trouble. If one gets rid of these habits one can think more clearly, and to think clearly is a necessary first step towards political regeneration: so that the fight against bad English is not frivolous and is not the exclusive concern of professional writers. I will come back to this presently, and I hope that by that time the meaning of what I have said here will have become clearer. Meanwhile, here are five specimens of the English language as it is now habitually written.

These five passages have not been picked out because they are especially bad — I could have quoted far worse if I had chosen — but because they illustrate various of the mental vices from which we now suffer. They are a little below the average, but are fairly representative samples. I number them so I can refer back to them when necessary:

> 1. I am not, indeed, sure whether it is not true to say that the Milton who once seemed not unlike a seventeenth-century Shelley had not become, out of an experience ever more bitter in each year, more alien (sic) to the founder of that Jesuit sect which nothing could induce him to tolerate.
>
> Professor Harold Laski (Essay in *Freedom of Expression*)

> 2. Above all, we cannot play ducks and drakes with a native battery of idioms which prescribes such egregious collocations of vocables as the Basic *put up with for tolerate or put at a loss for bewilder.*
>
> Professor Lancelot Hogben (*Interglossa*)

> 3. On the one side we have the free personality: by definition it is not neurotic, for it has neither conflict nor dream. Its desires, such as they are, are transparent, for they are just what institutional approval keeps in the forefront of consciousness; another institutional pattern would alter their number and intensity; there is little in them that is natural, irreducible, or culturally dangerous. But *on the other side*, the social bond itself is nothing but the mutual reflection of these self-secure integrities. Recall the definition of love. Is

not this the very picture of a small academic? Where is there a place in this hall of mirrors for either personality or fraternity?

Essay on psychology in *Politics* (New York)

4. All the 'best people' from the gentlemen's clubs, and all the frantic Fascist captains, united in common hatred of Socialism and bestial horror of the rising tide of the mass revolutionary movement, have turned to acts of provocation, to foul incendiarism, to medieval legends of poisoned wells, to legalize their own destruction to proletarian organizations, and rouse the agitated petty-bourgeoisie to chauvinistic fervour on behalf of the fight against the revolutionary way out of the crisis.

Communist pamphlet

5. If a new spirit is to be infused into this old country, there is one thorny and contentious reform which must be tackled, and that is the humanization and galvanization of the B.B.C. Timidity here will bespeak canker and atrophy of the soul. The heart of Britain may be sound and of strong beat, for instance, but the British lion's roar at present is like that of Bottom in Shakespeare's *Midsummer Night's Dream* — as gentle as any sucking dove. A virile new Britain cannot continue indefinitely to be traduced in the eyes, or rather ears, of the world by the effete languors of Langham Place, brazenly masquerading as 'standard English'. When the voice of Britain is heard at nine o'clock, better far and infinitely less ludicrous to hear aitches honestly dropped than the present priggish, inflated, inhibited, school-ma'amish arch braying of blameless, bashful mewing maidens!

Letter in *Tribune*

Each of these passages has faults of its own, but, quite apart from avoidable ugliness, two qualities are common to all of them. The first is staleness of imagery: the other is lack of precision. The writer either has a meaning and cannot express it, or he inadvertently says something else, or he is almost indifferent as to whether his words mean anything or not. This mixture of vagueness and sheer incompetence is the most marked characteristic of modern English prose, and especially of any kind of political writing. As soon as certain topics are raised, the concrete melts into the abstract and no one seems able to think of turns of speech that are not hackneyed: prose consists less and less of *words* chosen for the sake of their meaning, and more of *phrases* tacked together like the sections of a prefabricated hen-house. I list below, with notes and examples, various of the tricks by means of which the work of prose construction is habitually dodged:

DYING METAPHORS. A newly invented metaphor assists thought by evoking a visual image, while on the other hand a metaphor which is technically 'dead' (e.g., *iron resolution*) has in effect reverted to being an ordinary word and can generally be used without loss of vividness. But in between these two classes there is a huge dump of worn-out metaphors which have lost all evocative power and are merely used because they save people the trouble of inventing phrases for themselves. Examples are: *Ring the changes on, take up the cudgels for, toe the line, ride roughshod over, stand shoulder to shoulder with, play into the hands of, no axe to grind, grist to the mill, fishing in troubled waters, rift within the lute, on the order of the day, Achilles' heel, swan song, hotbed.* Many of these are used without knowledge of their meaning (what is a 'rift', for instance?), and incompatible metaphors are frequently mixed, a sure sign that the writer is not interested in what he is saying. Some metaphors now current have been twisted out of their original meaning without those who use them even being aware of the fact. For example, *toe the line* is sometimes written *tow the line.* Another example is the *hammer and the anvil*, now always used with the implication that the anvil gets the worst of it. In real life it is always the anvil that breaks the hammer, never the other way about: a writer who stopped to think what he was saying would be aware of this, and would avoid perverting the original phrase.

OPERATORS, OR VERBAL FALSE LIMBS. These save the trouble of picking out appropriate verbs and nouns, and at the same time pad each sentence with extra syllables which give it an appearance of symmetry. Characteristic phrases are: *render inoperative, militate against, prove unacceptable, make contact with, be subject to, give rise to, give grounds for, have the effect of, play a leading part (role) in, make itself felt, take effect, exhibit a tendency to, serve the purpose of,* etc. etc. The keynote is the elimination of simple verbs. Instead of being a single word, such as *break, stop, spoil, mend, kill,* a verb becomes a *phrase* made up of a noun or adjective tacked on to some general-purposes verb such as *prove, serve, form, play, render.* In addition, the passive voice is wherever possible used in preference to the active, and noun constructions are used instead of gerunds (*by examination of* instead of *by examining*). The range of verbs is further cut down by means of the *-ize* and *de-* formations, and banal statements are given an appearance of profundity by means of the *not un-* formation. Simple conjunctions and prepositions are replaced by such phrases as *with respect to, having regard to, the fact that, by dint of, in view of, in the interests of, on the hypothesis that;* and the ends of sentences are saved from anticlimax by such resounding commonplaces as *greatly to be desired, cannot be left out of account, a development to be expected in the near future, deserving of serious consideration, brought to a satisfactory conclusion,* and so on and so forth.

PRETENTIOUS DICTION. Words like *phenomenon, element, individual* (as noun), *objective, categorical, effective, virtual, basic, primary, promote, constitute, exhibit, exploit, utilize, eliminate, liquidate* are used to dress up simple statements and give an air of scientific impartiality to biassed judgements. Adjectives like *epoch-making, epic, historic, unforgettable, triumphant, age-old, inevitable, inexorable, veritable* are used to dignify the sordid processes of international politics, while writing that aims at glorifying war usually takes on an archaic colour, its characteristic words being: *realm, throne, chariot, mailed first, trident, sword, shield, buckler, banner, jackboot, clarion.* Foreign words and expressions such as *cul de sac, ancien régime, deus ex machina, mutatis mutandis, status quo, Gleichschaltung, Weltanschauung* are used to give an air of culture and elegance. Except for the useful abbreviations *i.e., e.g.,* and *etc.,* there is no real need for any of the hundreds of foreign phrases now current in English. Bad writers, and especially scientific, political and sociological writers, are nearly always haunted by the notion that Latin or Greek words are grander than Saxon ones, and unnecessary words like *expedite, ameliorate, predict, extraneous, deracinated, clandestine, sub-aqueous* and hundreds of others constantly gain ground from the Anglo-Saxon opposite numbers.[1] The jargon peculiar to Marxist writing (*hyena, hangman, cannibal, petty bourgeois, these gentry, lackey, flunkey, mad dog, White Guard, etc.*) consists largely of words and phrases translated from Russian, German or French; but the normal way of coining a new word is to use a Latin or Greek root with the appropriate affix and, where necessary, the -ize formation. It is often easier to make up words of this kind (*deregionalize, impermissible, extramarital, non-fragmentatory* and so forth) than to think up the English words that will cover one's meaning. The result, in general, is an increase in slovenliness and vagueness.

MEANINGLESS WORDS. In certain kinds of writing, particularly in art criticism and literary criticism, it is normal to come across long passages which are almost completely lacking in meaning.[2] Words like *romantic, plastic, values, human, dead, sentimental, natural, vitality,* as used in art criticism, are strictly meaningless, in the sense that they not only do not point to any discoverable objects, but are hardly even expected to do so by the reader. When one critic writes, 'The outstanding features of Mr X's work is its living quality', while another writes, 'The immediately striking thing about Mr X's work is its peculiar deadness', the reader accepts this as a simple difference of opinion. If words like *black* and *white* were involved, instead of the jargon words *dead* and *living*, he would see at once that language was being used in an improper way. Many political words are similarly abused. The word Fascism has now no meaning except in so far as it signifies 'something not desirable'. The words *democracy, socialism, freedom, patriotic, realistic, justice* have each of them several different meanings which cannot be reconciled with one another. In the case of a word like *democracy*, not only is there no agreed definition, but the attempt to make one is resisted from all sides. It is almost universally felt that when we call a country democratic we are praising it: consequently the defenders of every kind of rgime claim that it is a democracy, and fear that they might have to stop using the word if it were tied down to any one meaning. Words of this kind are often used in a consciously dishonest way. That is, the person who uses them has his own private definition, but allows his hearer to think he means something quite different. Statements like *Marshal Pétain was a true patriot, The Soviet press is the freest in the world, The Catholic Church is opposed to persecution* are almost always made with intent to deceive. Other words used in variable meanings, in most cases more or less dishonestly, are: *class, totalitarian, science, progressive, reactionary, bourgeois, equality.*

Now that I have made this catalogue of swindles and perversions, let me give another example of the kind of writing that they lead to. This time it must of its nature be an imaginary one. I am going to translate a passage of good English into modern English of the worst sort. Here is a well-known verse from *Ecclesiastes*:

> I returned, and saw under the sun, that the race is not to the swift, nor the battle to the strong, neither yet bread to the wise, nor yet riches to men of understanding, nor yet favour to men of skill; but time and chance happeneth to them all.

Here it is in modern English:

> Objective consideration of contemporary phenomena compels the conclusion that success or failure in competitive activities exhibits no tendency to be commensurate with innate capacity, but that a

considerable element of the unpredictable must invariably be taken into account.

This is a parody, but not a very gross one. Exhibit 3, above, for instance, contains several patches of the same kind of English. It will be seen that I have not made a full translation. The beginning and ending of the sentence follow the original meaning fairly closely, but in the middle the concrete illustrations — race, battle, bread — dissolve into the vague phrase 'success or failure in competitive activities'. This had to be so, because no modern writer of the kind I am discussing — no one capable of using phrases like 'objective consideration of contemporary phenomena' — would ever tabulate his thoughts in that precise and detailed way. The whole tendency of modern prose is away from concreteness. Now analyse these two sentences a little more closely. The first contains 49 words but only 60 syllables, and all its words are those of everyday life. The second contains 38 words of 90 syllable: 18 of its words are from Latin roots, and one from Greek. The first sentence contains six vivid images, and only one phrase ('time and chance') that could be called vague. The second contains not a single fresh, arresting phrase, and in spite of its 90 syllables it gives only a shortened version of the meaning contained in the first. Yet without a doubt it is the second kind of sentence that is gaining ground in modern English. I do not want to exaggerate. This kind of writing is not yet universal, and outcrops of simplicity will occur here and there in the worst-written page. Still if you or I were told to write a few lines on the uncertainty of human fortunes, we should probably come much nearer to my imaginary sentence than to the one from *Ecclesiastes*.

As I have tried to show, modern writing at its worst does not consist in picking out words for the sake of their meaning and inventing images in order to make the meaning clearer. It consists in gumming together long strips of words which have already been set in order by someone else, and making the results presentable by sheer humbug. The attraction of this way of writing is that it is easy. It is easier — even quicker, once you have the habit — to say *In my opinion it is a not unjustifiable assumption that* than to say *I think*. If you use ready-made phrases, you not only don't have to hunt about for words; you also don't have to bother with the rhythms of your sentences, since these phrases are generally so arranged as to be more or less euphonious. When you are composing in a hurry — when you are dictating to a stenographer, for instance, or making a public speech — it is natural to fall into a pretentious, latinized style. Tags like *a considera-tion which we should do well to bear in mind* or *a conclusion to which all of us would readily assent* will save many a sentence from coming down with a bump. By using stale metaphors, similes and idioms, you save much mental effort, at the cost of leaving your meaning vague, not only for your reader but for yourself. This is the significance of mixed metaphors. The sole aim of a metaphor is to call up a visual image. When these images clash — as in *The Fascist octopus has sung its swan song, the jackboot is thrown into the melting-pot* — it can be taken as certain that the writer is not seeing a mental image of the objects he is naming: in other words he is not really thinking. Look again at the examples I gave at the beginning of this essay. Professor Laski (1) uses five negatives in 53 words. One of these is superflu-ous, making nonsense of the whole passage, and in addition there is the slip *alien* for akin, making further nonsense, and several avoida-ble pieces of clumsiness which increase the general vagueness. Pro-fessor Hogben (2) plays ducks and drakes with a battery which is able to write prescriptions, and, while disapproving of the everyday phrase *put up with*, is unwilling to look *egregious* up in the dictionary and see what it means. (3), if one takes an uncharitable attitude towards it, is simply meaningless: probably one could work out its intended meaning by reading the whole of the article in which it occurs. In (4) the writer knows more or less what he wants to say, but accumulation of stale phrases chokes him like tea-leaves block-ing a sink. In (5) words and meaning have almost parted company. People who write in this manner usually have a general emotional meaning — they dislike one thing and want to express solidarity with another — but they are not interested in the detail of what they are saying. A scrupulous writer, in every sentence that he writes, will ask himself at least four questions, thus: What am I trying to say? What words will express it? What image or idiom will make it clearer? Is this image fresh enough to have an effect? And he will probably ask himself two more: Could I put it more shortly? Have I said anything that is avoidably ugly? But you are not obliged to go to all this trouble. You can shrink it by simply throwing your mind open and letting the ready-made phrases come crowding in. They will construct your sentences for you — even think your thoughts for you, to a certain extent — and at need they will perform the important service of partially concealing your meaning even from yourself. It is at this point that the special connexion between poli-tics and the debasement of language becomes clear.

In our time it is broadly true that political writing is bad writing. Where it is not true, it will generally be found that the writer is some kind of rebel, expressing his private opinions, and not a 'party line'. Orthodoxy, of whatever colour, seems to demand a lifeless, imitative style. The political dialects to be found in pamphlets, leading articles, manifestos, White Papers and the the speeches of Under-Secretaries do, of course, vary from party to party, but they are all alike in that one almost never finds in them a fresh, vivid, home-made turn of speech. When one watches some tired hack on the platform mechanically repeating the familiar phrases — *bestial atrocities, iron heel, blood-stained tyranny, free peoples of the world, stand shoulder to shoulder* — one often has a curious feeling that one is not watching a live human being but some kind of dummy: a feeling which suddenly becomes stronger at moments when the light catches the speaker's spectacles and turns them into blank discs which seem to have no eyes behind them. And this is not altogether fanciful. A speaker who uses that kind of phraseology has gone some distance towards turning himself into a machine. The appropriate noises are coming out of his larynx, but his brain is not involved as it would be if he were choosing his words for himself. If the speech he is making is one that he is accustomed to make over and over again, he may be almost unconscious of what he is saying, as one is when one utters the responses in church. And this reduced state of consciousness, if not indispensable, is at any rate favourable to political conformity.

In our time, political speech and writing are largely the defence of the indefensible. Things like the continuance of British rule in India, the Russian purges and deportations, the dropping of the atom bombs on Japan, can indeed be defended, but only by arguments which are too brutal for most people to face, and which do not square with the professed aims of political parties. Thus political language has to consist largely of euphemism, question-begging and sheer cloudy vagueness. Defenceless villages are bombarded from the air, the inhabitants driven out into the countryside, the cattle machine-gunned, the huts set on fire with incendiary bullets: this is called *pacification*. Millions of peasants are robbed of their farms and sent trudging along the roads with no more than they can carry: this is called *transfer of population* or *rectification of frontiers*. People are imprisoned for years without trial, or shot in the back of the neck or sent to die of scurvy in Arctic lumber camps: this is called *elimination of unreliable elements*. Such phraseology is needed if one wants to name things without calling up mental pictures of them. Consider for instance some comfortable English professor defending Russian totalitarianism. He cannot say outright, 'I believe in killing off your opponents when you can get good results by doing so'. Probably, therefore, he will say something like this:

> While freely conceding that the Soviet rgime exhibits certain features which the humanitarian may be inclined to deplore, we must, I think, agree that a certain curtailment of the right to political opposition is an unavoidable concomitant of transitional periods, and that the rigours which the Russian people have been called upon to undergo have been amply justified in the sphere of concrete achievement.

The inflated style is itself a kind of euphemism. A mass of Latin words falls upon the facts like soft snow, blurring the outlines and covering up all the details. The great enemy of clear language is insincerity. When there is a gap between one's real and one's declared aims, one turns as it were instinctively to long words and exhausted idioms, like a cuttlefish squirting out ink. In our age there is no such thing as 'keeping out of politics'. All issues are political issues, and politics itself is a mass of lies, evasions, folly, hatred and schizophrenia. When the general atmosphere is bad, language must suffer, I should expect to find — this is a guess which I have not sufficient knowledge to verify — that the German, Russian and Italian languages have all deteriorated in the last ten or fifteen years, as a result of dictatorship.

But if thought corrupts language, language can also corrupt thought. A bad usage can spread by tradition and imitation, even among people who should and do know better. The debased language that I have been discussing is in some ways very convenient. Phrases like *a not unjustifiable assumption, leaves much to be desired, would serve no good purpose, a consideration which we should do well to bear in mind* are a continuous temptation, a packet of aspirins always at one's elbow. Look back through this essay, and for certain you will find that I have again and again committed the very faults I am protesting against. By this morning's post I have received a pamphlet dealing with conditions in Germany. The author tells me that he 'felt impelled' to write it. I open it at random, and here is almost the first sentence that I see; '(The Allies) have an opportunity not only of achieving a radical transformation of Germany's social and political structure in such a way as to avoid a nationalistic reaction in Germany itself, but at the same time of laying the foundations of a co-operative and unified Europe.' You see, he 'feels impelled' to write — feels, presumably, that he has something new to say — and yet his words, like cavalry horses answering the bugle, group themselves automatically into the familiar dreary pattern. This invasion of one's mind by ready-made phrases (*lay the foundations, achieve a radical transformation*) can only be prevented if one is constantly on guard against them, and every such phrase anaesthetizes a portion of one's brain.

I said earlier that the decadence of our language is probably curable. Those who deny this would argue, if they produced an argument at all, that language merely reflects existing social conditions, and that we cannot influence its development by any direct tinkering with words and constructions. So far as the general tone or spirit of a language goes, this may be true, but it is not true in detail. Silly words and expressions have often disappeared, not through any evolutionary process but owing to the conscious action of a minority. Two recent examples were *explore every avenue* and *leave no stone unturned*, which were killed by the jeers of a few journalists. There is a long list of fly-blown metaphors which could similarly be got rid of if enough people would interest themselves in the job; and it should also be possible to laugh the *not un-* formation out of existence,[3] to reduce the amount of Latin and Greek in the average sentence, to drive out foreign phrases and strayed scientific words, and, in general, to make pretentiousness unfashionable. But all these are minor points. The defence of the English language implies more than this, and perhaps it is best to start by saying what it does *not* imply.

To begin with, it has nothing to do with archaism, with the salvaging of obsolete words and turns of speech, or with the setting-up of a 'standard English' which must never be departed from. On the contrary, it is especially concerned with the scrapping of every word or idiom which has outworn its usefulness. It has nothing to do with correct grammar and syntax, which are of no importance so long as one makes one's meaning clear, or with the avoidance of Americanisms, or with having what is called a 'good prose style'. On the other hand it is not concerned with fake simplicity and the attempt to make written English colloquial. Nor does it even imply in every case preferring the Saxon word to the Latin one, though it does imply using the fewest and shortest words that will cover one's meaning. What is above all needed is to let the meaning choose the word, and not the other way about. In prose, the worst thing you can do with words is to surrender them. When you think of a concrete object, you think wordlessly, and then, if you want to describe the thing you have been visualizing, you probably hunt about till you find the exact words that seem to fit it. When you think of something abstract you are more inclined to use words from the start, and unless you make a conscious effort to prevent it, the existing dialect will come rushing in and do the job for you, at the expense of blurring or even changing your meaning. Probably it is better to put off using words as long as possible and get one's meanings as clear as one can through pictures or sensations. Afterwards one can choose — not simply *accept* — the phrases that will best cover the meaning, and then switch round and decide what impression one's words are likely to make on another person. This last effort of the mind cuts out all stale or mixed images, all prefabricated phrases, needless repetitions, and humbug and vagueness generally. But one can often be in doubt about the effect of a word or a phrase, and one needs rules that one can rely on when instinct fails. I think the following rules will cover most cases:

   i. Never use a metaphor, simile or other figure of speech which you are used to seeing in print.
  ii. Never use a long word where a short one will do.
 iii. If it is possible to cut a word out, always cut it out.
 iv. Never use the passive where you can use the active.
  v. Never use a foreign phrase, a scientific word or a jargon word if you can think of an everyday English equivalent.
 vi. Break any of these rules sooner than say anything outright barbarous.

These rules sound elementary, and so they are, but they demand a deep change of attitude in anyone who has grown used to writing in the style now fashionable. One could keep all of them and still write bad English, but one could not write the kind of stuff that I quoted in those five specimens at the beginning of this article.

I have not here been considering the literary use of language, but merely language as an instrument for expressing and not for concealing or preventing thought. Stuart Chase and others have come near to claiming that all abstract words are meaningless, and have used this as a pretext for advocating a kind of political quietism. Since you don't know what Fascism is, how can you struggle against Fascism? One need not swallow such absurdities as this, but one ought to recognize that the present political chaos is concerned with the decay of language, and that one can probably bring about some improvement by starting at the verbal end. If you simplify your English, you are freed from the worst follies of orthodoxy. You cannot speak any of the necessary dialects, and when you make a stupid remark its stupidity will be obvious, even to yourself. Political language — and with variations this is true of all political parties, from Conservatives to Anarchists — is designed to make lies sound truthful and murder respectable, and to give an appearance of solidity to pure wind. One cannot change this all in a moment, but one can at least change ones own habits, and from time to time one can even, if one jeers loudly enough, send some worn-out and useless phrase — some *jackboot, Achilles' heel, hotbed, melting pot, acid test, veritable inferno* or other lump of verbal refuse — into the dustbin where it belongs.

-----

[1]An interesting illustration of this is the way in which the English flower names which were in use till very recently are being ousted by Greek ones, *snapdragon* becoming *antirrhinum, forget-me-not* becoming *myosotis*, etc. It is hard to see any practical reason for this change of fashion: it is probably due to an instinctive turning-away from the more homely word and a vague feeling that the Greek word is scientific. [Author's footnote.]

[2]Example: 'Comforts catholicity of perception and image, strangely Whitmanesque in range, almost the exact opposite in aesthetic compulsion, continues to evoke that trembling atmospheric accumulative hinting at a cruel, an inexorably serene timelessness . . . Wrey Gardiner scores by aiming at simple bullseyes with precision. Only they are not so simple, and through this contented sadness runs more than the surface bittersweet of resignation.' (*Poetry Quarterly*). [Author's footnote.]

[3]One can cure oneself of the *not un-* formation by memorizing this sentence: *A not unblack dog was chasing a not unsmall rabbit across a not ungreen field.* [Author's footnote.]

Knowing How to Think

ROYAL BANK LETTER

Next to breathing, thinking is arguably the most common of all human activities. We eat and sleep only at intervals; we walk or talk only part of the time. But as long as we are conscious, we think constantly. The ability to do so in the abstract — to have ideas — is what sets *homo sapiens* apart from the rest of creation. Descartes spoke for an entire species when he wrote, "I think, therefore I am."

According to Ralph Waldo Emerson, our very lives consist of what we are thinking all day long. Yet, considering how vital the mental processes are to human existence, it is remarkable how little is done to ensure that they are effectively exercised. We are told a great deal about *what* to think, but very little about *how* to think. This may be because most people regard thinking as something that comes naturally. They would no more seek instruction on how to use their minds than on how to use their veins.

But talking is a natural function too; and just as people can learn to express themselves more clearly, they can learn to think more clearly. The first recorded attempt to teach reasoning skills was among the philosophers of ancient Greece. Aristotle, for one, propounded certain formal laws of logic. These have since been widely disputed, but they formed an indispensable starting-point for the study of how to think.

Aristotle's work was carried on by scholars in the Middle Ages who developed a list of approaches to reasoning to be avoided. They called these fallacies — errors which have the deceptive appearance of making sense. They gave them Latin names which make them sound forbiddingly "intellectual." In fact, fallacies are common in everyday life. We are liable to slip into fallacious reasoning, or have our own thinking affected by it, at any time.

Take the fallacy the medieval scholars called *secudum quid*, which is nothing more than what we today would call jumping to conclusions. We visit a strange town and see two men reeling about on the streets; from these two instances we conclude that the town is full of drunkards. "People in this town are very rude, too," we think after being treated brusquely by the only local sales clerk we meet.

Gross over-generalizations like this may seem harmless, but they can lead to serious damage socially and politically. When applied to groups, they create misleading stereotypes. Two members of such-and-such a group are lazy and unreliable, therefore they are all lazy and unreliable; three members of another group are changed with stealing, therefore they are all criminals. There is a murder in an ethnic neighbourhood; we are frightened ever to go there, because everybody there is a potential murderer. It is from such crude labelling that vicious racial and sectarian prejudices arise.

A related over-generalization is the assumption that a localized and temporary opinion or sentiment represents a universal principle — that what we deem to be true here and now is going to be true everywhere and forever. This is often accompanied by the belief that what one deems to be good for oneself is good for the whole society.

Over-generalizations are the lazy man's substitute for rigorous thought, and mental sloth may be the only explanation for how widely some of them are accepted. In the 1950s, the press critic A.J. Liebling summarized the American newspapers' approach to foreign news this way: "Man go church, good man, no lie. Man not go church, man bad, lie. Communists bad, whatever they say lie." Scores of millions of people went along unquestioningly with that mindless line.

Many American lives were then being ruined by the over-generalization which guided Senator Joseph McCarthy's fanatical hunt for Communists: "If it waddles like a duck and it quacks like a duck, it must be a duck." The Senator and his henchmen raised to a high art the fallacious theory of guilt by association. Smith had lunch with Jones, who once attended a meeting of a Communist front group. Therefore both Jones and Smith are Communists.

Guilt by association incorporates erroneous correspondence, the assumption that a thing that has certain attributes in common with another will resemble it in all respects. If you were to believe that, you might also believe that whales, being mammals, can walk. It leads to the kind of thinking that ascribes a uniformity of opinion to every single member of a race, a religion, a sect, or a nation. Demagogues on personal power trips are only too happy to take advantage of this error to pretend that they speak for their entire group, which is of one monolithic mind.

Guilt by association also has elements of the fallacy in which ideas and things are mixed up with personalities. You may think, "That charity can't be a good cause because the man who runs it is an egotistical publicity hound." In fact, his lust for fame has nothing to do with his ability to run a charity, or with its worthiness. An awareness of this fallacy is handy in making judgments in politics, in which personalities are often confused with issues. You don't like that politician's appearance or his way of speaking. Therefore you reject his policies out of hand.

Personalities also come into play in what might be called the "you're a fine one to talk" fallacy. Under its spell people may absolve themselves of their faults on the specious grounds that others are just as bad as they are, or worse. A wife says she wishes her husband would not leave his socks on the bedroom floor. He retorts: "Yeah? And what about the dent you put in the car?" which is irrelevant to the question. Such cock-eyed connections are often made in political debates, deliberately or otherwise. They can be fatal in business, in which the management that concludes "we're no worse than anybody else" is courting bankruptcy.

Among the other fallacies that rest on irrelevancies is *circulus in probando* — arguing in circles. You can think in circles, too, without stating an argument aloud. Circular reasoning conveniently supplies its own authority. Someone might declare that Thackeray was a greater novelist than Dickens. Why? Because the most discerning critics say so. And who are the most discerning critics? Those discerning enough to discern that Thackeray was a greater novelist than Dickens, that's who!

Thinking in circles often entails joining an intellectual herd charging round and round. Everybody thinks such and such; it must be so for the simple reason that everybody thinks that it is so. A variation of this is basing a conclusion on an unprovable assumption. Fowler's *Modern English Usage* gives a grisly and ridiculous example: that fox hunting is not cruel because the fox enjoys the fun.

Baseless conclusions are sometimes palmed off as "self-evident truths." The phrase is a contradiction in terms since the word "evident" implies the presence of signs that point unmistakably to a conclusion. The less verifiable the "self-evident truth," the more fiercely those who subscribe to it will attack anyone who dares question it.

One tactic for defending a flawed piece of reasoning is to cite the endorsement of some prominent person or book. Of course, the validity of opinions does not necessarily depend on the fame or eminence of those who hold them. The principle applies equally to self-appointed gurus and impressive-sounding statistics, which can always be misinterpreted or deliberately skewed to support a certain cause. In his *Guides to Straight Thinking*, Stuart Chase quotes a sign in a British school that got to the heart of the matter: "The teacher could be wrong. Think for yourselves."

In our attempts to think for ourselves, we should refuse to be included in declarations that "everybody knows" something or other. Everybody else might indeed know it, but a critical thinker will withhold acknowledgement of a fact until it has been demonstrated satisfactorily. Similarly, if a speaker says that "most experts agree" on something, we have the right to ask: What experts? What precisely have they agreed on? Such challenges can be important because, as Bertrand Russell once observed, "Most of the greatest evils that man has inflicted on man have come through people feeling quite certain about something which, in fact, was false."

"It is better to know nothing than to know what ain't so," Josh Billings wrote. But how are we to distinguish between what is so and what "ain't?" Since people are always citing "the facts" to support their point of view, it helps to know what separates a fact from a mere notion. A few years back the California Department of Education defined a fact as "an understanding based on confirmed observations and inferences, and . . . subject to test or rejection." No one can unilaterally create a fact to fit their opinions, feelings or prejudices, as people frequently try to do.

Facts are elusive at the best of times. The great Canadian explorer and writer Vilhjalmur Stefansson illustrated the point by telling of a man coming into a house and saying, "There is a red cow in the front yard." Stefansson pondered the possibilities of error: "The observer may have confused the sex of the animal. Perhaps it was an ox. Or if not the sex, the age may have been misjudged, and it may have been a heifer. The man may have been colour-blind, and the cow . . . may not have been red. And even if it was a red cow, the dog may have seen her the instant our observer turned his back, and by the time he told us she was in the front yard, she may in reality have been vanishing in a cloud of dust down the road."

Because information is so fallible, scientists take five steps in attempting to establish what qualifies as knowledge and what does not: (1) asking questions; (2) making observations; (3) reporting results; (4) answering questions arising from those results; (5) revising assumptions in the light of the answers. Even then, they do not look for certainties, but for high probabilities. A scientist will say, "The evidence supports this hypothesis." He will not say: "This is the truth."

You can use the five-step system in your own efforts to think more logically, and also to assess the thoughts of others. Can they stand up to questioning and review? Have the assumptions implicit in them been revised to take account of the latest developments?

Some fairly reliable signals exist to indicate when people are on shaky logical ground. One is that they will refuse to listen to contrary arguments or evidence that might spoil their hypotheses. If forced to listen, they are likely to treat contrary arguments or facts not as challenges to the validity of their conclusions, but as attacks on their probity or dignity. In the marginal notes to a speech, an old Member of Parliament is said to have written: "Weak point. Emote!"

High on the list of fallacious tricks of rhetoric is one called *argumentum ad populum*, meaning an argument appealing to popular passions. It can usually be spotted by the splashing around of emotive abstractions like honour, dignity, and pride. You can be reasonably sure that you are being exposed to this type of propaganda if the message is couched in simplistic unitary terms: there is *one* problem, *one* solution, *one* indisputable body of evidence. Either there is one monstrous enemy, or there are enemies everywhere. In either case, the enemies all have the same traits.

The ability to detect a fallacious argument is the critical thinker's primary defence against demagoguery and brain-washing in advertising, politics and other public affairs. In a plea for the teaching of reasoning skills in grade schools, Toronto author and journalist Erna Paris wrote in *The Globe and Mail*: "Imagine a society in which children were taught to distinguish argument from emotion, and to evaluate information according to the quality of the evidence backing it up! We would still be faced with prejudice and a stubborn human unwillingness to see the other person's point of view. . . . But more of us would be equipped to resist the opinion manipulators, the weavers of superstition, and the propagandists with political or other agendas."

In the absence of such teaching except in specialized courses in philosophy, ordinary people must rely largely on horse sense to assure that they practise logic themselves and detect the lack of it in public discourse. There are, to be sure, a few books on the subject, and the larger encyclopedias have articles on logic describing the various fallacies and other intellectual tools. In broad terms, however, no one can go wrong by questioning all generalizations, looking for supporting evidence for every assertion made, and being on guard against extremes in thinking, whether in others or oneself.

On the personal side of the question, we would not be human if we did not occasionally allow our minds to go to extremes, if only when we are hurt or angry. The surest way to avoid extremes is to be aware of the danger of thinking in absolute terms. Absolutism thrives on words like "is," "are," "be," and "am," which lead people to confuse their interior judgments with exterior reality. "Statements such as 'this picture is beautiful' or 'the outlook is good' or 'this steak is overcooked' are not statements about the picture, the outlook or the steak, but the speaker's reaction to them," S.I. Haya-kawa wrote in his *Language in Thought and Action*. People are naturally inclined to mistake their impression of a thing or event for the thing or event itself — to mistake the map for the territory. "But, of course, no one can get outside the limitations of one's nervous system to see reality directly and absolutely objectively. If we could do this, we would never be fooled by magicians or optical illusions, and we would never misinterpret a situation."

By avoiding "is" and other absolute words, you can clarify your thinking. The distinguished semanticist Dr. Albert Ellis once gave some examples of how much more precisely and completely thoughts are constructed if one abstains from the verb form "to be": "John is lethargic and unhappy." / "John appears lethargic and unhappy in the office." / "John is bright and cheerful." / "John appears bright and cheerful at the beach." / "Mary is smart." / "Mary scored 160 on her IQ test."

Absolutist thinking seems to be a natural product of western culture, with its black-and-white view of the universe. Our legal system decrees that a defendant is guilty or not guilty; we vote either for one candidate or another; all too often, we can see only two ways of doing things, a right way and a wrong way; we are inclined to divide our tastes crudely into what we like and do not like. In relations with people who are not of our own kind, we think in terms of "them and us."

Aristotle's system of logic, which for centuries guided western thought, asserts that everything must be one thing or another. Like a light switch that is either on or off, it makes no allowance for degrees. This encourages what semanticists call "two-valued orientation." A typical two-valued judgment might be, "He who is not with me is against me." It does not contemplate the possibility that he could be with you on one issue and against you on another, or be with you at one time but against you at another when the circumstances have changed.

This all-or-nothing approach gives rise to childish judgments: "That is good, this is bad; they are right, the others are wrong; he is stupid, she is smart." It establishes an intellectual regime of "allness" in which people falling into certain categories are all deemed to think, feel or act in the same stereotypical way.

"Allness" can also affect one's thinking about oneself, as in, "They are all against me." It is associated with a lot of other absolute words: "*Nothing ever* goes right for me. I'll *always* be a failure. I *never* make *any* progress. *Everything* is falling apart for me. And *nobody* cares. *Everybody* is out for himself these days."

Absolutist thinking tends to reinforce "the power of negative thinking" because it sets up unrealistic expectations. In their personal relations, people under its influence expect others to treat them well or badly all the time, instead of treating them well some of the time, badly some of the time, and neither well nor badly some of the time.

Instead of seeing their own lives and those of others as processes undergoing constant change, they see them as static. Writing of a theoretical young man who has been going through a hard time and concludes, "I'll never get over this," Stuart Chase commented: "He thinks this unfortunate 'time' is all 'times.' Blinded by absolutes, he cannot see other 'times.' He believes his case is identical with all past and future cases in his life." He does not realize that "what has happened can never exactly repeat itself. No two contexts are the same."

The fallacious notion that what has happened before will happen again generates "pre-emptive thinking" intended to prevent its recurrence. Thus a young woman who has broken up with two or three men becomes convinced that, as far as men are concerned, she is "a failure;" because she believes this, all her relationships with men do indeed fail.

Self-defeating thoughts can hold us back from meeting our full potential, e.g.: "I won't approach the boss with that idea of mine because I'm sure to make a fool of myself." In this regard we would be wise to keep in mind Hayakawa's caution that what we think about anything — including ourselves — is not the reality of it: "One's self-concept is not oneself. It omits a great deal about oneself."

What you think of yourself and the world around you can literally be hazardous to your health. In recent years, experts on stress have determined that a person's self-concept plays a key role in how much stress he or she can take. If people jump to conclusions, take things personally, or fall for other fallacies, they will act as though everything around them is dangerous. This triggers the instinctive fight-or-flight response which causes unhealthy stress.

"Most folks are about as happy as they make up their minds to be," Abraham Lincoln said. Despite all the scientific, technological, and social advances made since Lincoln's time, his words remain true. External conditions can cause misery, of course, but the spiritual wellbeing of ordinary individuals depends more on their state of mind than on their circumstances. That state of mind can be improved by efforts to think more clearly, because by doing so we can eliminate baseless self-doubts and fears.

English as Second Language, English as First Love

STEPHEN BAKER

No doubt, English was invented in heaven. It must be the *lingua franca* of the angels.

No other language is like it. Nothing even comes close to it in sound, eloquence, and just plain common sense — and this from someone who spoke nary a word of it before reaching age 25, save for *Coke*, *OK* and *drugstore*.

Before my arrival in America, I was put through the paces of several languages, including my mother tongue, Hungarian. I was beginning to eat words for breakfast. It got so my brain would go into neutral just thinking about rules of grammar and pronunciation; I had recurrent nightmares about the collapse of the Tower of Babel with me as one of the lost babbling souls.

Then came English and with it, peace. Life had become bearable once again.

Let me tell you some of the reasons for my love affair with the English language. For starters, it has a vocabulary twice the size of its nearest competitor, German, which has less than half a million words. French follows, with the rest hopelessly behind.

"Who needs all those words?" you may ask. "The fewer, the simpler. Right?"

Wrong.

The larger the selection, the easier — and quicker — it is to get from one end of the sentence to the other. One word does the work of two or three. Speak or write English, and you are traveling on a verbal express. For example, take the King James Bible, and put it next to its German version — same typesize, same format. The German translation is more than 25 pages thicker, or almost 10%.

As a part-time writer, I now find myself celebrating every time I sit down at my word processor to write in my new language. I can hardly contain my enthusiasm. At long last, I can be mercifully brief and *still* say precisely what I mean. At my call are at least three quarters of a million words I didn't even know existed before learning English. For example, in my native Hungarian, jumpers could only *ugri* (jump). In North America, they can *leap, hop, vault, spring, bound, bounce, caper, prance, buck, trip, bob, skip* or even *go hippity-hop*. Does that mean English-speakers learned to jump more ways than Hungarian-speakers? No, but it makes for livelier speech.

You will be surprised to hear me say this: English is probably among the easiest languages to learn — because grammatically it makes sense. Anyone who tells you it isn't so should take a trip around the world and listen to tongues wagging. He'll be happy to be home again.

For one thing, our words are gender-free. A tomato is a tomato in North America. In France it takes on a female pronoun. In Spain it turns masculine. In Germany it remains neuter.

We get along on relatively few prepositions and we don't change them willy-nilly to better "harmonize" with the word they modify. Staples like *at, by, in, to, from* and *with* take care of most every contingency. Our adjectives do not form plurals or have cases. Best of all, we prefer short sentences to long and convoluted ones. Few of our writers would begin their paragraphs on top of the page only to finish them at the bottom — as some foreign writers do in their gleeful display of literacy.

In most countries, slang is greeted with the holding of the nose. Such confab, it is said, should be left to the Great Unwashed who don't know any better. The well-educated rely on "standard speech," the preferred parlance of television newscasters and debating parliamentarians, the schmooze of the intelligentsia who cringe at words such as *schmooze*.

Even our British cousins have a problem with the vernacular, such as the free-swinging Cockney or even the hyperbolic Irish. By and large, schools discourage such "aberrations" of the King's — or Queen's, depending on the gender of the incumbent monarch — English. Similarly, a great many Australians — a society that has long prided itself on its fiercely egalitarian values — have yet to allow outback-speak to seep into their everyday conversations, particularly at teatime. And as we all know, the class dialect of white South Africa so differs from the everyday patois of those from the homeland that it immediately identifies the speaker. The same is true in other parts of the world.

To this newcomer, the charm of North American speech lies precisely in its cheerful acceptance of all forms of speech. In fact, in this country the line between "correct" and "colloquial" speech has become so blurred as to be nearly imperceptible to all but the most consummate wordsmiths.

My heart thrills when I hear North American talk. Slang may be short on pedigree, and at times it tends to sound more like a primal scream, but who cares? The words are born out of need: they usually move into a vacuum. We welcome them regardless of origin. They come from everywhere, near and far, young and old, black, brown, yellow and white. Foreigners are often surprised to find an "old friend" in the midst of their new vocabulary. I remember my delight discovering the use of *gulyas* as I learned English, here used to define "a strange mixture of things." You know it as *goulash*. The word took me back to early days when no kitchen table-setting was complete without this Hungarian stew. As a boy obliged to finish anything put in front of him, I often wondered: was this wondrous concoction supposed to be a soup? Or a full-fledged main course? Or, mind-bogglingly, trying to be both? The answer still eludes me. Clever, these North Americans. What a great way to describe a complete mess.

While speakers (and writers) of other languages take pleasure in wallowing in adjectives and adverbs, North Americans would rather get on with the story. On this side of the Atlantic, verbs have it. Time is crucial in this country. North America thrives on action, prides itself on productivity. Speech habits reflect our national psyche.

I still recall lending a hand to a Chinese corporate executive client with a presentation he was asked to deliver to North American business executives. He liked my first draft but something seemed to trouble him. "Not enough nouns," he finally confessed. It appears that in the Orient, the clock ticks slower. Nouns stand still. They symbolize solidity, he explained; they are the pillars that hold up the building. Verbs, on the other hand, are ephemeral. They are at the mercy of the slightest breeze, just like a butterfly.

My special thanks for the conspicuous absence in this country of a National Academy in charge of speech.

France has such a group of learned men and women, the gotcha gang of proper usage. So does Germany, and even Britain. It is such an institution's responsibility — nay, mission — to keep out linguistic riffraff.

Wishing, of course, does not necessarily make it so. Not even the most determined efforts could keep *le drugstore, le parking, le covergirl* from entering the French language. Nor was the German literati particularly successful in keeping *der Drink* and *das Apartment* from crossing the Rhine.

I still remember the periodic purges of language while going to high school. In theory, it seemed a fine idea to keep Hungarian Hungarian. But as a practical matter we ended up with the pitiful remnants of a sheep shorn of its coat at the end of every such pogrom. Our homework assignments in Hungarian composition shrunk to their puniest ever — we literally found ourselves lost for words.

It is this nation's respect for the spoken word that makes North American-English dictionaries burst at their backstrip. New words enter the vocabulary almost by the day. A playful lot North Americans are when it comes to language. Nouns turn into verbs, verbs into nouns, adjectives into adverbs, adverbs into adjectives at the speakers' whim. We make expressions to fit our space, our mood, our needs. We toss words up in the air, flip them, watch them land, and fill them with goodies like so many pizza pies. New editions of dictionaries appear on this country's bookstores every two or three years; many become instant best-sellers. In other countries, a decade is more likely to pass between publication dates.

A multilingual Japanese businessman was once asked about his language preferences. "English, of course," he said with a smile. "In English I can always say to you, simply and without hesitation — *you*."

Considering the bewildering choice of honorifics in his native tongue, his sentiment was understandable. Protocol dictates that son, daughter, children, friends, brothers and sisters, seniors and juniors, and even household pets all answer to a different accost in the Land of the Rising Sun.

The free and uninhibited use of the second pronoun you in English pretty much stands alone among speakers of the world. North Americans should feel fortunate to be so blessed. The French, Dutch, Scandinavians and Russians have at least two ways of conversing with one another: familiar and unfamiliar, Germans have three; the formal *Sie*, the formal/familiar *Ihr*, and the familiar *du*.

Italians have a choice of four second-person pronouns, the Spanish five, and the Portuguese seven. In some Southeast Asian countries, the number hovers between ten and twenty.

Pity the speaker making a wrong choice. Such social blunders can have dire consequences; at the very least, they call for an apology. Vivid in my memory is the resounding slap meted out by my high-spirited Hungarian girl-friend who felt that my switching to the familiar *te* after a single perfunctory goodnight kiss at the door was just a bit premature.

Those born and raised here rarely appreciate the impact of this unassuming but handy little word. Quite possibly *you* represents one of the cornerstones of democracy. Because of it, cab driver or passenger, celebrity or ordinary citizen, worker or manager all converse on the same level playing field.

English is rapidly becoming the language of the world. More than 300 million consider it their native tongue — and even more than that speak it as their preferred second language. It is generally agreed that within a decade or so, English speakers will outnumber Chinese speakers, the current Pied Piper. Interestingly enough, speakers tried hard to *invent* such common speech for many a century. Esperanto amassed the largest following — about a million, still a far cry from the number of English speakers today.

North American English has become the principal "other" language in the classrooms of the world — a sure sign of further growth. Of all books published, more than half are written in English, as is 70% of global mail, 75% of cable messages, more than 10,000 newspapers, and almost as many magazines. Truly, English has become the "businessese," "medicalese," "legalese," "technologese" of the world.

Imagine! As an English speaker, I can now communicate with a barber in Debra Run, ask the waiter to serve kahve for breakfast in Istanbul, or ask for directions to the nearest public restroom in Moscow. Hungarian was never like this.

As far as I'm concerned, the time has come for the US to have its own "official language," and it should be English. I mean that from the bottom of my heart and the top of my brain.

English does not happen to be "my" language, but what difference does that make? I live and work — and vote — here and unless I understand what everybody is talking about, who am I to butt in with an informed opinion?

Now, I realize there are those who insist on their inalienable right to speak any way they please, loud or soft, fast or slow, English or Estonian. Conventional wisdom has it that ours is a land of newcomers, an ever-seething cauldron of divergent cultures. But listen to me, my fellow immigrants! Why should speaking English go against upholding longstanding, cherished traditions? No one stops you or me from donning our multicolorous native get-ups any time we're in the mood to do our Polka, fandango, Siebensprungs, csardas or whatever. What's that got to do with speaking the language of the land? Why not blend into the scenery just a smidgen? Let's count our blessings, my good friends; we have the best of two worlds.

Sure, I nurture my memories from the "old country." Like everyone else, I enjoy waxing nostalgic to my children. But I do so in *their* native language. Which happens to be English.

And you know something? My stories flow better.

Guilty verdict in the murder of the language

GEORGE GAMESTER

Welcome to The People's Court, friends. Today, **Judge Whopper** will deal with assaults on the language.

Case No. 1 is a class action against professional athletes. The charge: Murdering the Queen's English. Witnesses for the prosecution include **Harry Dean** of London, **Al Weinberg** of North York and **Edwin Kammin** of Toronto. Mr. Dean?

"I can't stand these jocks who cannot utter a sentence without saying 'you know.' Recently I counted 23 'yanows' in a single interview."

Mr. Weinberg?

"And why, oh *why*, must they pepper their inane answers with the word 'right?' 'So I shot for the corner, right? But he got his stick up, right? And that's the way it goes, eh?' *Arrrrgh!"*

Mr. Kammin?

"Next time I hear some bozo say 'This team is on a roll,' I'm going to ask: 'Kaiser, or onion?' "

And Judge Whopper's decision is: '*Guilty on all counts! Sentenced to a year of* **Don Cherry** *reruns!*"

Case No. 2 . . . say, where is Case No. 2? It seems to have gone missing . . . . "Aiyeee!"

You screamed, **Dorys Bernbaum** of North York?

"I certainly did! I feel like screaming every time I encounter the expression 'went missing.' People or things are either missing or not missing. They do not 'go missing!'"

Anything to add, **Cathy Iaboni** of Toronto?

"Yes. Why do people persist in saying something 'turned up missing?' How can something turn up if it is missing?"

And Judge Whopper's decision is: '*Guilty! Sentenced to a year of Leon's commercials.*'

Case No. 3 is unusual: Testimony from **John Duffy** of Toronto on behalf of **Gordon Black**, the Star reader who coined the expression 'chalk squeakers' for "unattractive or overworked words and phrases that produce a terrible grating sound on the brain." John?

"It *MAKES MY DAY* to see you undertaking this *AWESOME* task, *IN TERMS OF* monitoring the language.

"The *LEGENDARY* **George Orwell**, while *HONING HIS SKILLS* in '*Politics and the English Language,*' criticizes the *MINDSET* of those who use tiresome cliches and fly-blown metaphors.

"*ARGUABLY*, as a living language, the rules of structure are not *ETCHED IN STONE, HOPEFULLY,* your comments *AT THIS POINT IN TIME,* represent a saving *LIGHT AT THE END OF THE TUNNEL.*

"Meanwhile, *THE BOTTOM LINE* is that Orwell, the *POLITICALLY CORRECT* prophet of *THE NEW WORLD ORDER,* smiles down on your *MEANINGFUL WORK.*"

Revision or What Have I Actually Said?

JACQUES BARZUN

WHAT THE EYE DOESN'T CATCH, THE MIND GRIEVES AFTER

A good judge of the facts has declared: "All writing is rewriting." He meant good writing, for easy reading. The path to rewriting is obvious: when rereading after a shorter or longer lapse of time what one has written, one feels dissatisfaction with this or that word, sentence, paragraph — or possibly with the whole effort, the essay or chapter. If, as I shall assume, things are not totally bad, the rewriting affects only bits here and there. The criterion is as it has been throughout: Meaning. If words you have set down puzzle you once you have forgotten how they came to your mind, they will puzzle the stranger and you must do something about them — rediscover your meaning and express it, not some other or none at all.

The truths behind these reflections *guarantee* that the piece written at midnight on the eve of the deadline date will be bad. It is scarcely looked over in that desperate hour of fatigue and self-reproach; it is no piece of prose, but the possible embryo of one. Without time to reread and some calm thought to effect repairs, you defeat your purpose: the hastily cobbled thing you produce cannot succeed, whether its aim is to persuade, prove, enthrall, or merely show such powers of writing as you possess. Any of these ends can be achieved only after a series of revisions. Recall your experience as a student and imagine being allowed to go over your written final examination on three consecutive days, though without looking at your books or notes in between: the final final would surely be fuller, better organized, more intelligent than the first. You would have thought and remembered, filled gaps and corrected first impulses to a point well above your normal achievement when limited to a single try. Your article or report must be treated the same way. It must be gone over and patiently rewritten if it is to represent what you intend and what you can do.

Rewriting is called revision in the literary and publishing trade because it springs from *re-viewing*, that is to say, looking at your copy again — and again and again. When you have learned to look at your own words with critical detachment, you will find that rereading a piece five or six times in a row will each time bring to light fresh spots of trouble. The trouble is sometimes elementary: you wonder how you can have written it as a pronoun referring to a plural subject. The slip is easily corrected. At other times you have written yourself into a corner, the exit from which is not at once apparent. Your words down there seem to preclude the necessary repairs up here — because of repetition, syntax, logic, or some other obstacle. Nothing comes to mind as reconciling sense with sound and with clarity in both places. In such a fix you may have to start farther back and pursue a different line altogether. The sharper your judgment, the more trouble you will find. That is why exacting writers are known to have rewritten a famous paragraph or chapter six or seven times. It then looked right to them, because every demand of their art had been met, every flaw removed, down to the slightest.

You and I are far from that stage of mastery, but we are none the less obliged to do some rewriting beyond the intensive correction of bad spots. For in the act of revising on the small scale one comes upon gaps in thought and — what is a bad — real or apparent repetitions or intrusions, sometimes called *backstitching*. Both are occasions for surgery. In the first case you must write a new fragment and insert it so that its beginning and end fit what precedes and follows. In the second case you must lift the intruding passage and transfer or eliminate it. Simple arithmetic shows you that there are then three and not two sutures to be made before the page shows a smooth surface. If you have never performed this sort of work in writing, you must take it from me that it affords pleasure and satisfaction, both.

The Writer at Work

BRENDA CHOW *(student essay)*

I wish to invent a device. It would look innocuous enough, a mechanical thingamajig in a small leather case. But inside . . . inside it would hold the mystery of the mind, the power of thoughts and the force of emotion. There would be wires stretching out of it, to connect the case with your mind. I would call it The Thinker, and it would read your thoughts and transcribe them onto paper. Wouldn't it be wonderful? All your thoughts caught on paper, never a thought wasted. What efficiency!

Imagine the implications: the artist would simply conjure up an image, and it would magically appear on a screen. The scientist would be able to visualize equations; the photographer would take pictures in the maze of the mind. And a writer would not have to pick up a pen, but would brandish a tube of liquid paper instead.

It is a device which would be most useful to me. Sometimes, I remember things with ice-cold clarity, and the idea comes to me with hardly any effort at all. But then the words are caught somewhere in my mind, and when I sit at the computer terminal, the wonderful skein of imagery gets snarled within the sheltering embrace of logic. There is none of that beautiful marching precision of thought and the description gets lost somewhere in the tedious and pains-taking re-creation. Sometimes there is no idea, only a small phrase, and an elusive phrase at that. It haunts me, taunts me, until, out it comes, the perfect phrase. But what to do with it? It is only a useless sentence stored in my mind, biding its time for a good story.

Writing is frustrating. The words get stuck, the ideas won't come, the plot doesn't move . . .

I sit in front of the computer, its glowing cursor urging me on. The idea is slow to come. The radio plays old Springsteen, and suddenly there is a lightning flash, a sudden "eureka!", and the light bulb pulsates urgently over my head; a phrase pops into my mind. My fingers fly over the keyboard, and there is only the sound of the tapping keys for another two hours. The radio plays on — it could be Mozart, The Dead Milkmen . . . whatever. I remain oblivious. The words cascade to my fingertips effortlessly. It's as if my brain is wired into a creativity socket. At first, it's only a jumble of words, which then, of their own volition, form sentences and paragraphs. And, at the end, there is a story. It is a diamond in the rough. I go over it, gloating a little, and change sentences, alter paragraphs, ruthlessly delete whole sections. The whole middle is gutted, the ending discarded, and new ideas crowd my mind, new sentences glide onto the screen.

There, it is done, the first draft. But it gets more intense. Is "reputation" really the world I want? I decide to give it a little description. "He was anxious to rescue his impeccable reputation," I write. But that doesn't quite cut it. "Impeccable reputation" gives it a different flavour, but its taste is a little too bland. "Sterling reputation" bestows a different connotation altogether. Here, the ingredients blend uniformly. I am momentarily appeased. However, other sentences call to me, and I must play the medic, grimly making sharp, clean cuts to sever the gangrenous flesh. This part is the most agonizing. The incisions must be precise, the dead tissue carved out just so. It is a painful but necessary process.

After the story has been trimmed, without loss of main arteries and veins, the cosmetic alteration commences. The scapel lies neglected, while I pick up the make-up brush. First, a coat of foundation for consistency. Then, colours leap out of the jars: toothsome verbs, ripe with the red of crushed strawberries, the indigo blue of still skies. Nouns are crisp greens and dazzling yellows. Now, for the adjectives. They are shimmery and elusive. They are glints of the ocean, the smell of sun-warmed hay, the sound of honey dripping.

And still, the job is not done. I go through the whole story again, scrupulously fixing commas and semi-colons, adding a bit of description here, cutting out the rhapsody there. I must constantly check the Plausibility Meter. Are all wounds cauterized invisibly? Then, to the Interest Meter. Is the heart squeezing enough blood through the story? This is the most tiring part of editing. I must check the details again and again. It is a little line splicing frayed rope together again. The final step is to achieve wholeness, I must twist each separate strand together, tighter and tighter, until the naked eye cannot see where it once was eroded. When the seam is invisible, I know the chore is almost finished.

I look at the clock, and I am always surprised at how much time I spent writing three or four pages. I am exhausted, but it is a nice exhaustion. It is a peculiar kind of feeling, finishing a story. I can only describe it as being replete but empty. It's like finishing a marathon, breaking the white tape with arms upraised, and victory gushing up your body, until you are heady with it. It's like a weary swimmer swimming lap upon lap until the adrenalin rush is over and there is nothing left to give, and you sit on the edge of the pool panting, but wearing the golden mantle of accomplishment quietly around you.

When I finish a story it's the same feeling. The rush of excitement is over; the juice has run dry, and there is nothing left to give. All I have given is right there on the pages in front of me, and then the happiness crescendos and fills me — there is no more to the story, and that is the emptiness, but there is also a sense of glorious satisfaction that begins in my gut and soars up and up and up until I am spinning with the stars.

The finished product is beautiful. The words are lined up with militant accuracy, and none of the sweat and labour shows. There is only the message. And, sometimes, if you look very carefully, there is the writer standing in the twilight, eyes averted, hair askew, smiling foolishly.

2. The Classical Essay

KEY WORK:

"Where to draw the line?" — Mary Jo Leddy

ASSOCIATED READINGS:

"The Good Life" — Bertrand Russell
"Haunted by lives unlived" — David Helwig
"The Eichmann Trial in Retrospect" — Abba Eban
"Environmentalism and Civil Disobedience" — Des Kennedy
"How I Learned to Appreciate Sunday Afternoon Football *or*
   The Fine Art of Sandwich Making" — Sandra Bardocz
   (student essay)

If you record your thoughts and responses in a journal or a writer's notebook, then you are familiar with the conventions of the classical essay. And, if you have ever taken one of those entries and polished it for an audience other than yourself, then you have written the type of essay you will find in this section.

The classical essay was invented in the sixteenth century by the French writer, Michel de Montaigne, who published a collection of short prose writings in which he explored personal responses to various subjects and situations. No subject was too insignificant or too lofty to attract his attention. He called his writings "essais," a word which means "trials" or "attempts." All other more specialized forms of the essay have developed from this original form.

Classical essays share many characteristics and conventions with the Autobiography, Biography, Profile, and Narrative Essay and, like these other forms of the essay, provide researchers with a rich source of information and insight into an individual, society, or the human condition.

The Key Work, "Where to draw the line?," a tentative examination of the fine art of compromise, is a typical classical essay. The Associated Readings demonstrate the variety within the classical essay: "The Good Life" and "Haunted by lives unlived" are thoughtful personal speculations and reflections on life itself; "Environmentalism and Civil Disobedience" and "The Eichmann Trial in Retrospect" are passionate reflections on three important issues of our time. And, finally, the essay by a college student,

"How I Learned to Appreciate Sunday Afternoon Football *or* The Fine Art of Sandwich Making," demonstrates the lighter side of classical essay writing.

Conventions of the Classical Essay

Purpose	To explore and reflect on values and the meaning of experience
Audience	General: one's fellow humans, but often with a strong sense of self as audience as well
Tone	Tentative, questioning, reflective; may be either serious or humorous; more subjective than objective
Voice	Expressive and individualistic
Response	A sense of mental and emotional kinship
Language	LEVEL — Usually expressive; individual style is often apparent CHARACTERISTICS — May be first, second, or third person; often stylized, strongly rhetorical
Structure	Generally fluid, in keeping with reflective and tentative approach

BEFORE READING

1. In your journal or writer's notebook reflect on a moving experience that prompted you to explore its significance.

2. To what extent do Canadians seem willing to compromise to solve problems and deal with issues? Cite examples.

3. In pairs or small groups examine the conventions of the classical essay and consider why some people might find writing classical essays more to their liking than writing other essay forms.

Where to draw the line?

MARY JO LEDDY

Compromise. On one hand, it has been promoted as the great Canadian virtue; on the other, it has been decried as a dangerous national proclivity. The word compromise spells out the issue of national identity and purpose. It also compresses, for each of us, the question of substance and style of our lives. At some point, in some place, we all face the dilemma of whether or not to compromise.

In liberal democracies, the ability to compromise is considered one of the most important political virtues. A cursory review of history would seem to confirm the desirability of diluting any absolute principles in politics. The victims of crusades, inquisitions and the Holocaust are mute witnesses to the havoc wrought by unbending ideals and ideologies. In the relentless logic of totalitarianism, the necessity of compromising is eliminated by eliminating human beings.

Against this historical backdrop, the will to compromise seems enlightened and courageous. One of the most telling stories illustrating the cost of such compromise arises from a little known event during the First World War at the battle of the Somme. Two sides faced each other in the trenches, advancing and retreating by inches. Thousands died, were maimed for life and driven crazy in the process. Some, who had been left for dead in the middle of No Man's Land, began to pick themselves up and to care for one another in the trenches mid-way between the two opposing forces.

German and English soldiers struggled to help one another survive. They were called "the people of the middle." Ultimately, their very existence became a threat to the supreme sense of nationalism that was essential if the soldiers of either side were to continue to kill each other. In one of the most unusual agreements of wartime, the German and British leaders agreed to suspend hostilities for a morning in order to co-operate in gassing the "people of the middle."

Finding the middle ground, searching for common ground and making it an inhabitable space is sometimes highly costly.

In human relations, the inability to compromise also wreaks its own havoc. Many marriages fail because one or other or both of the partners refused to negotiate and compromise. In such situations, the inability or unwillingness to compromise is more a sign of weakness than of strength.

Yet, there is another lesson to be learned from modern history and from our own experience. There are times and places when the middle ground disappears, when common ground is an illusion, when compromise is a nicer word for coercion, when reconciliation means the abdication of responsibility.

Think of the Hitler era—what could compromise possibly mean in such a situation? People were either helping to make the Nazi system work or they were resisting it. Neutrality was impossible. Even the bystanders became complicit.

Another example: in the extreme economic disparities of many Latin American countries, those who are not struggling with the poor are contributing to their oppression. As Archbishop Oscar Romero of El Salvador discovered, it is impossible to remain above or beyond such a social conflict. The six Jesuit priests who were murdered in the university of San Salvador in November had come to understand that there are certain realities with which one should never be reconciled. These men refused to be reconciled with injustice, they refused to believe that the lives of their people were negotiable.

These and many other men and women demonstrate that genuine compromise can only be effected when the rights and interests of all are granted equal weight and legitimacy. When there is no such equality, the rhetoric of compromise serves only to camouflage the coercive tactics of the powerful. In a situation of inequality, the rights and the interests of the weaker are always compromised. Compromise becomes synonymous with capitulation. This is what the aboriginal peoples of our country have been trying to tell us for some time.

In human relationships this perversion of compromise has often prevailed. In marriage, one of the partners continually capitulates for the sake of "peace in the family." This is not peace. This is pacification. And there are far too many examples of those who have been ethically compromised "for the good of the company" or "in the interests of national security" or for some more dubious good.

In fact, we take heart from many people who have refused to compromise. Witness the wide-spread admiration for African National Congress leader Nelson Mandela and Czechoslovak President Vaclav Havel. We admire their refusal to negotiate or compromise with the powers that be. We recognize them as people with a bottom line. They seem precious and rare — especially in a culture such as ours, a consumer culture, where every value seems negotiable, every relationship seems as disposable as a paper cup.

History teaches us many lessons. Out of the seemingly contradictory experiences of our collective and personal lives, we can say only that there are times when we must compromise and times when we should not.

We cannot say in advance of any particular situation what stance we should take. But we have probably fallen victim to some political or psychological pattern if we either compromise in every situation or refuse to compromise in any situation. As Canadians, we are probably more likely to see compromise as a virtue. We are citizens living through the middle age of a middle power in the world. We tend to identify ourselves as inhabitants of the middle ground. Perhaps, personally and politically, we tend to compromise more than we should.

There must be some value, some principle, some person, some group, in our lives that is non-negotiable. If everything and everyone is negotiable, then we ourselves will ultimately become negotiable — in the eyes of others or perhaps even in our own eyes. If we do not know what we are willing to die for then we do not know what we want to live for.

I believe that there is within each of us some small, strong and even eternal point of our being that is beyond compromise. More than we know, this enables us to engage in authentic compromise with generosity of spirit and clarity of heart. I cannot prove to you that this is so. What we can do is to act on this belief, put it into practice and make it more so.

EXPLORING THE CLASSICAL ESSAY

1. Why does Leddy focus on compromise as such a significant factor for both individuals and nations?

2. a. How does Leddy distinguish between "times when we must compromise and times when we should not"?
   b. To what extent do you agree with her? Give examples from your own knowledge of history and your own experience.

3. Leddy demonstrates that there can be a perversion of "compromise" on both the political and personal levels. Explain what she means by this.

4. To what extent do you agree with Leddy's final assertion that "there is within each of us some small, strong and even eternal point of our being that is beyond compromise"? Justify your answer.

5. Show that, even though her tone is reflective, tentative, and questioning, Leddy has written a powerful essay.

EXTENSIVE STUDY

1. Read "The Eichmann Trial in Retrospect" by Abba Eban (p. 57), and show how his use of language and rhetorical devices intensifies the impact of his exploration of his topic and his reflections.

2. After reading Russell's "The Good Life" (p. 50), debate his contention that "the good life consists of love guided by knowledge."

3. a. Read "Environmentalism and Civil Disobedience" by Des Kennedy (p. 63) and "Dressed to Kill" by Robert Hough (p. 119), and discuss the extent to which you agree with the writers' reflections on the suggested methods, particularly the nonviolence model, for dealing with environmental issues.
   b. In role-playing pairs, conduct a debate between Des Kennedy and Robert Hough about ways of solving environmental problems.

4. Read "Haunted by lives unlived" (p. 55) and in pairs discuss the likelihood of your choosing to be friends with David Helwig.

5. a. Decide which of the classical essays you have read in this section was the most appealing to you. Support your decision with a list of reasons.
   b. Using your selected essay and the set of conventions, compose a set of four or five Tips to help an individual write an appealing classical essay.

THE WRITING FOLDER

1. In your journal or writer's workbook reflect on several of the following:
   - Mary Jo Leddy's thoughts on compromise
   - Abba Eban's query that "beyond this issue is the question of whether we are safe against a renewal of the tragedy" from the perspective of the 1990s
   - David Helwig's reflections on "the roads not taken"
   - Des Kennedy's thoughts on nonviolence as a way of achieving environmental goals

2. Develop one of your works above into a polished classical essay for publication in a specific magazine. Append a letter to the editor explaining why your essay is appropriate for this audience.

3. Write a classical essay in the same light-hearted tone that Sandra Bardocz created in "How I Learned to Appreciate Sunday

Afternoon Football *or* The Fine Art of Sandwich Making" (p. 69). Select a topic or subject of personal interest to you. You might even want to begin with Bardocz's first words: "My (dad, mom, brother, etc.) is the world's biggest. . . ."

INDEPENDENT STUDY

1. In consultation with your teacher-librarian, locate and examine literature on issues surrounding the Holocaust. Write an extended classical essay in response to your findings, reflecting on the Holocaust from an historical as well as a contemporary perspective. You may wish to use as a focal point Ebban's essay or Elie Wiesel's *Night* or *The Diary of Anne Frank*.

2. Read a collection of essays by and a biography or autobiography of a well-known classical essayist such as Bertrand Russell, Henry David Thoreau, George Orwell, Virginia Woolf, Stephen Leacock, H.G. Wells, or the more contemporary E.B. White, Gloria Steinham, Robertson Davies, Arnold Toynbee, Robert Fulford, Rachel Carson, V.S. Naipaul, June Callwood, or Doris Lessing. Write a detailed profile of the person, using his or her life to illuminate the concerns evident in the essays. Present your profile to the class. You may find it helpful to refer to the Autobiography, Biography, and Profile.

3. In consultation with your teacher and teacher-librarian, examine the nonviolence movement of the twentieth century, focussing on works and actions of Martin Luther King, Jr. or Mahatma Gandhi. Write a report or an essay on your findings and present it to the class for discussion.

TIMED READING AND WRITING

Read "Haunted by lives unlived" (p. 55), and answer the following questions in the time specified by your teacher:

1. Summarize the main point of the essay in two or three sentences.

2. To what extent does Helwig's style (diction, images, sentences, tone, voice) enhance the impact of the essay on the reader?

The Good Life

BERTRAND RUSSELL

There have been at different times and among different people many varying conceptions of the good life. To some extent the differences were amenable to argument; this was when men differed as to the means to achieve a given end. Some think that prison is a good way of preventing crime; others hold that education would be better. A difference of this sort can be decided by sufficient evidence. But some differences cannot be tested in this way. Tolstoy condemned all war; others have held the life of a soldier doing battle for the right to be very noble. Here there was probably involved a real difference as to ends. Those who praised the soldier usually consider the punishment of sinners a good thing in itself; Tolstoy did not think so. On such a matter no argument is possible. I cannot, therefore, prove that my view of the good life is right; I can only state my view and hope that as many as possible will agree. My view is this: *The good life is one inspired by love and guided by knowledge.*

Knowledge and love are both indefinitely extensible; therefore, however good a life may be, a better life can be imagined. Neither love without knowledge nor knowledge without love can produce a good life. In the Middle Ages, when pestilence appeared in a country, holy men advised the population to assemble in churches and pray for deliverance; the result was that the infection spread with extraordinary rapidity among the crowded masses of supplicants. This was an example of love without knowledge. The late war afforded an example of knowledge without love. In each case, the result was death on a large scale.

Although both love and knowledge are necessary, love is in a sense more fundamental, since it will lead intelligent people to seek knowledge, in order to find out how to benefit those whom they love. But if people are not intelligent, they will be content to believe what they have been told and may do harm in spite of the most genuine benevolence. Medicine affords, perhaps, the best example of what I mean. An able physician is more useful to a patient than the most devoted friend, and progress in medical knowledge does more for the health of the community than ill-informed philanthropy.

Nevertheless, an element of benevolence is essential even here if any but the rich are to profit by scientific discoveries.

Love is a word which covers a variety of feelings; I have used it purposely, as I wish to include them all. Love as an emotion — which is what I am speaking about, for love "on principle" does not seem to me genuine — moves between two poles: on one side, pure delight in contemplation; on the other, pure benevolence. Where inanimate objects are concerned, delight alone enters in; we cannot feel benevolence toward a landscape or a sonata. This type of enjoyment is presumably the source of art. It is stronger, as a rule, in very young children than in adults, who are apt to view objects in a utilitarian spirit. It plays a large part in our feelings toward human beings, some whom have charm and some the reverse, when considered simply as objects of aesthetic contemplation.

The opposite pole of love is pure benevolence. Men have sacrificed their lives to helping lepers; in such a case the love they felt cannot have had any element of aesthetic delight. Parental affection, as a rule, is accompanied by pleasure in the child's appearance but remains strong when this element is wholly absent. It would seem odd to call a mother's interest in a sick child "benevolence," because we are in the habit of using this word to describe a pale emotion nine parts humbug. But it is difficult to find any other word to describe the desire for another person's welfare. It is a fact that a desire of this sort may reach any degree of strength in the case of parental feeling. In other cases it is far less intense; indeed it would seem likely that all altruistic emotion is a sort of overflow of parental feeling, or sometimes a sublimation of it. For want of a better word, I shall call this emotion "benevolence." But I want to make it clear that I am speaking of an emotion, not a principle, and that I do not include in it any feeling of superiority such as is sometimes associated with the word. The word *sympathy* expresses part of what I mean but leaves out the element of activity that I wish to include.

Love at its fullest is an indissoluble combination of the two elements, delight and well-wishing. The pleasure of a parent in a beautiful and successful child combines both elements; so does sex love at its best. But in sex love, benevolence will only exist where there is secure possession, since otherwise jealousy will destroy it, while perhaps actually increasing the delight in contemplation. Delight without well-wishing may be cruel; well-wishing without delight easily tends to become cold and a little superior. A person who wishes to be loved wishes to be the object of a love containing both elements, except in cases of extreme weakness, such as infancy and severe illness. In these cases benevolence may be all that is desired. Conversely, in cases of extreme strength, admiration is more desired than benevolence: this is the state of mind of potentates and famous beauties. We only desire other people's good wishes in proportion as we feel ourselves in need of help or in danger of harm from them. At least, that would seem to be the biological logic of the situation, but it is not quite true to life. We desire affection in order to escape from the feeling of loneliness, in order to be, as we say, "understood." This is a matter of sympathy, not merely of benevolence; the person whose affection is satisfactory to us must not merely wish us well but must know in what our happiness consists. But this belongs to the other element of the good life — namely, knowledge.

In a perfect world, every sentient being would be to every other the object of the fullest love, compounded of delight, benevolence, and understanding inextricably blended. It does not follow that, in this actual world, we ought to attempt to have such feelings toward all the sentient beings whom we encounter. There are many in whom we cannot feel delight, because they are disgusting; if we were to do violence to our nature by trying to see beauties in them, we should merely blunt our susceptibilities to what we naturally find beautiful. Not to mention human beings, there are fleas and bugs and lice. We should have to be as hard pressed as the Ancient Mariner before we could feel delight in contemplating these creatures. Some saints, it is true, have called them "pearls of God," but what these men delighted in was the opportunity of displaying their own sanctity.

Benevolence is easier to extend widely, but even benevolence has its limits. If a man wished to marry a lady, we should not think the better of him for withdrawing if he found that someone else also wished to marry her: we should regard this as a fair field for competition. Yet his feelings toward a rival cannot be *wholly* benevolent. I think that in all descriptions of the good life here on earth we must assume a certain basis of animal vitality and animal instinct; without this, life becomes tame and uninteresting. Civilization should be something added to this, not substituted for it; the ascetic saint and the detached sage fail in this respect to be complete human beings. A small number of them may enrich a community; but a world composed of them would die of boredom.

These considerations lead to a certain emphasis on the element of delight as an ingredient in the best love. Delight, in this actual world, is unavoidably selective and prevents us from having the same feelings toward all mankind. When conflicts arise between delight and benevolence, they must, as a rule, be decided by a compromise, not by a complete surrender of either. Instinct has its rights, and if we do violence to it beyond a point it takes vengeance in subtle ways. Therefore in aiming at a good life the limits of human possibility must be borne in mind. Here again, however, we are brought back to the necessity of knowledge.

When I speak of knowledge as an ingredient of the good life, I am not thinking of ethical knowledge but of scientific knowledge and knowledge of particular facts. I do not think there is, strictly speaking, such a thing as ethical knowledge. If we desire to achieve some end, knowledge may show us the means, and this knowledge may loosely pass as ethical. But I do not believe that we can decide what sort of conduct is right or wrong except by reference to its probable consequences. Given an end to be achieved, it is a question for science to discover how to achieve it. All moral rules must be tested by examining whether they tend to realize ends that we desire. I say ends that we desire, not ends that we *ought* to desire. What we "ought" to desire is merely what someone else wishes us to desire. Usually it is what the authorities wish us to desire — parents, schoolmasters, policemen, and judges. If you say to me, "You ought to do so-and-so," the motive power of your remark lies in my desire for your approval — together, possibly, with rewards or punishments attached to your approval or disapproval. Since all behavior springs from desire, it is clear that ethical notions can have no importance except as they influence desire. They do this through the desire for approval and the fear of disapproval. These are powerful social forces, and we shall naturally endeavor to win them to our side if we wish to realize any social purpose. When I say that the morality of conduct is to be judged by its probable consequences, I mean that I desire to see approval given to behavior likely to realize social purposes which we desire, and disapproval to opposite behavior. At present this is not done; there are certain traditional rules according to which approval and disapproval are meted out quite regardless of consequences. But this is a topic with which we shall deal at some other time.

The superfluity of theoretical ethics is obvious in simple cases. Suppose, for instance, your child is ill. Love makes you wish to cure it, and science tells you how to do so. There is not an intermediate stage of ethical theory, where it is demonstrated that your child had better be cured. Your act springs directly from desire for an end, together with knowledge of means. This is equally true of all acts, whether good or bad. The ends differ, and the knowledge is more adequate in some cases than in others. But there is no conceivable way of making people do things they do not wish to do. What is possible is to alter their desires by a system of rewards and penalties, among which social approval and disapproval are not the least potent. The question for the legislative moralist is, therefore: How shall this system of rewards and punishments be arranged so as to secure the maximum of what is desired by the legislative authority? If I say that the legislative authority has bad desires, I mean merely that its desires conflict with those of some section of the community to which I belong. Outside human desires there is no moral standard.

Thus, what distinguishes ethics from science is not any special kind of knowledge but merely desire. The knowledge required in ethics is exactly like the knowledge elsewhere; what is peculiar is that certain ends are desired, and that right conduct is what conduces to them. Of course, if the definition of right conduct is to make a wide appeal, the end must be such as large sections of mankind desire. If I defined right conduct as that which increases my own income, readers would disagree. The whole effectiveness of any ethical argument lies in its scientific part, i.e., in the proof that one kind of conduct, rather than some other, is a means to an end which is widely desired. I distinguish, however, between ethical argument and ethical education. The latter consists in strengthening certain desires and weakening others. This is quite a different process.

We can now explain more exactly the purport of the definition of the good life with which this essay began. When I said that the good life consists of love guided by knowledge, the desire which prompted me was the desire to live such a life as far as possible, and to see others living it; and the logical content of the statement is that, in a community where men live in this way, more desires will be satisfied than in one where there is less love or less knowledge. I do not mean that such a life is "virtuous" or that its opposite is "sinful," for these are conceptions which seem to me to have no scientific justification.

Haunted by lives unlived

DAVID HELWIG

We are all followed through life by ghosts, but the ghosts I have in mind are not supernatural beings, at least not in the usual sense. They are not formed of ectoplasm or electricity or an altered flesh, and they are not the surviving traces of the dead. The ghosts I am thinking of are ghost selves, the lives we have chosen not to lead coming back to haunt us.

Everyone makes choices, every day, although some of these are more crucial than others, and at every point where a choice is made, another choice is not, and if our life is defined by the choices we have made, it is also haunted, at least in moments of thoughtfulness, by those that weren't.

Robert Frost has a poem called *The Road Not Taken*, which is about this. Years ago, when I was a teacher, I sometimes presented this poem to students. There is a line toward the end about taking the less travelled of two roads in a wood, and students liked to identify this as Frost's choice of a poetic vocation. Perhaps. But if the title means anything, what he's thinking about is the subtler question of the continuing existence of what was not done.

Such thoughts can come with very different sorts of emotion. How many lives are haunted by huge regrets? If only I had . . . married, not married, been braver, left sooner, worked harder . . . and so on. For those who feel like this, it must be hard not to remember Edith Piaf, who lived a painful and chaotic life and said of it, "I regret nothing." It is a dreadful thing, regret, that eats away the heart and must surely, in the name of sanity, be stifled in the energy of love for the choices made.

But what I was thinking of, when I first began to reflect on the ghost existences that haunt us, was something less painful. Even those who are able to accept the consequences of their choices with equanimity will be aware of untaken roads, and it is those that can be considered lightly, even playfully, to provide an enrichment to our being.

We have unlived lives in the realm of our personal and intimate existence, but also in our professional lives. Surely, there was a time when you thought of becoming . . . what? For myself, the existence I did not choose was that of a singer. There was a time, when I was in university, when such a thing might have been possible. I was offered a job as one of the professional soloists at a large church in downtown Toronto. If I had taken the job, gone on studying voice, who is to know?

But I was a high-strung and nervous young man, and singing in public — although I was vain enough to love the attention — was hard on me. At that age I already knew that I wanted to make myself a writer, and that was enough of a challenge. So I turned down the job offer and didn't sing seriously for 15 years.

That life, the one I didn't choose, does not exist, of course. I can speculate on whether in fact it was possible, whether my musicianship was sufficient, whether I might not have been daunted by difficulty, and soon enough such speculations become empty and depleting. Tell such a story once or twice and it starts to become a myth, a worn anecdote.

What happened, in my case, is that in later life I had a taste of things I had abandoned. A friend who is a church organist got me back to singing. I joined other choirs, sang more, studied voice for a while and got to make a good deal of joyful noise.

How often, I wonder, do people return to what has been loved and abandoned as an avocation? The guy who plays piano in the bar on weekends. The one who becomes an amateur hockey coach. Things have changed sufficiently in the roles of men and women in recent generations that the interplay of vocation and avocation in women's lives is probably more unpredictable. Still, I expect there are a lot of lost dancers in those aerobics classes. The mind remembers its past desires, and perhaps the body does as well.

Where does life happen? It's a question that often puzzles me. Does it only happen at the present moment, in the place where the body just now finds itself? Obviously not. We also live in memory and expectation, and both these things are, in some ways, forms of imagination. I can imagine those I love as they were or as they may come to be. Absent, they are present.

The moment when those two roads diverged, that too is now an imaginary moment, and the first few steps on the road untaken are as vivid as the first few steps on the one that was followed until new choices intervene, new decisions, and the merely hypothetical is left behind.

We have and should have an intense attentive loyalty to the here and now. Nevertheless, what exists in the vivid physical present is surrounded by a haze of memory, expectation, belief, fantasy. I suspect I am not alone in being unable, now and then, to distinguish a memory of a dream from the memory of an actual event. Both memories exist.

The singer I did not become, the athlete or dancer or actor you did not become, have an existence of some sort. Lost possibilities taunt us, amuse us, challenge us. The single life we are given is both too much and not enough. Even the most singular of us is plural, haunted by the ghost beings we own and are.

The Eichmann Trial in Retrospect

ABBA EBAN

He who cannot remember the past is doomed to repeat it.
GEORGE SANTAYANA

On a winter day in 1944 the head of an industrial concern in Berlin calmly signed the following letter to Gestapo headquarters:

> Following our verbal discussion regarding the delivery of equipment of simple construction for the burning of bodies, we are submitting plans for our perfected cremation ovens which operate with coal and which have hitherto given full satisfaction.
>
> We suggest two crematoria furnaces for the building planned, but we advise you to make further inquiries to make sure that two ovens will be sufficient for your requirements.
>
> We guarantee the effectiveness of the cremation ovens as well as their durability, the use of the best material and our faultless workmanship.
>
> Heil Hitler!
> C.H. Kori

There was a good reason for the writer's complacent mood. The places in which 'full satisfaction' had been given included Dachau and Lubin, where 'the best material and faultless workmanship' had efficiently converted the bodies of men, women, and children into piles of anonymous powdered ash. Why should not the Kori Corporation now receive the Belgrade business? Competition, however, was keen. The I.A. Topf Corporation was showing great technical ingenuity, as is clear from its terse note of February 12, 1943, to the 'Central Construction Office of the S.S. and the Police at Auschwitz':

Subject: Crematoria 2 and 3 for the camp.
We acknowledge receipt of your order for five triple furnaces, including two electric elevators for raising the corpses and one emergency elevator. A practical installation for stoking coal was also ordered and one for transporting ashes.

These documents, produced at the Nuremberg trials of Nazi war criminals and at the Eichmann trial in Jerusalem, are excellently typed. There was, of course, an adequate number of carbon copies for the files. One can imagine the respectable industrialists going off to their clubs in a fine glow of patriotic duty and commercial enterprise.

But there was no point in cremation furnaces without the human fuel. Not far away in his Berlin office, Adolf Eichmann was signing a briefer document. It was a telegram to his emissaries in occupied countries. It read simply: 'Children's transports can get under way.' The reference was to children who no longer had parents with whom to embark on the journey to Auschwitz for collective gassing. Even these presented problems. The Jerusalem court sat transfixed in silent horror as Attorney-General Hausner unfolded the story: 'You will hear evidence of tender infants pressed by their mothers to their bodies in the gas chamber so that they were not immediately poisoned, until the executioners came and threw them alive into the furnaces.'

This was standard practice. But a special routine was now necessary to organize the asphyxiation of Jewish children who had no parents to accompany them. How this worked in occupied France was factually described at the Jerusalem trial.

The children would arrive at the Drancy Camp packed in busses guarded by policemen. . . . On the arrival of the busses they would begin to remove the children and lead them in groups to the halls, the older ones holding the hands of the smaller children; or carrying them in their arms. They did not weep, the children; they walked terrified, disciplined, miserable, and complied with the orders like a flock of sheep, one helping the other. . . .

   On the day of deportation, they would be wakened at five o'clock in the morning. Irritable, half asleep, most of the children would refuse to get up and go down to the courtyard. The volunteer women would have to urge them, gently, patiently and so tragically, so as to convince the older children that they must obey orders and vacate the halls. On a number of occasions the entreaties did not help. The children cried and refused to leave their mattresses. The gendarmes would then enter the halls and pick up the children in their arms as they screamed with fear, struggling and grasping at each other. The halls were like a madhouse; the scene was too terrible for even the hardest men to bear.

In the courtyard they would call out the names of the children one by one, mark them off in the register, and direct them to the busses. When a bus filled up it would leave the camp with its cargo. Since many of the children remained unidentified and others would not answer to their correct or assumed names, they would include them in the convoy to make up the number.

Each convoy consisted of about five hundred children and five hundred adults chosen from the camp prisoners. Within a period of about three weeks, during the second half of August and the first part of September, 1943, four thousand children, thus made into orphans, were transported in this fashion to be exterminated with adult strangers.

Hauptsturmführer Roethke was present at these transports and would inspect personally the parading of the children, the roll call, and the loading into the busses.

The people of Israel are the sons, the daughters, the brothers, the sisters, the fathers, the mothers of the millions whose agony was re-enacted during the twelve months of the Eichmann trial. The procedures at every stage were marked by careful decorum and high legal scholarship. But behind the reserved procedures one could see the marching ghosts.

If you were a Jew in Europe during those years, and if Adolf Eichmann knew of your existence, your fate was inexorable. You would be rounded up with your family in Amsterdam or Paris, in Belgrade or Venice, in Budapest or Brussels, in Warsaw or Kiev. You would be put on a train for Auschwitz or Treblinka, and then either lined up naked with hundreds of others behind your neat pile of clothes while German soldiers shot you in the neck on the edge of a huge ditch or else herded into a shower room for mass asphyxiation. Your hair would be shorn beforehand, your gold fillings taken afterwards, your ashes used for fertilizer. You could be useful to the German war economy. Today the capital cities and villages of Europe contain ghostlike streets with their communal buildings, synagogues, and schools in which the bustle and laughter of living men, women, and children were choked by the grim ukase issuing from the sinister office in Berlin where Adolf Eichmann pored meticulously over his files, before affixing the most macabre signatures ever inscribed by mortal hand.

All this happened in recent memory. Anybody alive today over the age of thirty-five is in some way a part of this experience. For we belong to the unique generation that committed or suffered or failed to prevent these things. In each of the three contingencies we have a direct relationship to the drama. The theme of the Jerusalem courtroom was the unending tension between the sublime attributes of man's nature and his unlimited capacity to distort the human image. And in this conflict our generation has lived the moment of man's darkest defeat.

Some would have preferred not to evoke the past. Does not the tormented human imagination deserve respite from the assault of such memories? There are people of impeccable sincerity who advocate its oblivion. Mr. Victor Gollancz, for example, has written that 'The sooner we forget the cruelties of the past, the better.'

After millions of years of evolution, a species emerges on this planet endowed with the gift of memory and articulation. Man is the only animal able to transmit experience. And the transmission of experience is the central core of education and moral progress. Memory is the father of conscience. The issue is whether we should wipe from the tablets of memory the most vivid evidence of the consequences flowing from chauvinism, racial discrimination, and inhumanity.

The question must be answered in the name of the future, not of the past. Man is the only animal that has ever shown a tendency to destroy its own species. He may now become the first and only creature to devastate its habitat. He cannot afford to ignore any experience that throws light on the social consequence of his nature. 'The fundamental principle of all morality,' wrote Jean-Jacques Rousseau, 'is that man is a being naturally good, loving justice and order; that there is not any original perversity in the human heart and that the first movements of nature are always right.'

There may have been evidence for this outlook in the eighteenth century. It is less easy to reconcile it with the memory of ordinary men — tens of thousands of them — going calmly about their work of slaughter or writing solemn minutes in impeccable commercial jargon about the 'satisfactory' attributes of machines for burning bodies. The human conscience needs an alarm bell, not a sleeping pill.

The first lesson of the trial takes us back to the moral torment of our age. The horrors of Nazism sprang from a society in which high standards of science and technology were fostered. We are reminded here of the fallacy of a technical rationalism uninhibited by moral restraint. Man has probed deeply into the spectacle of nature, but he stands baffled before the incalculabilities of his own character. He has exercised command over his external realm but seems impotent to control his inner domain. Thus the age of scientific triumph is the epoch of confusion. Man is conscious of his lack of inner and outer harmony, obsessed by a sense of helplessness before the forces generated by his own creative imagination. He looks gropingly into the past in the hope of finding a beam of light to illumine his future.

It is for this future, and for its sake alone, that the trial was held. Its lesson and counsel affect every layer of social experience. It teaches how discrimination, taking root in small beginnings, leads to vast and uncontrollable disaster. The outrages of Auschwitz and Treblinka could not have occurred had there not been tens of thousands of men who became accustomed to look at other men as though they were not human at all. A man cannot murder others in cold blood, he cannot dash a baby to the ground or fling children into a furnace, unless he is first convinced that they are not a part of his own humanity.

The trial asks urgent questions about the limits beyond which racial incitement cannot be tolerated. This is the oldest dilemma of liberalism. If a society is free and tolerant, must it even tolerate attacks on its own toleration? If a society can suppress pornography without ceasing to be free, why is it forbidden to establish some criterion whereby ideas fatal to social morality may be denied the sanction of law? The indulgence granted the Nazi doctrine in the 1930's before it reached irresistible proportions stands as an ominous warning against inertia and apathy. In the Weimar Republic this indulgence flowed from the doctrine that there is no limit to the free dissemination of opinion — not even the limit of decency and survival. On the international plane, it sheltered behind a doctrine of sovereignty applied with such rigid pedantry as to inhibit effective international intervention. In the postwar world, lesser outrages have fortunately evoked a much sharper and more insistent international reaction.

In the particular terms of Jewish history, the trial represented Israel's assertion of the dignity and equality of Jewish life. The few voices that were raised against the verdict had not questioned similar action when the allied governments inflicted condign penalties on men who had not been responsible for a small fraction of Eichmann's butchery. There has been an insidious, if unconscious, assumption across history that Jewish lives are not enclosed within the same framework of law and social morality as the lives of other peoples.

It was probably in response to this background that the Jerusalem courts took care to remain in the orbit of the Nuremberg jurisprudence and of the legal practice of other nations outraged by Nazi violence. To have done anything else would have been to convict the allied and resistance powers of excessive severity. In a world in which the capital penalty still exists and in which the precedents for penalizing racial massacre have been so clearly and recently demarcated, any other course would have been a rebellion against the established juridical standards. Israel was created in order to make Jewish history flow in harmony with the universal procession of law — and not outside its realm, as in all previous generations. It is true that the Jerusalem courts had a particular message to write. But there was no clean slate on which to write it. I can personally testify that some in the legislative and executive branches who are passionate opponents of capital punishment felt inexorably that this was not the area in which to commence the writing of new law.

The news of Eichmann's most active operation — the gassing and burning of Hungarian Jews — reached the free world in the summer of 1944. The spokesman of that world brandished an impotent fist at the distant murderer:

> Prime Minister [Churchill] to Foreign Secretary, 11 July 1944.
> There is no doubt that this is probably the greatest and most horrible crime ever committed in the history of the world, and it has been done by scientific machinery by nominally civilized men in the name of a great State and one of the leading races of Europe. It is quite clear that all concerned in this crime who may fall into our hands, including the people who only obeyed orders by carrying out the butcheries, should be put to death after their association with the murders has been proved.

It is not a matter of vengeance. The children clutching each other's hands as they were herded into the slaughter chamber are beyond vengeance or expiation. The issue is whether the human society can be denied the ultimate right to banish from its midst those who massively violate its most sacred compassions. Beyond this issue is the question of whether we are safe against a renewal of the tragedy. We may become so if we save it from oblivion and deduce its lessons in the political, social, and educational domains.

The renaissance artists portrayed the human soul as being drawn upward and downward by elements in its own nature. Both the upward and the downward pull can be discerned in the life of our times. It is still not certain how the tension will be ultimately resolved. The story of this dark and evil assault enters the memory of man as one of his weapons in the struggle for the vindication of his essential humanity.

Environmentalism and Civil Disobedience

DES KENNEDY

I snapped awake to an insistent rapping on my van window. "The police are here!" a muffled voice called urgently. Pulling on my clothes, I stepped out into frigid darkness. Snow-covered mountains loomed up all around, and high above, cold stars glittered in the February sky. At the end of a narrow dirt road on which I was parked, the lights of a dozen RCMP cruisers flashed white and red against the night. There was a hubbub of voices and slammed car doors. Through the lingering fogginess of sleep, I sensed that some moment of truth had arrived.

We'd been camped out amidst the mountains of Vancouver Island for almost a week, about two dozen of us, blockading a mining road. A year earlier the provincial government had passed an order-in-council dramatically altering six of B.C.'s biggest wilderness parks. Thousands of hectares of wilderness were deleted entirely from the park system, and thousands more hectares were reclassified to "recreation area" status in which mineral exploration and other resource developments are permitted.

Strathcona Park, containing more than 200,000 hectares of Vancouver Island wilderness, had been one of the worst hit, but also one of the most fiercely defended. For over a year, the Friends of Strathcona Park had lobbied and petitioned Victoria to rescind the order-in-council. Answered with official lies, bullying and contempt, the group eventually notified the government that any new mineral exploration in the park would be met with civil disobedience. Then, in the early days of 1988, a mining company began moving drilling equipment into the park. Within hours, the Friends of Strathcona blockaded the remote access road, and for a week, protesters, police and miners faced each other across the blockade. Now the police had arrived in force, armed with an injunction and determined to break the blockade.

What evolved in the ensuing months became a textbook case of nonviolent resistance as a tool in environmental causes. Eventually successful, the experience leaves me with a firm conviction that significant environmental change in certain areas — generally where enormous potential profits are involved — may only be achieved by carefully orchestrated campaigns of nonviolent civil disobedience.

This conviction is not shared throughout the environmental community, and the deliberate use of lawbreaking tactics is often a hotly debated issue at environmental gatherings. I've heard representatives from some established environmental groups deride the use of civil disobedience for creating a "circus atmosphere" which ultimately discredits the movement. One wilderness group director told me his multimillion dollar organization wouldn't condone illegal acts because to do so would jeopardize its charitable tax status. On the other hand, groups like Greenpeace and the Sea Shepherd Society have a long history of using "illegal" (if sometimes not entirely "nonviolent") actions to tremendous effect.

As I sit at my desk writing this, almost two years after the Strathcona blockade, Gitskan natives in northern B.C. are maintaining road blocks against timber company incursions into their aboriginal homelands. Alberta's Lubicon people are threatening to shut down oil rigs on lands they know to be their own. The Temagami wilderness blockade continues in Ontario. The Innu of Labrador are dragged into court for resisting military assaults against their home environment. It seems to me entirely appropriate that native peoples, the most systematically oppressed of all Canadians, are now using the nonviolent model, because it is a device originally designed to liberate an oppressed class. As Albert Einstein observed, "Gandhi is unique in political history. He has invented an entirely new and humane technique for the liberation struggle of an oppressed people, and carried it out."

As the environmental movement continues discovering its roots in aboriginal wisdom, the often-parallel lines of environmental and native rights issues are finding their boldest expression in joint actions of nonviolent resistance to resource exploitation. I believe that the image of Haida elders being arrested on the logging roads of Lyell Island — as part of the joint native and nonnative effort to preserve the South Moresby area of the Queen Charlottes from logging — marked a decisive turning point in the history of native and environmental action in this country.

For Gandhi, civil disobedience was one component of satyagraha, "the Force which is born of Truth and Love;" mass education and mass noncooperation being the other two components. In deciding what, if any, role nonviolent civil disobedience should play in an environmental issue, the question must be asked: Are we looking at nonviolence primarily as a strategic tool, an effective mechanism for manipulating media, public opinion and political decision-making? Or is nonviolence for us, as it was for Gandhi, an "experiment in Truth," precipitating changes in attitudes and values far beyond the "winning" of some particular issue?

I recently attended a $100-a-ticket benefit in the opulent ballroom of a Vancouver hotel. Seventeen hundred people, decked out in tuxedos and evening gowns, grazed on fancy finger food and tippled at ubiquitous bars in order to save the Amazon rainforests. Rock musicians, politicians and T.V. personalities fluttered their high profiles. "Just because we're wealthy," declared the M.C. at one point, "doesn't mean we can't be environmentalists!"

On one level, she's absolutely correct. The evening was enormously successful, raising many thousands of dollars for tropical forests. But it occurred to me in the crush of glitterati that environmentalism, like nonviolence, is in its essence a matter of changing our lives. It includes, but goes far beyond, sorting the garbage into recyclable piles, and in its wider reach encompasses a "metanoia," a "turning away" from ostentatious display of wealth and privilege as giving significance to existence. It's now entirely self-evident that if the few of us at the top of the planetary food chain continue promoting a lifestyle of decadent elegance, the biosphere is doomed, no matter how much petty cash we fork over for noble causes. Some mischievous part of me wanted all those upscale environmentalists in the grand ballroom to have the experience of camping in primitive conditions, of being hauled away by the cops and locked in crowded jail cells for their convictions.

Back in the mountains of Strathcona Park in that cold February predawn, our ragtag group huddled to consider the RCMP ultimatum: clear the road or be arrested. After lengthy discussion, we developed consensus: If we all stood aside, the cause would be lost. If we all were arrested, our momentum would be lost. We opted to have three people arrested that morning and initiate a campaign of intermittent civil disobedience geared to attract increasing participation and public attention. Over the next six weeks, we organized a series of rallies drawing up to several hundred people to the park each weekend. Each rally ended with a smaller group of people risking arrest by forcing the mining company to shut down its drill rig. In total, 64 people were arrested in a dozen different incidents.

Suddenly, Strathcona Park was on the front pages of Vancouver newspapers and the lead item on regional T.V. news broadcasts. Membership in Friends of Strathcona Park ballooned overnight to about 3,000, making the Strathcona case the largest single-issue environmental cause in B.C. history. Eventually the mining company fled with its drill rig under cover of darkness, and the Vander Zalm government abandoned its ill-considered park plans.

As we surrounded, invaded and shut down the drilling rig time after time, not; then waited for hours for the RCMP to arrive, we had ample opportunity to reflect upon the psychology and strategic worth of nonviolence. Even in the bleakest weather, faced with hostile workers and cynical politicians, even as our numbers were carted off to jail and locked up, some for more than a week, we experienced a growing sense of power.

Perhaps because our society is generally so placid and proper in its public conduct, there comes a tremendous sense of exhilaration in refusing to accept the unacceptable. This is not the contrived rebellion of a multimillion-dollar rock concert, but rather a radical transformation of the coward most of us are trained to be. By crossing the line and saying "No!" we achieve a wonderful clarity about ourselves and about the culture of greed and fear in which we live. The taboos and myths of the acquisitive society seem to collapse like straw men, pathetic and contemptible.

Tracing personal power back to its headwaters, we find that it is not a commodity distributed among the wealthy and well-placed, drips of it trickling down to the underlings — but rather that power resides with us, with the earth, within the web of life. Nonviolence teaches that real power isn't *over* anything or anyone; it is power from within, the power of our place and all its interconnections. For those with the courage of their convictions, environmentalism and nonviolence are recognized as ultimately inextricable.

Empowered in nonviolence, one is able to stand unflinchingly before potentially violent people in potentially violent situations, because one is not trying to "beat" anyone or "win" anything. Of course you're trying to achieve something — say, for example, the preservation of a particular bit of ancient forest. The achievement is in the standing forest, not in the taunting of loggers who are trying to earn a living, nor even in the humiliation of a transnational timber outfit. Nonviolence changes the paradigm from a war against enemies to a collective and peaceful insistence that a principle be respected.

Larry Anderson, a member of the Vancouver Nonviolence Training Collective, has done nonviolence training sessions at a number of B.C. environmental hot spots. Says Anderson, "When I use the term 'nonviolence,' I mean the taking of assertive positive action while at the same time considering the needs and fears of my opponents." Anderson insists upon the importance of recognizing "that I am not the sole possessor of 'truth' in the conflict. Through my actions I seek a creative solution in which both parties are changed, in which a newer and deeper level of understanding and social cooperation is reached."

Nonviolence pokes and prods a situation, looking for small cracks through which connections can be made, for mutualities which might widen out into solutions, for areas where cooperation and understanding are possible.

Up at Strathcona Park, as the standoff intensified, the mining company brought in a crew of hefty security guards to arrest anyone interfering with its drill rig. Shortly after the guards arrived, I came up to our camp late in the evening. A mood of mutual fear and suspicion enveloped both camps. Confrontation seemed inevitable.

Supporters throughout the region had taken to sending us food to keep our camp fed, and the next morning by chance there arrived an enormous tray of Merville Triangles. These are an incredibly delicious pastry dessert made by a baker in the nearby community of Merville. Some little lightbulb blinked on in my mind. I took the tray of triangles and walked up to the pickup truck in which two security men were sitting, suspiciously watching our every move. I told them the delight of Merville Triangles transcended partisan considerations and invited them to help themselves. They hesitated for only a moment. Then as their eyes lit up and their oversized hands reached out, I saw them for what they were: two young, rather overweight men stuck doing an unpleasant job and perhaps unlikely to find one any better, and forgetting everything for the moment while they munched contentedly on triangles. After that we were able to communicate freely and each do what we were there to do without bitterness or anger.

Nonviolence teaches the futility of an endless boxing match of punch and counterpunch. It makes clear that to humiliate an opponent or beat an enemy is to participate in the culture of violence. As a particular environmental issue heats up, and media people come galloping, the temptation to stage a slugging match becomes ever stronger. A campaign of nonviolent civil disobedience directed at obtaining widespread media attention runs a constant risk of being nudged onto a battleground, simply because wars rate more coverage. To be successful, the campaign must resist other people's visions of what it is about.

Rather than wobbling all over to accommodate network news bites, the nonviolence model requires a clear articulation of its objectives and its place in the group's overall strategy. It needs a sense of empowerment which inspires hope and confidence, despite what may appear to be hopeless circumstances. It needs a flexible but firm structure for efficient decision-making and communication. It needs a sophisticated discipline best developed through nonviolence training. And, perhaps most importantly of all, it needs light-heartedness and humour so as not to take itself too seriously.

In the end, in this part of the world, powerholders can't do much more than lock people up as a form of intimidation. In the case of Strathcona Park, the provincial government found itself backed into a politically embarrassing corner by having its bluff called. Dozens of respectable citizens stepped forward, willing to be arrested and jailed — and remain in jail if necessary — until the politicians backed off.

Shelley Douglass, a veteran U.S. peace activist, writes about her days spent in jail: "The actual experience of jail, chosen in response to conscience, is comparative freedom. In choosing to make a statement of truth that puts us into jeopardy with the law, we deliberately break many of the bars that imprison us in our everyday lives. Arrest, trial and jail test our inner resources, challenge our relationships, and risk our jobs, reputations, and our ability to make choices. It is a freeing thing to feel ourselves stretched in this way, and to see that many of the "necessities" of our lives are in fact bars on a jail which hold us captive and hold, as well, our brothers and sisters around the world."

Beyond what participants derive from the experience personally, the ultimate success of civil disobedience lies in its contribution to a long-range strategy. I sometimes receive calls from enthusiastic environmentalists wanting advice on a planned "arrest-risk action" which has no strategic placement at all. These are people eager (or desperate!) to draw attention to a particular problem or to vent frustration at continued environmental abuses. But zeal alone is insufficient. You have to ask: What is the purpose of the event? Have other avenues been exhausted? How will civil disobedience, possibly resulting in arrests, advance the issue? What will be the follow-up? Will there be subsequent arrests? What would constitute "success" in this process? To charge off and be arrested without much likelihood of changing anything runs the risk of self-indulgence.

Similarly, it's tempting for some activists to get "stuck in protest" long after the actions have ceased to be effective, because the adrenalin rush of blockades, arrests and courtroom drama is far more intoxicating than painstaking organizational work. Civil disobedience ought to seriously inconvenience the opposition, and to do so must be one component of a larger strategy designed to change an exploitive system.

The true beauty of the nonviolence model is that it always finds its impetus and its power from an outraged and impassioned populace. Its ambition is to inform an ever-widening circle of people who will unite in demanding real policy change. The global environmental crisis into which we are now plunged goes far beyond "saving" some particular park or wilderness valley, no matter how spectacular. I believe that we need (and soon!) the environmental equivalent of recent mass demonstrations in eastern Europe, to shake the institutions of power down to their foundations and work a fundamental restructuring of the economic order, rendering it accountable to the realities of a finite biosphere. Such an ambition might seem unlikely, naive, absurd! But so did our position on that cold February predawn when there came an insistent rapping on my van window.

How I Learned to Appreciate Sunday Afternoon Football or *The Fine Art of Sandwich Making*

SANDRA BARDOCZ *(student essay)*

My dad is the world's biggest football fan. I'm not sure if it's because of the strategy involved in the game or because the games are played on Sunday afternoon, giving him an excuse to take time off from his domestic duties and entertain his secret passion — sandwich making.

As a kid, after I had successfully learned to play first base, hit, and throw like the Little Leaguer he knew I could be, I was indoctrinated into the Sunday afternoon football rituals. I was his last chance. After having two other daughters who wanted nothing to do with football, Dad attempted to pass down the truly meaningful things in life to me.

At one o'clock, sometimes at noon, after a morning of waiting, it would happen: the games would begin. Not just one, but three, four, even five at the same time. We'd sit and wait patiently while the announcers babbled on and on; then, with the opening kick-off, a tension rose over what seemed like the entire block. Gaze fixed on the TV, Dad would watch, scream, oooh, aaah, and curse.

At first I would question: "Don't they get hurt?" "Why do they get six points for a touch-down?" "What's a down? Offsides? Clipping?" "Why do they call a conversion a *conversion*, and a field goal a *field goal*?" Dad was always more than willing to answer my questions, as long as I asked them during commercials. However, when there was a crucial play, he would actually *offer* the information, usually during the playback. He treated me as if I knew what he was talking about. He would analyze the plays out loud, in such a way that it didn't take too long before I *did* know what he was talking about. Still, during the first few games, trying to remember all the questions I had during the plays (which guys in what colours did what to whom) and then to hold on to them until a commercial was quite a feat. In retrospect, I realize that he was really helping me to improve my concentration.

At half-time, we'd dash into the kitchen for The Sandwiches. I would bring cutting-boards, knives and bread to the TV room and Dad would bring the essentials — the cold cuts, the cheese, some pickles (hot peppers for him), and, of course, the mustard and mayonnaise. While he was arranging the sandwich materials, I would turn the dial to find the other games.

"Winnipeg and Edmonton are on Channel 7," he'd shout from the kitchen.

"But Chicago's at Green Bay and it's snowing," I'd offer.

"Okay," he'd confirm (I just loved it when it turned out that I'd had something valid to say), "but I've got some money on the San Francisco/Dallas game so let's see how they're doing; then we'll watch the Packers game."

So I'd find the channel with the Dallas game, and I'd keep him informed of the score.

We'd simultaneously watch the games and make sandwiches. To the lightly buttered rye bread he would apply a thin layer of mayonnaise. He was incredible — he could do this without taking his eyes off the game. At this point, I was concentrating on his sandwich making skills more than on the football, and I'd take my cues from him as to when to look up and catch the replays. On top of the mayonnaise would go some tomatoes: the more the better, was his philosophy. Lettuce and cheese would follow, and then the cold cuts. Here, too, more was better. Without moving his eyes from the screen, he would carefully choose just the right amount of roast beef, salami, and roast turkey. I didn't know how he could tell which cold cuts he was choosing. Maybe it was a secret ratio; anyway, he wasn't telling. All he would say was that one day I would know how he did it. The lid of the sandwich would, again, be a lightly buttered (never margarined) piece of bread, but this time it would be dressed with mustard. His sandwiches were art forms. I'd try and try to emulate his methods, but to no avail. His were always better. He'd have a beer, and I a Pepsi, and when each of us had a pickle in hand, the ritual was complete. My concentration could again focus on the football.

I'll never forget those Sunday afternoons. I don't own a TV, and, typically, my fridge is poorly stocked. But those days are occasionally relived when I make the trek to Unionville, to my father's house, where I can always count on the TV and the sandwiches. Now I have a beer, too, and my sandwiches are getting better. I think I'm beginning to understand how the cold cut trick works.

3. THE LITERARY ESSAY

KEY WORK:

> "Spiritual Longing in Laurence's Manawaka Women" —
> Leslie-Ann Hales

ASSOCIATED READINGS:

> "Robert Frost: The Way to the Poem" — John Ciardi
> "Forces of Corruption in *The Great Gatsby*" — Eva Manski
> (student essay)
> "Portraits of Women: The Quest for Self-Realization" — Sam
> Blythe (student essay)
> Tips on Writing a Literary Essay

As a senior English student, you have written this form of essay: a rigorously argued analysis of a literary work. You have observed that the literary essay develops from a clear, significant thesis statement which is supported by a harmonious balance of generalizations and specific textual references. You recognize certain conventions that this form of essay employs: an objective, scholarly tone that is written in the present tense using suitably formal standard English. Writing a literary essay is a challenging task, but it is rewarding because the form invites you to combine high-level thinking with personal response to a work of literature.

The essays and accompanying activities in this unit invite you to enhance your appreciation of the well-argued literary essay and refine your skills for future assignments. With tips from Ciardi and Tips on Writing a Literary Essay, you will build critical skills and enhance your ability to analyze literary works. By closely examining the work of students Blythe and Manski, you may become more adept at writing thoughtful introductions and conclusions, at linking each body paragraph to your thesis statement, and at smoothly integrating quotations. Finally, be sure to consult Tips on Your Writing Process on page 326 for help with the process of composition.

Conventions of the Literary Essay

Purpose   To argue the validity of an assertion

Audience   Specialized, educated

Tone	Objective, scholarly
Voice	Neutral
Response	Intellectually curious
Language	LEVEL — Formal, standard English CHARACTERISTICS — Largely factual, denotative
Structure	Thesis statement in paragraph one or two; highly structured format and paragraphs

BEFORE READING

1. In small groups, discuss your most successful experience with writing a literary essay and determine whether the process you followed was similar to that of your peers.

2. a. Brainstorm a set of criteria for developing an effective thesis statement.
   b. After reviewing the criteria, practise forming several thesis statements about a literary work you have studied.

3. Discuss with your teacher the conventions of the literary essay as outlined above and any modifications your teacher emphasizes such as use of third or first person, as well as the use of secondary sources and the preferred referencing style.

Spiritual Longing in Laurence's Manawaka Women

LESLIE-ANN HALES

Responding to Donald Cameron, who observed that there is a religious element in her fictional world, Margaret Laurence said:

> I don't know even what I mean by God, but I don't think, personally, that we do live in a universe which is as empty as we might think. A lot of my characters, like myself, inhabit a world in which they no longer believe in the teachings of the traditional church, but where these things have enormous emotional impact on them still, as they do on me. ... Part of the terrific impact of things like the

hymns derives from the fact that you learned these things in a much earlier era of your life, an era of rock-solid faith. Now you *lost* this: and part of the impact is not that you believe it, but you mourn your disbelief. This is Eden lost.[1]

Laurence's tentative wistfulness is even more apparent when she says that she does not "really believe that God is totally dead in our universe. . . ."[2] Both these statements suggest an almost reluctant belief in God, a belief which Laurence can only cautiously express: God is not totally dead and the universe not as empty as we might think. A more confident believer would affirm with assurance that God is alive and the universe full of God's presence. Laurence is unable to make any such assertive declaration. Yet the fact of God's existence, unfathomed, mysterious, and perhaps not completely dependable, is a fragile reality in Laurence's personal perspective.

Countering this tentative faith is Laurence's sorrowful sense that, God notwithstanding, human beings, ultimately, are sentenced to isolation, constantly thwarted in their attempts to touch each other. In the Donald Cameron interview, Laurence expressed the anguish of this human predicament:

> It's partly that I feel that human beings ought to be able, *ought* to be able to communicate and touch each other far more than they do, and this human loneliness and isolation, which obviously occurs everywhere, seems to me to be part of man's tragedy. I'm sure one of the main themes in all my writings in [sic] this sense of man's isolation from his fellows and how almost unbearably tragic this is.[3]

God may not be totally dead in our universe but, apparently however he is manifest, this in no way affects human relationships. This idea seems to represent a split in Laurence's stance since, on the whole, those who believe in God tend to think that the relationship with God provides a context, model, or way of understanding relationships with other people.

Whether Laurence's stance *really* has such a split, however, turns out to be much less certain if one examines how her personal perspective infiltrates her fictional world of Manawaka. Naturally the reader must be wary of identifying Laurence with her protagonists since, as novelist, she must be allowed the freedom to create characters who may have views radically different from her own. But in the Cameron interview, Laurence herself draws the parallel between her own beliefs and those of many of her fictional characters. It is at least evident that her Manawaka protagonists manifest a markedly similar tentative faith in God and that these protagonists are sentenced to the kind of isolation Laurence perceives to be the way of the world.

What the Manawaka protagonists do not realize is that there is an intimate connection between the way they understand the universe and God's place in it, and the way they relate, or fail to relate, with other people. Relationships do not develop in a vacuum; they are grounded in beliefs people have about themselves, other people, and the world in which they live. Whether Laurence states this systematically is not the question, for it is certainly true that her Manawaka novels demonstrate it consistently. Such frustrated communications as occur in these stories are not simply coincidental in a world where God's presence is posited with such hesitance and qualification. Rather this frustration results precisely from the protagonists' ambiguous response to God and his role in their lives.

Dostoyevsky raised the question of what happens in a world which has ceased to believe in God. How, he wondered, would people relate and how were their actions to be judged? Laurence's novels pose a different but, perhaps, related question: what happens in a world in which people believe that God is not totally dead but that his presence is only negative or indifferent? Indeed, why would one turn away from the human realm, if that is where anger and isolation begin and end, to the realm of a God who is, at best, indifferent? These questions are relevant with respect to the Manawaka novels, and the answer would seem to be that, although the protagonists would very much like to laugh God out of their universe, they are unable to do so. Their plight is that they transfer what happens in their relationships with other people to their relationship with God. But there is an important difference. Since they realize that other people, like themselves, have weaknesses, needs, and fears, the protagonists resign themselves to understanding, if not accepting, why a breakdown in relationship occurs. God, on the other hand, they believe to be all powerful. Therefore he should prevent such a breakdown. Apparently he does not, and for this reason, their relationships with him are marked by anger and fear. That they should cling to so negative a belief in God, all the while protesting that they do not believe at all, perhaps seems strange. However, it signifies that they desire more honest and loving communication not only with other people but also with God. They do not understand that they themselves make this impossible.

To spend time with the protagonists of the Manawaka novels is to have the feeling that one gets to know a family of sisters. Hagar Shipley, of course, is removed from the other protagonists by one generation, but in terms of her personality and the way she relates to other people, she is like the elder sister. Each of these women is a cauldron of conflicting emotions, conflicting responses, conflicting beliefs. With the possible exception of Rachel, who is a more timid woman in many ways, the Manawaka protagonists are strong-willed, proud, independent, tough survivors. Rachel shares these characteristics, but she is more muted, more repressed, more obedient to the expectations of society. At the same time, Hagar, Rachel, Stacy, Vanessa, and Morag are all emotional, sensitive, fragile, easily wounded, and somewhat superstitious with a superstition which is the distortion of their deep capacity for spirituality.

Laurence's novelistic technique for revealing the personalities of her protagonists allows the reader to see, simultaneously, both the apparently hard-boiled external self and the fragile inner being of the characters. One reason the Manawaka women move so realistically and credibly through Laurence's fictional world is that, not only their words, but also their thoughts, feelings, and fantasies are opened to the reader. Furthermore, the interwoven memory flashbacks to childhood, adolescence, and early womanhood eventually provide a rich context in which to understand the characters more fully. Indeed, it is only because Laurence makes the reader privy to so much of the protagonists' total selves that the consistent pattern of the intimate connection between relationships with other people and relationship with God is perceptible. In this pattern, the need to conceal what is inside, to hide vulnerability behind a mask of cavalier self-assurance or indifference, recurs. Hagar, recalling how she feared the dark because, for her, it "teemed with phantoms, soul-parasites with feathery fingers, the voices of trolls, and pale inconstant fires like the flicker of an eye,"[4] remembers what she did with her fear in front of her husband: "But I never let him, or anyone, know that."[5] Rachel talks to her lover, Nick, and remembers how feelings were handled in her family: " 'In my family, you didn't get emotional. It was frowned upon.' "[6] Stacy becomes worried and frustrated by her increasing sense of alienation from those around her: "What goes on inside isn't ever the same as what goes on outside. It's a disease I've picked up somewhere."[7] Vanessa, whose family motto is "be then a wall of brass," recalls how she longed to reach out to her father, but resisted doing so: "I stood beside him, wanting to touch the light-brown hairs on his forearm, but thinking he might laugh at me or pull his arm away if I did."[8] And Morag, retracing her past, is haunted by the lesson she learned so well so young: "Morag doesn't let on. If you let on, ever, you're done for."[9] Even these brief quotations indicate the pattern, for they are representative of how the Manawaka protagonists respond to other people.

However, as Stacy admits, what goes on inside is not the same as what goes on outside, and what is inside is a tremendous vulnerability, a sensitivity to rejection which each of these women finds necessary to guard jealously. As readers, we are privileged to see this side of the personality as well and, curiously, it is in this confusion, anger, pain, and isolation that the name of God keeps coming up. In other words, it is not in external dialogue but in internal monologue, reflections, and fantasies that God's ambiguous role in the lives of these women is revealed. As Laurence suggested in the Donald Cameron interview, none of the protagonists live in a world in which God is perceived as an informing presence. Yet none can wholly forget and dispense with God either. It is in this tension that Laurence's personal perspective qualifies the fictional world her protagonists inhabit. No one ever explains *why* God should be part of the picture. In fact, the presence of God seems to provoke only anger or fear. Invariably God is assumed by these women to be, if existent at all, removed, aloof, and indifferent, although there is always the possibility that God is at least interested enough in individuals to mock the hurtful things that happen to them.

Clinging to such a relationship with God seems odd and, of course, most of the protagonists would protest that they do not cling to it at all. But the fact of God as a being on whom one can vent one's frustration, or against whom one can rail, or even whose judgment one might fear, is undeniably present in the Manawaka novels. It is as true for Hagar, the woman who says she could never get the hang of praying, as it is for Morag, who suspects God does not care that little kids are being bombed in London during the war. Stacy, too, catches herself talking to God — again — and pauses to wonder why on earth she should be doing so:

God knows why I chat to you, God — it's not that I believe in you. Or I do and I don't, like echoes in my head. It's somebody to talk to. Is that all? I don't know. How would I like to be only an echo in somebody's head? Sorry, God. But then you're not dependent upon me, or let's hope not.[10]

Perhaps this does not sound like a particularly prayerful way to talk to God. Stacy would agree since she does not even know why she talks to God in the first place. She certainly does not expect these one-sided conversations to have any effect on her life, for she believes, with the other Manawaka protagonists, that she is alone in her struggles.

In many ways, Stacy MacAindra, suburban housewife with her salesman husband, her three children, her spreading waistline, her desire for a lover, and her almost hourly gin and tonic, seems the least likely of all the Manawaka protagonists to be chatting so familiarly with God. Yet, when her son, Duncan, nearly drowns shortly after Stacy has begun a love affair with a young man, her thoughts turn spontaneously to God, to the fear that God is punishing her for her actions:

> *God, if it was anything I did, take it out on me, not on him — that's too much punishment for me*
> — Judgment. All the things I don't like to think I believe in. But at the severe moments, up they rise, the tomb birds, scaring the guts out of me with their vulture wings. . . . I used to think about Buckle that he was as superstitious as a caveman. I didn't know then that I was, too.[11]

Until this moment, Stacy's conversations with God have been flippant. Now, when there is a crisis, she is no longer flippant for she perceives God as judge and jury. Panic notwithstanding, Stacy fears that the world is not, after all, chaotic and abandoned. Her fear of God is spontaneous and sudden, as if it has been lurking in the depths of her mind only to surface when something as "severe" and terrifying as the near death of her son occurs.

For Stacy, as for the other protagonists, it is next to impossible to reflect on life and believe that, if God exists, he is a God of mercy. If God exists, he is a cruel jester and a righteous judge, although he may not even care enough to bother judging. Hagar, in her more cynical moments, also sees a jester-God in her mind's eye.

> I see Him clad in immaculate radiance, a short white jacket and a smile white and creamy as zinc-oxide ointment, focussing His cosmic and comic glass eye on this and that, as the fancy takes Him. Or no

—He's many-headed, and all the heads argue at once, a squabbling committee.[12]

Why Hagar should bother to think about God at all if such a cynical portrait is the only one she can draw is not immediately clear. It is certainly not a portrait which can provide comfort for the dying old woman. It *does*, however, illustrate again the protagonists' tendency to transfer to God those characteristics which mark their other relationships. Yet Hagar does not rest entirely easy in this cynicism for, only moments before she describes God in this way, she wonders with far less effrontery about God's response to humanity: "What if it matters to Him, after all, what happens to us?"[13] Clearly when relationships break down, when one feels sentenced to isolation, when one's emotions are concealed behind a wall of stony silence, it is difficult to believe there is a God who actively cares about one's life. The point is that Manawaka protagonists always protest that they do *not* believe in God or that their belief is only, as Stacy says, superstition. Hence they should feel no need to repeat, in their loneliness, that God does not exist or, at least, is unconcerned with human affairs. That they *do* repeat this is a sign that, beneath their defiant stance of strength, they yearn for God to be involved in their world.

Precisely this conflict explains why the Manawaka protagonists make statements about God so riddled with contradiction. On the one hand, Hagar feels angry at God "for giving us eyes but almost never sight,"[14] but on the other, she stubbornly clings to the idea that she is irrevocably alone and so precludes opening herself to God exactly as she has prevented herself from opening up to other people:

> Pride was my wilderness, and the demon that led me there was fear. I was alone, never anything else, and never free, for I carried my chains within me, and they spread out from me and shackled all I touched. Oh, my two, my dead. Dead by your own hands or by mine?[15]

Hagar fears that she is largely responsible, if not for the deaths of her husband and son, then for the deaths of their relationships with her. She does not realize that she is similarly responsible for the death of her relationship with God, that she has shut God out just as surely as she shut out her husband and her son.

The barriers which the Manawaka protagonists inevitably raise between themselves and others do not suddenly crumble before

God. The fortress walls within which they hide are fortified against God and other people. Their understanding of the world demands that pride, independence, and self-sufficiency be cultivated because these are the only shields protecting them from pain; sadly, these shields also insulate them from joy. Laurence's protagonists demonstrate powerfully that these defences effectively quash attempts to trust and to love. Hence when they do think about God, they work on the same assumptions and stand defiantly stubborn, convinced that God simply does not care.

Hagar, Rachel, Stacy, Vanessa, and Morag all understand with terrible clarity the high price of such pride. In Vanessa's family no one is able to communicate honestly and, as her Uncle Terence says, "everybody to his own shield in this family."[16] This alienation causes Vanessa frequently to fear there is no rhyme or reason to anything that happens, much as Rachel bitterly suggests that, in the face of God's indifference, she should "celebrate confusion."[17] Vanessa shares this sense of the indiscriminate, random anarchy of events, and she also blames it on God: "I could not really comprehend these things, but I sensed their strangeness, their disarray. I felt that whatever God might love in this world, it was certainly not order."[18] Loneliness, alienation, estrangement all contribute to the feeling of being unrooted in the world. Rachel experiences this unrootedness in her dreams as the feeling of being a spectral photograph, "insubstantial, unable to anchor myself, unable to stop this slow nocturnal circling."[19] The world appears to her "blurred, artificial, indefinite, an abstract painting of a world."[20] Stacy looks in the mirror to make sure she really exists. For her, as for Rachel and Vanessa, using words becomes surreal, for words provide no access to other people: "I'm surrounded by voices all the time but none of them seem to be saying anything, including mine. This gives me the feeling that we may all be one-dimensional."[21] Even Morag, who does not so readily turn to thoughts of God, decides early that God is "no good" because he makes senseless, random decisions against which no one has recourse:

> She does not love God. God is the one who decides which people have got to die, and when. Mrs. McKee in Sunday school says God is LOVE, but this is baloney. He is mean and gets mad at people for no reason at all, and Morag wouldn't trust him as far as she can spit. . . . Does He really know what everybody is thinking? If so, it sure isn't fair and is also very spooky.[22]

The feeling of being disconnected, of being unable to touch other people (as Laurence believes to be characteristic of human relations) causes the feeling of insubstantiality, the randomness and chaos these women experience. They cannot perceive order or pattern if they are unable to get outside their own minds and connect with someone else.

The Manawaka protagonists do speak *about* God. Stacy chats *with* God, and even Morag, in all her unbelief, prays *to* God: *"Help me, God; I'm frightened of myself."*[23] Yet not once do any of them feel that God is listening, that he cares, or that he may be trying to reach them. They treat God as they have treated those who have sought to love them. Morag shares the fear which haunts all Laurence's protagonists. She cannot reach out or open herself for she cannot bear the desolation and humiliation of rebuff. In her heart, Morag cannot deny her daughter's angry charge: " 'You make me sick. You make me bloody sick. You're so goddam proud and so scared of being rejected. You're so stupid in that way, you really are.' "[24] But Morag's simple prayer, "Help me God," is offered more in panic than in faith, because accepting God's help would be letting on to him in a trusting way that she is frightened. And as Morag says, "if you let on, ever, you're done for."[25]

In her Manawaka protagonists, Laurence breathes life into fictional women who bear out what she said in her interview with Donald Cameron. People do not communicate with each other or touch each other as much as they should. But, and the "but" is important to Laurence, God is not totally dead in the universe. The Manawaka protagonists do not perceive in any logical way the connection between their estrangement from other people and their estrangement from God. Yet they repeatedly make this connection in less-guarded moments through their anger, their cynicism, and their "superstitious" fear of God. All unbidden, the desire to be grounded in relationship keeps cutting across the tangled knot of their unhappiness. Anger towards and cynicism about God are only the disillusioned and distorted expression of what these women actually desire in their lives. Hagar's recognition of what might have been shocks and grieves her, for it is now too late to do anything with her new understanding: "This knowing comes upon me so forcefully, so shatteringly, and with such a bitterness as I have never felt before. I must always, always, have wanted that — simply to rejoice."[26]

That none of the Manawaka protagonists ever uncover and nurture this lamented glimmer of faith, never trace it to its source, not in superstition, but in a recognition of what Hagar calls "the heart's truth,"[27] is probably a result of Laurence's own hesitation. The discovery that the universe truly *is* Godless and that honest communication between people really *is* impossible would be devastating to her protagonists. Perhaps it is also too overwhelming for Laurence to contemplate. Perhaps that is why she can only say that God is not totally dead. Yet even though the Manawaka protagonists are never able to take the tremendous risk of committing themselves to faith in a God who cares, their reluctant acknowledgment of God at all gives the lie to their cynicism. God is more real to them than they can admit, because Laurence is too honest a novelist to write him out of their lives entirely.

------

[1]Donald Cameron, *Conversations with Canadian Novelists — 1* (Toronto: Macmillan of Canada, 1973), pp. 111–12.
[2]Ibid., p. 111.
[3]Ibid., p. 105.
[4]Margaret Laurence, *The Stone Angel* (Toronto: McClelland & Stewart: New Canadian Library, 1968), p. 205.
[5]Ibid., p. 205.
[6]Margaret Laurence, *A Jest of God* (Toronto: McClelland & Stewart-Bantam Limited, 1979), p. 109.
[7]Margaret Laurence, *The Fire-Dwellers* (Toronto: McClelland & Stewart-Bantam Limited, 1969), p. 28.
[8]Margaret Laurence, *A Bird in the House* (Toronto: McClelland & Stewart Limited, 1974), p. 92.
[9]Margaret Laurence, *The Diviners* (Toronto: McClelland & Stewart Limited: New Canadian Library, 1974), p. 51.
[10]Laurence, *The Fire-Dwellers*, p. 57.
[11]Ibid., p. 266.
[12]Laurence, *The Stone Angel*, p. 93.
[13]Ibid., p. 90.
[14]Ibid., p. 173.
[15]Ibid., p. 292.
[16]Laurence, *A Bird in the House*, p. 87.
[17]Laurence, *A Jest of God*, p. 44.
[18]Laurence, *A Bird in the House*, p. 59.
[19]Laurence, *A Jest of God*, p. 21.
[20]Ibid., p. 106.
[21]Laurence, *The Fire-Dwellers*, p. 71.
[22]Laurence, *The Diviners*, p. 63.
[23]Ibid., p. 207.
[24]Ibid., p. 193.
[25]Ibid., p. 51.
[26]Laurence, *The Stone Angel*, p. 292.
[27]Ibid.

EXPLORING THE LITERARY ESSAY

1. Determine whether Hales effectively employs the literary essay's conventions. Cite specific examples.

2. Identify the writer's thesis as she develops it in her fifth and sixth paragraphs. Make sure that the key words "ambiguity" (or ambiguous) and "conflict" appear in your statement.

3. Suggest why Hales does not state her thesis in the introductory paragraph as is generally required in students' literary essays.

4. Demonstrate the process by which Hales effectively develops her thesis in paragraphs 7 through 16.

5. How does Hales sum up and encourage the reader to ponder these matters?

EXTENSIVE STUDY

1. According to Hales, Laurence's women portray the idea that our relationships derive from our views about ourselves and our place in the universe. Argue this idea, citing examples from your general knowledge.

2. Debate Laurence's contention that "being superstitious . . . is a distortion of . . . deep capacity for spirituality."

3. Read Russell's "The Good Life" (p. 50) and/or Thoreau's "Excerpt from *Walden*" (p. 174), and compare their approaches to life with Hales' observations about Laurence's protagonists.

4. Devise a list of criteria by which to judge a literary essay, culling tips from Mannes' "How Do You Know It's Good?" (p. 195) and Tips on Writing a Literary Essay (p. 100). Assess Blythe's or Manski's essay according to your criteria. You might compare your evaluation with the findings of other groups.

5. With a partner or in a small group, assume the roles of Hales, Blythe, or Ciardi and an interviewer on a television talk show. Explore relevant issues of thought, writing process, and criteria for evaluation.

THE WRITING FOLDER

1. Compose a response to one or more of the essays in this unit. For starting points, see the Tips on page 100.

2. Compose a literary essay on one or more works studied in this course. Consult with your teacher regarding the length and whether to use secondary sources.

3. Write a speech, lecture, or lesson plan entitled, "How to Write a Strong Literary Essay," for an audience of grade 9 and 10 students. You may wish to refer to the conventions of the Oral Essay to help prepare your speech or lecture.

INDEPENDENT STUDY

1. Read one or more novels by writers such as Margaret Laurence, D.H. Lawrence, Doris Lessing, Margaret Atwood, Penelope Lively, Margaret Drabble, Mary Wesley, Gustave Flaubert, John Irving, Larry McMurtry, or Leo Tolstoy. In an essay, compare the writer's depiction of males and the significance of their commonalities in their relationships with women.

2. Collect poetry that depicts people's spiritual questing. Write the introduction, prologue, or preface to your collection. Your project might include taped readings and/or some of your own verse. Consider poets such as Margaret Atwood, Al Purdy, T.S. Eliot, Gwendolyn MacEwen, or one of the Romantics.

3. Compare a writer's life quest as reflected in his or her (auto)biography with that of one of his or her fictional or dramatic characters. Consider writers such as George Bernard Shaw, James Joyce, Elizabeth Smart, Tennessee Williams, D.H. Lawrence, Margaret Laurence, Virginia Woolf, Emily Bronte, and Ernest Hemingway.

TIMED READING AND WRITING

1. Read Blythe's essay (p. 96), and outline its structure in the time stipulated by your teacher.

2. In pairs, construct a literature-based test question, and write the introductory and concluding paragraphs and the topic sentence of each body paragraph. See the Tips on Writing Examinations (p. 331) for help designing questions.

3. Write a short commentary for Blythe or Manski which would encourage further revisions. You may wish to review "Revision or What Have I Actually Said?" (p. 38).

Robert Frost: The Way to the Poem

JOHN CIARDI

Stopping by Woods on a Snowy Evening
by Robert Frost

Whose woods these are I think I know.
His house is in the village though;
He will not see me stopping here
To watch his woods fill up with snow.

My little horse must think it queer
To stop without a farmhouse near
Between the wood and frozen lake
The darkest evening of the year.

He gives his harness bells a shake
To ask if there is some mistake.
The only other sound's the sweep
Of easy wind and downy flake.

The woods are lovely, dark and deep.
But I have promises to keep,
And miles to go before I sleep,
And miles to go before I sleep.

The School System has much to say these days of the virtue of reading widely, and not enough about the virtues of reading less but in depth. There are any number of reading lists for poetry, but there is not enough talk about individual poems. Poetry, finally, is one poem at a time. To read any one poem carefully is the ideal preparation for reading another. Only a poem can illustrate how poetry works.

Above, therefore, is a poem — one of the master lyrics of the English language, and almost certainly the best-known poem by an American poet. What happens in it? — which is to say, not *what* does it mean, but *how* does it mean? How does it go about being a human reenactment of a human experience? The author — perhaps the thousandth reader would need to be told — is Robert Frost.

Even the TV audience can see that this poem begins as a seemingly simple narration of a seemingly simple incident but ends by suggesting meanings far beyond anything specifically referred to in the narrative. And even readers with only the most casual interest in poetry might be made to note the additional fact that, though the poem suggests those larger meanings, it is very careful never to abandon its pretense to being simple narration. There is duplicity at work. The poet pretends to be talking about one thing, and all the while he is talking about many others.

Many readers are forever unable to accept the poet's essential duplicity. It is almost safe to say that a poem is never about what it seems to be about. As much could be said of the proverb. The bird in the hand, the rolling stone, the stitch in time never (except by an artful double-deception) intend any sort of statement about birds, stones, or sewing. The incident of this poem, one must conclude, is at root a metaphor.

Duplicity aside, this poem's movement from the specific to the general illustrates one of the basic formulas of all poetry. Such a grand poem as Arnold's "Dover Beach" and such lesser, though unfortunately better-known, poems as Longfellow's "The Village Blacksmith" and Holmes's "The Chambered Nautilus" are built on the same progression. In these three poems, however, the generalization is markedly set apart from the specific narration, and even seems additional to the telling rather than intrinsic to it. It is this sense of division one has in mind in speaking of "a tacked-on moral."

There is nothing wrong-in-itself with a tacked-on moral. Frost, in fact, makes excellent use of the device at times. In this poem, however, Frost is careful to let the whatever-the-moral-is grow out of the poem itself. When the action ends the poem ends. There is no epilogue and no explanation. Everything pretends to be about the narrated incident. And that pretense sets the basic tone of the poem's performance of itself.

The dramatic force of that performance is best observable, I believe, as a progression in three scenes.

In scene one, which coincides with stanza one, a man — a New Englander — is driving his sleigh somewhere at night. It is snowing, and as the man passes a dark patch of woods he stops to watch the snow descend into the darkness. We know, moreover, that the man is familiar with those parts (he knows who owns the woods and where the owner lives), and we know that no one has seen him stop. As scene one forms itself in the theatre of the mind's eye, therefore, it serves to establish some as yet unspecified relation between the man and the woods.

It is necessary, however, to stop here for a long parenthesis: Even so simple an opening statement raises any number of questions. It is impossible to address all the questions that rise from the poem stanza by stanza, but two that arise from stanza one illustrate the sort of thing one might well ask of the poem detail by detail.

Why, for example, does the man not say what errand he is on? What is the force of leaving the errand generalized? He might just as well have told us that he was going to the general store, or returning from it with a jug of molasses he had promised to bring Aunt Harriet and two suits of long underwear he had promised to bring the hired man. Frost, moreover, can handle homely detail to great effect. He preferred to leave his motive generalized. Why?

And why, on the other hand, does he say so much about knowing the absent owner of the woods and where he lives? Is it simply that one set of details happened-in whereas another did not? To speak of things "happening-in" is to assault the integrity of a poem. Poetry cannot be discussed meaningfully unless one can assume that everything in the poem—every last comma and variant spelling—is in it by the poet's specific act of choice. Only bad poets allow into their poems what is haphazard or cheaply chosen.

The errand, I will venture a bit brashly for lack of space, is left generalized in order the more aptly to suggest *any* errand in life and, therefore, life itself. The owner is there because he is one of the forces of the poem. Let it do to say that the force he represents is the village of mankind (that village at the edge of winter) from which the poet finds himself separated (has separated himself?) in his moment by the woods (and to which, he recalls finally, he has promised to keep). The owner is he-who-lives-in-his-village-house, thereby locked away from the poet's awareness of the-time-the-snow-tells as it engulfs and obliterates the world the village man allows himself to believe he "owns." Thus, the owner is a representative of an order of reality from which the poet has divided himself for the moment, though to a certain extent he ends by reuniting with it. Scene one, therefore, establishes not only a relation between the man and the woods, but the fact that the man's relation begins with his separation (though momentarily) from mankind.

End parenthesis one, begin parenthesis two.

Still considering the first scene as a kind of dramatic performance of forces, one must note that the poet has meticulously matched the simplicity of his language to the pretended simplicity of the narrative. Clearly, the man stopped because the beauty of the scene moved him, but he neither tells us that the scene is beautiful nor that he is moved. A bad writer, always ready to overdo, might have written: "The vastness gripped me, filling my spirit with the slow steady sinking of the snow's crystalline perfection into the glimmerless profundities of the hushed primeval wood." Frost's avoidance of such a spate illustrates two principles of good writing. The first, he has stated himself in "The Mowing": "Anything *more* than the truth would have seemed too weak" (italics mine). Understatement is one of the basic sources of power in English poetry. The second principle is to let the action speak for itself. A good novelist does not tell us that a given character is good or bad (at least not since the passing of the Dickens tradition): he shows us the character in action and then, watching him, we know. Poetry, too, has fictional obligations: even when the characters are ideas and metaphors rather than people, they must be *characterized in action*. A poem does not *talk about* ideas; it *enacts* them. The force of the poem's performance, in fact, is precisely to act out (and thereby to make us act out emphatically — that is, to *feel out*, that is, to *identify with*) the speaker and why he stopped. The man is the principal actor in this little "drama of why" and in scene one he is the only character, though as noted, he is somehow related to the absent owner.

End second parenthesis.

In scene two (stanzas two and three) a *foil* is introduced. In fiction and drama, a foil is a character who "plays against" a more important character. By presenting a different point of view or an opposed set of motives, the foil moves the more important character to react in ways that might not have found expression without such opposition. The more important character is thus more fully revealed — to the reader and to himself. The foil is the horse.

The horse forces the question, Why did the man stop? Until it occurs to him that his "little horse must think it queer" he had not asked himself for reasons. He had simply stopped. But the man finds himself faced with the question he imagines the horse to be asking: What *is* there to stop for out there in the cold, away from bin and stall (house and village and mankind?) and all that any self-respecting beast could value on such a night? In sensing that other view, the man is forced to examine his own more deeply.

In stanza two the question arises only as a feeling within the man. In stanza three, however (still scene two), the horse acts. He gives his harness bells a shake. "What's wrong?" he seems to say. "What are we waiting for?"

By now, obviously, the horse — without losing its identity as horse — has also become a symbol. (A symbol is something that stands for something else.) Whatever that something else may be, it certainly begins at that order of life that does not understand why a man stops in the wintry middle of nowhere to watch the snow come down. (Can one fail to sense by now that the dark and the snow-fall symbolize a death-wish, however momentary, i.e., that hunger for final rest and oblivion that a man may feel, but not a beast?)

So by the end of scene two the performance has given dramatic force to three elements that work upon the man. There is his relation to the world of the owner. There is his relation to the brute world of the horse. And there is that third presence of the unownable world, the movement of the all-engulfing snow across all the orders of life, the man's, the owner's, and the horse's — with the difference that the man knows of that second dark-within-the-dark of which the horse cannot, and the owner will not, know.

The man ends scene two with all these forces working upon him simultaneously. He feels himself moved to a decision. And he feels a last call from the darkness: "the sweep / Of easy wind and downy flake." It would be so easy and so downy to go into the woods and let himself be covered over.

But scene three (stanza four) produces a fourth force. This fourth force can be given many names. It is certainly better, in fact, to give it many names than to attempt to limit it to one. It is social obligation, or personal commitment, or duty, or just the realization that a man cannot indulge a mood forever. All of these and more. But finally he has a simple decision to make. He may go into the woods and let the darkness and the snow swallow him from the world of beast and man. Or he must move on. And unless he is going to stop here forever, it is time to remember that he has a long way to go and that he had best be getting there. (So there is something to be said for the horse, too.)

There and only then, his question driven more and more deeply into himself by these cross-forces, does the man venture a comment on what attracted him: "The woods are lovely, dark and deep." His mood lingers over the thought of that lovely dark-and-deep (as do the very syllables in which he phrases the thought), but the final decision is to put off the mood and move on. He has his man's way to go and his man's obligations to tend to before he can yield. He has miles to go before his sleep. He repeats that thought and the performance ends.

But why the repetition? The first time Frost says, "And miles to go before I sleep," there can be little doubt that the primary meaning is: "I have a long way to go before I get to bed tonight." The second time he says it, however, "miles to go" and "sleep" are suddenly transformed into symbols. What are those "something-elses" the symbols stand for? Hundreds of people have tried to ask Mr. Frost that question and he has always turned it away. He has turned it away *because he cannot answer it.* He could answer some part of it. But some part is not enough.

For a symbol is like a rock dropped into a pool: it sends out ripples in all directions, and the ripples are in motion. Who can say where the last ripple disappears? One may have a sense that he knows the approximate center point of the ripples, the point at which the stone struck the water. Yet even then he has trouble marking it surely. How does one make a mark on water? Oh very well — the center point of that second "miles to go" is probably approximately in the neighborhood of being close to meaning, perhaps, "the road of life": and the second "before I sleep" is maybe that close to meaning "before I take my final rest," the rest in darkness that seemed so temptingly dark-and-deep for the moment of the mood. But the ripples continue to move and the light to change on the water, and the longer one watches the more changes he sees. Such shifting-and-being-at-the-same-instant is of the very sparkle and life of poetry. One experiences it as one experiences life, for every time he looks at an experience he sees something new, and he sees it change as he watches it. And that sense of continuity in fluidity is one of the primary kinds of knowledge, and one that only the arts can teach, poetry foremost among them.

Frost himself certainly did not ask what that repeated last line meant. It came to him and he received it. He "felt right" about it. And what he "felt right" about was in no sense a "meaning" that, say, an essay could apprehend, but an act of experience that could be fully presented only by the dramatic enactment of forces which is the performance of the poem.

Now look at the poem in another way. Did Frost know what he was going to do when he began? Considering the poem simply as an act of skill, as a piece of juggling, one cannot fail to respond to the magnificent turn at the end where, with one flip, seven of the simplest words in the language suddenly dazzle full of never-ending waves of thought and feeling. Or, more precisely, of felt-thought. Certainly an equivalent stunt by a juggler — could there be an equivalent — would bring the house down. Was it to cap his performance with that grand stunt that Frost wrote the poem?

Far from it. The obvious fact is that *Frost could not have known he was going to write those lines until he wrote them.* Then a second fact must be registered: *he wrote them because, for the fun of it, he had got himself into trouble.*

Frost, like every good poet, began by playing a game with himself. The most usual way of writing a four-line stanza with four feet to the line is to rhyme the third line with the first, and the fourth with the second. Even that much rhyme is so difficult in English that many poets and almost all of the anonymous ballad makers do not bother to rhyme the first and third lines at all, settling for two rhymes in four lines as good enough. For English is a rhyme-poor language. In Italian and in French, for example, so many words end with the same sounds that rhyming is relatively easy — so easy that many modern French and Italian poets do not bother to rhyme at all. English, being a more agglomerate language, has far more final sounds, hence fewer of them rhyme. When an Italian poet writes a line ending with "vita" (life) he has literally hundreds of rhyme choices available. When an English poet writes "life" at the end of a line he can summon "strife, wife, knife, fife, rife," and then he is in trouble. No "life-strife" and "life-rife" and "life-wife" seem to offer a combination of possible ideas that can be related by more than just the rhyme. Inevitably, therefore, the poets have had to work and rework these combinations until the sparkle has gone out of them. The reader is normally tired of such rhyme-led associations. When he encounters "life-strife" he is certainly entitled to suspect that the poet did not really want to say "strife" — that had there been in English such a words as, say, "hife," meaning "infinite peace and harmony," the poet would as gladly have used that word instead of "strife." Thus, the reader feels that the writing is haphazard, that the rhyme is making the poet say things he does not really feel, and which, therefore, the reader does not feel except as boredom. One likes to see the rhymes fall into place, but he must end with the belief that it is the poet who is deciding what is said and not the rhyme scheme that is forcing the saying.

So rhyme is a kind of game, and an especially difficult one in English. As in every game, the fun of the rhyme is to set one's difficulties high and then to meet them skilfully. As Frost himself once defined freedom, it consists of "moving easy in harness."

In "Stopping by Woods on a Snowy Evening" Frost took a long chance. He decided to rhyme not two lines in each stanza, but three. Not even Frost could have sustained that much rhyme in a long poem (as Dante, for example, with the advantage of writing in Italian, sustained triple rhyme for thousands of lines in *The Divine Comedy*). Frost would have known instantly, therefore, when he took the original chance, that he was going to write a short poem. He would have had that much foretaste of it.

So the first stanza emerged rhymed a-a-b-a. And with the sure sense that this was to be a short poem, Frost decided to take an additional chance and to redouble: in English three rhymes in four lines is more than enough; there is no need to rhyme the fourth line. For the fun of it, however, Frost set himself to pick up that loose rhyme and to weave it into the pattern, thereby accepting the all but impossible burden of quadruple rhyme.

The miracle is that it worked. Despite the enormous freight of rhyme, the poem not only came out as a neat pattern, but managed to do so with no sense of strain. Every word and every rhyme falls into place as naturally and as inevitably as if there were no rhyme restricting the poet's choices.

That ease-in-difficulty is certainly inseparable from the success of the poem's performance. One watches the skillman juggle three balls, then four, then five, and every addition makes the trick more wonderful. But unless he makes the hard trick seem as easy as an easy trick, then all is lost.

The real point, however, is not only that Frost took on a hard rhyme-trick and made it seem easy. It is rather as if the juggler, carried away, had tossed up one more ball than he could really handle, and then amazed himself by actually handling it. So with the real triumph of this poem. Frost could not have known what a stunning effect his repetition of the last line was going to produce. He could not even know he was going to repeat the line. He simply found himself up against a difficulty he almost certainly had not foreseen and he had to improvise to meet it. For in picking up the rhyme from the third line of stanza one and carrying it over into stanza two, he had created an endless chain-link form within which each stanza left a hook sticking out for the next stanza to hang on. So by stanza four, feeling the poem rounding to its end, Frost had to do something about that extra rhyme.

He might have tucked it back into a third line rhyming with the *know-though-snow* of stanza one. He could thus have rounded the poem out to the mathematical symmetry of using each rhyme four times. But though such a device might be defensible in theory, a rhyme repeated after eleven lines is so far from its original rhyme sound that its feeling as rhyme must certainly be lost. And what good is theory if the reader is not moved by the writing?

It must have been in some such quandary that the final repetition suggested itself — a suggestion born of the very difficulties the poet had let himself in for. So there is that point beyond mere ease in handling a hard thing, the point at which the very difficulty offers the poet the opportunity to do better than he knew he could. What, aside from having that happen to oneself, could be more self-delighting than to participate in its happening by one's reader-identification with the poem?

And by now a further point will have suggested itself: that the human-insight of the poem and the technicalities of its poetic artifice are inseparable. Each feeds the other. That interplay is the poem's meaning, a matter not of WHAT DOES IT MEAN, for no one can ever say entirely what a good poem means, but of HOW DOES IT MEAN, a process one can come much closer to discussing.

There is a necessary epilogue. Mr. Frost has often discussed this poem on the platform, or more usually in the course of a long-evening-after a talk. Time and again I have heard him say that he just wrote it off, that it just came to him, and that he set it down as it came.

Once at Bread Loaf, however, I heard him add one very essential piece to the discussion of how it "just came." One night, he said, he had sat down after supper to work at a long piece of blank verse. The piece never worked out, but Mr. Frost found himself so absorbed in it that, when next he looked up, dawn was at his window. He rose, crossed to the window, stood looking out for a few minutes, and *then* it was that "Stopping by Woods" suddenly "just came," so that all he had to do was cross the room and write it down.

Robert Frost is the sort of artist who hides his traces. I know of no Frost worksheets anywhere. If someone has raided his wastebasket in secret, it is possible that such worksheets exist somewhere, but Frost would not willingly allow anything but the finished product to leave him. Almost certainly, therefore, no one will ever know what was in that piece of unsuccessful blank verse he had been working at with such concentration, but I for one would stake my life that could that worksheet be uncovered, it would be found to contain the germinal stuff of "Stopping by Woods"; that what was a-simmer in him all night without finding its proper form, suddenly, when he let his still-occupied mind look away, came at him from a different direction, offered itself in a different form, and that finding that form exactly right the impulse proceeded to marry itself to the new shape in one of the most miraculous performances of English lyricism.

And that, too — whether or not one can accept so hypothetical a discussion — is part of HOW the poem means. It means that marriage to the perfect form, the poem's shapen declaration of itself, its moment's monument fixed beyond all possibility of change. And thus, finally, in every truly good poem, "How does it mean?" must always be answered "Triumphantly." Whatever the poem "is about," *how* it means is always how Genesis means: the word become a form, and the form become a thing, and — when the becoming is true — the thing become a part of the knowledge and experience of the race forever.

Forces of Corruption in The Great Gatsby

EVA MANSKI *(student essay)*

The theme of human corruption, its sources and consequences, is a common concern among writers from Shakespeare through J.D. Salinger. Some suggest it attacks from outside, while others depict corruption occurring from within the individual. In the case of *The Great Gatsby* and its protagonist's fate, Fitzgerald shows both factors at work. The moral climate of the Roaring Twenties, Daisy Fay Buchanan's pernicious hold on him, and Jay Gatsby's own nature all contribute to his tragic demise.

First, the loose morality of Dan Cody, Gatsby's unfortunate role model, and superficial people who flock to Gatsby's parties contribute to

Gatsby's downfall. Their examples encourage Gatsby's interpretation of The American Dream — his naive belief that money and social standing are all that matter in his quest for Daisy. The self-absorbed debutantes and their drunken escorts are among those who "crash" his extravagent soirées. As Nick Carroway tells us, "People were not invited — they went there." (p. 41) Prohibition notwithstanding, "the bar is in full swing . . . and casual innuendo and introductions forgotten on the spot." (p. 40) Shallow, corrupt people like Jordan Baker gossip with reckless abandon about their mysterious host. Their careless, superficial attitudes and wanton behaviour represent Fitzgerald's depiction of the corrupt American Dream.

Another force of corruption responsible for Gatsby's fate is his obsession with a woman of Daisy's nature. Determined to marry her after returning from the war, he is blind to her shallow, cowardly nature. He is unable to see the corruption which lies beyond her physical beauty, charming manner, and playful banter. That she is incapable of leaving her brutal husband, Tom, of committing herself to Gatsby despite his sacrifices, escapes him. As Nick observes, Gatsby's expectation is absurdly simple: "He only wanted her to tell him [Tom] that she never loved him." (p. 91) Daisy is not worthy of the pedestal on which he places her. Since she is hollow at the core, so is his dream which is based on a brief flirtation, nothing more.

Finally, Gatsby's own character — especially his willful obsession — contributes to his fate. Despite his naivete about Daisy and her friends who "are rich and play polo together," he, too, has been seduced by the lure of money and fame. Unable to control his obsessive desire to have Daisy, he cares little about the means by which he acquires the money to marry her. He associates with known criminals such as Myer Wolfsheim, appears to be involved with bootlegging, and is rumoured to have killed a man. Finally, he lies about himself and his family to enlist Nick's support of his grand quest. The means he uses to achieve his goal pervert his sacred dream. He prefers the pretty illusions he concocts to the harsh reality of the obsession he allows to corrupt his life.

Gatsby's character is probably the single most important factor in the story of his life and death. But Daisy and a society which rewards corruption play a part, too. F. Scott Fitzgerald's depiction of the soured American Dream dramatizes both internal and external forces at work in a modern tragedy about human potential for corruption.

Portraits of Women: The Quest for Self-Realization

SAM BLYTHE *(student essay)*

Central to Margaret Atwood's *The Edible Woman* and Margaret Laurence's *The Diviners* is the theme of psychological surfacing. For the female protagonists — Marian McAlpine and Morag Gunn — to achieve self-actualization, they must come to terms with three repressive factors: the restrictive needs of the men in their lives, their sexual relationships, and society's expectations of the female role. They must struggle through the expectations of others that interrupt the course of self-realization, with "tenacity and a will to survive"[1] and ultimately they insist on their independence.

First, the needs and demands of men hamper the self-actualization of women. In Atwood's *The Edible Woman*, Marian McAlpin is overwhelmed when she becomes aware of her apparent options: she can marry Peter, an urbane young lawyer, who needs a wife to complement his collection of guns, knives, and cameras, or she can align herself with the self-indulgent Duncan. Marian's discovery that her options are so confining, hampering factors in her quest for self-actualization, is striking. Marian realizes that she is being plastic-wrapped and consumed. Her knowledge nearly destroys her: she struggles desperately for her survival and for her sanity. Marian's survival depends on what the world will bring to her.

Marian feels increasingly consumed by her relationship with Peter. She reacts to her emotional turmoil by various inexplicable acts. She impulsively runs away from Peter after a dinner date. Later, at her friend Len's house with Peter, Marian seeks seclusion under Len's bed:

> My resentment at Peter for letting me remain crushed under the bed while he moved freely in the open, in the free air, jabbering away about exposure times, started me thinking about the past four months. (73)

Moreover, Peter's treatment of her when she later apologizes, is patronizing: he pats her head gently and refers to her as "baby."

Marian assumes "a submissive female role which demands passivity from her."[2] When Peter asks her when she would like to be married, she responds "in a soft flannely voice. . . . 'I'd rather leave the big decisions to you'." (87)

Often Marian needs to escape from Peter to Duncan, a colourless graduate student who looks like a boy of fifteen. She unconsciously picks up Duncan's ideas which hamper her self-actualization to a large extent. Under his influence Marian finds herself looking at the eating of meat as cannibalistic. She starts thinking of carrots as roots which make screams too low for the human ear to hear when they are pulled out of the ground. She wonders whether her body will reject all foods and cause her to starve to death.

In Margaret Laurence's *The Diviners*, writer Morag Gunn also must overcome the repressive factors in her life, that is, she must assume her own identity to achieve self-actualization. It is only in her forties when she is trying to cope with her daughter's identity crisis that Morag, through memorybank movies and snapshots, is able to arrive at an imperfect resolution of her quest for self-actualization.

Her first encounter with repression occurs after her parents' death. Although Morag lives with Christie and Prin Logan, she feels alienated from Manawaka, and has great difficulty accepting her dual heritage. Christie, the "Town Scavenger," indirectly hampers Morag's drive for self-fulfilment. Even as a child, Morag is acutely aware of the social constraints under which she suffers: Christie and his obese wife are social outcasts and the subject of cruel gossip. Her ambivalence toward Christie and Prin mounts during adolescence; she assumes a facade of tough indifference.

Morag's pride is wounded further by snide remarks about Christie, which prevent her from letting others know that she is vulnerable. On the first day of school, Morag learns a lesson that guides her throughout her life: "Hang on to your shit and never let them know that you are ascared." (28) Morag is repressed by an inability to communicate.

In addition, Morag's attempts to escape her past by fleeing Manawaka, receiving a university education, and marrying a professor, Dr. Brooke Skelton, only alienate her more from her roots and her quest. Her marriage to Brooke is Morag's most repressive male-female relationship. Brooke's need to dominate the relationship makes the possibility of Morag achieving her own identity inconceivable. Brooke's vanity, his egocentricity, and his need to manipulate are evident in his actions. Morag must order her appearance and arrange her writing schedule to suit his whims. She is his "child" (183), his "little one" (185), and his property: "You're mine. My woman. I'll protect you always" (182). He does not want her to finish her degree or choose her own friends. She must practise birth control because he does not want her child.

Hence, Morag makes the unhappy, unhealthy resolution to "do whatever [Brooke] wants," and "to conceal anything about herself which he might not like" (159). She depends on him for emotional as well as physical satisfaction: "Please don't ever leave me, Brooke. I couldn't bear it." (182) However, Morag soon becomes irritated as she is too strong-minded to play the role of the submissive wife for long: they divorce when Morag finally realizes that "I am not your child. I am your wife." (183) Morag's divorce from Brooke is her first step toward self-actualization.

The second major factor which impedes these two protagonists' quest is their sexual relationships with lovers. They use liaisons as a temporary release from loneliness or as a possible solution to their problems. These sexual relationships can threaten their autonomy — their emerging sense of self-direction.

In Atwood's *The Edible Woman*, Marian cannot define herself in relation to Peter, so she tries to define herself according to Duncan. The only role she can choose to accept is that of the helpful woman, willing to please others. Marian begins a sexual relationship with Duncan in an effort to resolve her feeling of being consumed, but discovers that no release of that kind occurs. However, Marian realizes that she has been oscillating from one man to the other. She abandons the characteristics that Peter wants to see in her only (later) to assume Duncan's vision of her. Marian decides that she has reached the very limit of her existence; defining oneself by the role one plays in one's lover's life does not make an individual whole. However, Duncan will not help her fight her way back from extinction:

> Don't ask me, that's your problem. It does look as though you ought to do something: self-laceration in a vacuum eventually gets rather boring. But it's your own personal cul-de-sac, you invented it, you'll have to think of your own way out. (264)

Duncan's response tells her that she must be thrown back on her inner resources and make her own authentic decision, thus allowing her self-actualization.

As a symbolic gesture of her new-found independence, Marian decides to bake a cake, and invites Peter over. This cake has an ironic meaning: Marian moulds it into the figure of a woman, clothes it in bright, pink frosting and adds a luscious pink mouth, green eyes and scrolls of hair. She sets it down in front of Peter, and says:

> You've been trying to destroy me, haven't you," she said. "You've been trying to assimilate me. But I've made you a substitute, something you'll like much better. This is what you really wanted all along, isn't it? I'll get you a fork. (284)

Thus, Marian discards her role as Peter's fiancée and assumes her own identity: she is no longer a delectable object for Peter's consumption, or a blank object sculpted to Duncan's taste.

In Laurence's *The Diviners*, Morag Gunn also attempts to liberate herself through sexual encounters with unsuccessful results. Her casual affairs, inspired purely by sexual need, are unfulfiling and intensify her loneliness. The two affairs that give her the most satisfaction are those that require limited commitment. Morag's second relationship of consequence with married artist Dan McRaith temporarily diminishes her loneliness. However, Morag's quest leads her to reject Dan's imposition on her writing time. Her fierce need for independence, which surpasses her fears and the loneliness of the path she chooses, is expressed in her authentic guideline: ". . . . just don't tell me what to do for my own good." (225)

The third and final factor which hampers these women's search is society's expectations for the female role. Society dictates that the role of the female is to be passive, submissive, and devoted to the needs of her family. In Atwood's *The Edible Woman*, Marian discards society's expectations. In the beginning, Marian amuses herself by turning conventional moral expectations upside down. She laughs at the "office virgins" and the trite explanations they give for their lack of experience:

> Millie from a solid girl-guide practicality ("I think in the long run it's better to wait until you're married, don't you?"), Lucy from social quailing ("What would people say,") . . . ; and Emmy, who is the office hypochondriac, from the belief that it would make her sick, which it probably would. (15)

However, Marian almost falls into the conventional, wifely role using the wifely formula "As Peter says" when she is engaged.

Marian escapes this trap when she realizes that she must assume her own identity. The cake Marian bakes in the form of a woman is a symbol of her rejection of society's expectations of the female role. When Marian's room-mate Ainsley sees the cake, she shrieks, "Marian! You're rejecting your femininity!" (286) What Marian is rejecting, in actuality, is femininity in the ways that Ainsley and Peter understand it.

In the same vein, Laurence's Morag Gunn explicitly rejects society's expectations of the female role. Even as a child, she is bold and brash. In an effort to have dates, Morag half-heartedly tries to play the socially acceptable female role of "aiming to please." (151) As a university student, she dates boys in whom she is not interested out of a sense of "being downgraded, devalued, undesirable" (151) if she doesn't participate in "the game." Although she needs sexual fulfilment, Morag holds back, for fear that a male might dismiss her as a cheap tramp. As a mature adult, Morag realizes the social restrictions imposed upon females, but refuses to submit to them. Morag's decision to have a child without the support of a husband, to write in a room of her own, and her refusal to accommodate herself to Dan's timetable are all important factors leading to her eventual self-realization.

The resolutions of the protagonists' struggles are both enigmatic and mature. Marian McAlpin is no longer someone "edible" but someone who eats: she is still within the cycle of production and consumption, and is able to affirm nothing more of herself than "I had steak for lunch, therefore I exist." Morag Gunn accepts Christie's centrality in her past and learns to appreciate his legacy: "Christie knew things about inner truths that I am just beginning to understand." (296) Morag must accept that the river flows both ways, that the water deepens and "keeps its life from sight." (370) The protagonists in each novel are offered an elusive peace. The quest for self-understanding has led Marian and Morag to a common resolution: the courage to "look ahead into the past, and back into the future, until the silence." (*The Diviners*, 370)

---

[1] V. Miner, "The Matriarch of Manawaka," *Saturday Night*, May 1974: 19.
[2] D.J. Doodley, *Moral Vision in the Canadian Novel* (Toronto: Clarke, Irwin and Company, 1979) 140.

TIPS ON WRITING A LITERARY ESSAY

1. Base your essay on a specific and significant question that you feel needs to be answered regarding the literary work.

2. Once you have such a question, brainstorm many possible answers. Think specifically about the work — for example, in fiction: themes, character development, plot and conflict, setting, and atmosphere.

3. Once you have a working thesis statement — essentially, your answer to the question — you may want to jot down a linear outline. If an outline does not take shape easily, you may want to push forward with your first draft. If you are using a computer you can easily rearrange this rough draft later, or you can cut and paste your essay from notepaper or typing paper.

4. Make sure the topic sentence for each paragraph deals with an aspect of your thesis statement. You may find it helpful to highlight crucial words in the thesis statement and the topic sentences. You may need to revise your thesis and rework the topic sentences as you rethink your answer.

5. Once you have all your paragraphs together, start revising: flesh out the details, cut and rearrange ideas, and write quotations in full with page numbers. You may want to consult "Revision or What Have I Actually Said?" (p. 38).

6. Next, you might discuss your essay with a partner. If possible, read it aloud. Often the ear detects flaws which the eye misses.

7. Try to save enough time to put the essay away for a few days. Your perspective will likely become more objective and you may notice contradictions and inconsistencies. Create a fresh draft from these corrections.

8. Read your revision aloud and pencil in editing changes, keeping a thesaurus and dictionary close at hand. Reread the wording of your thesis statement and check the topic sentence of each paragraph to make sure your argument hangs together.

9. Once again, you may want to exchange this draft with your partner who will likely be able to locate minor flaws.

10. The final version of your essay will probably differ greatly from your first draft. The time and effort you devoted to your composing process should pay off with an improved essay.

4. The Report

KEY WORK:

"Whole Brain Learning" — Margaret Hatcher

ASSOCIATED READINGS:

"How television is reshaping world's culture" — John Lippman
"Dressed to Kill" — Robert Hough
"Environmental Control of the Great Lakes" — Wendy Fox
   (student report)
Tips on Writing a Report

As you will see from the selections provided in this section, reports take many forms. They may be highly technical and academic for an audience in a specialized field or very general for the broad audience who gets its information mainly from the media. You will observe that the academic reports have many features in common with the social science essay whereas the more general reports have features in common with modern journalism. Since we live in what is called the "information age" we increasingly rely on reports to synthesize, communicate, and interpret this unending stream of information.

Because the length of a report is tightly circumscribed by the amount of information needed to accomplish its purpose, it must be carefully edited. Often, it employs word-saving devices such as the "bullet," or dot, before each item in a series to eliminate the need for full sentences. Frequently, the report's basic structure is outlined with a table of contents and/or headings and subheadings, and descriptions are replaced with figures, charts, tables, and other visual effects.

The Key Work, "Whole Brain Learning," is a carefully researched academic report, the type you will likely read and write at university. The Associated Readings demonstrate the importance of solid information in writing a convincing report and a variety of approaches to report writing. "Dressed to Kill," and "Environmental Control of the Great Lakes" were originally longer reports that here have been edited for length.

Conventions of the Report

Purpose   To inform, interpret, and, sometimes, to recommend

Audience   Specific or general, depending on the purpose

Tone	Usually objective, business-like, but may become persuasive through the logic of the recommendations
Voice	Silent or minimal
Response	Serious, but can be coloured by information and/or recommendations
Language	LEVEL — Generally fairly formal, but may vary, depending on the purpose and audience CHARACTERISTICS — Generally denotative and lacking in emotive language and often specialized and/or technical due to subject matter
Structure	Usually straightforward presentation of information, interpretation, and recommendations using headings and subheadings

BEFORE READING

1. What do you know about the theory of right brain, left brain thinking? Think about it, then share your thoughts with a partner.

2. Turn to Figure Two: Specialized Functions of Left and Right Sides of the Brain on page 107. Using your dictionary, study the material. Do you seem to have essentially a right brain or left brain approach to perceiving and processing information and sensations?

3. Examine the Conventions of the Report and list four or five subjects you might like to write about that would be suitable for this format.

Whole Brain Learning

MARGARET HATCHER

One of the more exciting and promising revolutions of our time is that of recent brain research and its mind-boggling implications for our education system. Recent brain/mind research offers undeniable evidence that we are taking the first steps toward understanding the latent, spectacular power of the mind. Yet we are tempted to ask: If our awareness is as pervasive, our brains as sensitive and infinitely complex, our memories as absorbent as research suggests, if we can indeed will changes in our physiology at the level of a single call as biofeedback and biosynergistic research indicate, why are we learning and performing at such mediocre levels?

While there are no easy, simple answers to this complex issue, it may be educators have ignored how the brain functions and have sought solutions elsewhere. In so doing, we may have neglected an organ of tremendous complexity and power. Recently, aided by new electronic tools, biomedical scientists, anthropologists, psychologists, and educators have sought to advance brain research and use this research to improve learning.

What are the educational implications of brain research?

INFINITE CAPACITY OF THE BRAIN

The brain is essentially a circuitry of interconnecting elements called neurons or nerve cells. Each neuron consists of three major parts: dendrites, cell body (soma), and axons (*see Figure One*).

Dendrites are spongy, antenna-like receptacles which conduct information from the neural field surrounding the neurons into the *cell body* (soma) where the information is coded and stored as a sensory image. When we need the information stored in the cell body, it is sent from the cell body along the *axon* and forms a *synapse*, an electrical quasi-juncture with a neighboring dendrite, thus transmitting information along the entire neural circuit.

The process we call "thinking" is actually the neural process of synaptic action. The simple act of blinking the eye takes about one million neural connections (Galyean, 1981). Researchers have concluded that "it is within the synapse itself that knowledge takes place" (Sagan, 1977; Teyler, 1978; Thompson, Berger, and Berry, 1980).

What is outstanding about the research on the neutral structure of the brain is the undeniable evidence of the apparently infinite capacity of the brain. Although estimates vary, Galyean summarizes research that indicates the brain is composed of ten to 100 billion neurons constantly firing and exchanging information among themselves (Hart, 1975; Sagan, 1977; Teyler, 1978). Add to this the fact that every neuron is capable of storing up to five billion bits of information (Galyean, 1981), whereas our most advanced computer chips can store only one billion. In addition, it is estimated that *each* neuron has ten to 100 thousand dendrites

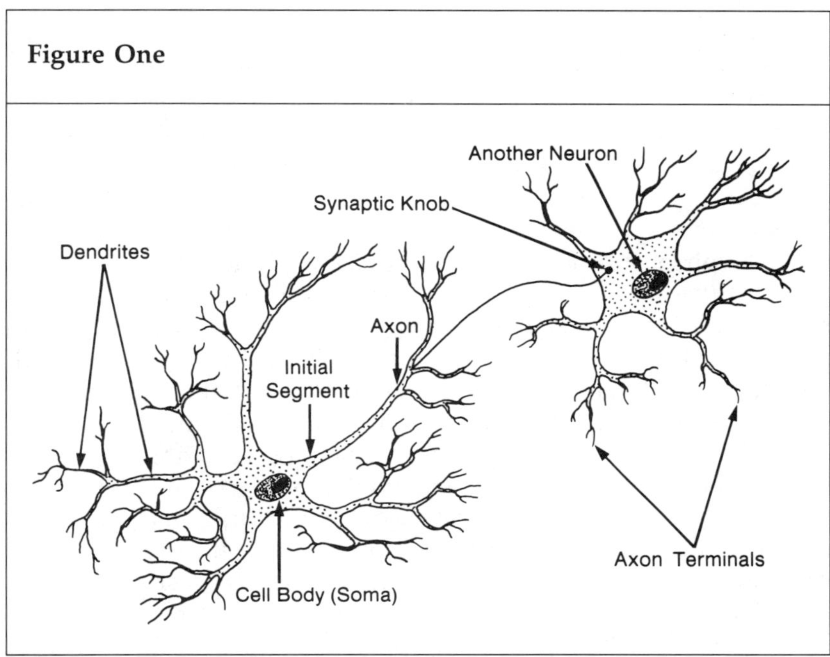

reaching to collect information, and each neuron, because of expansive dendritic branching, can connect with as many as 1,000 other neurons at any given moment (Galyean, 1981). According to Sagan, "Ten to 100 billion neurons interacting with a thousand each at one time implies that the brain is capable of processing from ten to 100 trillion bits of information in a lifetime." Since these are infinite numbers, from a mathematical point of view, it seems that the brain's capacity for learning is infinite. Leonard observes: "A brain composed of such numbers of neurons obviously can never be 'filled up'." Perhaps the more it knows, the more it can know and create. Perhaps, in fact, we can now propose an incredible hypothesis: *"The ultimate creative capacity of the brain may be, for all practical purposes, infinite."* (Leonard in Ferguson, 1973).

RIGHT BRAIN/LEFT BRAIN FUNCTIONS

One of the most exciting and dramatic findings of brain/mind research is that the right and left cortical hemispheres of the brain have certain specialized, predictable functions and process information differently. One of the first to report this "split brain" phenomenon was Robert Ornstein in the *Scientific American* in 1967. Other research followed (Bogen, 1969; Kinsbourne, 1980; Ornstein, 1972; Wittrock, 1978) and verified the thesis of *hemisphere differentiation*. By using brain scans of both cortices while subjects perform specific tasks such as daydreaming, counting, reading, writing, or drawing, researchers have been able to determine specialized functions for the right and left brains (*see Figure Two*).

Although each hemisphere has specialized functions, there is also a *bilaterality* of the brain, meaning that each hemisphere also shares some functions—both participate in most activities, but each hemisphere simply *processes* information differently. The corpus callosum, a bundle of nerves and fibers connecting the right and left cortices of the brain, functions to allow information perceived by one side of the brain to be received by the other. Without this, our right hand literally would not know what our left hand was doing.

In addition to specialized functions of the right and left hemispheres, other findings emerging from brain/mind research hold dramatic implications for personal growth and increasing our intellectual capacities. For example, we now know that the right brain cannot verbalize what it knows; its language is practically wordless, speechless. Information in the right brain is stored in images, senses, symbols, and metaphors. The left brain, on the other hand, must recognize and reformulate the images of the right brain into words before information in the right brain can be communicated. In short, the left brain is the "alphabet of the mind" (Galyean, 1981). The implications of that one fact alone are far-reaching. Like the dream we vividly experienced during the night, only to have it evaporate in the morning, the right brain world of intuitive, symbolic, holistic knowing is lost unless we capture it in words through the left brain.

Another significant finding relating to hemispheric differentiation is that, like a computer, the function of the left brain is to recognize, organize, and assimilate new information into *already existing frameworks*; its function is to recognize the relationship of stimulus to what it already knows. The left brain, in other words, is unable to create meaning or generate new ideas. It is from the right brain that new ideas, total contexts, creativity of meaning emerges. Hence, "without the right brain, there would be no idea; without the left brain, the idea would not be encoded, understood or communicated," observes Galyean.

Unfortunately, research indicates that our traditional educational system often emphasizes left hemispheric functioning to the

---

Figure Two. Specialized Functions of Left and Right Sides of the Brain.

Left Brain	*Right Brain*
1. Controls the right side of the body	1. Controls the left side of the body
2. Verbal/numerical	2. Visual/spatial
3. Logical/vertical	3. Perceptual/sensual/lateral thinking
4. Rational	4. Intuitive
5. Linear time	5. Space, infinity
6. Focus	6. Diffusion
7. Sequential/orderly	7. Spontaneous/creative
8. Analytic, the arrangement of parts	8. Gestalt, viewing the whole
9. Explicit	9. Tacit
10. Literal	10. Metaphorical/symbolic
11. Convergent	11. Divergent
12. Fact/Reality	12. Dream/fantasy/mystical

---

neglect and even denial of right hemispheric activity (Bogen, 1969; Frostig and Maslow, 1979; Wittrock, 1978). Also, tests are designed to measure predominantly left brain analytical skills as the major determinant of IQ, and often the creative individual who perceives holistically rather than analytically is left little opportunity to achieve well on most IQ tests. Only recently has research begun to attach equal importance to right and left brain learning styles (Brown, 1971; Galyean, 1981; Valett, 1977; Weinstein and Fantini, 1970).

The point of research on hemispheric specialization is *balance*; let us not neglect either hemisphere in favor of the other. The goal is to become equally familiar, equally proficient in both modes. Ornstein notes:

> Our highest creative achievements are the product of the complementary functioning of the two modes. Our intuitive knowledge is never explicit, never precise in the scientific sense. It is only when the intellect can begin to *process* the intuitive leaps, to explain and "translate" the intuition into operational and functional knowledge that the scientific becomes complete.
>
> (Ornstein, 1972).

Educational implications of "whole brain learning" are just now being explored. Some of the major techniques currently being used to tap the power of the right hemisphere and to form a bridge between right and left hemispheres include:

- **Synetics** is a new field of educational psychology that focuses on techniques teaching metaphorical thinking (Ferguson, 1973). The metaphor is a natural bridge between the right and left hemispheres because metaphors symbolically carry knowledge and make connections from the mute right brain so that it may be recognized by the left as being *like* something. Often the depth and significance of our experiences are related to the quality and intensity of our metaphorical insights, and indeed the more intense our experiences, the less words are useful. Also, metaphorical thinking is a key to *pattern* seeing, the ability to see relationships. Thus, to detect meaning from parts, to see wholes, the interrelatedness of things.

- **Multi-Sensory / Discovery / Experiential Learning Techniques**. Because the sense of space, the five physical senses, and body movement are all predominantly right brain processes, more and more educational strategies are involving total body experiences in learning. Discovery and experiential programs provide opportunities for learning by *doing,* for real-life situations within which students can find and solve problems that are relevant to their lives, and opportunities for observing and accomplishing skills/ concepts not possible in the classroom. Such activities provide the right hemisphere with the stimulus to activate and bridge whole brain functioning. Techniques involving body movement, improvisation, role-playing, multi-sensory expression, and synesthesia are all being used to facilitate learning.

  Some interesting research suggests that extra-sensory perception (telepathy, clairvoyance, precognition and psychokinesis) could also be viewed as a total combination of senses throughout the body so that the body as a whole acts as a perceptual organ. Research is in its infancy in relating this concept to intuitive and creative thinking processes, but the implications for education in the future are staggering.

- **Divergent and Creative Thinking Techniques**. Research tells us that the brain apparently does not require our conscious (left brain) effort to form bridges to creative (right brain) functions; it requires only our *attention,* our openness to let the information through and to recognize its significance. Because the left brain is logical and verbal, we often tend to listen and to give attention only to it. Divergent and creative thinking techniques rest on the premise of the significance of *open-focus.* These techniques emphasize the use of contradiction and paradox; problem-solving techniques; organizing skills; Gestalt techniques to focus on patterns and wholes rather than isolated parts; information processes that emphasize asking the right questions rather than having the right answers; open-ended problems/situations; use of discovery, exploratory and imagination games, "mind-benders," and other mind expansion devices; and futuristics. A recent study showed that creativity scores invariably drop about 90 percent between ages five and seven; by age 40 an individual is only about 2 percent as creative as at age five (Ferguson, 1973). This suggests that the almost total emphasis on logical, linear thought in our educational system may effectively suppress creativity.

USE OF EMOTIONS IN LEARNING

A fascinating area of brain research deals with the role of emotions in the process by which information is transmitted smoothly and rapidly throughout the brain's neural circuitry. The axons of each neuron are coated with a fatty substance called myelin. Several research teams have verified that heavily myelinated axons conduct information more rapidly from the cell body than do less myelinated axons (Galyean, 1981; Thompson, Berger and Berry, 1980). In addition, and even more significantly, independent studies conclude that myelin production is heavily affected by the presence or absence of two factors: *emotional closeness and enriched experiential learning environments* (Sagan, 1977). The educational implications of this finding are clear: if it is true that highly intelligent people have an abundance of healthy myelinated axons to assure smooth and rapid transmission of vast amounts of information, then *increased learning capacity might possibly be nutured through physical affection and enriched learning environments* (Clark, 1979).

Related to this finding is the relationship between emotions and thinking. We now know that the brain operates on an emotional bias system and on a programmatic basis. The information stored within the cell soma of each neuron represents not only isolated bits of information, but chains of information, or programs, as well (Hart, 1975). What merits careful consideration for educators is *how the brain selects its programs*. Research tells us that *the brain processes only that information that is perceived by the learner as helpful, interesting, rewarding* (Hart, 1975; MacLean, 1978, 1980; Sagan, 1977) *and/or "gamey"* (Wittrock, 1978). In short, our brain's chemistry seems to be controlled by inner images of pleasure or displeasure, and if the learning environment or the information is negative, it is not allowed passage, the stimuli are never encoded, never stored, never remembered, and consequently, never learned.

Thus, the way we perceive ourselves, the inner images we hold about ourselves, others, and our environment determine how we think, behave, and ultimately determine what we learn. Research and experience have long verified that intellectual output can be enhanced through increasing the quality and quantity of affective motivators such as desire, excitement, and social/cultural approbation. More and more these are tied to the degree of the learner's positive self-image, to exercising focused concentration on performing tasks well on a daily basis, and to seeing oneself as thoroughly successful, capable, and confident throughout the day. It seems evident that one of the major thrusts of education of the future will be to find ways of providing students with means of discovering their own intentions and sources of their own learning motivation.

ALPHA CONSCIOUSNESS

Research into how the brain prepares to receive new ideas and new material shows us that there must be sufficient flexibility for change to take place, for old behavioral patterns to mollify, eventually break down, and to create new forms and new patterns. The brain performs dissipative action (breakdown and creation) through the creation of electric waves. Brain wave patterns are based on four basic frequency ranges: *Beta* waves are most often recorded in the ordinary waking state of conscious or in analytical thinking and are most often recorded when left hemisphere tasks occur such as externally focused attention, goal orientation, and problem solving. Beta waves are short and rapid, and they allow little or no room for disturbance of already existing patterns.

Alpha waves, however, are emitted when we are deeply relaxed, engaged in daydreaming, reverie, creative endeavors, intuitive thinking, or symbolic expression. These waves shake up already existing patterns, allowing new ones to emerge. Galyean notes that "The alpha state is the *sine qua non* exponent of creativity, insight, and illumination" (Galyean, 1981). Also the alpha state is usually characterized by feelings of psychological integration and unity, and that, although the alpha state involves both hemispheres, the right hemispheric processes appear to be predominant. Studies have shown that highly intelligent people produce more alpha waves and work in an alpha state for longer periods of time than do persons of average intelligence (Galyean, 1981).

Delta waves are recorded most frequently during deep dream states. *Theta* waves are usually recorded during semi-sleep, characterized by creative insights, and are often associated with creativity and right brain functioning.

Researchers such as Galyean, Clark, and Ornstein have documented dramatic results in the use of inducing alpha consciousness through relaxation techniques, such as deep breathing and yoga, meditation techniques, such as inner focusing, centering, visualization and guided imagery. These alpha states influence both the rapidity and quantity of information being retained over long periods of time. More and more, it is becoming evident that it might be necessary to structure periods for creative incubation as a part of the standard curriculum, including such elements as time for reverie, guided imagery, mind/body integrative activities nuturing intuitive development, and meditation approaches, all of which quiet brain activity and increase synchronous brain activity.

If we accept overwhelming evidence offered us by brain research that we *are* smarter than we think, that we *are* capable of functioning far beyond the limits of ordinary three-dimensional existence, it follows that we, as educational leaders, have much rethinking to do about the educational premises on which our schools are founded. Educational methodologies derived from brain research are still in the neophyte stages of development and should be treated as such — much research into individual learning styles still needs to be accomplished.

However, one thing remains certain: the promises and expectations of actualizing the full spectrum of human potential loom enticingly before us. The great challenge for educators is to discover ways to expand the greatest of all human gifts — a clear, sharp, constantly expanding, centered mind — to teach others how to acquire and nurture this gift for themselves.

SELECTED READINGS

Battung, Diane, "An Educator's Guide to the Brain/Mind Revolution: Implications for Learning and Expanded Human Potential." Long Beach, California: KenZel, 1980.

Bogen, Joseph, "The Other Side of the Brain, I, II, III." *Bulletin of the Los Angeles Neurological Societies* 34, 3 (July 1969).

Brown, George, ed. *Human Teaching for Human Learning.* New York: Viking Press, 1971.

Clark, Barbara, *Growing Up Gifted.* Columbus, Ohio: Merrill Publishing Co., 1979.

Ferguson, Marilyn, *The Brain Revolution.* New York: Taplinger, 1973.

Frostig, Marianne, and Maslow, Phyllis, "Neuropsychological Contributions to Education." *Journal of Learning Disabilities* 8 (October 1979): 40–54.

Galyean, Beverly, "The Brain, Intelligence and Education." *Roper Review* (Fall 1981).

Galyean, Beverly, "Guided Imagery in Education." *Journal of Humanistic Psychology* (Spring 1981).

EXPLORING THE REPORT

1. a. Make an outline of the report on "Whole Brain Learning" (p. 103) showing that it follows the conventions referred to earlier. Incorporate Hatcher's headings and subheadings.
   b. What heading could have appeared before the paragraph on page 106 beginning, "Unfortunately, research indicates … ?" Why?

2. Divide the following tasks among four groups; each group should prepare a response to the task assigned. Then, regroup so that there is an "expert" in each of the areas who can share his or her expertise with the group.
   a. the theory of how we think
   b. why research argues that "the ultimate creative capacity of the brain may be infinite"
   c. the concept of "hemisphere differentiation," related findings, and the implications for "personal growth and intellectual capacities"
   d. the interrelationship between the brain's two parts

3. Briefly explain these terms and phrases: synetics, multisensory/ discovery/Experiential Learning Techniques, and Divergent and Creative Thinking Techniques.

4. Does Hatcher provide her readers with sufficient data to support her interpretation and recommendations? Explain.

5. Is Hatcher's tone appropriate for her audience and intended purpose? Give reasons.

EXTENSIVE STUDY

1. In small groups, explore your educational background and decide to what extent your particular experiences have enhanced and/or repressed your capacity to learn. What

changes to curriculum, school organization, and school structure and environment would you recommend to rectify any
weaknesses you have identified?

   (You may wish to begin by making a list of subjects that are
essentially right brain or left brain oriented.)

2. Improvise a scene, either serious or humorous, between a couple conscious of recent brain research who are determined that
   their child (or children) will develop balanced hemispheric ability. Refer to "Whole Brain Learning" (p. 103) as well as the
   review "Your Brain Has a Mind of Its Own" (p. 201) to help
   make your scene vivid.

3. Read the student report, "Environmental Control of the Great
   Lakes" (p. 128), and assess its quality using criteria developed
   from the Conventions of the Report (p. 102) and Tips on Writing
   a Report (p. 134).

4. Read "Dressed to Kill" (p. 119), a report on the conflict between
   animal rights activists and the fur industry.
   a. What research methods has Robert Hughes employed to
      explore this controversial issue?
   b. What conventions of report writing has Hughes broken, or
      at least bent, in this report?
   c. Has he written a balanced and fair report? Justify your
      answer.
   d. What are some criteria a person should have in mind when
      preparing a report using personal research and investigation?

THE WRITING FOLDER

1. In your journal or writer's notebook reflect on the ethical and
   moral implications of current brain research.

2. Compose a fictional dialogue involving a conflict between a left
   brain thinker and a right brain thinker on how to accomplish a
   group task.

3. Using the Conventions of the Report on page 102 and Tips on
   Writing a Report on page 134 as a guide, write a brief report on
   a school issue or a public controversy.

INDEPENDENT STUDY

1. Explore recent studies in brain research either individually or with a partner. Using your findings, write an academic or formal report on how this research could help you become a better English student. Base your referencing on the style employed in "Environmental Control of the Great Lakes" (p. 128).

   You may wish to consult your teacher-librarian and conduct a computer search for recent studies, papers, and articles.

2. Studies on the functions of the brain have led to research into the way we learn.

   In consultation with your teacher and teacher-librarian, locate and examine various studies and reports that have been done on learning styles. From these develop a questionnaire or survey to administer to the students in your study. Using the research material and the data from your questionnaire, write a report on your findings and present it to the class. (In your report you should make use of your data in the form of figures, diagrams, and charts.

3. Using "How television is reshaping world's culture" (p. 115) as a starting point, examine the impact of television and the media on contemporary life. Refer to such works as Neil Postman's *Amusing Ourselves to Death*, Gore Vidal's *Screening History*, Marshall McCluhan's writings, and Saul Wurman's *Information Anxiety*. Your teacher and/or teacher-librarian may suggest other titles and sources.

   Use this information to write a report, and then present it to the class.

TIMED READING AND WRITING

1. Read "How television is reshaping world's culture" (p. 115).
   a. Make a point-form summary of the report's main points.
   b. Why does the writer predict that the advent of world-wide satellite television in our age will have as great an impact on world culture as the invention of the printing press had on European culture in the Middle Ages?
   c. Outline the positive and the negative aspects of this world-wide phenomenon and predict further changes in technology which might occur in the next twenty years.

How television is reshaping world's culture

JOHN LIPPMAN

Historians looking at the 20th century from the next millennium will likely pinpoint 1945 as the most pivotal year since the voyage of Columbus.

Two nuclear bombs exploded over Japanese cities, providing a glimpse of the apocalypse. And an obscure British radar officer named Arthur C. Clarke found that it's possible to relay pictures around the world almost instantly by bouncing radio signals off a few satellites orbiting high above the Equator.

Both developments changed the course of humankind.

Asked once what had caused the stunning collapse of communism in eastern Europe, Polish leader Lech Walesa pointed to a nearby TV set. "It all came from there."

If it has helped topple totalitarian governments and promote democracy, television has also, for better or for worse, led a modern Crusade, spreading pop culture over the Earth as medieval knights once spread Christendom.

In fact, nearly 30 years after Canadian philosopher Marshall McLuhan coined the phrase "global village" to describe how the electronics revolution was shrinking the world and shortening the time between thought and action, the Media Millennium is at hand.

TV sets are more common in Japanese homes than flush toilets. Virtually every Mexican household has a TV, but only half have phones.

More than half of North Americans alive today may not remember a time without TV in their home. They're surprised if someone *doesn't* have 25 or 30 channels to choose from. But for much of the globe, television is still relatively new, and changing fast. Today, there is hardly any spot on Earth untrammeled by a satellite "footprint" — the area, sometimes spanning whole continents, within reach of signals from its parabolic antennas.

The rapid inroads of satellite-based "borderless television" are changing the way the world works, the way it plays, even the way it goes to war and makes peace. Even countries that have long limited what their citizens can watch on nationalized TV are slowly being forced to relax their vice-like grip.

Madonna writhes on MTV videos from Bahrain to Bangladesh. A deputy police chief in Moscow is distracted during an interview by Super Channel, a British cross between MTV and *Entertainment Tonight*, which blares incessantly in many Russian homes and offices. Dozens of pan-European satellite channels, beaming everything from highbrow French talk shows to Dutch pornography, trespass national borders without visas. *Los Simpsons* becomes a top-rated TV show in Colombia.

Spurred by technological advance and the worldwide trend toward privatization, a global TV economy is growing at a blistering rate. Consider:

* More than 1 billion TV sets now populate the globe, a 50 per cent jump over the last five years. The number is expected to continue growing by 5 per cent annually, and by more than double that in Asia, where half the world's population lives.
* Worldwide spending for television programming is now about $65 billion, and the tab is growing by 10 per cent per year, according to Neal Weinstock, media project director for the New York research firm Frost & Sullivan Inc. TV programs are a major U.S. export now worth about $2.3 billion annually.
* The number of satellite-delivered TV services around the world is more than 300 and climbing rapidly, says Mark Long, publisher of the *World Satellite Almanac*. Truly global "super channels" such as MTV reach hundreds of millions of households, while CNN is seen in 137 countries.
* Scores of new communications satellites are planned for launch in just the next five years, which will mean a huge jump in the number of space-borne TV channels.

The cultural, political and economic effects of this global television revolution are enormous.

Whether in the situation room at the White House or in living rooms at home, it is clear to viewers that television is no longer simply a limp witness to history.

Television is how most people now experience history, as happened when viewers watched live satellite pictures of U.S. troops landing on the beach at Mogadishu. Conversely, history is now shaped by television, a reality eloquently symbolized by East German youths when they hoisted MTV flags over the Berlin Wall as it was torn down.

Oxford political scientist Timothy Garton Ash dubs television "the third superpower" whose influence will only grow as satellites and cable revolutionize its content.

A complex set of problems and issues arise from that power.

Ash warns that borderless TV threatens to make even more painfully obvious the economic gulf between rich and poor nations. Diplomats in Libya contend that television is undermining Moammar Gadhafi by tempting the country's relatively poor and otherwise largely sheltered population with the consumer delights seen in Italian commercials.

Even more alarming to some is the prospect of a world full of couch potatoes. The French now spend more time watching TV than working. Spanish schoolchildren are heavier viewers than their American counterparts. In Canada, the Vancouver-based Media Foundation, which publishes a magazine called *Adbusters*, has launched a frontal assault on TV's incessant buy-buy message by producing and attempting to air "anti-consumption" commercials.

Some worry that TV watching will make the rest of the world lose its appetite for reading, as has already happened to two generations of North Americans.

With satellites beaming down literally hundreds of TV channels over whole continents and oceans, countries lose control over the information crossing their borders — an unstoppable migration of ideas, images and culture that raises basic questions about the meaning of national sovereignty in the modern world.

"The nation-state is less and less able to control what goes in and out of it," said Everrete E. Dennis, a media scholar and executive director of the Freedom Forum Media Studies Centre. "It really makes customs and other nuances from the past kind of irrelevant."

What is happening around the world is the outcome of nearly two decades of global deregulation, spreading capitalism and advances in technology that are making electronic communications perhaps the world's pre-eminent growth industry.

"Technology has made it possible to add a number of channels in a variety of ways," said Eli Noam, an expert in global television at Columbia University in New York. "And the old state-run broadcasting systems are running out of steam."

Many of the new channels are being financed by advertising generated from an increasingly industrialized world looking for new outlets for its consumer and manufactured goods.

In Europe, TV advertising is expected to more than double to $36 billion by the turn of the century. The Pacific Rim's nascent TV ad market, just emerging from years of heavy-handed government regulation, has already reached $14 billion. With worldwide satellite networks, the Holy Grail of marketing — global advertising — is finally a reality.

"In another five years, there will be a direct broadcast satellite all over the Arab world," said Abdallah Schleifer, professor of television journalism at American University in Cairo. "And whether (people) want it or not, everyone is going to have success."

Historically, empowered elites have sought to suppress the wider distribution of ideas, wealth, rights and, most of all, knowledge.

This is as true today as it was 536 years ago, when the German printer Gutenberg invented movable type to print the Bible. For two centuries afterward, government tightly controlled what people could read through the widespread exercise of "prior restraint."

Some governments still go to great lengths to make the news fit their purposes.

The Chinese government doctored videotape of the 1989 Tiananmen massacre, reversing the order of events to make it appear the killings were a justified reaction to mob violence.

If you can't lick 'em, some governments apparently feel, you may as well join 'em. There are presently more than 40 established or planned government-run satellite TV channels, many with the same propagandistic purpose as their terrestrial predecessors.

Egypt's Space Channel, for example, originally launched to entertain homesick Egyptian troops in the Saudi desert during the gulf war, is seen as a response to Middle Eastern Broadcasting's Pan-Arabic news channel, owned by Saudis with royal connections.

Like ambitious states that want to join the nuclear club, a country today barely ranks as a world-class power unless it lofts a satellite bearing its own acronym: Asiasat, Aussat, Turksat, Thaicom, Arabsat, Insat, Indonesia's Palapa and Spain's Hispasat, to name a few.

"It's frequently a question of political sovereignty, not just economic rationality," said Meherro Jussawalla, a research economist with the East-West Center in Honolulu. "Each country wants to control its own satellite system for domestic purposes."

Even more than on politics, however, the greatest influence of satellite television is on culture. Whereas it used to take decades or centuries for one culture to seep into another, television today can spread lasting images in a matter of seconds.

"Foolish programs coming in foreign languages to our cable television stations are as much a danger to us as some attacks on our frontier," threatening Israel's culture, heritage and language, Foreign Minister Shimon Peres said not long ago.

Ironically, Peres shares this concern with Islamic fundamentalists in Algeria who now call satellite receiving dishes — *les antennes paraboliques* in French — *les antennes diaboliques.*

But neither quotas nor religious edicts are likely to slow the onslaught of borderless television. Rather than homogenizing the world, it is possible that the revolution will instead lead to a greater diversity in programming, especially as developing states become more sophisticated in the use of the medium.

The global village won't be called "Dallas."

Dressed to Kill

ROBERT HOUGH

Ploughing through the crowd in his blue rayon trench coat, issuing directives in a deep, theatrical voice, Tony urges his people to stay together, to march in tandem, to show a united front. Josephine, meanwhile, governs the chants, her American accent amplified through a raised megaphone. *What's our mission? Fur abolition! What's our mission? Fur abolition!* Then . . . subtly . . . she introduces a different rhyme, insinuating new words into the vocal groove. *No more cages, no more traps, no more fur on human backs! No more cages, no more traps, no more fur on human backs!* Pinned to her grey polyester coat is a button reading, "Fur, The Ultimate Sadist Symbol."

It is a cold, clear morning early in February. Two hundred animal-rights activists circle a small stretch of Bloor Street west of Yonge, a stretch housing Toronto's ritziest clothing stores, upheld signs preaching their gospel. FUR IS DEAD! BARBARIC BLOOD FASHION! FUR ON YOUR BACK, BLOOD ON YOUR HANDS! Looking thin and bashful, Rob remains in the background, following the chants, clutching a placard reading FUR IS NOT CHIC. Shortly after noon, as a lone Voyageur bus unexpectedly pulls up, he detects a slight mood shift in the crowd, an expression of pleased surprise. Tony and Josephine are pointing, laughing; they find it humorous, this futile attempt to fight back, to defend the barbaric slaughter of innocent animals. "Lookit," Josephine says to Tony, gesturing at the trappers, natives, and furriers charging off the bus. "This is gonna be wonderful. . . ."

Rob, however, senses the situation could get weird; the newcomers are already storming off the bus in twos, poking their own signs to the sky, yelling at the activists. *Losers! Get a job! Liars!* Some are wearing business suits. Some wear native garb. Some wear the workmen jackets of a trapper. Many wear fur. Then there are the large, unshaven males who seem to have no connection with the fur industry; Josephine suspects they are unemployed northerners, hired by the fur industry to don mink coats and outscream pain-in-the-ass do-gooders in Toronto. Still, most of the anti-fur protesters remain confident. With only one busload, what are they gonna do? What *can* they do? In every living room in Metro, anti-fur activists will be shown vanquishing the animal-killers!

Minutes later, the next bus arrives.

And the next.

Others follow.

The animal-rights activists are soon outnumbered by a hundred, forcing them to scream louder. *Murderers! Get the dead animals off your backs! Losers!* Tony runs in manic circles, imploring his troops to turn away, to ignore them, to *please* people stick to your chants. A young activist and a trapper begin shoving. A woman has an earring ripped from her lobe. Josephine, three months pregnant, is thankful when the police move in, separating the throng, the two sides now sandwiched against each other, a filling of blue in between. Nose to nose, they bellow expletives, until police move the animal-rights activists to the other side of Bloor Street. The melee ends at two o'clock, when the pro-fur demonstrators finally depart; members of both factions hail the confrontation as a victory.

Few, however, describe it as a pivotal moment, as a turning point in the Canadian fur controversy. Of course, it is easy *now* to recognize the significance of the event: it was the first time the fur industry ever fought back in public, the first time it openly challenged people like Tony and Josephine and Rob, the first time it ever admitted that *hmmmmmmm, maybe those sign-toting misfits really are a threat.* And with two years' worth of hindsight, it is also easy to grade the fur industry's entire defence strategy, as one thing has since become abundantly clear.

Those misfits are winning.

Tony Smith is currently one of the highest-profile "animal-rights" activists in the country — a designation that bears explaining. Groups working for the betterment of animal life form a spectrum. Moderates are referred to as animal welfarists; they believe animals *can* be used by mankind, but only if treated as compassionately as possible. The Canadian Association for Humane Trapping, for example, feels it is ethically permissible to trap animals, yet it decries painful trapping methods, and has long been lobbying to ban leg-hold traps. Welfarism, surveys suggest, also approximates the national mood; most Canadians will squash a buzzing mosquito, but won't slowly yank its wings off first.

In the middle are animal protectionists, who want to reduce the degree to which humans dominate animals. Those in the World Society for the Protection of Animals, an international troop with its Canadian headquarters in Toronto, do not believe in killing animals for their fur, in eating animals (unless necessary for survival), or in using animals for most scientific research. They will, however, use leather and wool, eat dairy products, and visit the zoo. That pesky mosquito? They'd shoo it away a few times, then smear it to a pulp if it persisted.

Which brings us to the far end of the spectrum, a region occupied by such animal-rights groups as Canadians Against Fur, Action Volunteers for Animals, and ARK II. Many are vegans, consuming no animal products whatsoever. They generally wear nothing but cotton, plastic, or synthetics. For them, breeding is abhorrent, as is the practice of confining animals in zoos. Instead, they dream of restructuring the societal power structure so that all creatures — from the tiniest bug to a trumpeting bull elephant — enjoy the same rights afforded to Homo sapiens. A thirsty mosquito lands? An animal-rights activist questions whether it is ethical to wave off the insect, as it is merely performing its biological duty.

Not surprisingly, adherents of the animal-rights philosophy are the ones who picket, who demonstrate, who are dragged away by tired, stony-faced cops. With Tony, Josephine, and Rob acting as leaders, they conduct sit-ins in boutiques, in department-store fur sections, always joining forces to increase their numbers. These are the groups who protest at fur-farming conventions, who've tromped outside the Hudson's Bay at Yonge and Bloor so many times the pavement is grooved.

"Whenever fur is politicized," Tony says, "it works in our behalf. Fur serves a purpose. It is designed to be quietly admired. It is not meant to be a symbol of anything but self-indulgence. It's just not cut out for any kind of ethical battle." In other words, the fur industry is a convenient first step; because it disposes of animals in the name of fashion, it isn't as defensible as the meat industry or medical research. Once the fur industry is overcome, however, animal-rights activists will select their next target. That day, they can see, is nearing.

In the meantime, activists continue the battle, stopping fur-wearers on the streets, demanding that they remove their mink coat, their beaver hat, their fox stole. Others have invented different methods: some sneak anti-fur buttons into the pockets of fur coats. A few slap stickers on the backs of fur garments. One woman, having spotted a fur-wearer on a commuter train, stands and silently points at the offender during the entire ride. Whatever the method, it is this aggressiveness that best characterizes the animal-rights movement; like Jesus among the moneychangers, activists feel a divine mission to overrun an evil social order. And if they have to make enemies, so be it. "Soon," Tony warns, "it will be hard to wear fur downtown and not be reminded of your boorishness, your lack of class, your bad manners, your lack of consideration, your callousness." As he speaks, he jabs a sinewy finger in the air, as though bayoneting a foe.

The current archenemy, the figure most hated by animal-rights activists, is one David Sebben, marketing director for the Fur Trade Association of Canada (which is really the Ontario branch of the Fur Council of Canada, the body representing trappers, factory farmers, dressers, and furriers across the country). "A vile automaton," Tony Smith says of Sebben. "He's even more parasitical than the furriers. Furriers live in the bowels of other animals, while he lives in the bowels of the creatures who live in the bowels of other animals."

I arrange to meet Sebben in his Toronto office, a large panelled room coated with posters depicting gleeful men and women wearing fur. Whereas the animal-rights personnel I have met seem perpetually agitated, Sebben is an island of calm, a personification of Alfred E. Newman's "What, me worry?" He is also polite and accommodating, completely unlike the monster Tony described. "Anti-fur activism hasn't had an effect on sales," Sebben tells me, "and we know that. You can check the records."

Animal-rights groups, meanwhile, have their own studies showing the opposite. The only independent research available is from

Statistics Canada; while it had no actual sales data, its figures did show a forty per cent drop in the retail price of fur coats over the last eight years. According to Sebben, this has been caused by a glut of Scandinavian furs. Mind you, *every* furrier I talked to maintained that fur still enjoys a sterling image, despite some ominous indicators. Between 1985 and 1990, fur sales have dropped ninety per cent in Holland, seventy-five per cent in Switzerland, and seventy-four per cent in Britain, countries that just happen to have the most active anti-fur movements. The Hudson's Bay Company — an organization built upon the fur trade — stopped retailing furs. Creeds, one of Canada's biggest single-store fur outlets, collapsed. Stars who have publicly denounced fur include k.d. lang, Brigitte Bardot, Candice Bergen, Rosanna Arquette, the Go-Go's, Daryl Hannah, Ally Sheedy, and Bob Barker. "The Young and the Restless" has carried a disclaimer at the beginning of each show: furs depicted are not real. "Wheel of Fortune" no longer gives fur as prizes. The makers of "Barbie" list her as an animal-rights volunteer in her most recent curriculum vitae. Still, Sebben maintains it is merely coincidental that in the fall of 1990 the Fur Council launched a three-year PR campaign; using print and radio ads, the council is spending "a significant amount" to "get the real facts on the table."

"Let me show you something," Sebben says. He pulls out a standard leg-hold trap, its chains clanking as he sets it. He inserts his fingers, and the sinister-looking jaws snap shut. He doesn't flinch. "You see? Animal-rights activists tell you it will break a coyote's leg! But my fingers are a lot thinner." Kinder, gentler traps are a common defence of the fur industry: ninety per cent of fur-bearing animals are now taken in instant-kill traps, while the remainder are caught in leg-hold traps padded with a space-age plastic. If that isn't enough, fur-reps proudly state, more humane traps are being developed every day by a government-funded body called the Fur Institute of Canada. The strategy is clear; by convincing the public that the fur business is cruelty-free, the industry is attempting to adopt a "welfarist" image, putting it in tune with Mr. and Mrs. Average Canadian.

Sebben resets the trap and pushes it across the desk. "You wanna try?" I am hesitant. Then, with a deep breath, I insert my fragile digits, the steel tines slamming closed on my knuckles. He is right. It doesn't hurt. A minute later, as the ends of my fingers start to throb, he reaches over and releases me.

"See?"

We discuss the other key points of the Council's PR campaign. Furs, he tells me, are environmentally friendly (because they are renewable resources, as opposed to oil-based synthetics). Fur coats are not frivolous. (As Fur Council literature states, fur is "nature's most beautiful solution to the challenges of winter.") Animals raised on fur ranches are well cared for. (Otherwise, poor pelts would result.) Endangered animals are not used (though there is evidence suggesting that lynx and wolverine have been depleted by trapping). Three of the arguments, however, are more germane: the fur industry is a cornerstone of Canada's history, the fur industry provides jobs for natives, and, if wild animals weren't trapped for fur, they would be trapped by Environment Canada to control wildlife populations. This is what makes the Canadian fur controversy compelling: in Europe there is no fur-trade tradition, no guilt complex over aboriginal treatment, and far less wildlife to control.

The most sensitive topic within this insane rubric called "the fur controversy" is, of course, aboriginal survival. As one of the Fur Council pamphlets reads: "The fur industry maintains a unique tradition and culture for thousands of Canadians who still live from the land. . . ." Animal-rights activists, on the other hand, insist that native survival is a convenient smoke-screen, an opportunistic dodge. "Listen," I was told again and again, "read *Defense of the Fur Trade!*" at which point I'd be handed a 1985 government report prepared by a market-research firm. (True enough, it does contain some mighty damning evidence: "Defense of aboriginal cultures," the document reads, "could be a good counterbalance to anti-fur or anti-trapping campaigns. . . .")

"Of course," I would then be told, "you must also talk to Paul Hollingsworth." Hollingsworth is the spokesperson of Native Animal Brotherhood, a small minority of natives who oppose fur trapping. This is what I learn, on the day Hollingsworth drives in from his home in Guelph: the bulk of the profit generated by fur trapping is absorbed by manufacturers and furriers, not by Indian trappers. Ergo, fur is symbolic of the white man's oppression of natives. Aboriginals, Hollingsworth feels, should get out of fur altogether, and build economic infrastructures in which *they* derive the profit. His argument is logical, attractive. But I am intrigued for another reason; despite what the anti-fur forces told me, Hollingsworth is more a native-rights advocate than an animal-rights activist.

"Listen," I finally say, "we both know the fur industry uses natives as a justification for the fur trade. Do you ever feel your group is used by animal-rights activists?"

"Oh yeah," he answers. "Both sides are holding up their token natives." As he says this, he leans back and smiles, as though amused by my naivety.

Native recruitment is, after all, a single tactic in a war brimming with suspected conspiracies, with behind-the-scenes alliances. Four anti-fur groups, including the World Society for the Protection of Animals, have had their charitable status reviewed by Revenue Canada; Michael O'Sullivan, the group's Canadian director, swears it was the result of fur-industry prompting. Four years ago, the fur-protest arm of the Toronto Humane Society had a series of print ads challenged by the Canadian Advertising Federation. Ainslie Willock, that arm's former director, also claims the investigation was prompted by the fur industry. On the other hand, Paul Magdar maintains the fake-fur industry is funding animal-rights groups. Brian Davey, deputy grand chief of the Nishnawbe-Aski Nation in Northern Ontario, suspects a fraternity between animal rights and research-and-development companies; with land claims predicated on trap lines, the end of trapping could mean a field day for corporations wishing to explore native land.

These are allegations I became accustomed to hearing — allegations charged with contempt, with scorn, both sides assuming moral superiority. With one exception, there was no desire to understand the other side, no recognition that maybe, just maybe, discussion was warranted. Ironically, the exception was Rob Eastwood, a slight young man with wire-framed glasses, an earring, and a brush cut. Rob is president of Canada's most infamous animal-rights group, ARK II.

"ARK II is abolitionist in every respect," he says, taking the same seat at my kitchen table that Tony occupied the previous week. "We feel that humans and animals are on the same level. Because we're all part of the same planet, and we're all interconnected, we all — in total fairness — should be treated equally." A twenty-nine-year-old clerk, Rob was first enamoured of a cocker spaniel who roamed around his grandfather's cottage. But it wasn't until he visited a Humane Society anti-fur exhibit, where he saw photos of bloodied animals writhing in traps, that his consciousness was pricked. He began going to demos, reading books, attending AVA meetings. After a year as an AVA board member, he made a switch. At the time, ARK II was larger, better organized, more militant. Its founding president, Vicky Miller, had conducted a twenty-eight-day hunger strike outside the Heart and Stroke Foundation to protest the use of chimpanzees in medical research. ARK II activists, wearing cat and mouse costumes, had staged a sit-down at a vivisectionist convention in Toronto's Westbury Hotel. Their style was inventive, elaborate, defiant, seductive. "ARK II did things before everyone else in animal-related issues," Rob says. "No-one else was doing civil disobediences when ARK II was doing them."

Though ARK II now maintains a lower profile, mostly because it is no longer the only demo-oriented group in town, Rob remains a dogged worker in the animal-rights movement. His persona, however, differs from that of activists like Tony and Josephine. He speaks too softly to be an effective orator. He does not confront fur-wearers on the street. His answers are filled with conciliatory words: *that's a tough question* or *I have a problem with that as well* or *yes, that is a challenge for our side.* Most importantly, he was the only one I talked to who didn't expect me to believe that the fur controversy — a controversy that is threatening Canada's oldest profession — is simply a case of the other guy being morally bankrupt and entirely stupid.

"There's a big wall between the two forces," he says at the end of our meeting. "What I would like to see is more communication between the trappers themselves and the animal-rights movement. That way *we* could see what goes on at a trap line, and that way, maybe we could understand. I don't think any of us know enough about each other."

In this conflict of strangers, I can't help but recall the comments of two people I telephoned. The first came from skier Laurie Graham, who, along with four other Canadian athletes, promoted fur during the 1988 Olympics. Later, she said she was "no longer comfortable with the fur wearer's image." The second came from Judy Stoffman, who at the time was fashion editor of *The Toronto Star.* "My own feeling is that fur is a dying industry, which in many ways is unfortunate." The fur industry, it seems, committed the gravest of errors: it underestimated the opponent. For fifteen years, anti-fur activists marched, protested, and bulk-mailed while the industry remained mute. Even when they halted the seal hunt, fur representatives figured — perhaps *hoped* is a better verb — the problem would evaporate, like a bad dream. Now that they're finally fighting back, it may be too late. Even Princess Di no longer wears fur — a million print ads would have a rough time neutralizing that kind of symbolism.

The fur industry faces another dilemma: the issue is precisely where the anti-fur forces want it. Now that intense mutual hatred has developed, national debate is impossible. And so, both sides are lashing out, attempting to strike an emotional chord wherever possible. Under these Aussie-style rules, the anti-fur forces have an overwhelming advantage. They are the ones with photos of animals hanging inverted from tree traps, struggling to chew through mangled limbs. They are the ones with films of fur-ranched minks groping helplessly in their own excrement. And while fur-industry reps can loudly protest that those traps have been outlawed for decades, that those fur-farm photos were taken outside Canada *fer the lovva Christ*, it hardly matters. The visual material still registers, deep within the viewer's brain. Meanwhile, the fur industry's main strategy — painting animal-rights activists as dynamite-wielding radicals — has proved ludicrous. At every public demonstration, the peaceful complexion of the animal-rights contingent is revealed. So while animal-rights activists may or may not be the deserving winners in this ethical brawl, they certainly — at this point at least — have the superior weapons.

I know, I met the individuals. Animals-rights activists, if nothing else, are persuasive. Tony, Josephine, and Rob consider activism their true calling, and they work hard at it. They get good at it. They are so loquacious, so tireless, so self-righteously indignant — after a while I caught myself thinking *hmmmm . . . maybe I've missed something here*. Furriers, on the other hand, are more adept at cutting patterns, at measuring seams, at picking over pelts in Montreal warehouses. It is simply not in their nature to wage ideological war. This, more than arrogance, could explain their initial reluctance to enter the fray; facing a foreign battlefield and a bloodthirsty opposition, they adopted the worst strategy imaginable. They decided to wait and see.

Environmental Control of the Great Lakes

WENDY FOX *(student report)*

INTRODUCTION

Canadians and Americans alike are proud of our Great Lakes, and in years past, used them to their fullest potential. Unfortunately, our pride has led to this resource being naively exploited. Too many people are unaware of the present threat to the life of the Great Lakes, and still more of those who are informed, including the governments, are not doing enough about it.

THE GREAT LAKES — A VAST RESOURCE

The Great Lakes shared by Canada and the United States are a valuable resource to both nations. The five lakes — Superior, Huron, Michigan, Erie, and Ontario — are connected by rivers, forming the largest freshwater system in the world, and holding nearly one-fifth of the freshwater on the planet. Their headwaters begin in the middle of the continent and travel 3800 km to the Atlantic Ocean.[1] They are bordered by the provinces of Ontario and Quebec in Canada, and eight states in the United States — Minnesota, Wisconsin, Illinois, Indiana, Michigan, Ohio, Pennsylvania, and New York.

Centuries ago, people began using the Great Lakes for a wide variety of purposes, including boating, fishing, swimming, drinking water, shipping, industrial processing, and waste disposal. Since then, over forty million citizens in both countries depend on the Great Lakes for their industrial, economic, and recreational livelihood. Unfortunately, this exploitation of the waters also has led to their pollution. The water quality of the lakes has rapidly deteriorated.[2]

WHAT WENT WRONG?

The pollution in the Great Lakes has been called "gross and foul" by the International Joint Commission. The Commission also submitted that the "situation along the frontier is generally chaotic, everywhere perilous, and in some cases disgraceful."[3] Shockingly, this statement was not issued as recently as one might think; it was made in 1918.[4]

Water pollution can come from many different sources, including long-range air pollution from industrial smokestacks and incinerators, as well as pesticide sprays picked up by winds and carried across the continent. Hazardous chemicals can also wash off the land, from inadequate sewer systems, cars, pets, farms, and land that has been contaminated by careless storage of hazardous materials. Finally, Great Lakes pollution is also caused by spills. In 1988 the Ontario government's Spills Action Centre reported over 300 spills of oils, chemicals, wastes and other contaminants in the lakes and tributaries. In the 1980s, the U.S. Coast Guard reported an average of over 500 spills annually.[5]

Along the Niagara banks are two hundred toxic waste dumps, including the world's largest storehouse of cancer-linked dioxin (a combustion by-product), and at least 22 of these sites are leaking into the water. Among these is the Love Canal, a municipality built atop a dump containing more than 20,000 tonnes of chemicals. Love Canal was evacuated when mysterious illnesses and deformities were found in local children. People are now returning since it has been named "habitable" by authorities and the dump "contained." The Niagara River is just one of the 42 sites along the Great Lakes System designated as "Areas of Concern" by both Canada and the United States.[6]

It is particularly necessary to avoid contamination from persistent toxic substances because of the long retention time of the Lakes, the period of time during which the water stays in the Great Lakes before being flushed out. Lake Superior, the largest and deepest, has a retention time of 200 years.[7] As well, the chemicals are part of a deadly toxic cycle: the pollution evaporates, washes through the soil, and travels with winds for thousands of kilometres, eventually ending up in the food we eat, and thus in our bloodstreams and body tissues. While not all of the pollutants in the lakes are dangerous, their combined and cumulative effects are unknown. Scientists say they may lead to long-term health problems, more cases of cancer, brain damage, and birth defects.[8]

PAST AND PRESENT ATTEMPTS FOR CONTROL

In 1909, Great Britain and the United States signed the Boundary Waters Treaty, concerning all waters which form or cross the border between the United States and Canada. Its purpose was to settle present and prevent future disputes regarding the use of such boundary waters, and ensure free navigation. The Treaty stated "boundary waters and waters flowing across the boundary shall not be polluted on either side to the injury of health or property on the other."[9] Especially important, the Treaty created the International Joint Commission, established in 1912, to deal with boundary water problems, including those of the Great Lakes. In 1916, the Commission first raised pollution concerns.[10] The Commission was, and continues to be, composed of three members each from Canada and the United States.

In 1964 the Commission was asked to perform an in-depth study of Lake Erie, Lake Ontario, and the St. Lawrence River. It was then to report its findings and recommend solutions to the two governments. A serious pollution problem was reported in the Lower Lakes, and Lake Erie was declared "dead." But the Commission found that there was little information about the other lakes, or information about the extent of water pollution from land drainage. Subsequently it recommended two special studies: the first to determine the quality of water in Lakes Huron and Superior, and the second to determine how much pollution comes from the careless use of the land, and was later asked to carry out these studies. Finally, it called for an international clean-up of the Lower Lakes. As a result, Canada and the United States signed the first Great Lakes Water Quality Agreement in 1972.[11]

The 1972 Great Lakes Water Quality Agreement was a dramatic step, a step rarely taken between two sovereign governments. It provided the necessary focus for a co-operative, co-ordinated international clean-up. It focussed on problems created by excess phosphorus and other nutrients being released into the Great Lakes, causing an overwhelming growth of algae. Not only did this cause beaches to be laden with smelly seaweed, but more significantly, the algae consumed the dissolved oxygen in the water and caused fish to suffocate. The central promise of the Agreement therefore was the reduction of phosphorus released into the Great Lakes by building sewage treatment plants, reducing phosphates in detergents, and controlling run-off from rural and urban areas. Both governments spent billions of dollars in the attempt to solve point source (industrial and municipal discharge) problems.[12] Over five years there was to be an expected 50% reduction in pollution; Canada spending $250 million, the larger United States to spend $2 billion. The Great Lakes began to show definite signs of progress. Sewer treatment plants were built on both sides of the border and by the 1980s almost all communities were served.[13] Lake Erie came back to life and the others were much less affected by excess algae growth. However, the pollution was merely slowed, not stopped. Now there was an even greater threat: toxic contaminants, endangering the health of fish, wildlife, and humans.[14]

Because Great Lakes water quality is a shared provincial and federal responsibility, Canada and Ontario signed the Canada-Ontario Agreement Respecting Great Lakes Water Quality in 1971. The Ontario Ministry of the Environment and Environment Canada are presently lead agencies working together to prepare the Remedial Action Plans called for in the 1987 Protocol.[15]

1978 GREAT LAKES WATER QUALITY AGREEMENT AND 1987 PROTOCOL

From 1977 to 1978, the first Agreement was reviewed. The governments looked at increasingly significant problems: toxic substances in fish and wildlife, the extent of land drainage pollution, and the influence of air pollution on water quality. In 1978, Pierre Trudeau and Richard Nixon signed the second Great Lakes Water Quality Agreement. It was called an "outstanding, precedent-setting document."[16] Under the Agreement the parties state that it is their purpose "to restore and maintain the chemical, physical and biological integrity of the waters of the Great Lakes Basin Ecosystem."[17] At the time of signing, 76% of the industries in the United States, and only 50% of Canadian industries were complying with their government's requirements of discharges into the Great Lakes, while 89% of Canadian municipalities and only 64% of American municipalities were conforming to the requirements.[18]

The Great Lakes Water Quality Agreement applies to the five Great Lakes, connecting channels (St. Mary's, St. Clair, and Niagara Rivers), and the St. Lawrence River up to the point that it ceases to form the boundary between the two countries (near Cornwall, Ontario and Massadena, New York). The Great Lakes System refers to streams, rivers, lakes, tributaries, and other bodies of water draining into the Great Lakes Ecosystem, including "interacting components of air, land, water, and living organisms, including humans."[19]

The Agreement introduced two new concepts: the "ecosystem" and "zero discharge" philosophies. The "ecosystem" approach was meant to help the two parties realize that the Great Lakes are one water body that cannot be separated, and therefore toxic chemicals do not stop at the border, and hopefully encourage co-operation among the states and the provinces.[20] It also calls on both Canadian and American governments to virtually eliminate the input of persistent toxic substances into the Great Lakes Ecosystem: "the philosophy adopted for control of inputs of persistent toxic substances shall be zero discharge."[21]

RECOMMENDATIONS

The Federal Government has presently devised the Great Lakes Action Plan, with $125 million dollars devoted to saving the Great Lakes through three specific areas: Preservation, Health Effects, and Clean-up. As well, the 1987 Protocol has strengthened the co-ordination of federal, provincial, and state actions.[22] But now some tangible action must take place. Greenpeace has implemented a Great Lakes Project working on a Zero Discharge Campaign. Greenpeace demands that the governments adjust all federal, state, provincial, and municipal laws to implement the zero discharge principle, and reconstruct the International Joint Commission so that it is the sole authority for ecosystem management of the Great Lakes Basin.[23] Greenpeace admits that completely ending all toxic pollution will take years to achieve, but recommends three steps that the two governments can begin immediately:

1. End chlorine-based bleaching by the pulp and paper industry, which discharges hundreds of millions of pounds of persistent toxics called "organochlorides" into the lake each year. These toxics could be virtually eliminated by halting the use of chlorine to bleach pulp white.
2. Ban new incinerators in or near the Great Lakes basin, recognizing that existing incinerators must be phased out. This would eliminate the 50% of toxics in the Great Lakes that enter through the air, and through ground water contaminated by toxic ash.
3. Establish sunset permits for all industrial processes that use or produce persistent toxic substances. Such permits would set a fixed date after which processes that use or produce persistent toxic chemicals must be changed or eliminated.[24]

CONCLUSION

Even though there have been recognizable achievements towards improving the water quality of the Great Lakes, their pollution remains a very serious threat to organisms and the environment itself. Part of the problem is that the job of trying to clean them comes under the jurisdiction of at least twelve different governments at all different levels. They have all the tools of modern bureaucracy: a binational treaty, two major agreements, several additions and revisions, thousands of studies, millions of dollars, and the infinite ability to talk about stopping pollution, without actually stopping it. The procedural system for control is excellent, but the product is not good. Bias exists among bureaucrats towards technological control, while the focus should be on stopping the contamination as proposed in the Agreement. As well, the obscurity of the International Joint Commission reflects their limited power. Public acceptance of pollution must be ratified; though the dump was not removed and the area not declared safe, people moved back to the Love Canal. Perhaps, most importantly, enforcement of anti-pollution laws must improve. In Canada at the present time, most of the rules restricting pollution are still guidelines, not enforceable standards. Many industries escape easily or fail to be prosecuted at all.[25] The Great Lakes must be saved before it is too late.

---

[1]Minister of Supply and Services, *Clean Waters* (1990), p. 2.

[2]International Joint Commission, *Great Lakes Water Quality Agreement*, p. 3.

[3]David Israelson, "Dying Lakes Tangled in Red Tape," *Toronto Star*, January 13, 1990, p. A14.

[4]*Ibid.*

[5]Minister of Supply and Service, *Op. cit.*, p. 3.

[6]David Israelson, *Loc. cit.*

[7]Tim Eder and John Jackson, *A Citizen's Guide to the Great Lakes Water Quality Agreement* (Buffalo, 1988), p. 30.

[8]David Israelson, *Loc. cit.*

[9]Tim Eder and John Jackson, *Op. cit.*, p. 1.

[10]David Israelson, *Loc. cit.*

[11]International Joint Commission, *Op. cit.*, pp. 3-4.

[12]Tim Eder and John Jackson, *Loc. cit.*

[13]David Israelson, *Loc. cit.*

[14]Tim Eder and John Jackson, *Op. cit.*, p. 2.

[15]Canadian Government, *Working Together For The Great Lakes*.

[16]Tim Eder and John Jackson, *Loc. cit.*

[17]Canadian Government, *Great Lakes Action Plan*.

[18]International Joint Commission, *Loc. cit.*

[19]Tim Eder and John Jackson, *Op. cit.*, p. 3.

[20]Greenpeace, "Summary of Recommendations," *Water For Life — The Tour of the Great Lakes* (Canada, 1989), p. 4.

[21]Zero Discharge Alliance, *Zero Discharge Alliance*.

[22]Canadian Government, *Loc. cit.*

[23]Greenpeace, *Loc. cit.*
[24]Greenpeace Lakes Project, *Zero Discharge Campaign.*
[25]David Israelson, *Loc. cit.*

TIPS ON WRITING A REPORT

Planning

Reading Your Audience
- Who is likely to read this report?
- What is the best format to use for this audience?

Purpose
- What is the purpose of this report?
- What essentially do you want it to say?
- Have you collected all the necessary information?

Drafting

Structure and Organization
- Have you based the order of your material on the audience's needs?
- Have you clearly integrated your information into your text?
- Have you said what you wanted to say and no more?
- Have you used graphics and illustrations to help your audience interpret your written text?

Editing and Polishing

Style
- Are your sentences and paragraphs clear and unambiguous?
- Have your avoided using jargon and trendy fashionable expressions?
- Have you explained technical words, where necessary?
- Is your tone appropriate for the information/findings you are reporting?
- Is your tone appropriate for your audience?

Design
- Is your design attractive and easy to read?
- Have you helped your audience find the information they need, using subheadings and/or a table of contents?
- Can your reader easily connect your graphics and illustrations with the written text?

Checking with Your Audience

- Have you asked a sample reader or group of readers to check your draft document?

Adapted from *A User's Guide to Plain Language*, Ontario Ministry of Education, Literacy Branch, June 1992.

5. The Narrative Essay

KEY WORK:

"The Sea and Me" — Alan Pearson

ASSOCIATED READINGS:

"Canadian Experience" — Meera Shastri
"Frozen delights with the Inuit" — Douglas McArthur
"The Breakfast Battles" — Marilyn Kwan (student essay)
Tips on Writing a Narrative Essay

You will find that the essays in this section have a great deal in common with those in the Classical Essay and the Autobiography, Biography, and Profile units. As with those essays, you will likely gain a sense of emotional intimacy and a shared experience which is conveyed through the writer's voice and a host of rhetorical devices often found in short stories.

Narrative essayists voice their purpose through the use of extended anecdotes and stories drawn from their personal experience. In some instances the writer may explicitly state a thesis. However, more often the writer is not able or does not wish to put the meaning of the experience explicitly into words. Instead, he or she relies on the reader to infer it from reading about the experience itself. The Key Work, "The Sea and Me," demonstrates the typical qualities of a narrative essay. The Associated Readings provide other perspectives on the narrative essay. "Canadian Experience" has been edited for length.

Conventions of the Narrative Essay

Purpose	To communicate a significant experience in order to enlighten and perhaps persuade or move readers
Audience	Various
Tone	Often reflective and personal: may be either serious or humorous, subjective, or objective
Voice	Strongly individualistic
Response	A sense of intimacy or shared experience

Language   LEVEL — Formal through informal and colloquial
    CHARACTERISTICS — Strongly expressive; images are
    often striking and individualistic

Structure   May be chronological, but often is altered for dra-
    matic or emotional impact

BEFORE READING

1. Suggest why storytelling has been used as an important instructional method throughout history.

2. Compare the Conventions of the Narrative Essay with those of
   the Classical Essay and the Autobiography, Biography, and
   Profile.

3. Reflect on a significant experience which led to personal growth.
   You may wish to share it with a partner.

The Sea and Me

ALAN PEARSON

As my life has progressed I have come to see that time is the great
destroyer, that its soft dissolving work goes on day after day,
moment by moment. But I've learned that memory is the great
preserver, that it can give back to us, in modified form, what time
takes. That being so, I've always felt pressed to live in a way that
would provide interesting things to look back on.

One of my fondest memories is of my first sea voyage. It is not
that the voyage surpassed all the other adventures of my life, but
it is my first real adventure and held all the excitement that comes
when, for the first time, one leaves home for abroad. The trip began
in the late 1950s, when an old freighter I'd elected to sail on nosed
its way out of the Liverpool docks in England at midnight and
inched its way to centre stream and the outgoing tide of the Mersey
River. I knelt on my narrow bunk and stared out of the porthole,
watching the dockside sheds and cranes slide by. I was 20 and had
found employment as the freighter's junior engineer.

As the ship moved toward the ripply flow of the Mersey's deep channel, all you could hear over the hum of the generators was the occasional slap of water against the ship's plating and, now and again, the peremptory blast of our tug's horn.

Presently I could see the opposite side of the wide river mouth, the string of lights along the promenade and even my parents' house; weeks would pass before I would see my home and family again. The tug's horn blasted again, and I thought of how many times in the past I had responded to that sound as I lay awake, my imagination taking me off to some romantic part of the world.

Soon we would reach the yawning mouth of the Mersey estuary, where a few buoy lights endlessly blinked in a black void of splashing waves. Tomorrow we would reach Glasgow and, after a couple of days there, head south through the Bay of Biscay and then make a sharp left at Gibraltar into the blue Mediterranean, a sparkling playground for frolicsome dolphins.

On the way to Glasgow my work on watch was explained. I was to check engine temperatures and to start and stop various pumps for various crucial reasons. The tricky job was to start number 2 electric generator and make sure the electric power was running through the switchboard as I subtracted power from number 1 generator. This operation required a nice balancing of two gauges on the switchboard and the tripping of a switch. The idea was to make sure the generators — the source of the ship's electrical supply — were used evenly.

The following day — New Year's Eve — we reached Glasgow and, being the most junior officer, I was required to stay on board and change over the generators at midnight. I would have an "experienced oiler" with me and so, I was told, had no need to worry.

When the time came for me to carry out my chore, I did so with a nervousness I should not have concealed, because, presumably, it led my "experienced oiler" to relax his vigilance. The consequence was that I failed to balance the gauges properly, and when I tripped the switch there was a blinding flash followed by a burning smell. Every light on the ship went out and, in the engine room, darkness fell like a cape. With a clatter of hobnailed boots the "experienced oiler" ran off with the cry, "Strike a light, now you've done it."

My stomach muscles clenched as I stood in the funereal darkness, paralyzed with fear. I felt as though I'd pushed the button that would, at any second, start World War III.

I had no idea how to put things right, so I stood there sick and aging. There was a clatter on the overhead grating, and the slim beam of a torch cut the darkness. Then I heard the captain's booming voice, "What in God's name is going on down there?" I hadn't a clue, so I wailed back something to that effect, "Well, start the bloody emergency generator," he commanded with a roar. I would have been delighted to if only I'd known where it was and how to use it.

Then one of those amazing strokes of good fortune that one reads about but seldom encounters occurred: the ship's electrician appeared on the scene (when by all calculations he should have been out on the town). He explained later that he'd been returning to the ship when to his astonishment he'd seen all the deck and mast lights gutter out "right before me bleedin' eyes." That's when he'd thought of me and had run as fast as he could. Within minutes after his arrival in the engine room, power was restored; however, the damage I'd inflicted on innocent machinery kept him busy for many days.

At 20 you feel a minor humiliation keenly — this one was a major one. I had expected to be fired and sent home by train the following day, but surprisingly I was kept on.

Unfortunately this episode was only the beginning of my humiliations; almost immediately after it I became afflicted with chronic seasickness.

The Bay of Biscay in winter is a place of high drama, especially if you're in a small freighter as I was. From the moment we entered this area, the ship heeled over so severely that I thought it would rotate completely. Then its bow nosed deep under water, only to rise up, water running from it, with agonizing slowness and pause with a shudder as it met a towering wave that rose before us like a gun-metal wall three storeys high.

To walk to the mess for meals (if you could face them) meant, on occasion, having one foot on the ground and the other on a bulkhead that tilted over at a 45-degree angle. To work in the engine room involved tortuous point-to-point movements. And all the while broadside waves thudded against the open skylight and sent down sheets of icy water.

At such moments I should have worried about the ship's seaworthiness, splitting weld seams, popping rivets and such, but I was so glutted with seasickness that I didn't care — my stomach seemed to be splitting. Consequently I was, to my shame, only able to carry on a fraction of my allotted chores. Most of my watch was spent flat on my back close to the ship's centreline, where the side-to-side oscillations were minimal. And it was here, several times a day, that my condition was silently noted by scornful brother officers.

Meals were by now out of the question as I retched almost continually. I subsisted on dry crackers and oranges brought by a steward. "Don't retch on an empty stomach or you'll do yourself an injury," was his advice as he reeled in and out of the wildly swaying frame of my cabin doorway.

Contributing to my nausea was the sickening odor created by the combined smells of diesel oil, coffee and cigarettes, which was never absent from the living quarters.

"Get fresh air," I was told by the steward, so I went on the boat deck and breathed deeply on icy wind, but it gave no solace to a stomach sensitive to a millimetre of movement in any direction. Eventually I discovered, by accident, that the gut-clenching effect of singing at the top of my voice restored a degree of comfort to my stomach (this has not been documented in any scientific paper so far). Fortunately, there were no witnesses, apart from a gull or two, as I hoarsely sang in the teeth of a wind that snapped the tarpaulins over my head and knifed through my woolly sweater.

Once in the Mediterranean, the sea settled, but although my seasickness abated it did not go away. Our ports of call were to include Beirut, Alexandria, Famagusta, Cyprus and — our first stop — Iskenderun, Turkey. But uppermost in my mind was not the exotic sights and sounds of Arabs, souks and minarets, but the relief of once again standing on terra firma (the more firm the less terror).

I was now able to get on with work in the engine room, which, among other things, included pumping tanks by means of a steam-driven reciprocating pump that would, unaccountably, run away with itself, the reciprocating arm thrashing wildly. My "experienced oiler" redeemed himself for his cowardice in Glasgow by showing me how, by judicious placement of a heavy spanner, the pump could be made to resume its regular rocking motion. "That's something they don't put in books," he chuckled, "but it works like a charm, don't it?"

And so the days proceeded.

Even before I sighted the brush-covered limestone hills of Turkey, I could smell the thyme-scented landscape. It came as a faint thread of vegetation fragrance, riding on a clear wind that fanned across the sea. As we approached the shore, we could see the dusty white road at the foot of a towering massif, where, here and there, an isolated house was visible. The odor by now had changed to an interesting mix of creosote, tobacco and dust. We reduced engine speed and edged up to a massive earth-and-rocks jetty, where a couple of giraffe-necked cranes stood beside an irregular line of bulky cargo. Men, clad in shabby overcoats that came down to their ankles, could be seen at work on the jetty and the road — soldiers apparently. There didn't seem to be a community nearby; the reason for our berthing here was a mystery. But who cared? All I cared about was that, at long last, I was abroad.

By late afternoon, I was dressed in my new American-style suit, ready to go ashore. To my chagrin nobody wanted to go with me. "What will you do when you're ashore?" they asked. Then the second engineer pointed out in a mild way that the weather wasn't too promising and suggested that perhaps I shouldn't go. But I didn't care about the weather; I was eager to set foot in a new country and headed for the gangplank.

I walked along the jetty, came to the dusty white road and followed it, observing the wild hills around me and breathing in the exciting new odors.

An open truck stopped, and I was offered a ride by a gang of ferocious, mustached workmen. I accepted and was soon speeding along the road. The workmen questioned me; they thought I was an American. A conversation of sorts took place.

In a few minutes they let me off in the middle of an ancient and primitive village with open-front shops where merchants sat cross-legged and stared at me in my American-style suit, as though I'd come from another planet. Nobody else had on a decent suit, no shop had anything I might want, and there wasn't a woman in sight. "Visually drab" were the words that best described the town. After a few minutes I decided I might as well head back to the ship; I was glumly aware that I had a featureless walk ahead of me.

When I arrived back at the jetty the workmen had long since gone, and it was dark. The only sign of life came from a sort of watchman's shack, where a brazier burned cheerfully against the darkness. I looked over to my ship, and there it was — gone.

The first emotion that flooded over me was blind panic. Then came the thought that maybe someone else had done a number on the electric generators. I peered hard into the darkness, but there was no escaping the sickening knowledge: the ship was well and truly gone.

Presently I saw it, riding at anchor some distance from shore. The realization that I would have to spend the night on the jetty swept over me in a demoralizing way, and I remembered the second engineer's words — "maybe you shouldn't be going ashore." Presumably the ship was offshore because of anticipated bad weather. As I stood on the shelterless jetty, I felt the first splotchy raindrops blow in from the sea.

After a considerable amount of fearful vacilation I found myself communicating, in sign language, with an ancient watchman who had a face lined like the block on which my father used to chop wood. He was amused when he learned of my predicament and kindly allowed me to share his cramped quarters for the night; it was in this place that I spent the dark hours, listening to heavy rain drum on the leaky roof made of enameled tin, advertising Coleman's mustard.

I rose from a bed of sacking just as dawn was about to break, full of muscular pains and with a sleepless-night hangover; my new American-style suit no longer looked new.

As I looked out to sea I saw the freighter maneuvering deliberately to a new position. And while it was some time before my ship was tied up once again alongside the jetty — and though my stomach grumbled for lack of food — I was calm now the fear of abandonment was over.

Part of the reason for my composure was that during the night I'd had time to consider the peculiarity of my small adventure in this alien land. And I had awakened early enough to witness a dawn of pale saffron light deepen to flush with gold the dark recesses of the looming hills around and sprinkle with gleams of light a vast expanse of calm sea.

I'd had time to reflect on what was to be sure a small plight. For someone of my age and background, however, it had opened enchanting vistas. I had found myself at the edge of Asia and in the heart of unpredictable experience. I was poised also on the edge of a new life, one that would be different from all that had gone before — a better one if only I could keep the courage to live with more spontaneity than good sense usually prescribes.

The rest of my first trip to sea was to be mercifully free of disasters and rich enough in new experiences, though none of them imprinted itself on my memory and imagination as this past night had done. And as for the light of the dawn I'd watched from the jetty, I realize now that it signaled for me more than a new day.

EXPLORING THE NARRATIVE ESSAY

1. a. What do Alan Pearson's opening comments about time and memory reveal about his character?
   b. What are the potential advantages and disadvantages of living one's life the way he has?

2. Account for the fact that Pearson vividly describes the discomfort and humiliations he suffered on his first sea voyage, yet he describes it as "one of my fondest memories."

3. What is the pivotal experience in the narrative? Justify your answer.

4. To what extent do you think Pearson has captured the essence of youthfulness in relating this story of his own youthful adventure?

5. Show that Pearson has demonstrated the ultimate skill of the narrative essayist — that is, entertaining, enlightening, and moving his reader by combining the elements of storytelling with vivid detail.

EXTENSIVE STUDY

1. Alan Pearson's narrative essay focusses on a "rites of passage" story, one in which he left home for the first time and dealt with life on his own. By drawing parallels with Pearson's story of going to sea, consider how going to university might be viewed as a "rites of passage" adventure. (You may wish to refer to some of the readings in the Essays About University Life.)

2. a. Read "Canadian Experience" by Meera Shastri (p. 145), and identify the positive and the negative elements in her experience.
   b. Suggest how the school system might ease the immigrants' transition into Canadian life.

3. Assess the effectiveness of Marilyn Kwan's style — sentences, diction, imagery — for accomplishing her purpose.

4. In what way are Alan Pearson in "The Sea and Me" and Douglas McArthur in "Frozen delights with the Inuit" (p. 152) alike in their reactions to experiencing a different culture from their own?

5. The narrative essay writer is often described as a person on whom "nothing is lost." To what extent do the essayists you have read in this unit support this description?

THE WRITING FOLDER

1. Write a narrative essay based on a significant personal experience. (You may wish to write about the experience you related to a partner in the prereading activity.)

2. Assume the role of Mrs. Pearce in "The Breakfast Battles" (p. 156), and write about the experience from her perspective.

3. Write a personal response to one essay in this unit.

INDEPENDENT STUDY

1. In consultation with your teacher and teacher-librarian, assemble an anthology of "rites of passage" narrative essays. Write
   • a *Preface* that introduces the anthology
   • a brief, one-paragraph profile to introduce each writer, and
   • a thought-provoking question as a lead into each of the essays.
   One of the selections should be a "rites of passage" essay about you.

2. Explore the Canadian immigrant's experience by reading a collection of essays in which the writer tells about his or her encounter with Canadian culture. You may wish to begin with such writers as Neil Bissoondath, Bharati Mukherjee, and Austin Clarkson. Or, consult your teacher, teacher-librarian, and/or an ESL teacher about the names of other writers. See also John Lombardi's speech, "Fiercely Canadian" (p. 260), and Stephen Baker's "English as Second Language, English as First Love" (p. 32).

3. Read several collections of narrative essays and analyze the works' literary qualities. Then write a variety of essays in that mode. For example, consider collections of narrative essays by writers such as E.B. White, Tom Wolfe, Emily Carr, Margaret Laurence, Stephen Leacock, Frantz Fanon, Pierre Elliott Trudeau,

Helen Keller, Andrienne Clarkson, Robertson Davies, or other essayists identified by your teacher or teacher-librarian.

TIMED READING AND WRITING

1. a. Read "Frozen delights with the Inuit" (p. 152) and write a one-paragraph synopsis of the writer's experience, ensuring that you reflect the author's tone and voice.
   b. Using Douglas McArthur's essay as a guide, write a letter or a flyer to promote Inuit Adventures.

Canadian Experience

MEERA SHASTRI

People constantly ask me why I came to Canada. I wish I could reply that it was a desire to be a part of this great country, but that was not the reason.

I grew up in an upper middle-class (East) Indian home and was fiercely patriotic. My goal was to become a teacher and educate the illiterate masses of India. To prepare myself for this profession, I went to university. How can I explain to my Canadian friends that the institution of arranged marriages, unheard of in Canada, was responsible for my emigration to Canada? Yes, I had decided that my parents would choose a life partner for me. I know that most Canadians will be shocked at that statement, but I have seen how dearly my parents love one another and how successful their arranged marriage has been.

My parents corresponded with many people and eventually heard of Ray. Our horoscopes, which had been prepared and based on planetary positions at the precise moment of birth, were hourly compared by an astrologer who declared us to be highly compatible. Ray and I were brought together, and my first reaction was: "Oh, God! I hope my parents approve of him!" Perhaps it was what is called "love at first sight", but I will not give my intuitive reactions such a glorified expression.

I had been under the impression that Ray was studying and training in the United States and Canada and would be coming back to

India. It came as a shock, therefore, when he mentioned he had just emigrated to Canada and would be returning to look for his first job. My heart sank. Immigration seemed so final and involved giving up so much. I nearly backed out of the marriage, but my parents pointed out that they had migrated from Southern India to Northern and that had been a major step. Northern and Southern India are poles apart linguistically and culturally — dress and food are totally different as well.

Although our parents were from the south, both Ray and I had been raised in the north, and we spoke three different languages — not dialects — fluently. Because we had traveled back and forth visiting grandparents each year, we were equally at home in both parts of the country and thus, had retained our southern heritage. Taking all this into consideration, I finally allowed my initial hesitation to vanish and decided to marry Ray and emigrate to Canada.

Little did I realize that I would be coming to a country where people would refer to me as an East Indian; a large percentage of the population would have the preconceived notion that I stank; that I couldn't speak English; that my house would reek of curry and that I should consider myself lucky to find a job as a berry picker or at most, a nurse's aide. I must admit it took a while for my bubble to burst and for me to realize what most Canadians thought of the East Indian immigrant.

My first impression of Toronto was great. Immigration staff at the airport seemed brusque at first, but became very friendly when they found I could speak English. I was very impressed by the way they handled everything with a minimum of red tape — a contrast to India.

Ray expected me to be gasping in wonder at everything I saw in the city, but when you have read about life in the western world and have been exposed to it through the media, the reality does not surprise or delight you in the same way. What impressed me the most was the cleanliness which was a stark contrast to Bombay or Calcutta where I grew up.

The first adjustment I had to make was to the weather. I had left the tropics and walked into a blizzard! I stood outside in the snow, savouring the delights of my first snowflakes. Within a week of my arrival in Toronto, I realized that the sari was not a practical outfit for the Canadian winter and took to wearing pants. It was just a short while before I began to feel self-conscious about wearing saris even when the weather was good. Now I wear pants most of the time, but to this day I have not been able to wear a skirt. The sari was designed to conceal rather than reveal, and I am inhibited about showing my legs.

My first lessons in humility began when I looked for a job. The University of Toronto graciously evaluated my Master's degree and gave it the equivalent of a Bachelor's at their university. Without a teaching certificate, however, I could not teach in this country so I decided to enter the clerical force. Unfortunately all new immigrants must have faced the Catch-22 situation of requiring "Canadian experience" for a job and needing a job to get that experience. I suppose I was luckier than most new immigrants because I could speak English fluently with little trace of accent. In fact, several people pointed this out to me and with delight, I mentioned it to my husband. He retorted: "The next time someone says you speak good English, you should say, 'so do you'." I was shocked at his cynicism, but I understand it now because I have heard people say it patronizingly. There is no rule that says an immigrant should speak "pidgin" English! I can imagine what my son's reaction would be twenty years hence if someone said to him: "You speak good English!"

My first proper job interview was for a junior clerical position in a Downsview factory, in a Toronto suburb. I learned my interviewer was a Mr. Mishra which indicated he was of East Indian origin. His first statement after he introduced himself was that he did not come from India and had never been there. He was an Australian immigrant. He seemed to feel I would take advantage of the fact that we had common ancestors and he took great pains to convince me that we had nothing in common. Because I was there on the basis of my qualifications and not my race, his attitude irritated me. He barely touched on my ability and suitability, and in the half hour I was there, related his own views on immigration and expounded in great detail the shortcoming of immigrants from India.

Needless to say, I was not hired. Although I was not disappointed at not getting the job, this incident sowed the seeds of doubt in my mind. Would my children and grandchildren someday be subjected to this, and would they feel ashamed of their Indian ancestry the way Mr. Mishra obviously did? Because I was an optimist, I pushed away such thoughts then, but today I am convinced that most second- and third-generation immigrants react this way, and my child is not going to be an exception.

After a week of filling out forms and making phone calls, I finally found something. An insurance company where I had applied in answer to an ad, called me for an interview which lasted three hours and included tests. I sailed through everything without trouble and got the job. It was just a junior clerical position, but I was delighted for I had proved to Ray that a new immigrant without experience could get office employment.

At last I was exposed to the Canadian business world and loved every minute of it. My work proved far more exciting than I had expected. For the first time in my life, I was involved with the vagaries of a computer and found it fascinating. Within a month I was teaching the girl who had trained me better ways of doing the job. Luckily she didn't resent it.

I mentioned to Ray that about fifty per cent of my co-workers were immigrants and remarked how fair my employers were. In his usual cynical way he retorted that their salary level would never attract Canadians.

Six months later I was offered a ten per cent raise. I wasn't happy about it because I felt I had proved myself and deserved more.

"You claim you are doing a great job and that you are almost indispensable. Why don't you go and ask for a better salary?" Ray goaded.

Although I had been prepared to work for less, Ray egged me on to see the manager and state my case. He was very sympathetic and even though it involved certain technicalities, he went to the "top brass". Two months later I was given a fifty-four per cent retroactive raise and told my position had been up-graded two levels. It was a great victory, and I felt quite smug. Ray was suitably impressed.

While my work experience was improving, our social life, however, was practically non-existent. Neither one of us had any family in the city. In addition, Ray had spent four years in the United States as a student and a worker and had felt he had been accepted there as a professional. Yet here in Canada he was an immigrant first, and his professional status was resented by some of his colleagues who saw immigrants in menial roles. I tried to assure him it was his imagination, but I don't think my words had any effect. Already the seeds of discontent had been sown in his mind, nurtured by stories of rampant racism in the press and in our circle of friends. Soon Ray began talking of returning to India. I was shocked by his defeatist attitude and tried my best to dissuade him. However, the idea was still in his mind.

One evening when I arrived home from work, I saw a message scrawled in bold letters at the entrance to our apartment building.

"PAKI GO HOME!" It was the first time we had seen it so close to home, and it really disturbed and hurt us. We were living in a posh residential neighbourhood and the thought that we had neighbours in the area harbouring such feelings was too much to stomach. Thus I fell in eagerly with Ray's plans to return to India, and within three months we had wound everything up and were saying good-bye to Canada.

Miraculously, Ray got a fairly decent job within a few weeks of our arrival, and we were all set to start a new life. Within a few days, however, we discovered that our lifestyle would be drastically altered by another factor — I was pregnant. In addition, our stay in Canada had made us misfits for the Indian way of life. Although we had been prepared for this, we still had to make a lot of sacrifices.

Toward the end of my pregnancy, I moved in with my parents in another city while Ray continued at his job. He found it more and more frustrating for his colleagues were continually sneering at him for his Canadian ideas. Just a month before Sameer (Sam) was born, Ray came to see me and broached the subject of returning to Canada. He was quite convinced this was the best course for both of us and our unborn child. I was shocked and so were our families. All our efforts to persuade him to stay met with failure. It wasn't a case of the "grass being greener somewhere else". Ray had thought it out carefully and had come to a decision. I had to support him and give in.

I will never know what caused it, but after Sam was born, I changed and about three months later had a complete nervous breakdown. With the help of electric shock treatment and drugs, I was restored to some semblance of normalcy after five months of therapy. During one of these sessions, I blurted out that I did not want to leave my family again. Perhaps this affected my feelings, for this time I did not look forward to living in Canada with the eager enthusiasm of the first time. Even though I was more worldly wise and less naive than before, I was apprehensive.

Ray left for Vancouver after I had been pronounced fit, and it was a good six months before he was able to find a job and our son and I could join him. For the first few months Ray's salary was barely enough to cover our basic needs, but we were optimistic that things would improve. This time I did not look for work because I preferred to look after my son until he was at least two years old.

One day as I was walking down the street with Sam in his stroller, a man stuck his head out of a passing car and yelled, "I hate f — ing Pakis; they stink! Why don't you go home?"

It is difficult to express how one feels at a moment like this so I will not even attempt to do so. With time, however, one learns to develop a thicker skin, but the hurt never goes. And yet I have to say that there had been times when I was out with Sam and people had stopped to say: "Oh, what a cute child!" or "What gorgeous eyes!" These remarks went a long way in assuaging my fears and helped to ease the pain of the other stupid insults.

Meanwhile Sam was growing up a beautiful and intelligent child. What filled our hearts with delight was purchasing a house for him to grow up in. Despite being so far from our families, everything seemed worthwhile here in Canada because we felt certain that Sam would have a better life in this great country. It was in our first home that an event occurred I shall never forget.

It was our first Christmas, but because we are Hindus, this holiday had no religious significance for us then. Today we do have a little tree with gifts for Sammy, but then he had been too small, and all we did was send cards to our friends. We had also sent a card to our neighbours, Fred and Alison. Imagine our surprise to find a gift for Sammy on our doorstep when we awoke on Christmas morning.

At about 4:00 p.m. that afternoon, Fred walked into our house and found us watching TV.

"TV on Christmas day!" he boomed. "I can't have that. Get ready and come over to our place. Alison is cooking a great dinner, and you must join us."

And just like that we were part of an intimate family Christmas dinner! We were deeply touched and from that day on felt an integral part of Canada.

It was only after I was working again and Sammy was at a day-care centre that I realized he was going to have problems, too. I had always thought that because he was growing up in Canada, he would be spared much of the agony of wondering if he would be accepted in Canadian society. Suddenly one night last year he asked me, "Mom, how come I'm white at home and become brown when I go to daycare?"

This incident drove home rather forcefully the point that he and maybe his children and grandchildren would be different as well. I dismissed the question as natural childish curiosity and didn't think he was being sensitive. However, I was wrong because one day he asked, "Mom, if you and Dad had lived in Canada when I was born, would I look like a Canadian?"

I tried to tell him he *was* a Canadian and that he *did* look like me, but he was not convinced. "Oh, come on, don't kid me. I don't look white," he said.

I felt like a real hypocrite then. Yes, he would have to sort out a lot of problems in his little mind in the years to come, and all I could do was hope that he would develop a sense of belonging.

He's just a child, but he is incredibly patriotic. He takes great pleasure in singing "O, Canada" at every opportunity. He is annoyed that all his favourite TV shows are made in United States and not Canada. His face lights up when he sees a maple leaf. I have every reason to believe that in him Canada has a citizen to be proud of, but . . . I have been doing much soul-searching and I find that his up-bringing is definitely not Canadian. We have tried our best to assimilate into the outside world, but at home we are still very much Indian. Our food, our music, our religion, everything is different. How can we expect our child not to be confused?

Then there is the issue of stereotyping. Ray goes to a very good barber near our home who is a jovial type. But whenever he sees Ray, he asks: "So what sawmill do you work in?" Ray has told him repeatedly that he works as a management consultant, but the man just can't seem to accept this. I have also been asked several times if I work as a nurse's aide. Now there is nothing demeaning in these professions, but I find it a little irksome that people should jump to the conclusion that I am capable of doing only certain kinds of jobs.

I have talked to several Canadian "WASPS", who are close friends, about these issues, and their reaction has almost always been: "I'm not a typical Canadian because I'm not a racist at all, but. . . ." My conclusions based on several such discussions are that the average Canadian's attitude toward the immigrant is — "They can't help the way they look, so we'll accept that, but that's as far as we'll go. They will have to accept our ways and mannerisms in everything else. If not, they can do what they like in the privacy of their home, but outside they should conform."

Therefore, this is the approach I have chosen for myself. At home I am almost entirely Indian, but outside I ape every Canadian mannerism possible. I must confess that since there is no definite Canadian identity, this is quite difficult. Of one thing I am convinced and that is the "ethnic mosaic" is a myth.

Our lives now are typical immigrant success stories. Ray and I both have jobs where we are respected, and we live in our own home in a very respectable neighbourhood. We have an adorable child, but are we really happy? Will we ever regret our decision to make Canada our home?

Sammy's future is what will decide that. The decision to come here was ours, but the consequences are something he will have to face. We don't want him subjected to emotional hurt he wasn't responsible for, but will we be able to prevent it? Only time will tell.

Frozen delights with the Inuit

DOUGLAS McARTHUR

Expedition weight long underwear. Thermal turtlenecks. Wool socks. Gortex gloves. This, I thought, jamming the gear into my duffle bag, would be unlike any winter vacation I had experienced. Was I ready for it? Would I survive it? Would it be fun?

I have always loved the Arctic in summer when endless sunlight drenches the vast, empty landscape. But winter was another matter. Over the next few days in the Ungava Peninsula of northern Quebec I would travel by snowmobile, sleep in an igloo and visit one of Canada's least-known natural wonders — a massive crater created millions of years ago when a meteorite crashed into Earth and exploded. It sounded both fascinating and frigid.

I was to supply basic cold-weather clothing specified on a hand-out list. The tour operator, Inuit Adventures, would provide the hard-core stuff: insulated boots, waterproof pants and a parka, all designed to withstand temperatures of 40 below.

Five of us would make the early April journey: Michael Sorensen, an adventurous German businessman; Stephen Ashton from the tour company's head office; Inuit guides Lucassie Nappaluk and Josepi Qiisiq, and myself.

The first night was spent in comfort at the Wakeham Bay Co-op Hotel in the small Inuit community of Kangiqsujuaq, formerly Wakeham Bay. Run by an Inuit corporation, the hotel has the feel of a private home. Guests congregate in the kitchen/livingroom to prepare their own meals, watch TV and share their impression of the North.

It was basic accommodation but it took on the allure of a luxury resort when I thought of what was to come. The next night would be spent in the middle of a frozen wasteland — in a house built of snow.

It was clear, crisp and sunny in Kangiqsujuaq the following morning but out on "The Land" a blizzard had seized control. Like generals planning a battle, Nappaluk and Qiisiq sat at the kitchen table consulting maps and using a two-way radio to gather intelligence about the storm's progress. Our departure, they announced, would be delayed indefinitely.

At 3 p.m., they decreed it was safe to go.

I was given the option of driving a snowmobile or of being towed behind one in a *komatik*, a hybrid cousin of a dogsled used to carry supplies and extra passengers. My decision came quickly when I learned that on one of last year's trips Ashton, an experienced snowmobile driver, got separated from the rest of the party during a blinding snowstorm.

I would be delighted to go as a passenger, I said. Sorensen made the same decision. It was the safe but bumpy choice. We set out with three snowmobiles. Ashton and our two guides were the designated drivers.

My seat was on top of the sleeping bags and between the luggage and food boxes, inside a wooden box with canvas top, scarcely bigger than a coffin. I could look out toward the rear and freeze my nose or close the flap and be warm in the darkness. When we sped up or slowed down, I teetered forward and backward. When we hit rocks or bumps of snow and ice, I was thrown repeatedly against the wooden sides.

For the first half hour, the scenery was fabulous as we headed across the frozen bay between two ridges of low mountains and ascended a steep grade to a plateau. Then suddenly, our whole world turned white. There no longer seemed to be any north or south, left or right or up or down. There was only snow, snow and more snow, the faint glimmer of snowmobile headlights behind us and the even fainter glimmer of a far-away sun. Occasionally, but only briefly, the curtain of white parted long enough to reveal the shadowy forms of caribou, usually in groups of three to eight, somewhere off in the distance.

How our guides found their way, I'll never know. They stopped frequently to consult about landmarks that I could not even see, to take compass readings and to look at maps.

We were getting close to the crater they informed us at 8:30 when they stopped to build our home for the night. The sun was just beginning to set but the weather had started to clear. The temperature was −20°C.

The creation of an igloo is a work of art, a technical wonder, an act of magic. Watching one appear before your eyes is a mystical experience.

Qiisiq did most of the work, carving out building blocks from the snow beneath his feet and arranging them in a circle around him. He worked deftly with a handsaw, much like the one I use to topple the family Christmas tree.

Once the ring of foundation blocks was in place, Qiisiq shaped its top into a spiral. Each future tier continued the pattern, and the snow wall gradually took shape in a continuous circular pattern, like an orange peeled without a break. Qiisiq disappeared from view as the igloo wall grew higher, but the single candle that lighted his work made the whole structure glow in the darkness. He fitted the final block into place directly above his head. Then he tunnelled his way out, forming the front door in the process.

While Qiisiq was using the snow for building blocks, Nappaluk placed a chunk of the same material in a pot, boiled it and made tea.

With the igloo completed, Qiisiq offered to build an "igloo loo" if anyone felt the need. We all passed, and our Inuit guides busied themselves furnishing the interior of our home. By the time we crawled into our snow house on hands and knees, it looked as exotic and welcoming as a sultan's tent. It was also cozy and warm.

Near the entrance was a low area that served as our kitchen, furnished with a Coleman stove and a naphtha lamp. Beyond was a raised snow shelf that was both sitting area and bedroom. Five sleeping bags were laid out on top of a thin mattress that was separated from the snow bed by a layer of caribou skins over a ground sheet. A small hole in the ceiling provided ventilation.

Dinner was hardly typical northern fare. Ashton heated up some *osso buco* — stewed veal shank in a rich sauce — supplied by a caterer in Montreal. Qiisiq shared bannock baked by his mother. Of course there was more tea.

Being the tallest, I was assigned to sleep in the middle, my head toward the snow wall. Ashton and Sorensen were on each side of me, their faces at my feet. The Inuit guides took the outside, again sleeping head to foot with their neighbour.

There was a moment of claustrophobic panic when the doorway was sealed shut with snow. Would my weak bladder last through the night? Thankfully it did. The last thing I heard before falling asleep was Qiisiq and Nappaluk saying prayers in Inuktituk. I awakened to them talking on the two-way radio.

Following a breakfast of porridge and coffee, our snowmobile cavalcade ascended the raised outer rim of the Nouveau-Quebec (New Quebec) Crater, a startling formation in the stark, flat Arctic landscape. A circular depression some 3.4 kilometres in diameter and 400 metres from top to bottom, the crater contains a lake 267 metres deep.

Used as a navigational aid during the Second World War, it was originally named the Chubb Crater after Frederick Chubb, a prospector whose interest in the strange hole helped spur a 1951 expedition by the Royal Ontario Museum.

Looking down into the doughnut-shaped crater, the bottom seemed only a short walk away. But as we descended the slippery slope on foot, we realized looks can be deceiving. Our guides took the lead, advising us to follow in their footsteps to avoid sliding.

The lake at this time of year was buried under snow and ice, but our guides knew that Arctic char lived in the water below. Completely cut off from outside waterways, the lake continues to sustain a fish population that may date back to post-glacial flooding.

Using a shovel and metal bar, Qiisiq dug a well-like hole through $2\frac{1}{2}$ metres of snow and ice. The open water gushed up below his feet, briefly exposing a char, some 20 centimetres long. Later he put down a line and hook, but the fish wisely ignored it.

The ride home seemed even rougher and bumpier than the trip out. But the sky was clear and the caribou were easier to spot. We stopped for a stand-up lunch of ham and cheese sandwiches.

It was 9 p.m. and dark when we returned "home" to the settlement. I was glad to be back in our humble hotel. One night in an igloo had been a marvellous experience. Two nights might have seemed an ordeal.

The Breakfast Battles

MARILYN KWAN *(student essay)*

Sunday morning at Centenary Hospital. Light, the colour of warmed cider, wafting into the sixth-floor lounge. Curled into a chair with a magazine, and the soft, slow drift into sleep . . .

Uh-oh. Nurse alert.

I snap to attention and slink into the supply room, pretending to prepare ice water. The harried nurse corners me between the sink and the syringe supply.

"Can you feed Mrs Pearce, 606B, please?" She grips me by the wrist and tows me towards the room.

"Actually . . ." I say, trying to prize her fingers off my wrist. ". . . I don't know how to feed."

"It's very simple. Put food onto the utensil and empty the contents into the patient's mouth. Here." The nurse thrusts a bib at me.

"But what if she spits or throws up or — ?" Her rubber-soled shoes are already out of sight. I sigh, and trudge to 606B.

Yuck! A sagging sack of bones, clothed in brown-spotted skin. Clammy hands painted with greasy yellow bruises. Porous skin crawling with sated bacteria . . . The things I do for a beefy résumé.

I delve into a box near the sink, and snap on a pair of latex rubber gloves.

Nothing's supposed to get by these babies. Let's hope I don't need a rabies shot or anything.

I descend on Mrs Pearce, bib brandished.

"Hi there! How's it going?"

No answer.

Great, she doesn't talk.

I scoop up some porridge. "Open up." Her mouth remains closed, and the spoon hovers in mid-air.

What should I do?

I insert the spoon between clamped lips. The mush spills down her chin as I watch helplessly. I hear the squeak of the nurse's shoes behind me and I make a couple of backhanded swipes at Mrs Pearce's chin.

"How's it going?" the nurse asks me rhetorically.

"Okay, I guess. She won't eat."

"Just leave it." The nurse flaps off with an impatient wave. I abandon the full tray for my ice water duties.

Spend much more time on this, and I might have to sacrifice my break.

"How was the hospital?" my sister asks me at dinner.

"I gave out ice water and stuff."

"You spend the whole morning giving out water?" my dad asks.

"Sure. Sometimes I feed people."

"What're you doing next week?" my dad persists.

"Feeding. Giving out ice water."

"Again?"

"That's what I do."

"Why don't you volunteer in the labs?"

"I want to *talk* to the patients."

"How can you talk to them if they're eating?"

Three weeks later, I'm still asking myself that question. I'm standing in front of Mrs Pearce, arms upraised like a surgeon before operating. The labs are looking better and better every day. Well, the sooner I get this over with, the sooner I can leave.

"Hello, Mrs Pearce. How are you today?"

Her blue eyes stare unwaveringly at me.

"Well, let's get on with it. I don't have all day. Let's try to beat our record, okay?"

I snap on a pair of gloves, and the smell of overcooked eggs wafts into my nostrils. I poke gingerly at the yellow mass, which has the consistency of paste. Spearing some of the gelatinous goop onto a fork, I aim for Mrs Pearce's mouth.

"Open up," I coax, waving the egg tantalizingly in front of her. Her lips don't budge. "Open up. C'mon, I don't have all day." Still no relenting.

What can I do? I've tried.

I peel off the gloves, and head for the supply room to give out ice water. With a little bit of luck, I might be able to manage an hour and a half long break.

"How did Mrs Pearce do?" the nurse asks.

"She won't eat."

"Did you get some of that porridge into her? Her blood sugar's a little low."

"She's diabetic?"

"Yep. Do me a favour, and try to get some juice into her, at least."

"Okay." My fingers squirm into the gloves again.

I can't believe this. The one patient I have to feed not only doesn't eat, but is diabetic. Now I have to make *her eat.*

I brandish a spoonful of Cream of Wheat in front of Mrs Pearce.

"You gotta eat, okay? I want you to eat every bite on this tray. Now, open up." I pry open her lips and insert the spoon. Half of the mush dribbles down her chin.

At least some of it went in.

Doggedly, I scoop up some more porridge, and wait for her to gulp some air. When her mouth slackens, I am poised for action. This hit and miss strategy lasts for an hour and a half. Flicking off my gloves, I survey my handiwork.

Porridge? Check. Eggs? Check. Juice? Check. That's a wrap, people, see you next week.

Satisfied, I troop off to do ice water.

"So what did you do today?" my dad asks at dinner.

"Gave out ice water."

"Again?"

"And fed Mrs Pearce."

"I'm sure you can switch if you want."

Pediatrics sounds good. I'll only have to play with the kids. I don't have to feed them, don't have to give them ice water . . . But who gives up after a day on the job? Not me. I'll show her who's boss.

"Reporting for duty," I snap at the mirror in the Auxiliary lounge. Grimly, I fix the starched collar of my volunteer uniform. It's week seven, and still there's no significant development in the Breakfast Battle. Today, I decide. Today must be the turning point. I whip a stiff salute to myself, and march upstairs. No more Ms Nice Guy.

Surveillance shows the enemy strapped into a wheelchair. Ammunition, in form of porridge, scrambled eggs, and juice. There's no going back now.

Malevolently, I pull on gloves. *Show no fear.*

"Hi there, Mrs Pearce. Beautiful day, isn't it? I hope you're ready to eat." I circle the chair stealthily.

"You gotta eat your porridge. Here we go." I manoeuvre the spoon into position.

You've met your match, Pearce. No one gets past me.

"Ready?"

I advance the spoon into the starting position.

"Set?"

The spoon picks up speed.

"Go!"

In a series of intricate flight patterns, I make a couple experimental passes. Mrs Pearce looks totally unmoved. With a deft movement of my wrist, I bank into a shallow dive. Right on target. The spoon makes contact with her mouth which drops open with sheer surprise.

"She shoots, she scores," I crow.

Mrs Pearce splutters and chokes. Fish-like, her mouth gapes and puckers. Evilly, I lie in wait, anticipating the moment she'll come up for air. When she does, I'll be ready for her.

"Gotcha!" The loaded spoon flashes through the air.

Going into the final round, the score is tied. Shoot out at centre ice. Will it be Kwan or Pearce? Place your bets, ladies and gentlemen. The audience is speechless. Kwan makes the play — the puck glides over the ice — it veers toward the goal — does it go in? — it's going in — it's going in — it's in!

When a kitchen employee comes for the tray, I present her with three empty containers. She is unimpressed.

Okay. So maybe a lot of the food did land on the bib, but at least half of it did go down to her stomach. Definitely a victory.

"Reporting for duty," I say to my mirror image. It's week twenty in the Breakfast Battle, and the Allied Forces are gaining territory fast. I smile, and salute briskly. It's time to get down to business.

Mrs Pearce is propped up in her chair. I could be wrong, but I think I see a resigned shake of the head as I walk in. What's she thinking? Probably consigning me to hell.

I string a bib around her with a practised hand. "Are you hungry today?"

No answer. I snap on gloves and pick up a spoon.

"You know the routine, Pearce. Let's get started."

Kwan takes the face-off at centre ice. She wends her way through the defence. She's smoking! She hurtles through the defence like they don't even exist. She's going for the goal — she's close, but Pearce blocks her with a vicious bodycheck. Kwan goes down. But Pearce is slapped with a two-minute penalty, and the goal's clear for Kwan. She punches holes in the defence, and makes an easy score on the net. It's gonna be a close game, folks. Stay tuned . . .

Breathing heavily, I emerge victorious again, after an hour and a half. But she's getting into better shape. I'd better train harder for the next game. I pull off the gloves.

"Good game, Pearce," I say.

Tired blue eyes staring at me from a shrunken head. Hanks of hair plastered limply onto her skin. Trapped inside an uncooperative body. Too tired to live, unable to die. Maybe, just maybe . . .

My hand crawls out furtively and snakes around her fingers.

Fingers unpadded with flesh. Soft and cool, like a rainy day in spring. Rough spots where the IV needle has punctured the skin.

I sit with her until her hand is warm and she is asleep. Bathed in the brittle winter sunshine, she is oddly angelic.

"I'll see you next week," I whisper.

"Give out some more water?" my dad asks at dinner that night.

"Did some feeding, too."

"You can switch. Why don't you ask that supervisor of yours?"

"Actually, I kinda like what I'm doing."

My dad's eyebrows jerk up.

It's week thirty in the Breakfast Battle. Mentally, I review the latest intelligence. Surveillance reports show heavy reinforcements along the border. But I'm ready.

Grinning at my reflection, I stride upstairs.

"Yo, Mrs Pearce . . ." I stop on the threshold.

The bed is empty.

"Mrs Pearce?"

Where is she?

A nurse brushes past me.

"Excuse me."

"Yeah?"

"I was going to feed — that is, I usually feed Mrs Pearce — and she's not — "

"She died, honey. Last week."

Week thirty in the Breakfast Battle. And the ground war is over.

TIPS ON WRITING A NARRATIVE ESSAY

1. Select an experience that had a strong impact on you and that you want to communicate.

2. Concentrate on engaging and entertaining your reader. Use detail and description to communicate your experience clearly and vividly. Remember, the narrative essayist is a keen observer, one on whom "nothing is lost."

3. Let the experience speak for itself. The reader should be enlightened, moved, or persuaded through the force of the narrative. If

you wish to state your thesis explicitly, keep it brief. Avoid editorializing, offering asides to the reader, concluding with a paragraph that spells out what it all meant, or telling the reader how to feel.

4. Work your narrative toward a climax or "moment of truth" which crystallizes the experience for both you and your reader. Remember that essentially you are telling a story and stories work best when they leave the reader feeling emotionally satisfied.

5. Polish, polish, polish. The narrative essayist reveals himself or herself not only through the telling of the experience but also through the way in which it is told. Your voice should shine through the strength of your style and presentation. In the end, it is a picture of the world as you see it and live it that your are presenting to your reader.

6. The Autobiography, Biography, and Profile

KEY WORK:

"Harriet Tubman: The Moses of Her People" — Langston
   Hughes

ASSOCIATED READINGS:

"Excerpt from *Walden*" — Henry David Thoreau
"The Victory of 'Calamity Nell': a profile of Nelly McClung"
   — Mary Nemeth
"Dr. Norman Bethune: A Canadian Hero" — Michelle
   Patterson (student essay)
Tips on Writing an Autobiography, Biography, or Profile

You probably have read many autobiographies, biographies, and
profiles in your years in school. These "true stories," which are a
clever blend of fact, anecdote, and dialogue, often produce work
that reads like fiction. In fact, as in the narrative essay, the writer
often uses the elements of fiction — suspense, building to a climax
through one or more conflicts, irony, and the reconstruction of
events which reinforce character details. Both Hughes' biographical tale about the legendary Harriet Tubman and Patterson's portrait of the well-known Norman Bethune fulfil all these criteria
and, as a result, provide interesting reading.

Because the autobiography, biography, and profile focus on an
individual's life and reveal his or her experiences and responses,
you will find that this type of writing shares certain characteristics
and conventions with the classical and narrative essays. Within the
form itself, the essential difference between an autobiography and
a biography, whether in the form of a full-length portrayal or a
brief profile, is in the depth of perspective they present. Each provides a rich source of information on the life of an individual, but
without the biographer's filter, the objective camera's eye is gone.

The profile, a special form of autobiography or biography, is a brief sketch or verbal portrait of an individual. You may be asked to write a profile to accompany a job or university application. The Associated Readings contain profiles of influential Canadians.

Conventions of the Autobiography, Biography, and Profile

Purpose   To explain, explore, describe, and provide insights into the life of an individual

Audience   Various

Tone   Depends on the writer and his or her relationship with the individual who is the subject of the work. As a result, the tone can be reverential, humorous, mocking, ironic, even belligerent.

Voice   Usually strong in autobiographies, but less strong in biographies so as not to overshadow the individuality of the person being written about

Response   A sense of intimacy or shared experience sometimes verging on conspiracy by sharing hitherto unknown details and secrets

Language   LEVEL — A wide range, from formal through informal to colloquial

CHARACTERISTICS — Either first person "I" or third person "he" or "she"

Structure   Usually chronological, but the chronology may be reorganized for dramatic or emotional impact

BEFORE READING

1. Relate to a partner a true story about a significant person in your life.

2. Who might be an interesting subject for a biography? Justify your choice.

3. What qualities should an effective leader possess? Are these qualities universal and timeless or specific to a culture and era?

Harriet Tubman: The Moses of Her People

LANGSTON HUGHES

Biography
She could have been content with her own freedom, but she wasn't.
Time and time again, she risked her life to free hundreds of slaves
in the South.

"Then we saw the lightning, and that was the guns; and then
we heard the thunder, and that was the big guns; and then we
heard the rain falling, and that was the drops of blood falling; and
when we came to get in the crops, it was dead men that we
reaped." So the escaped slave, Harriet Tubman, described one of
the battles of the Civil War in which she took part, for she was in
the thick of the fighting. Before the War Harriet Tubman devoted
her life to the cause of freedom, and after the War to the advancement of her people.

She was born in Maryland a slave, one of eleven sons and
daughters. No one kept a record of her birth, so the exact year is
not known. But she lived so long and so much was written about
her that most of the other facts of her life are accurately recorded.
She was a homely child, morose, willful, wild, and constantly in
rebellion against slavery. Unlike Phillis Wheatley[1] or Frederick
Douglass,[2] Harriet had no teaching of any sort, except the whip.
As a little girl, on the very first day that she was sent to work in
the Big House, her mistress whipped her four times. Once she ran
away and hid in a pig sty for five days, eating the scraps thrown
to the pigs. "There were good masters and mistresses, so I've heard
tell," she once said, "but I didn't happen to come across any of
them."

Harriet never liked to work as a servant in the house, so perhaps
because of her rebellious nature, she was soon ordered to the fields.
One day when she was in her early teens, something happened
that affected her whole life. It was evening, and a young slave had,
without permission, gone to a country store. The overseer followed
him to whip him. He ordered Harriet to help tie him up. As Harriet
refused, the slave ran. The overseer picked up a heavy iron weight
from the scales and threw it. But he did not hit the fellow. He
struck Harriet's head, almost crushing her skull, and leaving a

deep scar forever. Unconscious, the girl lingered between life and death for days. When at last she was able to work again, Harriet still suffered fits of unconsciousness. These lasted all her life. They would come upon her at any time, any place, and it would seem as if she had suddenly fallen asleep. Sometimes in the fields, sometimes leaning against a fence, sometimes in church, she would "go to sleep," and no one could wake her until the seizure had passed. When she was awake, this did not affect her thinking. But her master thought the blow had made her half-witted. Harriet continued to let him believe this. Meanwhile, she prayed God to deliver her from bondage.

When she was about twenty-four years old, she married a jolly, carefree fellow named Tubman, who did not share her concern for leaving the slave country. A few years later, when her old master died, Harriet heard that she and two of her brothers were to be sold, so they decided to run away together. It was dangerous to tell anyone. Harriet had no chance to let even her mother know directly. But on the evening that she was leaving, she went about the fields and the slaves' quarters singing:

> When that old chariot comes
> I'm gwine to leave you.
> I'm bound for the Promised Land. . . .

And the way she sang that song let her friends and kinfolks know that to Harriet the Promised Land right then meant the North, not Heaven. That night she left the Brodas Plantation on the Big Buckwater River, never to return. Before dawn her brothers became frightened and went back to the slave huts before their absence was discovered. But Harriet went on alone through the woods by night, hiding by day, having no map, unable to read or write, but trusting God, instinct, and the North star to guide her. By some miracle she eventually got to Philadelphia, found work there, and was never again a slave.

But Harriet could not be happy while all her family were slaves. She kept thinking about them. So some months later, she went back to Maryland, hoping to persuade her husband to come North with her. He said he did not wish to go. She led others Northward, however, and, within two years of her own escape, she had secretly returned to the South three times to rescue two brothers, a sister and her children, and a dozen more slaves. The Fugitive Slave Law of 1850 now made it dangerous for runaways to stop anywhere in the United States, so Harriet led her followers to Canada, where she spent a winter begging, cooking, and praying for them. Then she returned to Maryland to rescue nine more Negroes.

During the first years of her own freedom, Harriet spent most of her time showing others how to follow in her footsteps. Her fame as a fearless leader of "freedom bands" spread rapidly. Shortly, large rewards were offered by the slaveholders for her capture. But she was never captured, and she never lost any of her followers to the slave catchers. One reason for this was that once a slave made up his mind to go with her and started out, Harriet did not permit any turning back. Perhaps her experience with her two brothers when she first ran away accounted for this insistence. Her method of preventing frightened or weak travelers on the freedom road from returning to slavery, and perhaps being whipped into betraying the others, was simple. Harriet Tubman carried a pistol. When anyone said he could not, or would not, go on, Harriet pulled her gun from the folds of her dress and said, "You *will* go on — or you'll die." The strength or the courage to continue was always forthcoming when her faltering companions looked into the muzzle of Harriet's gun. Through swamp and thicket, rain and cold, they went on toward the North. Thus everyone who started out with Harriet Tubman lived to thank her for freedom.

Long before the Civil War came, so many slaves were escaping and so many white people in the North were helping them, that the routes to freedom became known as the Underground Railroad. Secret "stations" where escaping slaves might be hidden, warmed, and fed were established in houses, barns, and sometimes even churches along the way. The Quakers were especially helpful and active in this regard. And a strong Anti-Slavery Society supported such activities. Slave owners were losing thousands of dollars worth of slaves by escape every year. Harriet Tubman became known as a "conductor" on the Underground Railroad. She was not the only "conductor," but she was the most famous, and one of the most daring. Once she brought as many as twenty-five slaves in a single band to freedom.

Another time she had in her party of runaways a big strong slave worth $1500. His name was Josiah Bailey, and the Maryland countryside was plastered with posters offering a reward for his capture. There were ads in the papers for his return. On the way through New York City, a friend of freedom recognized Bailey from the description in the papers and said, "I'm glad to meet a man whose head is worth fifteen hundred dollars!" Josiah was so shocked at being recognized and so afraid that he would be captured that a mood of deep despair descended upon him, and he would not speak the rest of the trip. When the train was carrying the runaways across the bridge at Buffalo into Canada, Bailey would not even look at the wonder of Niagara Falls. But when they got on free soil and he was finally safe, he burst into song, and nobody could stop him from singing. He cried that at last, thanks to God, he was in Heaven! Harriet Tubman said, "Well, you old fool, you! You might at least have looked at Niagara Falls on the way to Heaven."

Harriet had a great sense of humour. She enjoyed telling the story on herself of how, not being able to read, she once sat down and went to sleep on a park bench right under a sign offering a big reward for her capture. When she began to make speeches to raise money for the cause of freedom, she often told jokes, sang, and sometimes even danced. She might have been a great actress, people said, because without makeup she could hollow out her cheeks and wrinkle her brow to seem like a very old woman. She would make her body shrink and cause her legs to totter when she chose to so disguise herself. Once, making a trip to Maryland to rescue some relatives, she had to pass through a village where she was known. She bought two hens, tied them by their feet and hung them heads down around her neck, then went tottering along. Sure enough, a slave catcher came up the street who might, she thought, recognize her, tottering or not. So she unloosed the squalling chickens in the middle of the street and dived after them, purposely not catching them so she could run down the road in pursuit and out of the slave catcher's sight, while all the passers-by laughed.

Sometimes, knowing that her band of fugitives was pursued by angry masters, she would get on a train headed South — because nobody would suspect that runaway slaves would be going South. Sometimes she would disguise the women in her party and herself as men. Babies would be given a sleeping medicine to keep them quiet and then wrapped up like bundles. Sometimes she would wade for hours up a stream to throw the hounds off scent. . . . Often when all seemed hopeless — although she never told her followers she had such feelings — Harriet would pray. One of her favorite prayers was, "Lord, you've been with me through six troubles. Be with me in the seventh." Some people thought that Harriet Tubman led a charmed life because, within twelves years, she made nineteen dangerous trips into the South, rescuing slaves. She herself said, "I never run my train off the track, and I never lost a passenger."

Her father and mother were both over seventy years of age when she rescued them and brought them North to a home she had begun to buy in Auburn, New York. At first they stayed in St. Catharines, Canada, where escaped slaves were safe, since in 1833 Great Britain had declared all slavery illegal. But it was too cold for the old folks there. And Harriet's work was not on foreign soil. She herself seemed to have no fear of being captured. She came and went about the United States as she chose, and became so famous that, although she never sought the spotlight, it was hard for her not to be recognized wherever she was. Once at a great woman's suffrage meeting where her old head wound had caused her to go sound asleep in the audience, she was recognized, and awoke to find herself on the platform. Her speech for women's rights was roundly applauded. In those days neither Negroes nor women could vote. Harriet believed both should, so she followed the woman's suffrage movement closely.

In appearance "a more ordinary specimen of humanity could hardly be found," but there was no one with a greater capacity for leadership than she had. Among the slaves, where she walked in secret, Harriet began to be known as Moses. And at the great public meetings of the North, as the Negro historian William Wells Brown wrote in 1854, "all who frequented anti-slavery conventions, lectures, picnics, and fairs, could not fail to have seen a black woman of medium size, upper front teeth gone, smiling countenance, attired in coarse but neat apparel, with an old-fashioned reticule or bag suspended by her side, who, on taking her seat, would at once drop off into a sound sleep. . . . No fugitive was ever captured who had Moses for a leader." She was very independent. Between rescue trips or speeches, she would work as a cook or a scrubwoman. She might borrow, but she never begged money for herself. All contributions went toward the cause of freedom in one way or another, as did most of what she earned.

But when the Civil War began and she became a nurse for the Union Armies, and then a military scout and an invaluable intelligence agent behind the Rebel lines, she was promised some compensation. Technically she was not a registered nurse, and being a woman, she could not be a soldier. Yet she carried a Union pass, traveled on government transports, did dangerous missions in

Confederate territory, and gave advice to chiefs of staffs. But she never got paid for this, although she had been promised $1800 for certain assignments. To Harriet this made no difference, until after the War she badly needed money to care for her aged parents. Petitions were sent to the War Department and to Congress to try to get the $1800 due her. But it was never granted.

Harriet Tubman's war activities were amazing. She served under General Stevens at Beaufort, South Carolina. She was sent to Florida to nurse those ill of dysentery, small pox, and yellow fever. She was with Colonel Robert Gould Shaw[3] at Fort Wagner. She organized a group of nine Negro scouts and river pilots and, with Colonel Montgomery, led a Union raiding contingent of three gunboats and about one hundred fifty Negro troops up the Combahee River.[4] As reported by the *Boston Commonwealth*, for July 10, 1863, they "under the guidance of a black woman, dashed into the enemy's country, struck a bold and effective blow, destroying millions of dollars worth of commissary stores, cotton and lordly dwellings, and striking terror into the heart of rebeldom, brought off near eight hundred slaves and thousands of dollars worth of property." Concerning Harriet Tubman, it continued, "Many and many times she has penetrated the enemy's lines and discovered their situation and condition, and escaped without injury, but not without extreme hazard."

One of the songs Harriet sang during the War was:

Of all the whole creation in the East or in the West,
The glorious Yankee nation is the greatest and the best.
Come along! Come along! Don't be alarmed,
Uncle Sam is rich enough to give you all a farm.

But Harriet Tubman never had a farm of her own. Her generous nature caused her to give away almost all the money she ever got her hands on. There were always fugitives, or relatives, or causes, or friends in need. She was over forty years old when Abraham Lincoln signed the Emancipation Proclamation, making legal the freedom she had struggled to secure. She lived for almost fifty years after the War was over. Some people thought she was a hundred years old when she died in 1913. Certainly she was over ninety.

A number of books have been written about her. The first one, *Scenes in the Life of Harriet Tubman,* by Sarah H. Bradford, appeared in 1869, and the proceeds from its sale helped Harriet pay for her cottage. She wrote her friend, Frederick Douglass, who had hidden her and her runaway slaves more than once in his home in Rochester, for a letter about her book. In his reply he compared their two careers:

> The difference between us is very marked. Most that I have done and suffered in the service of our cause has been in public, and I have received much encouragement at every step of the way. You, on the other hand, have labored in a private way. I have wrought in the day — you in the night. I have had the applause of the crowd and the satisfaction that comes of being approved by the multitude, while the most that you have done has been witnessed by a few trembling, scared, and footsore bondsmen and women, whom you have led out of the house of bondage, and whose heartfelt *God bless you* has been your only reward. The midnight sky and the silent stars have been the witnesses of your devotion to freedom and of your heroism.

When years later, in her old age, a reporter for the *New York Herald Tribune* came to interview her one afternoon at her home in Auburn, he wrote that, as he was leaving, Harriet looked toward an orchard nearby and said, "Do you like apples?"

On being assured that the young man liked them, she asked, "Did you ever plant any apples?"

The writer confessed that he had not.

"No," said the old woman, "but somebody else planted them. I liked apples when I was young. And I said, 'Someday I'll plant apples myself for other young folks to eat.' And I guess I did."

Her apples were the apples of freedom. Harriet Tubman lived to see the harvest. Her home in Auburn, New York, is preserved as a memorial to her planting.

----

[1]Phillis Wheatley: Born in Africa, she came as a slave to Boston. She later gained recognition as a poet.
[2]Frederick Douglass: Born into slavery, he escaped to freedom in the North.
[3]Robert Gould Shaw: the commander of a free Negro regiment from Massachusetts.
[4]Combahee River: in South Carolina.

EXPLORING THE BIOGRAPHY, AUTOBIOGRAPHY, AND PROFILE

1. Has Langston Hughes successfully observed the conventions of this form of writing? Cite evidence for each writing component.

2. Quote the sentence that expresses Hughes' thesis and explain how this sentence relates to the title.

3. Tubman's courage and humility dominate this biographical profile. Demonstrate how Hughes achieves this impression through judicious selection and organization of both diction and material.

4. What relative weight did Tubman apparently assign to each of the following: God, circumstance, and personal control? How did these attitudes apparently affect the nature of her life?

5. What does the structure of this biographical profile have in common with the structure of the narrative essay?

EXTENSIVE STUDY

1. This library exercise will acquaint you with reference sources of use in this course and future university and college arts and science courses. Your teacher may ask the teacher-librarian to introduce the class to appropriate resources and, perhaps, assess this orientation's success. Major references include:
   - special encyclopedias (e.g., Benét's *The Reader's Encyclopedia*)
   - handbooks and special reference tools (e.g., *A Reader's Guide to Literary Terms*)
   - biographical and/or historical references (e.g., *Who's Who in Canada* and *The Literary History of the United States*)
   - abstracts and indexes (e.g., *Reader's Guide to Periodical Literature*)
   - specialized dictionaries which provide rules and examples of language usage (e.g., Fowler's *A Dictionary of Modern English Usage* and Bernstein's *The Careful Writer*)

   Working in pairs, locate answers to the questions listed below. Take point-form research notes.
   a. Find biographical data about Hughes that may provide clues about his interests, credibility, and biases.
   b. Locate at least one other biographical profile about Harriet Tubman. What details are presented differently or omitted? Speculate on possible reasons for the differences.
   c. Identify the Quakers.
   d. Record the title of a source containing the Fugitive Slave Law of 1890.

   e. Find the titles of two other books about Tubman or the escape of slaves from the southern United States.

   f. Note five facts about Frederick Douglass's life.

   g. Identify Moses and his role in the Promised Land.

   h. Record the names of two famous slave catchers.

   i. Write definitions of biography and autobiography as literary forms.

   j. Quote the rule about the usage of the word "but" which suggests that Hughes has employed it correctly in his sentence beginning, "But Harriet could not be happy . . . ".

   Compare your findings with another pair of students. Consult your teacher or the teacher-librarian about any problems you encountered.

2. In small groups, explore these questions. You might take notes on your conversation for subsequent discussion with another group.

   a. How did you feel about Harriet Tubman, the woman, after reading the essay? Why?

   b. Which of Tubman's traits could have contributed to her success in contemporary society, as demonstrated by effective leaders today?

3. a. Read the biographical profiles of Nelly McClung and Dr. Norman Bethune and compose a list of attributes they share with Tubman.

   b. Define the characteristics of a hero. Which of these criteria do the persons mentioned above share? Which of the standards in your definition apply to the Greek and Shakespearean hero and which are peculiar to our time and culture?

4. a. Read the "Excerpt from *Walden*" by Henry David Thoreau (p. 174) and explain what lessons in living we can learn from his life.

   b. To what extent do you think it is possible to put these lessons into practice in contemporary society?

5. Compose a dialogue or role-play a scene from one of the following topics:

   a. Adrienne Rich (see Essays About University Life), Emmeline Pankhurst (see The Oral Essay), and Nelly McClung on women's issues

b. Harriet Tubman, Norman Bethune, and Nelly McClung on the importance of being committed to a cause in one's life

c. Nelly McClung, Harriet Tubman, and Norman Bethune reflecting on their places in history and their impact on history

d. Your interview with one or more of the people profiled in this unit

THE WRITING FOLDER

1. Write a personal response to one of the works in this unit.

2. Interview someone you admire and know well, perhaps a member of your own family, and write a biographical profile of that person's life that could be submitted to a local newspaper.

3. Prepare a profile to accompany your postsecondary school application.

INDEPENDENT STUDY

1. Read two biographies of a famous person or one biography and one autobiography. Compare the depictions of the individual in question, considering point of view, bias, focus, omissions, interests, and interpretation.

   You may wish to focus on one of the well-known individuals profiled in this unit or consider such people as Pablo Picasso, Emily Carr, Martin Luthur King, Jr., Zelda or Scott Fitzgerald, Nelson Mandela, Marie Curie, Andy Warhol, William Shakespeare, Georgia O'Keefe, Emily or Charlotte Brontë, Samuel Beckett, Mao Tse-tung, Pierre Elliott Trudeau, Wayne Gretzsky, Mackenzie King, Virginia Woolf, Anne Frank, Mother Teresa, Laurence Olivier, Helen Keller, Margaret Mead, Albert Camus, Bertrand Russell, Indira Gandhi, Carl Jung, or Simone de Beauvoir.

2. Read material about how to write a biography or profile. Write an original work of biography about a living person you know whom you believe to be worthy of such attention. Base your work on in-depth interviews with the individual and with

others who know or have known him or her. Be sure you establish the universal dimension of the project.

3. Read at least two books about either Harriet Tubman, Nelly McClung, or Dr. Norman Bethune. (If the person has written an autobiography, be sure to include it as one of the works.) Compare the quality of the works in terms of accuracy, completeness, detail, biases, and overall interest and readability.

TIMED READING AND WRITING

1. Write a personal essay which begins with either of:
   If I had met Harriet Tubman (or another heroic figure), the
      first thing I would want to ask her is . . .
   Or
   The best way to meet a challenge is . . .

2. Summarize Michelle Patterson's profile of Dr. Norman Bethune in approximately half a page.

Excerpt from Walden

HENRY DAVID THOREAU

. . . When first I took up my abode in the woods, that is, began to spend my nights as well as days there, which, by accident, was on Independence Day, or the Fourth of July, 1845, my house was not finished for winter, but was merely a defence against the rain, without plastering or chimney, the walls being of rough, weather-stained boards, with wide chinks, which made it cool at night. The upright white hewn studs and freshly planed door and window casings gave it a clean and airy look, especially in the morning, when its timbers were saturated with dew, so that I fancied that by noon some sweet gum would exude from them. To my imagination it retained throughout the day more or less of this auroral character, reminding me of a certain house on a mountain which I had visited a year before. This was an airy and unplastered cabin, fit to entertain a travelling god, and where a goddess might trail her garments. The winds which passed over my dwelling were such as sweep over the ridges of mountains, bearing the broken strains, or celestial parts only, of terrestrial music. The morning wind forever blows, the poem of creation is uninterrupted: but few are the ears that hear it. Olympus is but the outside of the earth everywhere.

The only house I had been the owner of before, if I except a boat, was a tent, which I used occasionally when making excursions in the summer, and this is still rolled up in my garret; but the boat, after passing from hand to hand, has gone down the stream of time. With this more substantial shelter about me, I had made some progress toward settling in the world. This frame, so slightly clad, was a sort of crystallization around me, and reacted on the builder. It was suggestive somewhat as a picture in outlines. I did not need to go outdoors to take the air, for the atmosphere within had lost none of its freshness. It was not so much within-doors as behind a door where I sat, even in the rainiest weather. The Harivansa[1] says, "An abode without birds is like a meat without seasoning." Such was not my abode, for I found myself suddenly neighbour to the birds; not by having imprisoned one, but having caged myself near them. I was not only nearer to some of those which commonly frequent the garden and the orchard, but to those wilder and more thrilling songsters of the forest which never, or rarely, serenade a villager, — the wood thrush, the veery, the scarlet tanager, the field sparrow, the whip-poor-will, and many others.

I was seated by the shore of a small pond, about a mile and a half south of the village of Concord and somewhat higher than it, in the midst of an extensive wood between that town and Lincoln, and about two miles south of that our only field known to fame, Concord Battle Ground; but I was so low in the woods that the opposite shore, half a mile off, like the rest, covered with wood, was my most distant horizon. For the first week, whenever I looked out on the pond it impressed me like a tarn high upon the side of a mountain, its bottom far above the surface of other lakes, and, as the sun arose, I saw it throwing off its nightly clothing of mist, and here and there, by degrees, its soft ripples or its smooth reflecting surface was revealed, while the mists, like ghosts, were stealthily withdrawing in every direction into the woods, as at the breaking up of some nocturnal conventicle. The very dew seemed to hang upon the trees later into the day than usual, as on the sides of mountains.

This small lake was of most value as a neighbour in the intervals of a gentle rain-storm in August, when, both air and water being perfectly still, but the sky overcast, mid-afternoon had all the serenity of evening, and the wood thrush sang around, and was heard from shore to shore. A lake like this is never smoother than at such a time; and the clear portion of the air above it being shallow and darkened by clouds, the water, full of light and reflections, becomes a lower heaven itself so much the more important. From a hill-top near by, where the wood had been recently cut off, there was a pleasing vista southward across the pond, through a wide indentation in the hills which form the shore there, where their opposite sides sloping toward each other suggested a stream flowing out in that direction through a wooded valley, but stream there was none. That way I looked between and over the near green hills to some distant and higher ones on the horizon, tinged with blue. Indeed, by standing on tiptoe I could catch a glimpse of some of the peaks of the still bluer and more distant mountain ranges in the northwest, those true-blue coins from heaven's own mint, and also some portion of the village. But in other directions, even from this point, I could not see over or beyond the woods which surrounded me. It is well to have some water in your neighbourhood, to give buoyancy to and float the earth. One value even of the smallest well is that when you look into it you see that the earth is not continent but insular. This is as important as that it keeps butter cool. When I looked across the pond from this peak toward the Sudbury meadows, which in time of flood I distinguished elevated perhaps by a mirage in their seething valley, like a coin in a basin, all the earth beyond the pond appeared like a thin crust insulated and floated even by this small sheet of intervening water, and I was reminded that this on which I dwelt was but *dry land*.

Though the view from my door was still more contracted, I did not feel crowded or confined in the least. There was pasture enough for my imagination. The low shrub oak plateau to which the opposite shore arose stretched away toward the prairies of the West and the steppes of Tartary, affording ample room for all the roving families of men. "There are none happy in the world but beings who enjoy freely a vast horizon," said Damodara[2], when his herds required new and larger pastures.

Both place and time were changed, and I dwelt nearer to those parts of the universe and to those eras in history which had most attracted me. Where I lived was as far off as many a region viewed nightly by astronomers. We are wont to imagine rare and delectable places in some remote and more celestial corner of the system, behind the constellation of Cassiopeia's Chair, far from noise and disturbance. I discovered that my house actually had its site in such a withdrawn, but forever new and unprofaned, part of the universe. If it were worth the while to settle in those parts near to the Pleiades or the Hyades[3], to Aldebaran or Altair[4], then I was really there, or at an equal remoteness from the life which I had left behind, dwindled and twinkling with as fine a ray to my nearest neighbour, and to be seen only in moonless nights by him. Such was that part of creation where I had squatted;

> There was a shepherd that did live,
>   And held his thoughts as high
> As where the mounts whereon his flocks
>   Did hourly feed him by.

What should we think of the shepherd's life if his flocks always wandered to higher pastures than his thoughts?

Every morning was a cheerful invitation to make my life of equal simplicity, and I may say innocence, with Nature herself. I have been as sincere a worshipper of Aurora[5] as the Greeks. I got up early and bathed in the pond; that was a religious exercise, and one of the best things which I did. They say that characters were engraven on the bathing tub of King Tching-thang to this effect: "Renew thyself completely each day; do it again, and again, and forever again." I can understand that. Morning brings back the heroic ages. I was as much affected by the faint hum of a mosquito making its invisible and unimaginable tour through my apartment at earliest dawn, when I was sitting with door and windows open, as I could be by any trumpet that ever sang of fame. It was Homer's requiem; itself an Iliad and Odyssey in the air, singing its own wrath and wanderings. There was something cosmical about it; a standing advertisement, till forbidden, of the everlasting vigor and fertility of the word. The morning, which is the most memorable season of the day, is the awakening hour. Then there is least somnolence in us: and for an hour, at least, some part of us awakes which slumbers all the rest of the day and night. Little is to be expected of that day, if it can be called a day, to which we are not awakened by our Genius, but by the mechanical nudgings of some servitor, are not awakened by our own newly acquired force and aspirations from within, accompanied by the undulations of celestial music, filling the air — to a higher life than we fell asleep from; and thus the darkness bear its fruit, and prove itself to be good, no less than the light. That man who does not believe that each day contains an earlier, more sacred, and auroral hour than he has yet profaned, has despaired of life, and is pursuing a descending and darkening way. After a partial cessation of his sensuous life, the soul of man, or its organs rather, are reinvigorated each day, and his Genius tries again what noble life it can make. All memorable events, I should say, transpire in morning time and in a morning atmosphere. The Vedas[6] say, "All intelligences awake with the morning." Poetry and art, and the fairest and most memorable of the actions of men, date from such an hour. All poets and heroes, like Memnon[7], are the children of Aurora, and emit their music at sunrise. To him whose elastic and vigorous thought keeps pace with the sun, the day is a perpetual morning. It matters not what the clocks say or the attitudes and labours of men. Morning is when I am awake and there is a dawn in me. Moral reform is the effort to throw off sleep. Why is it that men give so poor an account of their day if they have not been slumbering? They are not such poor calculators. If they had not been overcome with drowsiness, they would have performed something. The millions are awake enough for physical labour; but only one in a million is awake enough for effective intellectual exertion, only one in a hundred millions to a poetic or divine life. To be awake is to be alive. I have never yet met a man who was quite awake. How could I have looked him in the face?

We must learn to reawaken and keep ourselves awake, not by mechanical aids, but by an infinite expectation of the dawn, which does not forsake us in our soundest sleep. I know of no more encouraging fact than the unquestionable ability of man to elevate his life by a conscious endeavour. It is something to be able to paint a particular picture, or to carve a statue, and so to make a few objects beautiful; but it is far more glorious to carve and paint the very atmosphere and medium through which we look, which morally we can do. To affect the quality of the day, that is the highest of arts. Every man is tasked to make his life, even in its details, worthy of the contemplation of his most elevated and critical hour. If we refused, or rather used up, such paltry informations as we get, the oracles would distinctly inform us how this might be done.

I went to the woods because I wished to live deliberately, to front only the essential facts of life, and see if I could not learn what it had to teach, and not, when I came to die, discover that I had not lived. I did not wish to live what was not life, living is so dear;

nor did I wish to practise resignation, unless it was quite necessary. I wanted to live deep and suck out all the marrow of life, to live so sturdily and Spartan-like as to put to rout all that was not life, to cut a broad swath and shave close, to drive life into a corner, and reduce it to its lowest terms, and, if it proved to be mean, why then to get the whole and genuine meanness of it, and publish its meanness to the world; or if it were sublime, to know it by experience, and be able to give a true account of it in my next excursion. For most men, it appears to me, are in a strange uncertainty about it, whether it is of the devil or of God, and have *somewhat hastily* concluded that it is the chief end of man here to "glorify God and enjoy him forever." . . .

---

[1] A Sanskrit epic poem of the fifth century A.D. Thoreau and Emerson were both interested in Eastern and Near Eastern religious literature.
[2] The Hindu divinity, Krishna.
[3] *Pleiades, Hyades,* constellations.
[4] *Aldebaran, Altair,* bright stars.
[5] The Greek goddess of dawn.
[6] The sacred literature of the Hindus.
[7] Son of Aurora; his statue is reputed to emit a harp-like sound at sunrise.

The Victory of 'Calamity Nell': a profile of Nelly McClung

MARY NEMETH

Inside Alberta's towering sandstone legislature building, at the far end of the east-wing hallway, hangs a photograph of a handsome middle-aged woman with curly hair, a strong chin and thin, determined lips. In her day, critics called Nellie McClung a "lady terror" or "Calamity Nell." Admirers called her a heroine. She led the campaign to win the vote for women, became one of the first women elected to the Alberta legislature and helped wage a court battle to prove that Canadian women were legally "persons." Meanwhile, she married, raised five children, published 16 books and delivered fiery speeches across Canada and the United States. To Elaine McCoy, now Alberta's 46-year-old minister responsible for women's issues, McClung is "a role model" whose commitment to social change is as relevant today as it was two generations ago.

During the battle for women's suffrage, McClung argued that the vote would usher in a new era of equality and justice. But in the years before her death in 1951, she wrote of her disappointment at the slow pace of change. In fact, it was not until the late 1960s that a new wave of feminism surged onto the national scene with a message as radical as McClung's had been in her time. McCoy was at the University of Alberta by then — an ambitious young law student convinced that all barriers to women's advancement had crumbled. "I thought that the doors were open," says McCoy. "I was naïve. Here I am 23 years later, and there's still a wage gap, there's still sexual harassment and family violence. We don't have true equality. We've inherited all of those issues."

And yet, so much has changed since 1873, when McClung was born in Chatsworth, Ont., and women — lumped in with lunatics and criminals—were still denied the right to vote. McClung's family moved to an isolated homestead in southern Manitoba when she was six years old. Pioneer life shaped her fiercely independent spirit and later inspired her folksy, homespun novels. After finishing the eighth grade, she taught school in Manitou, Man., where she met and married Wesley McClung, a pharmacist. "They had a very happy marriage," says Marcia McClung, the couple's 48-year-old granddaughter, who owns a Toronto public relations firm. "Wesley had been brought up by an emancipated woman and he was very proud of Nellie."

Wesley McClung's mother, Annie, was an ardent activist. Nellie soon joined her in the temperance cause, campaigning for universal suffrage in the belief that women's maternal instincts would compel them to ban the demon alcohol as soon as they won the vote. Opponents of women's suffrage argued that politics would take women away from their duties at home, and they often accused McClung of neglecting her family. "I wish you could see the proportion of my mail that tells me to go home and darn my husband's socks," she wrote a friend. Still, McClung's married respectability, her pretty hats and witty speeches made her more socially acceptable than some of her more radical colleagues.

In 1911, when the McClungs moved to Winnipeg, Nellie's political horizons expanded. Already a skilled orator, she began campaigning for better factory conditions and women's rights to family property. During Manitoba's 1914 election campaign, she played a leading role in the battle to unseat Conservative Premier Rodmond Roblin, who had rejected women's suffrage. She stumped the countryside and took part in a popular mock parliament in which she played premier to a fictious delegation of men. "Man is made for something higher and better than voting," she told the delegates, mimicking Roblin's tone. "Politics unsettle men, and unsettled men means unsettled bills — broken furniture, and broken vows."

The McClungs had moved to Edmonton by the time the new Liberal government gave Manitoba women the vote in 1916. Saskatchewan and Alberta followed the same year; British Columbia and Ontario in 1917, Nova Scotia and the federal government in 1918. "More has happened in the last four years and a half," McClung wrote in 1919, "than in the 400 years that preceded that time." In 1921, McClung won a seat in the Alberta legislature as a member of the Liberal opposition. She crusaded for women's rights and prohibition. When the prohibition campaign failed, wrote *The Edmonton Journal*, she "scorched the government with acidulated and bitter tongue."

Later, she joined four other women to fight the famous Persons Case. Under the British North America Act, only "persons" could sit in the Senate, and the Supreme Court of Canada ruled in 1928 that that did not include women. Undaunted, the five women took the case to the Privy Council in Britain—and won. Later, McClung served on the CBC's first board of governors and was a delegate to the League of Nations in 1938. She continued writing until her death in 1951, at 77.

After helping to bring the vote to more than half of the Canadian population, McClung was largely forgotten until a feminist revival in the 1960s. "It's been two steps forward and one step back," says 68-year-old Alberta Liberal MLA Bettie Hewes. Women now, she adds, must join the battle where the early suffragists left off. "I feel some obligation to them because of what they accomplished," says Hewes. "I feel some duty to live up to their legacy."

Dr. Norman Bethune: A Canadian Hero

MICHELLE PATTERSON *(student essay)*

We Canadians often lament our paucity of heroes and myths on which to build our cultural folklore. True, we have our maple leaves and our beaver, and thanks to Pierre Berton, the story of our railway. But especially since Wayne Gretzsky crossed the border, we envy Americans their epic heroes — their Davy Crocketts, Daniel Boones, and Abraham Lincolns.

Dr. Norman Bethune is just such an epic figure — an uncompromising person who dedicated his life to the passionate pursuit of a cause. Indeed, since Prime Minister Trudeau named him a Canadian of "historical significance" in 1972, he has become a popular figure in Canadian mythology, along with Louis Riel and Jacques Cartier. And, nearly twenty years later, even movie-makers jumped on the bandwagon with a film mythologizing Bethune.

Bethune was driven by a passionate desire to combat injustice. Long before Canada's universal medical insurance, he challenged his colleagues to provide equality of access to health care. But he was not a simple altruist: his intense need to achieve, explore, and create was often overshadowed by an internal struggle between self-doubt and over-confidence. Bethune was a complex man whose character and achievements were the product of his medical and political beliefs and his artistic and literary interests.

Part of Bethune's drive may be attributed to his family background. Born into a family tradition of successful professionals in Gravenhurst, Ontario, he apparently felt considerable pressure to make a statement with his life. Frequent moves with his clergyman father coupled with a volatile, self-absorbed nature effectively inhibited him from forming close friendships, and may help account for his restless adult wanderings.

Bethune's medical career and early marriage began in Detroit where he impressed his colleagues with his charm and hard work. However, his flirtation with the conventional medical community was as brief as his marriage. Recovering from a bout of tuberculosis in 1927, he was determined to change his life.

First, he returned to Canada, making an international name for himself in tubercular research at the Royal Victoria Hospital where he also invented surgical instruments still used today. Here he developed a reputation of a difficult individualist who pandered to no one and rashly criticized established medical practice. He characterized the Canadian medical system as "a luxury trade," adding that Canadians were selling "bread at the price of jewels." Along with several avant-garde colleagues, he drew the blueprints for a system of universal health care much like we have today. Although his ideas were denounced as "grandiose," "impractical," and "crack-brained," even his detractors admired his dedication and surgical skill.

Unsatisfied by his medical achievements, he expressed his frustrations through the arts. He dabbled in painting, producing bold, intense work. But it was his poetry and short stories which spoke most clearly of his conflicts. Indeed, during the Depression, he discovered Communism through the poets and artists with whom he identified.

A tour of the USSR in 1931 convinced Bethune he'd found an answer to human degredation and inequality. Despite his dislike of groups and regimentation, Bethune impulsively joined the party in 1936 and he sailed to Spain to fight Fascism with other creative idealists such as Ernest Hemingway and George Orwell.

On the front, Bethune's bold leadership saved thousands of lives. Within ten days of his arrival, he established plans for a mobile blood clinic. But, once again, his volatile character got in the way when the Republican government assumed control of his transfusion unit. Unable to work in this structure, he returned to Canada to raise funds for his unit in Spain.

Perhaps his happiest challenge was to come, however. Bethune soon found a new cause in providing medical services in China which had been invaded by the Japanese. Persuading Mao Tsetung that he'd be most useful at the conflict-ridden border region, he assumed control of medical services. For the first time in his life, the "fit" was right. He wrote, "It is true I am tired, but I don't think I have been so happy in a long time . . . I am doing what I want to do." Despite the dangers of guerrilla warfare, limited supplies, and inadequate sanitation and personnel, he remained enthusiastic.

Touring China in his mobile medical unit for nearly two years, he saved many lives, inventing makeshift medical tools as he went along. Ironically, the one thing he could not create—rubber gloves—cost him his life. On November 12, 1939, he succumbed to blood poisoning after cutting his ungloved finger during surgery.

Bethune was a driven individual as most heroes are—driven to act by complex internal and external factors. Clearly, his quest to serve others was not the product of simple altruism. It satisfied intense psychological needs to lead, to rectify social inequalities of his time. Regardless of his motives, Bethune's legacy of dedication to a vision qualifies him for Canada's Hall of Heroes.

TIPS ON WRITING AN AUTOBIOGRAPHY, BIOGRAPHY, OR PROFILE

1. *Know your subject.* No biography, autobiography, or profile can have a strong impact if the writer does not have a thorough knowledge of his or her subject. Make sure your information comes from a variety of sources so that you have a clear knowledge of and insight into your subject, and are not unduly influenced by one perspective. For example, if you are interviewing someone in order to write their profile, also try to interview others who know that person.

2. *Have an appreciation for your subject.* Appreciation does not necessarily have to be positive and glowing. You can appreciate a person's achievements without necessarily liking that person. Because appreciation determines your attitude toward your subject, it is significant in creating the work's voice and tone. For example, Mary Nemeth's appreciation of Nelly McClung is evident in the care she takes to give the reader insight into McClung's personal as well as her professional life.

3. *Get beneath the surface.* Even the most ordinary individual becomes interesting in the hands of a skilled observer. Look for an angle, an insight, an experience that reveals the individual beneath the surface. Remember, a short anecdote reveals far more about an individual than a lot of dry data or surface information.

4. *Consider the best way to present your material.* You must organize your material to help reveal the character and achieve the greatest dramatic and emotional impact on your reader. Generally, the order for a biography, autobiography, or profile is chronological, but not necessarily.

5. *Use language that is appropriate to your subject and your intended audience.* The language you use should reflect your subject. For example, compare the language used in the Nelly McClung profile with that used in the Dr. Norman Bethune profile. As well,

when writing a biography or biographical profile, you should let the subject speak for himself or herself in addition to others who might know or have known the individual. Quotations and dialogue add a sense of truth to the work.

The Tips on Writing a Narrative Essay (p. 160) might also be of help.

7. The Review

KEY WORK:

> "The spell of a Shakespeare lover" — Robertson Davies (a review of *The Life and Times of William Shakespeare* by Peter Levi)

ASSOCIATED READINGS:

> "How Do You Know It's Good?" — Marya Mannes
> "Your Brain Has a Mind of Its Own" — Janice Dineen (a review of *The Brain Has a Mind of Its Own* by Richard Restak)
> "Her life entire" — Douglas Glover (a review of *Cat's Eye* by Margaret Atwood)
> "How Atwood creates novels that are mortuaries" — Ray Conlogue (a review of *Cat's Eye* by Margaret Atwood)
> Tips on Writing a Review

Because you lead such a busy life, reviews or short excerpts in advertisements can help you decide what books to read, what plays or films to see, and what concerts to attend. In fact, an influential reviewer or critic often has a profound impact on the success or failure of an endeavour.

A good review informs the audience about the nature of the work and its creator(s) and suggests whether the endeavour is worthy of attention. It also establishes a tone that is appropriate for the audience for whom it is intended. A good review also permits the personal voice and stance of the writer or speaker to stand out. It is this latter quality that often sets good reviews apart as works of art in themselves.

As a busy student, you should consider how reviews can help your research process. For example, a book review will quickly indicate if that book will help with your research. As well, examining several reviews of the same material will help you explore different perspectives on the topic. The Key Work, a review by Robertson Davies of a new book on Shakespeare, exhibits all the qualities of a good review. The first Associated Reading, "How Do You Know It's Good?" by Marya Mannes delineates the criteria for being a good reviewer or critic. The remaining reviews demonstrate other important qualities and the importance of examining more than one review in order to gain a well-rounded perspective of a work.

Conventions of the Review

Purpose	To evaluate, appraise the worth of
Audience	Varied, but often specialized
Tone	Varied, often depending on reviewer's perceived quality of material
Voice	Strong and often highly individualistic
Response	Varies from serious to humorous response
Language	LEVEL — Varied, depending on material and intended audience CHARACTERISTICS — Often highly specialized
Structure	Can vary in order, but must include a summary and develop an opinion

BEFORE READING

1. Complete this role-play in pairs.

   Imagine that you and a friend have just seen a specific movie or watched a particular television show and you are sitting together afterwards discussing it.

   Your friend says, "Well, what did you think of it?"
   "It was really good," you reply enthusiastically.
   Your friend looks you in the eye and says, "How do you know it's good?"

   Continue the dialogue for five minutes, articulating the principles behind your definition of "good."

2. What is the key difference in purpose between a report and a review? (If you have not already examined The Report, you may want to refer to the notes in Unit 4.)

3. In groups or as a whole class identify the reviewer's or critic's responsibilities to the work and to the audience.

The spell of a Shakespeare lover

ROBERTSON DAVIES

It may as well be said at the beginning as at the end of this review: Peter Levi, Oxford Professor of Poetry, has written a very good book about William Shakespeare, and you will find it fresh and pleasant to read.

But why would anybody write another book about Shakespeare when already great libraries groan under the weight of volumes about every aspect of the poet's life and art? Levi has an excellent answer: "The whole point of writing a biography of Shakespeare at all is to try to relate his life to his writings and his writings to his life . . . All that a writer like myself, who is not a professional Shakespearean, can hope to do is to offer a fresh, partial point of view, prolegomena, a few new or unregarded crumbs for the general pile, a first step for someone younger who may be just starting." And as evidence of the partiality of which he speaks, he declares that Shakespeare "is the most enjoyable and the greatest poet I have ever read, and the most interesting, because he can do more in poetry with his little finger than I can in a lifetime, because of his exhilarating unevenness, and exemplary mixture of concentration and carelessness, his images, his phrases, his characters, and his dramatic contradictions."

Levi is an enthusiast, and he wants to infect us with his enthusiasm. As I am already an enthusiast I am not open to this spell, but readers who still wonder what all the fuss over Shakespeare is about will find this book a happy, genial and persuasive explanation.

What does he mean by "a professional Shakespearean"? He means such scholars as Sidney Lee, E.K. Chambers, Dover Wilson, C.J. Sisson and many others who have given their lives to minute examination of Shakespeare's works, to textual criticism and reconstruction, to ferreting out the minutest details that relate to the poet's life; these are the people to whom we owe the fine editions on which our appreciation of the poet rests, and for which modern, serious productions of the plays draw their strength.

But of course Levi is modest; he knows a great deal about Shakespeare, and as a critic he speaks with an authority which not all the noteworthy scholars can rival, because he is himself a poet, and a man of broad sympathies, open to the esthetic and emotional impact of the great work as not every scholar may be.

As a poet himself, and an acknowledged authority on that subject, he devotes a good deal of his discussion to Shakespeare's poetic techniques and the innovations by means of which he enlarged the scope of poetry in his own time, and set a mark of excellence in that art which has not since been surpassed. Levi is gentle with his subject; he spares no time for that royal critic, King George III, who exclaimed to Fanny Burney: "Was there ever such stuff as a great part of Shakespeare? Only one must not say so! But what think you? — what? — is there not sad stuff? — what? — what?"

If we take Shakespeare whole, and take him seriously, we must agree with the frank King. There is indeed sad stuff, but there is also stuff that is unsurpassed in dramatic and lyric power. Shakespeare must have written at great speed to do all that he did in what we should regard as a short professional career. He wrote under stress of time, and under the demands of his professional colleagues. Actors have no poetic conscience, and theatre managers are slave-drivers; the miracle of Shakespeare is that he could do what he did in rough theatrical conditions. What sort of man was he?

We know a great deal more about Shakespeare than we know about most of his contemporaries. There is a substantial body of documentary material which gives us a picture of his quality as a man of business and his prudence about money. There are a good many references to him in the writings of his fellow poets, and they show him to have been neither a shrinking violet nor yet a man who involved himself in literary and political rows. We know quite a lot about his family, his forebears and his children, about his ambition to establish himself as a gentleman with a fine house and a coat of arms, about where he lived, and what we can derive from these things about how he lived. We know who were his friends and patrons.

But his admirers have never thought this enough. They want to know about his innermost secrets and have attempted to divine these things from his works. Although many of these searchers are learned people, they have often been coarse, foolishly imaginative and frequently downright silly about what they think they have found. Peter Levi is firm in dismissing much that passes as Shakespeare biography.

Was Shakespeare a homosexual? Building on matter to be found in the sonnets, many writers have said so, and now that homosexuality is enjoying a vogue of popularity after a long period of condemnation, this opinion has become almost accepted fact. But Levi denies that there is any reason to suppose that he was on terms beyond strong friendship with his patron Southampton, which led to warmth of expression no more extreme than that with which Alfred Tennyson wrote of his friend Arthur Henry Hallam. Nobody has ever seriously asserted that Tennyson and Hallam were physical lovers; such devotion was, and is, frequent among men of powerful sensibility in every walk of life, without being homosexuality in the modern acceptance of the term. Not "gay" in the fashionable misuse of the word. Indeed, Levi presents Shakespeare as a man of chaste life, on excellent terms with his wife, and a fond father; much evidence supports this opinion and there is nothing but guesswork to contradict it. There are people to whom the notion of a chaste poet is incredible; they wish Shakespeare to have been what they themselves would be, given his genius and his opportunities — or so they like to think.

Was Shakespeare a Catholic? Levi accepts evidence, which is not conclusive, that his parents were married in that faith, but Shakespeare does not seem to have been a man who ran, in his public life, against the stream of his time, and Catholicism was very dangerous in the age of Elizabeth and James I.

Was Shakespeare a drunkard? No evidence, says Levi, though many people think that a poet who is not a drunkard is less a poet in consequence.

Did Shakespeare believe in the supernatural? Certainly he knew Reginald Scot's Discoverie Of Witchcraft and made good use of it, but that book was not pro-witchcraft in its tone. It was, by the way, reprinted in 1930, edited by the much-abused but invaluable Montague Summers, and Levi does not seem to know this. Certainly witchcraft, ghosts and supernatural beings served Shakespeare well, for they allowed him to deal with elements in human experience which were not, before the coming of depth-psychology, approachable by other means.

May we learn anything of Shakespeare's life from the tone of works he wrote at particular periods of his career? Serious, otherwise sensible scholars have allowed themselves great liberty in describing various "periods" of the poet's life, when they assume that he was melancholy because of the death of his father, or his son, or his brother. What they do not know is that creative force is not directly related to outward circumstances. In another art, for instance, we know that Mozart wrote sublimely serene music at times when his outward life was heavy with anxieties and tragic forebodings. Molière wrote splendid comedy when beset by ill health and domestic anxiety. Dare we assume that because Shakespeare sometimes wrote bitterly about love that he was at the outs with Anne Hathaway? Because the poet speaks ill of syphilis, need he have had it?

Levi is particularly good on the absurdity of such speculations. Shakespeare had his ups and downs, no doubt, like the rest of us, but we simply cannot tell how or if it affected his work.

We all tend to create Shakespeare, as we do God, in our own image. Samuel Johnson postulated a Johnsonian Shakespeare, who occasionally had to be rebuked for descents into what the Doctor called "unresisting imbecility." To Frank Harris, the playwright was a boozer, a wencher, a man of violent passions. To Bernard Shaw he was a man of irrepressible gaiety of whom he says, with admirable frankness, "I am convinced that he was very like myself." Has Peter Levi created a Shakespeare in his own image?

Certainly he has given us a reasonable, credible Shakespeare, not marred by romantic guesswork, though he does suggest that we may form a notion of what Shakespeare's aristocratic patron Southampton looked like by observing his descendant, the Princess of Wales, who has, says Peter Levi, "a trick of the eyes" which was that of the poet's dear friend. This writer is great on cousinships, connections and descents, as were the Elizabethans. As a biographer of Shakespeare he has the uncommon advantage of an unsleeping sense of humor; he loves not only the poet's wit but also his merriment, and his bawdry.

More precise scholars than he have lacked this clue to Shakespeare's mind, as they have lacked an understanding of music. Levi knows English poetry, and the poetry of Shakespeare's time especially, through and through, and he appreciates it as one who is himself a poet and not simply a critic. Because he is so discreet in using the provable facts about Shakespeare, and forebears to make dangerous leaps from fact to speculation, we forgive him occasional "temerarious ruminations," as he calls them, such as when he speculates that late in his life Shakespeare and Ben Jonson, carousing in the Mermaid Tavern, may have wakened the infant Milton, who was born a few houses away, in 1608. We enjoy, with this biographer, his inability to resist a fascinating, seemingly irrelevant fact, such as that Shakespeare's daughter, Susanna, when she had colic, was given an enema of a pint of heated sherry, by her physician husband John Hall; we are glad to know that "this presently brought forth a great deal of Wind, and freed her from all Pain."

Is this really irrelevant? Does not Shakespeare's daughter's bout of wind somehow humanize the greatest of English poets, and bring him nearer? Levi thinks so, and this reviewer agrees.

Peter Levi will trouble some readers. He dislikes Coriolanus, which happens to be a favorite of mine. He admits that his opinion of some of the plays has been influenced by fine stage performances, which will give austere scholars fits, for they cannot bear to think that the player might know a few things they have missed. But all in all, this delightful book can be recommended, not perhaps as all you will ever want to know about Shakespeare, and certainly not as a substitute for reading his works, but as an admirable place to start on that endless splendid voyage of discovery.

EXPLORING THE REVIEW

1. Prove that Davies has the following qualities of a good reviewer: a specialized knowledge of the area represented by the work being reviewed and the appropriate specialized language to deal with the material and concepts.

2. Why does Davies think that the author, Peter Levi, has sufficient credentials to write a book on Shakespeare?

3. To what extent is Davies' voice evident in this review? Explain its impact on the review.

4. a. What does Davies see as some of the weaknesses in Levi's biography?

   b. Does Davies support this observation convincingly? Explain.

5. Using this review as a guide, establish a set of principles or criteria for writing a thorough review.

EXTENSIVE STUDY

1. Peter Levi's book and Robertson Davies' review raise a number of questions and issues about William Shakespeare. In pairs, role-play an interview between either Levi and Shakespeare or Davies and Shakespeare in which you raise some of those questions and issues. ("Shakespeare" may wish to refer to some of the characters in his plays to illustrate his point.)

2. Read Marya Mannes' essay, "How Do You Know It's Good?" (p. 195).
   a. What does she say is the role of the reviewer or critic in judging a work?
   b. What does she say are the reviewer's two "keys to your judgement in all the arts"?
   c. To what extent do you agree with Mannes' advice to the reviewer? (You might wish to compare her criteria with the criteria you established from the Davies' review.)

3. Read Janice Dineen's review, "Your Brain Has a Mind of Its Own" (p. 201) and assess the extent to which it is a "good" review by applying the two "keys to judgement" described by Marya Mannes and any other criteria you have developed.

4. Compare the two reviews of Margaret Atwood's novel, *Cat's Eye*, by Douglas Glover (p. 204) and Ray Conlogue (p. 212) using the following headings:
   • knowledge of subject and writer
   • revelation of contents of the book
   • judgement of quality of the book
   • merits of the review itself as a piece of writing

5. Locate and read two reviews of the same movie or concert in two different newspapers or magazines.
   a. Note the similarities in and differences between the two reviews.
   b. Consider the intended audiences for each publication.
   c. Using criteria you developed in Exploring the Review and/ or from reading Mannes' "How Do You Know It's Good?" (p. 195), determine which is the better review and why.

THE WRITING FOLDER

1. Using criteria established in this section as a guide, write a "good" review of a current work you are reading or studying.

2. Write an imaginary interview in which Margaret Atwood talks with either Ray Conlogue or Douglas Glover about his review.

3. Not all reviews are positive. Adopt the persona of a bemused or outraged critic and review a book, play, or movie of your choice, either real or invented. Use irony, satire, or other appropriate rhetorical devices.

INDEPENDENT STUDY

1. Read two or more of Atwood novels (including *Cat's Eye*) and support or refute Conlogue's assertion that Atwood writes novels that are "mortuaries."
   - You may work with a partner.
   - Research other reviewers' perspectives on the novels.
   - Your response could take the form of an essay or a combined oral presentation and written submission. If you work with a partner, you might wish to set up a debate.

2. Read Richard Restak's book, *The Brain Has a Mind of Its Own*, and at least two reviews of it. Write a comparative assessment of Janice Dineen's review based on your analysis of the book and the reviews.

3. View two or more film versions of *Hamlet* (or another Shakespearean play) and, in consultation with your teacher-librarian, locate and read reviews of them. Write a report on your analysis of the films, concluding with your recommendation as to which movie provides the best film version of the play to date.

TIMED READING AND WRITING

1. Read the review "Your Brain Has a Mind of Its Own" (p. 201) and summarize the reviewer's assessment in roughly one hundred words.

2. Read Douglas Glover's review of Margaret Atwood's *Cat's Eye* (p. 204) and assess the effectiveness of his imagery in reinforcing the tone of the review.

3. This is a timed *viewing* and writing task:
   View a film of your choice and, assuming the role of a newspaper reviewer with an immediate deadline, write an on-the-spot review.

How Do You Know It's Good?

MARYA MANNES

Suppose there were no critics to tell us how to react to a picture, a play, or a new composition of music. Suppose we wandered innocent as the dawn into an art exhibition of unsigned paintings. By what standards, by what values would we decide whether they were good or bad, talented or untalented, successes or failures? How can we ever know that what we think is right?

For the last fifteen or twenty years the fashion in criticism or appreciation of the arts has been to deny the existence of any valid criteria and to make the words "good" or "bad" irrelevant, immaterial, and inapplicable. There is no such thing, we are told, as a set of standards, first acquired through experience and knowledge and later imposed on the subject under discussion. This has been a popular approach, for it relieves the critic of the responsibility of judgment and the public of the necessity of knowledge. It pleases those resentful of disciplines, it flatters the empty-minded by calling them open-minded, it comforts the confused. Under the banner of democracy and the kind of equality which our forefathers did *not* mean, it says, in effect, "Who are you to tell us what is good or bad?" This is the same cry used so long and so effectively by the producers of mass media who insist that it is the public, not they, who decides what it wants to hear and see, and that for a critic to say that *this* program is bad and this program is good is purely a reflection of personal taste. Nobody recently has expressed this philosophy more succinctly than Dr. Frank Stanton, the highly intelligent president of CBS television. At a hearing before the Federal Communications Commission, this phrase escaped him under questioning: "One man's mediocrity is another man's good program."

There is no better way of saying, "No values are absolute." There is another important aspect to this philosophy of *laissez-faire*: It is the fear, in all observers of all forms of art, of guessing wrong. This fear is well come by, for who has not heard of the contemporary outcries against artists who later were called great? Every age has its arbiters who do not grow with their times, who cannot tell evolution from revolution or the difference between frivolous faddism, amateurish experimentation, and profound and necessary change. Who wants to be caught *flagrante delicto* with an error of judgment as serious as this? It is far safer, and certainly easier, to look at a picture or a play or a poem and to say, "This is hard to understand, but it may be good," or simply to welcome it as a new form. The word "new" — in our country especially — has magical connotations. What is new must be good; what is old is probably bad. And if a critic can describe the new in language that nobody can understand, he's safer still. If he has mastered the art of saying nothing with exquisite complexity, nobody can quote him later as saying anything.

But all these, I maintain, are forms of abdication from the responsibility of judgment. In creating, the artist commits himself; in appreciating, you have a commitment of your own. For after all, it is the audience which makes the arts. A climate of appreciation is essential to its flowering, and the higher the expectations of the public, the better the performance of the artist. Conversely, only a public ill-served by its critics could have accepted as art and as literature so much in these last years that has been neither. If anything goes, everything goes; and at the bottom of the junkpile lie the discarded standards too.

But what are these standards? How do you get them? How do you know they're the right ones? How can you make a clear pattern out of so many intangibles, including that greatest one, the very private I?

Well for one thing, it's fairly obvious that the more you read and see and hear, the more equipped you'll be to practice that art of association which is at the basis of all understanding and judgment. The more you live and the more you look, the more aware you are of a consistent pattern — as universal as the stars, as the tides, as breathing, as night and day — underlying everything. I would call this pattern and this rhythm an order. Not order — *an* order. Within it exists an incredible diversity of forms. Without it lies chaos. I would further call this order — this incredible diversity held within one pattern — health. And I would call chaos — the wild cells of destruction — sickness. It is in the end up to you to distinguish between the diversity that is health and the chaos that is sickness, and you can't do this without a process of association that can link a bar of Mozart with the corner of a Vermeer painting, or a Stravinsky score with a Picasso abstraction; or that can relate an aggressive act with a Franz Kline painting and a fit of coughing with a John Cage composition.

There is no accident in the fact that certain expressions of art live for all time and that others die with the moment, and although you may not always define the reasons, you can ask the questions. What does an artist say that is timeless; how does he say it? How much is fashion, how much is merely reflection? Why is Sir Walter Scott so hard to read now, and Jane Austen not? Why is baroque right for one age and too effulgent for another?

Can a standard of craftsmanship apply to art of all ages, or does each have its own, and different, definitions? You may have been aware, inadvertently, that craftsmanship has become a dirty word these years because, again, it implies standards — something done well or done badly. The result of this convenient avoidance is a plenitude of actors who can't project their voices, singers who can't phrase their songs, poets who can't communicate emotion, and writers who have no vocabulary — not to speak of painters who can't draw. The dogma now is that craftsmanship gets in the way of expression. You can do better if you don't know *how* you do it, let alone *what* you're doing.

I think it is time you helped reverse this trend by trying to rediscover craft: the command of the chosen instrument, whether it is a brush, a word, or a voice. When you begin to detect the difference between freedom and sloppiness, between serious experimentation and egotherapy, between skill and slickness, between strength and violence, you are on your way to separating the sheep from the goats, a form of segregation denied us for quite a while. All you need to restore it is a small bundle of standards and a Geiger counter that detects fraud, and we might begin our tour of the arts in an area where both are urgently needed: contemporary painting.

I don't know what's worse: to have to look at acres of bad art to find the little good, or to read what the critics say about it all. In no other field of expression has so much double-talk flourished, so much confusion prevailed, and so much nonsense been circulated: further evidence of the close interdependence between the arts and the critical climate they inhabit. It will be my pleasure to share with you some of this double-talk so typical of our times.

Item one: preface for a catalogue of an abstract painter:

"Time-bound meditation experiencing a life; sincere with plastic piety at the threshold of hallowed arcana; a striving for pure ideation giving shape to inner drive; formalized patterns where neural balances reach a fiction." End of quote. Know what this artist paints like now?

Item two: a review in the *Art News*:

". . . a weird and disparate assortment of material, but the monstrosity which bloomed into his most recent cancer of aggregations is present in some form everywhere. . . ." Then, later, "A gluttony of things and processes terminated by a glorious constipation."

Item three, same magazine, review of an artist who welds automobile fragments into abstract shapes:

"Each fragment . . . is made an extreme of human exasperation, torn at and fought all the way, and has its rightness of form as if by accident. *Any technique that requires order or discipline would just be the human ego.* No, these must be egoless, uncontrolled, undesigned and different enough to give you a bang — fifty miles an hour around a telephone pole. . . ."

"Any technique that requires order of discipline would just be the human ego." What does he mean — "just be"? What are they really talking about? Is this journalism? Is it criticism? Or is it that other convenient abdication from standards of performance and judgment practiced by so many artists and critics that they, like certain writers who deal only in sickness and depravity, "reflect the chaos about them"? Again, whose chaos? Whose depravity?

I had always thought that the prime function of art was to create order *out* of chaos — again, not the order of neatness or rigidity or convention or artifice, but the order of clarity by which one will and one vision could draw the essential truth out of apparent confusion. I still do. It is not enough to use parts of a car to convey the brutality of the machine. This is as lavishly representative, and just as easy, as arranging dried flowers under glass to convey nature.

Speaking of which, i.e., the use of real materials (burlap, old gloves, bottletops) in lieu of pigment, this is what one critic had to say about an exhibition of Assemblage at the Museum of Modern Art last year:

Spotted throughout the show are indisputable works of art, accounting for a quarter or even a half of the total display. But the remainder are works of non-art, anti-art, and art substitutes that are the aesthetic counterparts of the social deficiencies that land people in the clink on charges of vagrancy. These aesthetic bankrupts . . . have no legitimate ideological roof over their heads and not the price of a square intellectual meal, much less a spiritual sandwich, in their pockets.

I quote these words of John Canaday of *The New York Times* as an example of the kind of criticism which puts responsibility to an intelligent public above popularity with an intellectual coterie. Canaday has the courage to say what he thinks and the capacity to say it clearly: two qualities notably absent from his profession.

Next to art, I would say that appreciation and evaluation in the field of music is the most difficult. For it is rarely possible to judge a new composition at one hearing only. What seems confusing or fragmented at first might well become clear and organic a third time. Or it might not. The only salvation here for the listener is, again, an instinct born of experience and association which allows him to separate intent from accident, design from experimentation, and pretense from conviction. Much of contemporary music is, like its sister art, merely a reflection of the composer's own fragmentation: an absorption in self and symbols at the expense of communication with others. The artist, in short, says to the public: If you don't understand this, it's because you're dumb. I maintain that you are not. You may have to go part way or even halfway to meet the artist, but if you must go the whole way, it's his fault, not yours. Hold fast to that. And remember it too when you read new poetry, that estranged sister of music.

> A multitude of causes, unknown to former times, are now acting with a combined force to blunt the discriminating powers of the mind, and, unfitting it for all voluntary exertion, to reduce it to a state of almost savage torpor. The most effective of these causes are the great national events which are daily taking place and the increasing accumulation of men in cities, where the uniformity of their occupations produces a craving for extraordinary incident, which the rapid communication of intelligence hourly gratifies. To this tendency of life and manners, the literature and theatrical exhibitions of the country have conformed themselves.

This startlingly applicable comment was written in the year 1800 by William Wordsworth in the preface to his *Lyrical Ballads*; and it has been cited by Edwin Muir in his recently published book, *The Estate of Poetry*. Muir states that poetry's effective range and influence have diminished alarmingly in the modern world. He believes in the inherent and indestructible qualities of the human mind and the great and permanent objects that act upon it, and suggests that the audience will increase when "poetry loses what obscurity is left in it by attempting greater themes, for great themes have to be stated clearly." If you keep that firmly in mind and resist, in Muir's words, "the vast dissemination of secondary objects that isolate us from the natural world," you have gone a long way toward equipping yourself for the examination of any work of art.

When you come to theatre, in this extremely hasty tour of the arts, you can approach it on two different levels. You can bring to it anticipation and innocence, giving yourself up, as it were, to the life on the stage and reacting to it emotionally, if the play is good, or listlessly, if the play is boring; a part of the audience organism that expresses its favor by silence or laughter and its disfavor by coughing and rustling. Or you can bring to it certain critical faculties that may heighten, rather than diminish, your enjoyment.

You can ask yourselves whether the actors are truly in their parts or merely projecting themselves; whether the scenery helps or hurts the mood; whether the playwright is honest with himself, his characters, and you. Somewhere along the line you can learn to distinguish between the true creative act and the false arbitrary gesture; between fresh observation and stale cliché; between the avant-garde play that is pretentious drivel and the avant-garde play that finds new ways to say old truths.

Purpose and craftsmanship — end and means — these are the keys to your judgment in all the arts. What is this painter trying to say when he slashes a broad band of black across a white canvas and lets the edges dribble down? Is it a statement of violence? Is it a self-portrait? If it is *one* of these, has he made you believe it? Or is this a gesture of the ego or a form of therapy? If it shocks you, what does it shock you into?

And what of this tight little painting of bright flowers in a vase? Is the painter saying anything new about flowers? Is it different from a million other canvases of flowers? Has it any life, any meaning, beyond its statement? Is there any pleasure in its forms or texture? The question is not whether a thing is abstract or representational, whether it is "modern" or conventional. The question, inexorably, is whether it is good. And this is a decision which only you, on the basis of instinct, experience, and association, can make for yourself. It takes independence and courage. It involves, moreover, the risk of wrong decision and the humility, after the passage of time, of recognizing it as such. As we grow and change and learn, our attitudes can change too, and what we once thought obscure or "difficult" can later emerge as coherent and illuminating. Entrenched prejudices, obdurate opinions are as sterile as no opinions at all.

Yet standards there are, timeless as the universe itself. And when you have committed yourself to them, you have acquired a passport to that elusive but immutable realm of truth. Keep it with you in the forests of bewilderment. And never be afraid to speak up.

Your Brain Has a Mind of Its Own

JANICE DINEEN

So you think you're a civilized, reasonable human being? In the face of a threat, you will examine all the options and do the well-bred thing?

Well, meet Richard Restak, the doctor who knows all about the beast you really are.

Deep below the civilized layers of your brain lies the primitive limbic system which hasn't changed in thousands of years. Human behavior has evolved away from the caveman, but not this bit of your brain. The limbic system is something we all share with jungle animals.

Here's what Restak says about the darker depths of his own brain: "I'm certain that all kinds of chained and muzzled demons lurk in the murky outer banks of my brainscape." The socialized parts of the brain live in an uneasy truce with these creepy-crawlies, he suggests.

In a situation that feels very threatening, anyone may find the limbic system rousing itself to create a panic attack, a sudden outburst of rage, or a show of aggressive or violent behavior.

Restak, 49, calls it "the fiction of the reasonable man" — the theory that, when you're under severe stress, your limbic system can mug the civilized parts of the brain, and take right over.

It's one of the thoughts that unfolds entertainingly in *The Brain Has a Mind of Its Own* (Harmony Books), his latest book about the insides of people's heads. It's a collection of 41 short essays setting out the most readable of the things he has learned and theorized in his years in brain medicine.

He's a Washington, D.C., neurologist and psychiatrist, so he works with both the brain and the mind.

His mom wanted him to be a writer. His dad pressed him to be a doctor. He's balancing careers to please everyone by writing books about his medical specialty.

Restak writes about adventures of the brain that everyone can recognize, such as the state he calls information overload. That's when you have so many things to remember some of them just seem to fall out of your head. It's like a telephone switchboard getting jammed because of too many calls on Mother's Day.

When your brain's circuits get jammed with too much information, Restak says, you show some of the symptoms of information overload. You start out getting irritable, or bored and unresponsive, and you find you can't make even the simplest of decisions. Eventually you can be overwhelmed by a feeling of "so what?" about everything.

The only way to recover, he says, is to cut yourself off from new information for a while, because any that you hear will be disorienting and confusing. Unplug the TV and the radio, and steer conversations into restful areas. For self-protection, he says, free yourself as much as possible from the junk food of information — the material full of bulk and trivia but lacking in any intellectual value.

In fact, Restak declares, television news can be bad for your mental health on a daily basis. Reading about a personal tragedy or a natural disaster is a completely different experience from seeing video images of it. Reading sends the information through the part of the brain that deals with language, reason and logic. This helps to deal with the information in a reasonable way.

Seeing video pictures of it, however, bypasses the reasoning part of the brain and has an enormous psychological impact. "We resonate to it in the right hemisphere of our brain," Restak explains.

The fear, horror and outrage this can stir up becomes more than a person can cope with. To protect itself, the brain will eventually shut down. "Hideous images cease to arouse any emotion except, perhaps, boredom," he says.

Watching stark, shocking, bloody pictures numbs the sensitivities. It results in personal insensitivity to the plight of people suffering hunger, unemployment, pain and death, he says. The violence and horror on television and in movies has "injurious effects on our brains and mental health," he adds.

"It's okay to read it in the newspaper. That's a different brain reaction. But TV news changes our brain function." He calls its depictions of violence "obscene."

A person's whole outlook on life is influenced by pathways in the brain forged by the way you act and circumstances you live in, Restak says, making it more natural for you to react with either hostility or compassion. For example, Mother Teresa finds it easier to be kind and compassionate than to be angry and competitive because her neuronal pathways have been tracked into habits of kindness.

Others may find they have tracked themselves into habits of anger and aggression, and the neuronal paths in their brains now automatically send them in that direction.

"Lawyers, and others whose lifestyles are focused on conflict and dissent, really have to make a big extra effort if they want to do something gentle," he says. "There is nothing soft or tender in these people. Their whole style of life is conflict and aggression. We know the brain works in the way made easier by the paths that have been set. Essentially, we are what we do.

"It's not impossible to change, but it's very hard."

People living in big cities are more liable to set neuronal paths of impatience, frustration, cynicism and anger, according to Restak. Traffic, crowds, strangers cutting in on you in line or trying to cheat you, and similar metropolitan scenes from daily life can take their toll on the structure of the brain.

Studies also suggest that a gentle, loving environment has a positive impact on the brain, he says, and history tells us the same thing.

People are defined by their actions, though, not by their thoughts, Restak observes. Everyone has things they don't want to think about, and everyone finds these thoughts dancing up to the surface, teasing and tormenting from time to time. Health issues, fears about the past and future, difficult relationships, money problems, worries about physical appearance, and rejection and loneliness are some common ones.

The more you try to control and banish these thoughts, the more it ends up causing you mental anguish. In a mild form, this means that the more you struggle to try to get to sleep, the more likely you are to toss and turn all night. In more severe forms, the struggle to eliminate unwanted thoughts can lead to some kinds of mental illness such as depression or severe obsession.

The answer Restak offers is deciding to accept whatever thoughts arise in the disturbing area and willingly giving them room in your head. This denies them the status of unwanted thoughts, robs them of their power and gives you a new feeling of freedom. Eventually, he says, you become bored by the thoughts and they no longer arise.

One of the most uplifting messages in Restak's book is that it's possible to deliberately become smarter. "There's no question about that," he states. He writes that activities, habits and interests not only define personalities, but also affect the physical structure of our brains.

It's not necessarily true that the bigger your brain, or the more brain cells you have, the smarter you are. Someone with a smaller brain and fewer brain cells may actually have a higher intellectual function than another person with a big brain and lots more brain cells. Charlemagne had a bigger brain than Einstein, but Einstein had the greater intellectual gift.

The key seems to be how numerous and intricate your brain cell networks are, even the cells that are far away from each other. And you can improve your networks by enriching your environment, interests and activities. By developing new talents and taking up new interests, Restak says, you can literally change your brain for the better.

New information and new abilities can stimulate improvement in the brain at any time of life, including old age.

Her life entire

DOUGLAS GLOVER

Margaret Atwood's public image is huge. She's an icon and a target; she's the blank sheet everyone gets to write on. She's the face on the construction-site wall that everyone gets to deface — moustache, halo, horns, the works.

When Elaine Risley, the acclaimed Canadian painter-heroine of Atwood's new novel, *Cat's Eye*, comes upon a defaced poster of herself on a Toronto street corner, she thinks:

> I have achieved, finally, a face that a moustache can be drawn on, a face that attracts moustaches. A public face, a face worth defacing. This is an accomplishment.

This is vintage Atwood, dry, deadpan, and deadly. She writes jokes with as many barbs as a sea urchin. But Risley is not Atwood — or is she? Risley and Atwood are the same age. They share an entomologist father, parents from Nova Scotia, and childhood summers spent in the northern Ontario woods. Atwood loves to play hide-and-seek at the place where autobiography and fiction meet, always ensuring there is a back door open for quick escapes. The front matter for *Cat's Eye* contains the following disclaimer.

> This is a work of fiction. Although its form is that of an autobiography, it is not one.

Cat's Eye is Atwood's seventh novel. It is dense, intricate, and superb, as thematically diverse and complex as anything she has written. It is what you might expect from a writer at mid-career, mid-life: a portrait of the artist, a summation of what she knows about art and people. It is also an Atwoodian *Under the Volcano*, a vision of Toronto as Hell.

On one level (in Atwood novels, it is always necessary to specify levels), *Cat's Eye* is about the life of Elaine Risley, artist, painter of neorealist works pleasantly reminiscent of Jack Chambers and a raft of other Canadian painters (Atwood gives a list). Risley's life splits into two parts: up to age nine, and after age nine. This is because, for this novel at least, Atwood has adopted the psychological truism that our personalities are more or less set by the time we are five (or six, or nine). "Get me out of this," thinks a middle-aged Risley, late in the novel. "I'm locked in. I don't want to be nine years old forever."

What happens to Risley up to age nine is gruesome. Her earliest memories are Edenic, her family wandering happily like nomads through northern Ontario, sleeping in tents, searching for the insects that feed her father's research. When she is eight, however, the Risleys move to Toronto, to an unfinished house near one of the many ravines that cut through the city's geography. To her new schoolmates, little Elaine is a primitive, a freak.

Three friends, Carol, Grace, and Cordelia (variously associated in the novel's image pattern with the three muses or the three witches in *Macbeth*), take it upon themselves to socialize her, to teach her their language ("twin sets" and "pin curls"), games (cutting up Eaton's catalogues for scrapbooks), proprieties (girls don't climb ladders for fear of showing their underpants) and religion (Grace Smeath's pinched and pious family invites Risley to their church).

But the project soon reveals itself as insidious, as something like the childish reign of terror in Golding's *Lord of the Flies*. Cordelia, especially, torments Risley, humiliating her, tripping her up over words (words like *bugger* and *kike*), forcing her to submit to trials, even a mock burial. Risley begins to eat herself (chewing her fingers, her hair, tearing the skin off her feet); she has fainting spells. "Cordelia," she thinks, "you have made me feel I was nothing."

At nine, she suffers a nervous breakdown—or mystical vision—when Cordelia forces her to descend into a ravine haunted by "bad men" (unseen child molesters) and polluted by the runoff from a nearby cemetery (atoms of dissolved dead people). Fainting with terror, Risley falls through the thin creek ice, then sees the Virgin Mary (variously through the book: Our Lady of Perpetual Help, Our Lady of Perpetual Hell, the Virgin of Lost Things, and so on) wearing a blue robe, with her red heart clutched to her breast, floating down from an ancient, rotting foot-bridge to comfort her.

This is the climax of the first half of *Cat's Eye*. Following Atwood's psychological paradigm, Risley represses everything— "I've forgotten things, I've forgotten that I've forgotten them.... I've forgotten all the bad things that happened."

A few days later, she returns to school, but the whole tone of her world has altered. She remains friends with Cordelia, but her friendship is distant and cynical. She develops a "mean mouth," a razor-sharp wit with which to flay her playmates. Her secret, the past she has forgotten, gives her an edge. She and Cordelia trade places, the tormented becoming the tormentor. Years later, when Cordelia calls her from an asylum where she has been locked up for attempted suicide, Risley refuses to help.

Risley's first painting instructor calls her an "unfinished woman."

> You can draw objects very well. But as yet you cannot draw life . . . Both are necessary. Dirt and soul . . . There must be passion.

Of course, he's wrong; he's telling Risley this to get her in bed (which he does). Risley's objects are her passion and her salvation. When objects from her childhood — a silver toaster, a wringer washing machine, a cat's-eye marble, three girls, Grace Smeath's mother stretched on a couch, the Holy Virgin on a bridge — come unbidden to her canvases, she thinks:

> I know that these things must be memories, but they do not have the quality of memories . . . They arrive detached from any context; they are simply there, in isolation . . . I have no image of myself in

relation to them. They are suffused with anxiety. The anxiety is in the things themselves.

On the surface (in Atwood novels it is always necessary to specify, etc.), Risley remains very much a mirror of her generation: emotionally aloof yet ambitious, she decides to be a painter, has affairs, marries another painter, bears a child, flirts with the women's movement, separates, and escapes to Vancouver. Her relationship with her first husband, Jon, is one of the delights of this book, harrowing, comic, good-hearted and sly — note especially the way Jon flits from fad to fad only to end up making sci-fi movies in Hollywood while Risley stubbornly sticks to her own "reactionary" agenda and becomes a great artist.

But Risley's real life, the life of her emotions, the life of the luminous, grotesque, mythic creatures of her childhood, has gone underground, only to reappear in her pictures. The drama of the second half of *Cat's Eye* climaxes when Risley attends the first retrospective show of her work. All the images of her childhood are there, hung in a Toronto gallery appropriately named Sub-Versions; her paintings are like stations of the cross, her past recapitulated in her art. And the last painting of all, the keystone and culmination of her oeuvre, a picture called *Unified Field Theory*, is Risley's childhood vision — Risley in the ravine, the Virgin floating above the bridge.

Cat's Eye is Risley's Progress, the journey of her soul; when she visits the ravine the day after her retrospective, she is cured. The locus of her breakdown is no longer charged or mythic.

> There was no voice. No one came walking on air down from the bridge, there was no lady in a dark cloak . . . The bridge is only a bridge, the river a river, the sky a sky. . . .
>
> Risley has healed the rift, banished the ambiguity of language, rediscovered her self (or selves — the lost Cordelia, the child Elaine, Grace . . .) in the univocal meaning of things.

Although *Cat's Eye* is not autobiography, in a sense Atwood is teaching her readers how to read *her*. All Atwood's novels are alike in this: they contain highly complex patterns of images. Usually the title of the novel is hinged to its dominant pattern — in *The Edible Woman*, Marian's anorexia, in *Surfacing*, the narrator diving into a lake to look for Indian petroglyphs, in *Life Before Man*, Lesje's dinosaur fantasies, in *Bodily Harm*, cancer, surgery, torture.

The passion, joy, and craft that Atwood pours into these patterns reminds me of something the fictional poet John Shade says in Vladimir Nabokov's novel *Pale Fire*:

> I feel I understand Existence or at least a minute part of my existence only through my art in terms of *combinatorial delight*.

Or it reminds me of the American experimental novelist John Hawkes who once wrote:

> Structure— verbal and psychological coherence— is still my largest concern as a writer. Related or corresponding event, recurring image and recurring action, these constitute the essential substance or meaningful density of writing.

But Atwood is no experimentalist; her novels are reactionary, i.e., conventionally realistic in the same sense that in *Cat's Eye* Risley calls her paintings "reactionary." Risley's paintings are representational; she uses traditional techniques like underpainting and concentrations of egg tempera to give them a "luminous flatness." Atwood's originality is very much Risley's originality— they both produce startling effects by a somewhat daring juxtaposition of experimental (image patterns) and traditional (plot, character) devices.

Atwood's mass-audience appeal derives from a reading of her novels as conventional narratives, as good stories, with meaningful characters and contemporary themes. Her audience (and her critics) see her variously as a feminist Boadicea, a flag-draped nationalist, or a yuppie bard. The experimental side of Atwood, her self-conscious manipulation of images, her attention to language, makes her critics (and mass audience) uncomfortable. It seems somehow too intellectual, too calculating. Hence, Atwood's other reputation as the Ice Queen of Canadian Literature, e.g., (from reviews of her previous books) ". . . I found myself in awe of the stylistic grace and precision of this cold pastoral and yet . . ." "In fact it's astonishing what a funny, entertaining book she has written without any of that warmth. When this ice-jam breaks, what an even more astonishing book she will write." "Margaret Atwood's new novel is a departure, quite different from its predecessors, though immediately recognizable as coming from the same mind, by the grace of its style, the penetration of its wit, and the emotional chill that pervades it."

I'm sure Atwood can live with herself as Ice Queen, though it must be irritating to be so underestimated. Reflecting on her former teacher Northrop Frye, Atwood once wrote how reassuring it was to turn to his essay

> on Emily Dickinson, which presents her neither as a White Goddess, despite her manner of dressing, nor as a feeble neurotic, but as *a skilled professional who knew exactly what she was doing.*

I emphasize those last 10 words because I suspect this is precisely how Atwood would prefer to be known herself. If you assume she knows what she's doing, if you assume Atwood's great art is in her art, then a new way of reading her reveals itself.

You reread *Cat's Eye* with a slight squint so that instead of reading the story of Elaine Risley, you watch for the images that repeat. You reread with a pencil in your hand, reading backwards and forwards so that you begin to notice that a blue cat's-eye marble appears on page 396 and on pages 61, 95, 139, 140, 143, 153, etc. This should be fun; think of it as a game of golf. Atwood drives off the tee on page 61 and then walks down to page 95 and hits a three iron ahead to 139, then chips to 140, and so on until she holes the ball (image) on 396.

Patterns emerge. On page 396, Risley finds the cat's-eye marble inside a red purse inside a steamer trunk full of family memorabilia. (This novel, Risley's retrospective, you might say, is a steamer trunk full of family memorabilia.) You try to find all the red purses (the tee for red purses is on 53). You notice that Atwood repeatedly associates red purses with hearts. Then, on 406, you read this description of that keystone painting, *Unified Field Theory*.

> She is the Virgin of Lost Things. Between her hands, at the level of the heart, she holds a glass object: an oversized cat's eye marble, with a blue centre.

Feverishly, you flip the pages until you come to where Risley looks at the cat's-eye marble in the purse and sees her "life entire." Which means that Risley, the painter, has painted the Virgin of Lost Things (lost as in Risley's memories) holding Risley's life to her heart, and suddenly this shiver of combinatorial delight begins to travel down the back of your neck.

But the cat's-eye marble complex is only an instance of eye imagery that tees off on page 2 when Cordelia, Risley's childhood tormentor and alter ego, rolls her "grey-green eyes, opaque and glinting." There's a radio with "a single green eye" like a cat's-eye marble and a veritable swamp of pickled ox-eyes, heads like eyes, not to mention dead turtles with hearts like eyes.

At a certain point the golf-game analogy will break down. Sometimes Atwood's image patterns seem like nuclear chain reactions; one atom splits another, which splits two others, which split four others. This is how she manages to create such complexity — juxtapositions and associations mount geometrically. (Atwood herself likes to play with the idea of language as disease — words are contagious, images metastasize.) One image (cat's-eye marble) hits another (radio with a green eye), which hits another (signals from space), which hits another (time, curved space, strings of light, the universe), which hits another (a jar of cat's-eye marbles that Risley describes as a "jar of light").

The image ramifies, transforms, slips (*slippage* is one of the words that post-Saussureans like to use). The cat's-eye marble becomes an image of the universe of modern physics as much as it is an image of Risley's entire life. It is an image of *everything*, or everything is infected with cat's-eye marbleness. So that in *Unified Field Theory*, the painting, the Virgin of Lost Things holding the cat's-eye marble to her heart is described as

> a woman dressed in black, with a black hood or veil covering her hair. Here and there on the black of her dress or cloak there are pinpoints of light. The sky behind her is the sky after sunset; at the top of it is the lower half of the moon. Her face is partly in shadow.

The Virgin of Lost Things is the Universe, the night sky, or the moon (that ambiguous "Her" is a wonderful touch) — the Virgin Mary becomes the female lunar goddess, the mother of all things.

But that's not all — hold on to your hats. Flip the pages again. You'll find Cordelia's face described as "a blurred reflection of the moon" and her name translated as "Heart of the moon." Risley's childhood enemy is both the lost *and* the Virgin of Lost Things!

Cat's Eye spirals in on itself, or implodes. It becomes so self-referential that it begins to feel like the dilemma of the Cretan barber who said, "I am lying." It becomes a logically impossible novel, an antinovel, a novel, to paraphrase Nabokov, that proves the impossibility of novels.

At this point it becomes something like pure art.

Writing a novel at this level of self-consciousness is a highly risky business. What is at risk, for Atwood, is her novel's verisimilitude, its quality of appearing to be real, the very quality that attracts her mass audience.

Atwood's solution to this problem is inspired. All her sensitive female narrators are neurotic (usually they are more or less cured by the end of the book). It's an axiom of modern psychology that neuroses occur when a person cannot face certain traumatic events and emotions. The traumatic events and emotions are hidden in the unconscious only to reappear in symbolic forms. Meaning occurs at the point where the plane of language meets the plane of the unconscious. As Risley says, "A lot of my painting then began in my confusion about words."

Atwood's characters live in a fetishized universe. Neurotic symbols obey dream laws — laws of association and juxtaposition — which are just the same as aesthetic laws. Atwood manipulates the fetishized universe of her narrators as though it were a poem. On one level (in Atwood novels it is always etc.), it is psychoanalysis; on another, she is creating art. But the art is safely cocooned inside the framework of psychological realism. When Risley goes out on the streets of Toronto she carefully disguises herself as a "non-artist."

To ask what this all means only ratifies a ridiculously reductive impulse. No doubt some critic will want to nail it down, nail image patterns to themes. Someone will say *Cat's Eye* is about the psychic healing power of art. Someone else will say it is Atwood's leap into religion, that she has finally, at 48, come to terms with her own mortality and God (and, as one would expect with Atwood, God is a woman). Still another will say she has adopted some notion about Zen and modern physics, that we are all one with the universe.

But you could pull a dozen themes out of *Cat's Eye* and not exhaust it (and not be true to the book — like the blind men with their marvellous elephant).

Risley calls her painting *Unified Field Theory*; she gets the physics from her scientist brother. She doesn't really think physics; she thinks images. So you don't get any help from Risley. But the novel's references to field, language as an entity, and to secret or encoded messages are clues to a complex theory of language. Words (people, the world) exist in self-referential fields of meaning; they are messages on a chain of messages.

As a writer, when she is actually sitting at her desk composing, Atwood knows that there is no meaning, that meaning only *happens* when you put two things together. Perhaps the truth of the matter is that Atwood means simply to say that the world is ineffably complex, but that it is not a symbol, that it refers to itself, that the novel is a book (and not an autobiography), the bridge a bridge, the sky a sky.

How Atwood creates novels that are mortuaries

RAY CONLOGUE

Scott Symons recently argued in The Idler that Margaret Atwood's obsession with control leads to books which "are not a fount of emotional renewal so much as a slaughterhouse for emotions."

This astringency, so at odds with the usual adulation, led me to read her most recent novel *Cat's Eye.*

In this book, the narrator, Elaine, describes the world from a high window no fewer than three times in the first 40 pages, an angle from which "the pedestrians appear squashed from above, like deformed children . . ." This is the beginning of a *nausée* that continues throughout the book. For Elaine, Lake Ontario is a toxic sewer and the Rocky Mountains "of the sunset-and-sloppy message variety." However, it is not her thanatic or death-obsessed nature that is striking, but the author's unawareness of it.

This is apparent in the other characters' failure to take note of Elaine's balefulness. She is not only the narrator of her world, but the *creator* and *controller* of it. The novel's world is an artifact of Elaine's mind.

In terms of gender politics, the worst villainy is done by a cabal of little girls led by the quasi-psychopath Cordelia, while Elaine's brother Stephen is warmly drawn. Male bodies are beautiful, but Cordelia's sisters are "alien and bizarre, hairy, squashy, monstrous."

The unkindness toward women is not merely physical. Elaine observes that they "pass hard, legitimate judgments, unlike the purblind guesses of men, fogged with romanticism. . . . Women . . . can neither be deceived nor trusted."

There is sympathy for the demise of traditional male behavior. Schoolboys have "that baffled look, like a night dweller gone blind in the sunlight." Her first husband, Jon, denied custody of their child, "calls long distance, his voice ... plaintive with ... an archaic sadness that seems, more and more, to be that of men in general."

But her view of women's hardness is a veiled compliment, and her sympathy for men is cold. Men are Other, and if women are hurt by them it is because they fail to see this. "I did not ascribe any intention to these men. They were like rocks. . . . If you slipped you'd cut yourself, but it was no use blaming the rocks."

However, Elaine *chooses* to see men as opaque. "Knowing too much about other people puts you in their power, they have a claim on you, you are forced to understand their reasons for doing things and then you are weakened."

Here is why the men in Atwood's novels are unmemorable. She has a faultless talent for exterior observation—tics and habits and attitudes — but she will not inhabit their minds. This would be "weakness," a loss of control.

She wants us to like Stephen, the brother, but refuses to individuate him. He is, for example, obsessed with war games because he is a boy. I couldn't help remembering the boy in *The World According to Garp*, similarly obsessed but for a personal reason: he has heard his father died in war. Which is more believable?

Cordelia is better drawn, but when after her defeat by Elaine— "energy has passed between us, and I am stronger" — she ends up mentally crippled in the Dorothy Lyndwick Rest Home, there is no compassion.

Elaine says she loves her daughter ferociously, but the description of them together is dead and affectless, a recitation of chores: I walk Sarah, I lift Sarah inside. I get her a glass of milk.

Her husband, by contrast, "scoops Sarah up, gives her a kiss, tickles her face with his beard." And what does Elaine think of this? "He has a way of putting the two of them into the same camp, in pretended league against me, that annoys me more than it should."

It is nowhere written that a novelist must be upbeat or humanist. But it says something about Canadians that our most celebrated author creates novels which are mortuaries. They are full of acute recollection, but lifeless. Dialogue is wooden, spoken not by individuals but by strangulated puppets. Woven into Elaine's rich gown of thought, these dialogues take on a spurious life. But one can't imagine of Atwood the thing that novelists say so often — "the characters took over and wrote it themselves!"

There is indeed an obsession with control behind the books. It was at one time beguiling, a display of skittish brilliance. But in *Cat's Eye* it is as triumphant as death.

TIPS ON WRITING A REVIEW

1. Reread Marya Mannes' rules concerning the role of the reviewer or critic in judging a work.
2. Be thoroughly acquainted with the work and the writer. Factual errors detract from the reviewer's credibility.
   - Use quotations from the work to provide a sense of the contents and the writer's style.
   - Refer to the writer and his or her life and times when it would help the reader understand the context of the work. Notice how Douglas Glover does this in his review of *Cat's Eye* (p. 204).
3. Provide the reader with enough information to familiarize him or her with the contents of the work, but be sensitive as to how much you should reveal.
   - For nonfiction give as much information on content as space will permit.
   - For fiction, do not reveal too much of the content or you will spoil the work for the reader.
4. In your judgement of the work — which is at the heart of the review — consider:
   - the quality of the work. Your review will be enhanced if you are able to compare the work or the achievement with others that it resembles.
   - whether or not to focus on any perceived faults in the work. Notice how skilfully Davies supports his critique.
   - the audience who may find this work appealing. Phrases such as "If you like this type of . . ." or "People who have an interest in . . ." are helpful in giving your reader information he or she might need.
   - your own biases and criteria. Revealing your own biases and the criteria you have applied to the work can be helpful to the

reader. However, do not focus on your own biases to the extent that the reader might disqualify you from providing a carefully considered opinion.

5. Present the review as a piece of writing that has merit in itself.
   - Make sure your review engages, captivates, or entertains the reader. Polish your sentences, diction, and imagery so that your own voice comes through.
   - Be sure to follow the review's conventions.

8. Contemporary Journalism

KEY WORK:

"Academic Rigour or Rhetorical Flash?" — Thomas Hurka

ASSOCIATED READINGS:

"Letter of Response to Thomas Hurka" — Sandford Borins
"Why dogs are the cat's pajamas" — John Riley
"A dogged defence of our feline friends" — James Taylor
"Curbing hockey's brawlers" — Editorial
"Why Talk Shows Won't Shut Up" — Barbara Grizzuti
   Harrison
"Journalese for the Lay Reader" — John Leo

If you look around your home, you may be surprised by the variety of magazines, newspapers, bulletins, and periodicals you find. Because these publications compete for readership, articles are often selected for their ability to sell the publication to audiences ranging from your little brother, the model plane enthusiast, to your mother, the economist. Since this consideration may override the contents' merits, you should reflect on a publication's possible biases and vested interests to weigh the value of the works in that publication. Matters of bias may be cause for concern, since estimates suggest that over 60 percent of our information originates in print journalism.

The essays in this unit (with the exception of Leo's work) originally appeared as works in influential media publications. They represent several of the most common types of print journalism: the column, the editorial, and the specialized article. Hurka's column and Borins' response are general interest works. Riley's and Taylor's whimsical exchange represents articles which readers submit for publication. "Curbing hockey's brawlers" is an editorial, a formal piece of writing which appears unsigned on the editorial page and argues one perspective. Harrison's article is an example of the social issues raised in popular magazines. No doubt you have observed the print journalism scattered throughout this book.

Each of the types of specialized writing (columns, articles, etc.) found in contemporary journalism has its own conventions. The conventions of the column are the focus for the conventions of this unit.

Conventions of Journalism — The Column

Purpose   To inform, entertain, argue, interpret

Audience   General through specialized

Tone   Serious and rational through whimsical and subjective

Voice   Often strongly expressive but may be neutral and objective

Response   Informed, entertained, moved

Language   LEVEL — Often informal, colloquial, breezy but may be formal, standard English
               CHARACTERISTICS — Often rhetorical and anecdotal, easy to read

Structure   Often long sentences (especially the lead, or first, sentence) composed of short paragraphs

BEFORE READING

1. a. Bring to class a favourite magazine or newspaper. With a partner, examine it for: the publisher, the intended audience, and the possible biases or leanings.
   b. Discuss your findings with classmates, considering the possible implications for the reliability of your reading material.
   c. Assess the value of the articles as a source of solid research information.

2. In small groups, brainstorm a list of controversial topics about which you might express your opinion in an editorial, a letter to the editor, or a column. Store the list in your writing folder for future consideration.

3. Review the conventions of the column outlined above. With a partner, speculate about the probable conventions for the editorial or article.

Academic Rigour or Rhetorical Flash?

THOMAS HURKA

Philosophers haven't always been impressed with journalists —
"They vomit up their bile and call it newspaper," said Friedrich
Nietzsche. But journalism can reply in a similar tone about aca-
demics: "They can't hiccup without adding 10 pages of footnotes."

Academic and journalistic writing certainly differ. Scholarly
prose is long on care and short on charisma. Journalists — especially opinion-piece writers — trade rigour for rhetorical flash.

Some differences are obvious. Academic writing has long sentences, a ponderous tone, and apparently pointless jargon.
("According to Derrida, dialectical logic represses difference by
putting closure on the process of exteriorization.") But often these
traits spring from an admirable concern for method. The academic
writer wants to state a position precisely, which sometimes
requires inventing new words. And he or she wants to *prove* the
position. This requires a sober tone, so it's clear one's argument is
doing the persuading, not some rhetorical trick.

By contrast, journalism is bright and breezy, a pleasure to ingest.
But how nourishing is it? Although opinion pieces have an opinion, often it's presented as the only possible opinion. Dissenting
views at best provide the occasion for sarcasm or ridicule. (When
has Barbara Amiel seriously considered an argument for socialism,
or This Magazine listed a single benefit of free trade?) As for a
careful, step-by-step presentation of an argument, that would be
just too boring.

How you write depends on whom you write for. The academic
assumes an audience that is already fascinated by the topic but
will be stubbornly skeptical. The journalist envisages readers who
start out uninterested — hence the need for a catchy lead and an
entertaining style — but who, once hooked, will cheer almost anything you say.

As an academic, you've worked for years on a topic, so of course
it's fabulously important. How could anyone who knows anything
need persuading of that? Besides, if readers had the good taste to

pick up The Journal of Romantic Poetry, they're sure to want to know all about Wordsworth and Cross-Dressing.

But if academic readers are easy to interest, they are bears to persuade. They have intellectual defences — a veritable Maginot Line of doubts and objections—that you have to storm to establish a position.

In the sciences, you do this with experimental design, giving tests of significance and enough detail that doubters can replicate your results themselves. Elsewhere it calls for footnotes — when you've said something's true, readers can check that it's so. And persuasion demands that sober tone. You have to state objections to your thesis in the strongest possible form and then show you can answer them.

Journalists aren't as arrogant as academics — they don't assume that what they're interested in (or have been told to write about) is a not topic for everyone. They try to create interest by tying their subject to people's lives or to recent events in the news. Hence the human-interest openings to foreign correspondents' reports ("Carmelina strolls across the clearing, a child in one arm and a gun in the other"). They're an attempt to hook readers who otherwise couldn't care less.

Journalists also realize that readers who start a piece can give up in the middle, so they keep their language lively. In opinion pieces, this often means going for the strongest opinion possible and flailing all dissenters — the more colourfully the better. But then the tone leaves little room for serious supporting argument. And how entertaining would it be to explain all the good points made by people on the other side?

The result is political journalism of the Barbara Amiel-This Magazine kind — rhetorical point-scoring to amuse the converted, but incapable of persuading someone who doesn't already buy the party line. It's a kind of cheerleading for the home political team, the Free-Market Flyers or the Lefty Maple Leafs.

In academic writing, what's most important are your arguments, not the opinion they support; in journalism, opinion is king. That's what's been toughest for me writing in this space — the pressure to state opinions even if I can't justify them fully. It's time to get back to Nietzsche and his cronies and let someone else have a crack.

EXPLORING THE ESSAY

1. To what extent has Hurka effectively employed the conventions of the column? Give specific examples.

2. a. Identify Nietzsche, Wordsworth, Maginot Line, *This Magazine*, and Barbara Amiel.
   b. What does each reference contribute to the overall effectiveness of his essay?

3. a. Paraphrase Hurka's thesis.
   b. To what extent does his own journalistic prose illustrate his thesis? Cite specific examples.

4. Hurka refers to specific journalistic techniques such as the lead. After determining the criteria of a sound lead, assess the effectiveness of his opening.

5. Hurka claims journalistic prose is noted for its "rhetorical flash"; it is "bright and breezy and easy to ingest." In partners or small groups, locate specific examples in his work which support this description.

EXTENSIVE STUDY

1. In small groups, compare the academic and journalistic styles of writing as they appear in this or other texts. Note specific ways the essays differ in style and structure and account for these differences in terms of purpose and audience. Consult examples such as:
   a. academic
   - Rich's "Claiming an Education" (p. 297)
   - Blythe's "Portraits of Women" (p. 96)
   - Manski's "Forces of Corruption in *The Great Gatsby*" (p. 94)
   - Neville's "Native Canadian Land Claims and Sovereignty" (p. 287)
   - Hatcher's "Whole Brain Learning" (p. 103)
   - Fox's "Environmental Control of the Great Lakes" (p. 128)
   b. journalistic — any essay in this unit
   - Lipman's "How television is reshaping world's culture" (p. 115)
   - Hough's "Dressed to Kill" (p. 119)
   - Labatt's "Violence against women" (p. 266)
   - Helwig's "Haunted by lives unlived" (p. 55)

2. a. With a partner, assess the extent to which Borins has effectively countered Hurka's arguments. Make specific reference to each step in Hurka's and Borins' arguments.
   b. Compose an outline for a letter or column in which Hurka responds to Borins' column.

3. Read "Knowing How to Think" (p. 24), and determine the success with which Hurka and/or Borins have followed the suggestions for rational argument.

4. a. Rewrite "Journalese for the Lay Reader" (p. 235) in standard English.
   b. Speculate on George Orwell's views about the quality of journalism selected for this text.

5. After reading Riley's euolgy of dogs and Taylor's spirited defence of cats, complete one or more of the following tasks:
   a. prepare tongue-in-cheek debates which argue similarly trivial, even absurd, issues such as the relative merits of apples and oranges
   b. assess the strengths of each according to stated criteria for contemporary journalism
   c. in pairs, research and role-play a serious response to two sides of an issue.

THE WRITING FOLDER

1. Compose a personal response column or a letter to the editor for Harrison's article, responding to specific issues which you disagree with or support.

2. Rewrite an academic essay for a specific mass media publication or a piece of journalism for an academic audience, observing appropriate conventions. You might work with one of your own essays or choose a piece from this text.

3. a. Compose an interview in which television host Thomas Hurka chats with Sandford Borins, George Orwell (p. 12), and at least two other authors such as Harrison (p. 231) or Lippman (p. 115), about the influence of media on contemporary language, thought, and values.
   b. Express your ideas on the above subject in an editorial for a specific publication.

INDEPENDENT STUDY

1. Analyze the language of a specific type of print journalism. You might:
   a. Compare the slant or bias in front-page reporting of the same issue by two reputable papers.
   b. Compare language strategies employed by two or more special interest columnists who write for the same or different publications (e.g., June Callwood, Michelle Landsberg, Greg Quill, Carol Goar, Thomas Hurka, John Allemang, Milt Dunnell, Peter Goddard, or Richard Needham).

2. Conduct a study of a particular newspaper or a Canadian magazine such as *Maclean's*, *Saturday Night*, or *Canadian Forum*. Analyze it in terms of the "look" or image it maintains through its content (articles, special features, and advertising), its style, and its point of view. Determine its target audience and, using the information you have gained in your research and information from this unit, write a series of editorials, columns, and book reviews that might appear in that publication.

3. After reading several sources about the ethics of journalism, write an essay in which you analyze the ethics of press coverage of a controversial or sensitive issue over a period of time. Consider issues such as violence in sport or on prime-time television, the depiction of minority or special interest groups, AIDS, date rape, the quality of contemporary education, land use for cattle grazing, or censorship.

TIMED READING AND WRITING

1. Read "Curbing hockey's brawlers" (p. 229) and write a letter to the editor in response to the issues raised.

2. Write a letter to the editor stating your position on the extent to which the government should regulate the media. (If you have read "How television is reshaping world's culture" (p. 115), you may want to refer to the issues it raises.)

3. Compose a spirited defence of cats or dogs (or another animal).

Letter of Response to Thomas Hurka

SANDFORD BORINS

In his final Fifth Column last week, Thomas Hurka told us why he feels academic writing is so boring. I've always enjoyed Mr. Hurka: he penned a good column. Now that he is going back to writing scholarly articles, it would be a pity if he renounces the literary talents he demonstrated weekly and begins churning out sleep-inducing prose. Unlike Mr. Hurka, I would maintain that good scholarship and good writing are not incompatible.

Mr. Hurka's main point seems to be that newspaper columnists are allowed to present one-sided opinions, while academics must take into account all possible counter-arguments to their theses. In Mr. Hurka's mind, this weighing and sifting of the evidence seems to produce boring writing. Must it?

In his classic study of government decision-making during the Cuban Missile Crisis, one of the many ideas Professor Graham Allison of Harvard expounded was what he called "the 51-49 principle." That is, in a competitive world, politicians and bureaucrats are forced to state their positions much more confidently than if they were detached judges. They act as advocates, arguing an uncertain 51-49 case as though it were a certain 100-0. The world is full of advocates, whether they are lawyers, managers or newspaper columnists.

The very nature of the academic publishing process puts limits on Prof. Allison's "51-49 principle." Before an article can be published in an academic journal, it is reviewed by several referees, who are not told the author's identity. (Nor does the author know who they are.) Undoubtedly the referees will raise questions, and these must be answered before an editor will accept an article for publication. As a consequence, articles often become encumbered with footnotes intended to satisfy the referees' concerns.

Do the requirements of building logical arguments and responding to referees' concerns mean that academic writing must be boring?

If some academics have acquired a reputation for dull writing, it is for reasons that can easily be remedied, simply by applying some of the principles of effective writing. For example, nothing requires academics to write in long, run-on sentences. Nothing requires them to write in massive paragraphs that transform entire pages to visually undifferentiated blocks of print. There is no reason to prefer the anonymity of the passive voice to the vividness of the active.

As an occasional referee of other academics' manuscripts, I can recall some that present a distorted version of the "51-49 principle." When a case is really quite clear, they undercut it with meaningless qualifiers, phrases like "to be sure," "on balance," "in a very real sense," and so on. Such phrases are a distracting clearing-of-the-throat for these sufferers of a self-induced literary catarrh. I find myself wishing they would just get on with the argument.

It is quite legitimate for the academic brethren to use the journalist's various hooks to capture the reader's attention. I recall a political science paper on voting behaviour with the aphoristic title Closeness Only Counts in Horseshoes and Ballroom Dancing. The opening paragraph can also contain hooks. For example, "The conventional wisdom of astronomers is that the Earth is flat. Here's why they are all wrong." There are myriad ways to start an article that will make colleagues sit up and take notice. A modicum of literary marketing is all that's needed.

There are academic writers whose prose flows lucidly, helping us understand what are often subtle and complicated concepts. The two I feel epitomize this clarity of expression are Sigmund Freud and John Maynard Keynes. For literary style, Freud's *Civilization and its Discontents* and Keynes's *Essays in Persuasion* should be required reading for any professor and for the lay reader as well.

The canons of academic writing don't require wave upon wave of sparkling one-liners. On the other hand, they should not permit turgidness, excessive use of jargon, or simply bad writing.

Recently, there has been a recognition in the academic world that good communication is important. For examples, I see more and more colleagues attending seminars and learning ways to improve their communication in the classroom.

The logical next step would be to pay more attention to communication on the printed page. I think this is something Mr. Hurka and those few other academics who have real literary talent could teach the profession. Perhaps there may be a small business for Mr. Hurka here. At any rate, I hope he brings a literary style to his writing on ethics that will be a standard for his colleagues.

Why dogs are the cat's pajamas

JOHN RILEY

There are some sensitive topics that I suspect will provoke heated debate for centuries to come: abortion, capital punishment and euthanasia, to name a few. It is conceivable, though, that these issues may one day be resolved; perhaps at some point there will be no crime or we'll all live for eternity.

There is, however, one controversial question people assume will never be resolved: Which are better, dogs or cats? Not so. I plan to demonstrate irrefutably that there is a definitive answer to the question, and it barks.

Starting with the premise that the basic purpose of owning a pet is to have a friendly animal companion, dogs trump cats hands, er, paws down. Canines are mostly playful, dopey and trustworthy. Felines, on the other hand, tend to be aloof, cunning and suspicious. It is true a cat will swat at a ribbon suspended above its head; but this is not play, it is merely an extension of their reflex instinct to kill (see below).

Dogs are giving creatures; they will see you through divorces and firings and endure your endless rants about how unfair the world is. Like your distant cousin Eddie, cats appear only when they want something. Once they've emptied your wallet and cupboards, it's back in the van and on with the great mooching tour for Eddie and the cat.

Cat lovers argue that cats are more self-reliant than dogs. While certainly this is true, it seems a rather pointless quality in a pet. The whole object of having a pet is to develop a mutually rewarding relationship between animal and person. I get the impression that if you could train a cat to use a can opener and a flush toilet, it wouldn't have much use for human beings.

Cat owners also love to boast that cats are self-cleaning. Big deal, so is my oven, but you don't see me plastering snapshots of it all over the wall of my office cubicle. Besides, for sheer joyous pandemonium, nothing quite compares with giving a dog a bath. Afterwards, the dog will race around the house as if it is possessed by mad spirits while strains of the William Tell Overture play in your head.

The great thing about dogs is that they have utility; they can be trained. Dogs can be taught to fetch things and perform tricks, providing endless hours of amusement. Lest you cat lovers believe that such a trait is exploited merely for the frivolous enjoyment of dog owners, I offer the example of Seeing Eye dogs. Even if you could teach a cat the nominal aspects of leading the blind, I shudder to consider the mayhem that would ensue if a mouse scampered through a busy intersection while a cat was performing such duties.

Ah, say cat lovers, catching mice — there's a utilitarian service performed by felines on behalf of people who find their abodes overrun by pesky rodents! Perhaps. But it's not as if cats catch mice in the interests of assisting humanity. It's no accident that the word "catch" begins with c-a-t. Cats just catch — and kill — mindlessly and without purpose. Mice, rats, birds — the cat is the animal kingdom's equivalent of a serial killer.

I will admit that cats may be "smarter" than dogs, if only in an unscrupulous and underhanded way. For example, one of the most wily villains in the old *Batman* television series was Catwoman. I can't image that a foe named Dogman would have provided the Caped Crusader with much of a challenge; a few loving scratches administered behind the ears and Dogman would have immediately rolled over and discarded his plans to destroy Gotham City's priceless art collection.

Another way in which dogs are superior to cats is that they come in vastly more shapes and sizes. Except for those overstuffed hairballs, Persians, mostly a cat is a cat is a cat. On the contrary, it's hard to believe the Chihuahua and the St. Bernard are even members of the same species. Such wide variety gives you the freedom to choose the dog most suitable to your personality, lifestyle and apartment size.

But the attributes of dogs I love best are their unselfishness and bravery. Dogs are renowned for their countless feats of daring and heroics, immortalized by such fictional canine luminaries as Lassie, Old Yeller and Rin Tin Tin. Nobody uses the word "brave" and "cat" in the same sentence. The words most commonly associated with "cat" are "that darn."

On balance, there can be no question that dogs are superior to cats. Oh, I'm sure there are some slighted feline-lovers out there wailing like cats in heat that I have ignored such heinous canine atrocities as rabid pit bulls, overturned garbage cans and the mine-fields of dog droppings around most public parks and private lawns. These apologists thus conclude that the debate remains at a minimum unresolved. So what is the definitive proof that makes my case irrefutable?

Well, last summer I was in the park with my handsome and noble golden Labrador, when a cat was just about to pounce on a tiny gosling of our country's unofficial national bird, the Canada goose. My canine companion, having been trained to guard, inter-ceded on my command to protect the young, helpless bird. So not only did my pal save a life, but in his own small way served his country. Name a darn cat that can claim as much.

A dogged defence of our feline friends

JAMES TAYLOR

I do not usually write to newspapers. I think that those of us who read newspapers deserve what we get. The reporting on the econ-omy, the Constitution, death and mayhem—all this I endure with-out comment. But I cannot remain silent in the face of John Riley's article on this page last week—Why Dogs Are The Cat's Pajamas.

His thesis is that dogs are "superior" to cats because they are friendlier, they can be trained and they are available in many vari-eties. He is wrong on all counts.

First, dogs are not friendlier, nor, indeed, are they even capable of being friendly. In part, people mistake dogs' dependency on their masters (cats do not have masters) for friendship. More importantly, the ability to be a friend implies a capacity to choose otherwise. Dogs have no such capacity.

Dogs are (as Mr. Riley in a rare insight observes) both "playful" and "dopey." Pathologically so, except for those whom inbreeding has turned into pathological killers. But being pathologically play-ful and dopey is not being friendly. It is a disorder. Apparently, some people like it (although some do not — the expression "let sleeping dogs lie" is a direct reference to the degree of distaste mankind holds for this disorder) but it has nothing to do with friendship.

Dogs are incapable either of showing friendship or not showing it. They are simply dogs — playful and dopey — all the time.

Dogs bounce. They drool. They wag. They pant. They nuzzle. It means nothing. It is just being a dog. Very much like mailboxes sit or politicians lie. Properly understood, none of these behaviours is good or bad. It is just what they variously do.

Cats, on the other hand, are discriminating. They choose. Some people (presumably Mr. Riley included) they even disdain. To some they show various degrees of affection. Cats are capable of showing friendship and may do so (or may not). It is precisely the ability to withhold friendship that makes a cat capable of friendship.

Mr. Riley apparently likes his relationships broadly drawn. Fair enough. He undoubtedly prefers whoopee cushions to paradox. To each his own. But we ought not confuse the tragic result of inbreeding with advantage.

Second, Mr. Riley extols dogs because they can be trained. Actually, he says "they have utility; they can be trained."

Cats are markedly more intelligent than dogs and accordingly *could* be trained — if they wanted to be. Cats, however, decline to conduct themselves as clowns or robots or — well, let's say it, dogs — to please humans. Cats are companions. They seek mutuality. They expect to be treated with respect.

The only companionship comparable to that of a cat is that of a spouse. My spouse is the best of companions. She is capable, to quote Mr. Riley, of being "taught to fetch things and perform tricks, providing endless hours of amusement." Mr. Riley however, would be disappointed in her, because she does not do these things. She is a companion. A co-equal. We fetch things and perform tricks (if you'll excuse the expression) together. She is a true cat among persons.

Third, Mr. Riley rhapsodizes about what he describes as the "variety" of dogs. He apparently finds subtle distinctions a little difficult (although he is able to recognize the difference between a Chihuahua and a St. Bernard). He undoubtedly orders three-alarm chili in Mexican restaurants, plays Bartok (at high volume) on his stereo and has a fondness for Picasso. But variety is not only found in such extremes.

A trained palate will prefer the more subtle and exquisite experience of a mimosa salad to tobasco. A trained ear likely prefers the understatement of a Haydn to discordant noise. A trained eye might pass over a Picasso, but is likely to linger on a Renoir.

Mr. Riley confuses variety with extravagant extremes. He is apparently incapable of seeing the real cat within the cat form.

Unlike dogs, cats think and choose. It is apparent from Mr. Riley's vicious attack that they do not think to choose him. Why? We need look no further than his sad description of what he esteems in dogs.

He describes an experience when, on his command, his dog interceded to protect a gosling from a cat. You would expect a playful and dopey dog, dispatched by a master to implement without question the master's desire, to interfere with the survival of the fittest. A cat would not. Rather it would rightfully fix Mr. Riley with a stare that said, "If you want to work up a sweat saving geese from cats, feel free. As for me, I'm for gravity and the rest of the natural order of things."

Curbing hockey's brawlers

EDITORIAL

Meeting yesterday in Florida, the National Hockey League's board of governors approved some overdue changes to the rules of professional hockey. Coincidental minor penalties will no longer cancel one another out, a change that will force both teams to play an exciting two minutes with five players a side instead of six. A minor penalty will be assessed for diving: attempting to persuade the referee you've been tripped when you haven't been. The league also toughened the rules on high-sticking, which will now be defined as any stick contact above the waist. But the most important and controversial change is designed to curb fighting. The NHL introduced a tough new game-misconduct penalty for instigating a fight. This does not go as far as some wanted, but it should act as a considerably more powerful deterrent than the current two minutes in the box for starting a punch-up.

Admittedly, many people are not going to like this anti-fighting measure. Those who would prefer to tolerate fighting put forward several arguments:

FIGHTING IS A SAFETY VALVE: According to this theory, players in a tough, contact sport like hockey need to let off steam every once in a while. But why does no other rough-and-tumble team sport — football and rugby come to mind — feel the need to confer semi-legal status on mid-game fisticuffs? If hockey players really needed a safety valve, then one would expect to see most players fighting, and frequently. Instead, fights usually occur between the league's small number of dedicated pugilists. Glen Sather, Edmonton General Manager, last year speculated that 10 per cent of the players do 90 per cent of the fighting. If it's a safety valve, it's one the vast majority of NHLers rarely use.

FIGHING IS PART OF THE GAME: Though some people are in the habit of forgetting, the NHL already bans fighting. It earns its practitioners an automatic five-minute misconduct, and can also cost them an extra penalty for instigation, not to mention additional misconducts for leaving the bench to join a fight or for being the third man in a fight. Because of these latter two rules, an extra participant hardly ever joins a two-man fight, and bench-clearing brawls have become more common to baseball than hockey.

FIGHTING IS NEEDED TO ENFORCE THE RULES: The proponents of this theory hold that the incidence of high-sticking and other dangerous infractions would get out of control unless teams occasionally took the law into their own hands to protect their players. This view at least has a certain logic to it. But instead of tolerating fighting, there is a simpler and more effective way to ensure respect for the rules: arm hockey's officials with the power to adequately penalize illegal play.

The "pro-fighting lobby" at the NHL governors meetings had pushed for tougher rules on spearing, cross-checking, butt-ending, high-sticking and slashing, saying that these are a far graver problem than fighting. The "anti-fighting" group, in contrast, sees fighting as a serious blight that undermines hockey's attempts to increase its popularity in the United States. Both sides are right. The ideal outcome of the governors meeting would have been for both sides to have achieved their goals.

Why Talk Shows Won't Shut Up

BARBARA GRIZZUTI HARRISON

"Right now," Van Halen sings, "a mad man is wandering the streets of the town you live in." And you don't have to go far to find him: He may at this moment be in full public view—an audience member . . . a caller-in . . . even, one might be forgiven for believing, a talk-show host.

The landscape of talk shows is strange indeed. Here we are, being asked to spend trillions to explore space, when true howling-at-the-moon madness—stunning sterility combined with dazzling anomalies, cocooned craziness, frenzy that is at the same time stasis — is no further away (along with FCC-sanctioned brawls and voyeurism) than the remote control. One has, for one's out-of-body, out-of-mind, other-planetary experiences, only to watch Sally Jessy Raphael, Geraldo Rivera, Phil Donahue, Montel Williams, Jenny Jones. Of course, there's always Oprah — wily, teary, down-home Oprah. And now there's Jane, a bouncy, girlsy newcomer who dresses in Alice in Wonderland pastels when she does not choose to embody Shabby Chic — a trader of insults in a high-voltage, buzz-saw voice; a practitioner of instant intimacy who drapes her skinny arms around her rowdy teenage audience.

Silence, on the evidence, found its last spokesman (so to speak) in John Wayne. And the love that dared not speak its name has pitched its high-decibel voice over more talk shows than New York City has mice, homosexuality in all its manifestations being a topic almost as popular as weight (Skinny Women Say They Can't Get a Date; Beauty Pageant for Large Women), but not quite as popular as Ivana Trump (her Tragedy, Dignity and Triumph) and Dolly Parton.

I am in the soup. In the talk-show soup. I have watched so many talk shows in my undisciplined life — and, in the last couple of weeks, more talk shows than I have brain cells (which are rapidly dying off as a result) — that I am packing to go to the Galápagos Islands to rejoice in the company of tortoises.

If you watch talk TV as much as I do, you will have the questionable pleasure of hearing discourse on midget tossing; on husbands who try to kill their wives with snakes; (endlessly) from and about welfare recipients; on interracial this's and that's (People Who

Prefer Friends From Another Race; Interracial Couples Scorned by In-laws); on children who kill; on male stress syndrome; on therapy for "love" triangles; on kept women (women are, one way or another, often pitted against one another on talk shows); on a girl expelled from a shopping mall for wearing a short skirt. Also, Chippendale Dancers. In this strange netherworld, questions like *Why didn't you kill your husband?* actually begin to seem plausible and not impertinent.

Why do we watch?

We need to know how others live — so as to know how to live ourselves. We need myth, we need wonder, we need fairy tales, we need prescriptions for living, we need to define our own "normality" by the normality — or abnormality — of others. We used to tell tales around the fire. We used to read books. Then came the couch and the remote — and the comfy platitudes by which, in lieu of religious prescription, we live.

Why would we care to watch the fattest human being on earth, the tallest h.b., the shortest and the tattooed man? These are freak shows. Most talk shows are freak shows. We watch the disfigured of body and mind. We say: There but for the grace of God go I. Does our compassion mask contempt? Maybe yes; maybe no. There are as many reasons for watching talk shows as there are talk shows.

In the '40s, my mother used to listen to a radio show called *Queen for a Day*, in which poor — financially poor — wretches vied for gifts (washers, canned food); the woman who excited the most applause by virtue of her story's being the saddest got the loot. There's something of that, too, in today's TV talk shows. We live, we are told, in a classless society. Of course, we don't. We live amidst profound societal cleavages. We live in different pockets, strangers to one another. The talk show allows us to observe those differences — one day, Leona Helmsley; the next, feudin'/fussin' couples from the Ozarks.

We look for similarities. We look for differences.

On a local talk show, I watched — horrified, but mesmerized — a "square-off" between two groups: long-taloned, big-haired women from Brooklyn and New Jersey; and demure, upwardly mobile female preppies. Class warfare. Stereotypes? Yes. But something more: Makeup and hair artists tarted the preppies up, gave them big hair and Lycra, and toned the others down with L.L. Bean clothes and blunt cuts. And we had: metamorphoses, transformations. . . . We used to have fairy tales. Now we have "role reversals." Children

Who Hate Their Step-parents is our version of a fairy tale like Cinderella. But in a debased form. Oedipus vulgarized.

We used to have exorcisms; town halls; public hangings. Now we have talk shows, where everyone is a judge, the jury, an inquisitor, a prosecutor. People feel no qualms about standing up and saying: "I commend you." . . . "I applaud you." . . . "I condemn you." Everybody's an expert; everybody's God.

We used to have diversions. In the '30s, people's minds were taken off their lack of dough by madcap movies like Carole Lombard comedies and Busby Berkeley musicals. In this recession, we have a talk-show host called Jenny Jones who drags on "experts" to tell us how to survive unemployment: "Deal with your anger. Get over the anger. . . . Be an adversity specialist. . . . Read classified ads." If this information is helpful, I'm Brooke Astor. Is unemployment a psychological problem? Give me a break.

Talk show: I Can't Forgive My Mother. Talk Show: Lazy Son-In-Law Makes Wife Work. Talk show: Husbands Who Are Like Al Bundy. We used to have intact families. We used to have plays like *Our Town*. Now we have Oprah and Sally Jessy, who, about as often as I wash my hair, stage "reunions" — reunions of mothers who abandoned their children; reunions of one-night stands. Is all of America lonely? It is brutal to think that for many viewers, Oprah and Sally Jessy *are* family. And indeed, Oprah and Sally Jessy are incredibly — but to a controlled extent — self-revelatory. They want us to know that they love us.

Love. Words don't mean much on talk shows. I have noticed, now that I'm talk-show saturated, how much everybody's vocabulary owes to them. Language and concepts are debased; values are unexamined; we speak in pop-psych clichés: *dysfunctional, emasculate, defeminize*. "I've always been very spiritual, but I've never prayed," says one guest. What the hell does that mean? "People are doing well with the way their head is at this time," a host proclaims; meaning, exactly what? A kept woman on Joan Rivers' show announces that she has a "father complex," and that a rich and famous man gives her "validation" and that she's "addicted, like an alcoholic and a drug addict." She learned to talk from talk shows. She certainly couldn't have thought these things up by herself.

On talk shows, sentences end with words like *so . . . but . . . like . . . you know*. People get "tramantized" [sic] and "tooken" [sic], or they're "into denial" . . . which is okay, because, as one hears countless times a day on talk shows, "you don't have to blame yourself." Of course, you're also told to "take responsibility for your own life." And nobody asks you to reconcile these apparently antithetical imperatives.

I suppose it could be argued that talk shows extend the boundaries of what's possible — or at least, of what it's possible to imagine: A 14-year-old boy marries a 44-year-old woman; and we ask, Could I do that? Would I? A woman walks into sex shops, "adult" video stores alone. Could I do that?

Well, maybe. But it's at least as likely that people watch talk shows to feel like insiders — watch Joan Rivers, and you, too, will have the answer to Whatever Happened to John Travolta? Listen to a talk show of your choice to discover what it's like to be abducted by Aliens (by which I do not mean by talk-show hosts).

We listen. We mock. We receive a liberal education. Of a sort.

I'm going to make a distinction here (something that talk shows, which confuse the eccentric with the neurotic, the crazy with the wonderful and weird, seem intent upon *not* doing). Both Geraldo and Donahue had shows that dealt with compulsions and obsessions. Geraldo's show featured a lady who kept pet rats and snakes (she trained rats for the movies, as it happened) and a lady who had 80 cats. Also a woman (in real trouble) who couldn't stop washing her hands. Geraldo seemed not to see she was different in kind from the cat lady and the rat lady, both of whom were happy with their lives and animal appendages. Phobias have become, I am sorry to say, trendy. Nevertheless, Donahue's show dealt with authentic human suffering. He did not deal with this problem voyeuristically or sensationally — or with inappropriate whimsy: He understood that debilitating panic attacks, phobias and compulsions are, as he said, "the most common mental-health problem in the United States." He understood one could fear one might "go crazy, just drop dead, lose control"; he understood the overwhelming anxiety of someone who felt, on her way to the mailbox, "the way people feel when they're pushed out of a plane."

About Donahue: Although I think of talk shows as one massive organism with many tentacles, he does distinguish himself, from time to time, from his fellows in the genre he can be said to have created. His interviews with Clinton and Brown were sassy and aggressive and revealing: Nobody else on the circuit would take on the hard issues of an electoral campaign; he has the stuff. He has it; and in the past, almost daily, he used it. But as time went by, and he appeared to lose ground to the sob sisters of the talks, Donahue (who has said he refuses to be a martyr to the ratings) has apparently chosen to downplay the restless side of his intelligence and . . . well, *pander* is the only word: During one sweeps week, he wore, on a program about cross-dressers, a skirt. Pity. I wonder if I only imagine that he seems sad.

Still, Donahue is smart enough to speculate about the nature of what he does. On a painful program about the harvesting of organs from a child born with only a brain stem, he provided a good answer as to why we watch talk shows: It "obliges us all to look in the mirror and say: What would I do?" Yes. "We're trying to put the Talmud, the Bible and lots of other great writings in a one-hour show," he said. Yes. We used to have God. Now we have Donahue.

But Jeffrey Dahmer, the monster who killed and ate bodies, provided a better reason: According to a psychologist testifying at his trial (on Court TV — my favorite "talk show"), he said, "Is there anyone else in the world like me?"

That is the question we all ask. And that is why we watch talk shows.

Journalese for the Lay Reader

JOHN LEO

Journalese, the native tongue of newsgatherers and pundits, retains a faint similarity to English but is actually closer to Latin. Like Latin, it is primarily a written language, prized for its incantatory powers, and is best learned early, while the mind is still supple. Every cub reporter, for instance, knows that fires rage out of control, minor mischief is perpetrated by Vandals (never Visigoths, Franks, or a single Vandal working alone) and key labor accords are hammered out by weary negotiators in marathon, round-the-clock bargaining sessions, thus narrowly averting threatened walkouts. The discipline required for a winter storm report is awesome. The first reference to seasonal precipitation is "snow," followed by "the white stuff," then either "it" or "the flakes," but not both. The word snow may be used once again toward the end of the report, directly after discussion of ice-slicked roads and the grim highway toll.

Every so often, an inexperienced reporter attempts to describe a dwelling as "attractive" or "impressive." This is incorrect. In journalese, all homes are either modest or stately. When confronted with a truly ramshackle fixer-upper, knowing scribes will deflect attention to the surrounding area, describing the residence as "off the beaten track" or "in a developing area," that is, a slum. Distaste for the suburbs is conveyed by mentioning "trimmed lawns and neat flower beds," thus artfully suggesting both compulsiveness and a high level of intolerance for life in its hearty, untrimmed state.

Journalese is rich in mystic nouns: gentrification, quichification, greenmail, dealignment, watershed elections and apron strings (the political coattails of a female candidate). But students of the language agree that adjectives do most of the work, smuggling in actual information under the guise of normal journalism. Thus the use of soft-spoken (mousy), loyal (dumb), high-minded (inept), hardworking (plodding), self-made (crooked) and pragmatic (totally immoral). A person who is dangerous as well as immoral can be described as a fierce competitor or gut fighter, and a meddler who cannot leave his subordinates alone is a hands-on executive. When strung together properly, apparently innocent modifiers can acquire megaton force. For instance, a journalist may write, "A private, deliberate man, Frobisher dislikes small talk, but can be charming when he wants to." In translation this means, "An antisocial, sullen plodder, Frobisher is obnoxious and about as articulate as a canteloupe." The familiar phrase "can be charming" is as central to good journalese as "affordable" is to automobile ads and "excellence" is to education reports. It indicates that Frobisher's charm production is a rare result of mighty exertion, yet it manages to end the revelation about his dismal character on an upbeat note. . . .

9. The Oral Essay: The Formal Speech

KEY WORK:

> "Capital Punishment" — T.C. (Tommy) Douglas

ASSOCIATED WORKS:

> "Militant Suffragists" — Emmeline Pankhurst
> "Why Are Americans Afraid of Dragons?" — Ursula K. Le Guin
> "I Have a Dream" — Martin Luther King, Jr.
> "Fiercely Canadian" — Johnny Lombardi
> "The Task of the Poet" — Henrik Ibsen
> Tips on Writing and Delivering an Oral Essay

Most likely you have delivered a formal speech to your classmates, or have listened to one being delivered. From these experiences you know that formal speeches are carefully scripted pieces of writing. It probably will not come as a surprise to you that many public figures, particularly politicians, do not write their own speeches; instead, they use the services of a professional speech writer.

A formal speech is essentially an oral essay. Many formal speeches appear in print form after their original delivery, as is the case with the speeches in this unit and the speech in the unit on University Life. However, the focus and style of oral essays differ from the typical written essay, because the writer's primary concern is the immediate physical presence of the audience. The writer/speaker must establish a rapport with the audience through familiarity with the subject, appropriate tone, and effective delivery.

Formal speeches are a rich source of research information. The Key Work, "Capital Punishment," delivered by Tommy Douglas to the Canadian House of Commons during the 1960s debate on abolishing the death penalty in Canada, contains important information and historical perspective. As you read the other speeches in this unit, note the audience and the context in which each was delivered.

Conventions of the Oral Essay: The Formal Speech

Purpose	To persuade and/or inspire and/or motivate
Audience	Usually an audience of peers or like-minded individuals
Tone	Ranges from serious to humorous
Voice	A strong sense of the occasion and the collective identity of the speaker and the audience
Response	Ranges from deep reverence to light-hearted enjoyment
Language	LEVEL — Appropriate for the occasion and the audience CHARACTERISTICS — Usually personal, "I" and "we"; connotative and strongly rhetorical
Structure	Often straightforward direction

BEFORE READING

1. Discuss the issue of capital punishment, either in opposing pairs or small groups. After a specified time, a spokesperson from each pair or group should summarize the discussion.

2. In your journal or writer's notebook, relate your most memorable experience in delivering or listening to a speech.

3. Working in small groups, brainstorm the qualities of a good speech. Make sure you consider both content and delivery. You may wish to use the Conventions listed above as a guide for your discussion.

Note: Since this is an oral essay, if possible you should listen to someone deliver the speech before examining it in detail in print. See Exploring the Oral Essay (p. 245), question 1.

Capital Punishment

T.C. (TOMMY) DOUGLAS

There are times, Mr. Speaker, when the House of Commons rises to heights of grandeur and becomes deeply conscious of its great traditions. I think this debate has been one of those rare occasions. There has been a minimum of rancour and there has been no imputation of motives because I think that the abolitionists and retentionists alike have been sincerely searching their consciences to see if we can honestly resolve a moral problem. This problem is, how can we abolish a brutal punishment without endangering the safety of society?

I am in favour of the motion to abolish capital punishment and I am also supporting the amendment to put it on a five-year trial basis. I doubt that there is much new that can be said in this debate. The entire field has been well covered but I should like to put very briefly four reasons for my opposition to capital punishment. The first is that capital punishment is contrary to the highest concepts of the Judaic-Christian ethic. I do not propose to go into theological arguments, but both in this debate and in the discussions which have taken place outside the House many people have been quoting Scripture in support of retaining the death penalty.

It is always a dangerous practice to quote isolated passages of Scripture. The Bible has been quoted in times past to support slavery, child labour, polygamy, the burning of witches, and subservience to dictators. The Scriptures have to be viewed as a whole. The Bible is not one book; it is many books. It does not have a static concept. It represents man's emerging moral concepts as they have grown through the centuries.

It is true that the Mosaic law provided the death penalty for murder. It is equally true, if one looks particularly at the 20th chapter of the book of Leviticus, that the Mosaic law provided the death penalty for 33 crimes including such things as adultery, bestiality, homosexuality, witchcraft and sacrificing to other gods than Jehovah. It seems to me that those who want to pick out isolated texts from the Bible in support of retaining the death penalty for murder have to be equally consistent and ask that the death penalty be retained for all the other crimes listed in the Mosaic law.

Of course, those who take this position overlook several facts. They overlook, first of all, the fact that the Mosaic law was an advanced law for the primitive times in which it was formulated. It was later succeeded by the Hebrew prophets who introduced the idea of justice superseded by mercy, the possible redemption and reestablishment of the individual. They overlook the fact that if any nation in the world ought to feel itself bound by Mosaic law it should be the state of Israel. The state of Israel abolished the death penalty many years ago except for Nazi war criminals and for treason committed in times of war. The religious hierarchy of the state of Israel enthusiastically supported the Knesset in abolishing the death penalty in that country.

But for those of us who belong to the Christian religion it seems to me we have to remember also that the Christian religion went far beyond the Mosaic law. In the days of the founder of Christianity the Mosaic law still obtained. This law decreed that a woman taken in adultery could be stoned to death. We should remember the statement of Jesus of Nazareth when he came upon a group of people preparing to stone such a woman to death. He said, Let him who is without sin among you cast the first stone.

When the crowd has dwindled away so that only the woman was left he said to the woman, "Go and sin no more." It seems to me that this is the ultimate culmination of the Christian concept of the application of mercy and the possible redemption of the individual.

My second reason for opposing capital punishment is that I believe capital punishment brutalizes the society that uses it without providing any effective deterrent that cannot be provided equally well by life imprisonment. I believe that any society that practises capital punishment brutalizes itself. It has an effect upon that society and I do not believe that society can rid itself of murderers by itself becoming a murderer. Surely if brutality would deter the committing of a crime Great Britain should have been a place of law-abiding citizens because a little over 150 years ago there were over 200 crimes for which an individual could be put to death. Instead of making Britain a nation of law-abiders it was a country where crime abounded, where human sensibilities were dulled by the public execution of criminals. It is rather significant that in that day, as in this, it was often the juries who were more humane than the lawmakers. It was only because juries refused to convict, knowing the terrible punishment which would follow, that the lawmakers were forced 150 years ago to remove the death penalty from a great many of the crimes for which it had been prescribed.

All of the evidence which can be gathered seems to indicate that the death penalty is not a unique deterrent and that life imprisonment can be equally effective. . . .

I readily agree, Mr. Speaker, that quoting endless statistics is not going to prove either the case for abolition or the case for retention, but there certainly seems to be no convincing volume of evidence which would satisfy any unbiased individual that abolishing the death penalty has resulted in an upsurge of homicide or that those states which have retained the death penalty are any freer of capital crimes than those which have not.

After all, Mr. Speaker, who is it that the death penalty deters? It has certainly not deterred the man who commits murder. Will it deter him in the future? Surely he can be deterred in the future by being incarcerated for the remainder of his life. Who is deterred if this man is hanged? Is he to be hanged as an example to the rest of the community? I can conceive of nothing more immoral than to break a man's neck as an example to other people, but if that is the argument then surely, as the Leader of the Opposition [Mr. Diefenbaker] said yesterday, we ought to have public executions.

The hon. member for Winnipeg South Centre [Mr. Churchill] said that the fear of death will deter men. The fear of death will deter normal men but when a man commits murder, is he normal? Can we understand the motivation that causes a man to take a human life? When a man commits homicide, does he sit down and assess whether he is committing it in a state that has capital punishment or in a state that has abolished capital punishment? I think not. In the main the man who commits homicide is the man who is mentally ill; the man who kills does not make the common, rational judgments that are made by the average individual.

An individual who has become so mentally sick that he will take another life or ravage a child is certainly not a mentally healthy or normal individual.

The third reason I am opposed to capital punishment, Mr. Speaker, is that I believe there are better ways to ensure the safety of society. I completely disagree with the hon. member for Winnipeg South Centre who argued that we must be concerned about the safety of the public. When he asks which is the more important, the life of an innocent person who may be killed or the life of a murderer, there is no doubt that the life of the innocent person is the more important. But is the fact that we break a man's neck any guarantee that innocent people will not be hurt?

We are not suggesting removing the penalty. We are saying that the penalty which ought to be retained is one that will do the two things which are important. First of all, it must be a penalty which will remove the convicted person from human society as long as that person is likely to be a menace to the safety and well-being of his fellow-men. Second, that person should be given an opportunity to receive whatever psychiatric treatment and rehabilitation is possible in the light of his own particular circumstances.

What we have to decide is what we are trying to do, Mr. Speaker. Are we thinking purely of punishing somebody because they have done wrong? Are we thinking purely in punitive terms? Are we thinking purely in terms of vengeance or retribution? Or are we thinking of the two things I have mentioned, first, the safety of society by incarcerating the convicted murderer for life and, second, the possible rehabilitation and redemption of that individual? There is additionally the third great advantage that if society has made a mistake it is possible to rectify the mistake because justice is a human institution and like all human institutions it is liable to error.

I maintain that society has no right to take from a man something which it cannot restore to him. If society makes a mistake and confines a man to prison, depriving him of his freedom, when that mistake is found out society can at least restore to him his freedom and provide him with some compensation for the years he has been incarcerated. But if we hang a man and then find that a mistake has been made there is nothing at all which can be done to make amends.

My quarrel with the death penalty is that it is purely a negative attempt to promote the safety of society. We need to adopt positive measures to promote the safety of society. For instance, we need better law enforcement. In both Canada and the United States every year a great many unsolved crimes are committed. One of the best deterrents is for the criminal to know that if he does commit a crime he will be found out, that he will be incarcerated and put in a place where he can no longer be a menace to the community. We need quicker crime detection methods. For some types of crimes, particularly for those involving psychotics, there ought to be indeterminate sentences.

We all recall a case a few years ago in which a man sexually assaulted a child. He was sentenced to five years in jail. To my mind this was ridiculous because it was based purely on the punitive concept and not out of regard for the safety of the community. It was assumed that at five years less one day, when he was in jail, he was a menace but at five years plus one day he was no longer a menace. Such an individual ought to be sentenced to be kept out of circulation until such time as a panel of judges, psychiatrists and social workers are as certain as a human person can be that the individual is no longer a menace to the safety of the community. I think that in many cases indeterminate sentences to keep out of circulation psychotics who are likely to commit crimes would be of great advantage. In the case I referred to the man got out of jail after five years. Within six months he had not only assaulted another child but had killed the child in the process. Had that individual been sentenced to an indeterminate sentence in the first instance he would not have committed this second heinous crime.

If we want genuine deterrents in this country we need a program of penal reform for the segregation of prisoners and for their rehabilitation so that young first offenders do not go to jail to take what is virtually a postgraduate course in crime.

Let us face the fact that when we talk about retaining capital punishment as a deterrent we are really trying to take the easy way out from solving our problems. In the long run society often gets the criminals it deserves.

Why do we have criminals? What is wrong with the society that produces criminals? Some years ago when I was attending Chicago University I remember that every newspaper in the United States had a heading, "Where Is Crawley?" Crawley was a young gunman who was being hunted across the United States for a series of murders.

A very great columnist in the United States wrote a column which he headed, "Why Is Crawley?" He said that the people of the United States, instead of asking "Where Is Crawley?", ought to take a little time out to ask "Why Is Crawley?" The columnist went over his history. He came from a broken home which the father had deserted and where the mother was out working all day. The boy lived on the streets. He was part of a gang of hoodlums. He was sent to a reformatory and then was back on the streets. He was without proper education and without any counselling. He was sent to jail and associated with hardened criminals. He came out of jail twice as tough as when he went in. By 19 he was a hardened criminal. By the time he was 21 he was a killer. He was finally shot down by the police who were trying to capture him.

I suppose one of the most lamentable murders in our times has been the killing of President John F. Kennedy. Yet, when one reads the story of the man who is believed to have been responsible for his death, we find that when Lee Oswald was a boy in school he was recommended to undergo psychiatric treatment because of the dangerous psychotic tendencies he then displayed. But there were not enough psychiatrists to look after all the children in that particular part of New York city and this boy was not treated. This boy grew up with his psychotic tendencies expanding, and he is believed to have been responsible for extinguishing one of the brightest lights of our generation.

If we really want to tackle the problem of eliminating crime, we must tackle the problem of the slums which breed crime and we must tackle the problem of the lack of psychiatric clinics to take care of psychotics and persons who may become criminally dangerous. We need the kind of penal reform that will make possible the rehabilitation of first offenders with proper probation and parole. We need to go to the roots of the cause of crime and to ask ourselves what it is that produces the murderer in society. . . .

My final point is that I am opposed to capital punishment because I believe that the measure of a nation is the manner in which it treats its misfits and its offenders. Capital punishment has already been abolished in most of the advanced nations of the Western world. The abolition of capital punishment has come to be taken as the hallmark of a nation's conscience. I want to see Canada take this great forward step, and I want to make a special appeal to the members of the House to consider how important for Canada and for its future will be the vote we shall take tonight.

I should not want to be in the shoes of the Prime Minister and the members of his cabinet who have to face up to this very difficult problem. Nobody has been hanged in Canada since 1962. If the motion tonight is defeated the government is going to be in an awkward position. Either it will have to commute those sentenced to death to life imprisonment, knowing that the House of Commons has just rejected a motion suggesting the abolition of the death penalty, or it will have to take the defeat of the motion as an expression of opinion and allow the death sentences to be carried out.

I urge the members of the House to consider the predicament which faces the Prime Minister and the cabinet. I want to urge the House to give a five-year trial to the abolition of the death penalty. If the fears that have been expressed prove to be warranted, if there is an upsurge in the rate of homicide, if we are faced with an increase in crime rate, then in five years the members of the House of Commons who are here then can allow the death penalty to become effective again simply by taking no action. But I would urge that we give this a chance, that we step into line with the progressive countries of the world which have already abolished the death penalty.

What I plead for is that we pass this resolution tonight, with the amendment, which will declare in principle that the House is in favour of abolishing capital punishment and replacement with life imprisonment. If we do that then I believe the House of Commons will have won a great victory, not a victory that will be accompanied by the blaring of trumpets or the rolling of drums but a victory in that we will have taken a forward, moral step and left behind one of the last relics of barbarianism. We will be moving forward to a more humane approach in dealing with crime.

EXPLORING THE ORAL ESSAY

1. While listening to Douglas's speech, make outline notes. In pairs, compare your notes with attention to how concisely and clearly they summarize the content.

2. After listening to Douglas's speech, answer the following questions in small groups or as a class.
   a. To what extent do you think Douglas's speech would have moved and persuaded his audience — the members of the House of Commons? Justify your answer.
   b. To what extent does this speech have the power to persuade and move today's audiences, such as yourself? Explain.

3. Douglas bases his opposition to capital punishment on four reasons. Divide into four groups and have each group select one of those reasons, analyze the logic of Douglas's thinking, and report the analysis to the class.

4. How effectively do you think Douglas dealt with those arguments in favour of capital punishment?

5. Demonstrate that Douglas has effectively used strongly connotative language and a range of devices such as rhetorical questions, balance and parallel structures, irony, and repetition to help sway his audience.

EXTENSIVE STUDY

1. "Militant Suffragists" (p. 247) is part of an address which Emmeline Pankhurst delivered in Hartford, Connecticut, on November 13, 1913.

   a. How appropriate are Pankhurst's metaphors of herself as a soldier and a convict in the context of her speech?

   b. How fitting is Pankhurst's comparison of the "war" to win the vote with the American Revolution and the Civil War?

   c. How does Pankhurst make use of language and emotion to sway her audience?

   d. Which, if any, parts of this speech are still valid in today's society? Justify your answer.

2. Read and, if possible, listen to the speeches of Martin Luther King, Jr.

   a. Compare the rhetorical devices employed in each and compare their effectiveness in terms of intended purpose and audience.

   b. Which speech do you prefer? Account for your reaction.

   c. What makes a speech "memorable" for you?

3. Read Ibsen's "The Task of the Poet" and consider the relevance for today's students.

4. Read the speech by Ursula K. Le Guin (p. 251) and debate the truth of her premise that "The American boy and man is very commonly forced to define his maleness by rejecting . . . the absolutely human faculty of the imagination." Does her statement hold true for the Canadian boy and man?

5. Select two speeches from this unit and explain how each writer has created a tone that was entirely appropriate for the audience and the occasion.

THE WRITING FOLDER

1. Write an evaluation of the effectiveness of Ursula K. Le Guin's style in "Why Are Americans Afraid of Dragons?" (p. 251); consider the sentence structure, diction, and imagery.

2. Write a short formal speech on the importance of the right to vote. In pairs, polish each other's speech before delivering them either to each other or to a larger audience.

3. In your journal or writer's notebook, assess your strengths as a public speaker.

INDEPENDENT STUDY

1. Locate articles on speech writing and use them as a guide to research and "ghost write" a fairly lengthy speech or series of speeches for a contemporary or historical figure. Your research should include reading extensive autobiographical and/or biographical material.

2. Develop a how-to project entitled, "The Art of Speech Making." Include both model speeches and advice. Consult with your teacher-librarian regarding how-to texts and collections of important speeches.

3. John Diefenbaker, Emmeline Pankhurst, Tommy Douglas, Nelly McClung, Agnes McPhail, Martin Luther King, Jr., and Malcolm X are known public speakers. Read the speeches and a biography or the autobiography of one of these individuals (or another of your choice) and write an essay examining the individual's talents as a speech maker.

TIMED READING AND WRITING

1. a. Assess the effectiveness of Johnny Lombardi's speech, "Fiercely Canadian" (p. 260) by examining the sentences, diction, and imagery in terms of the audience and the occasion.
   b. Read Meera Shastri's "Canadian Experience" (p. 145) and, in the role of Shastri, write a personal response to Lombardi's speech as if she had been a member of Lombardi's audience.

2. Read "Claiming an Education" by Adrienne Rich (p. 297) and summarize it in approximately 300 words.

Militant Suffragists

EMMELINE PANKHURST

I do not come here as an advocate, because whatever position the suffrage movement may occupy in the United States of America, in England it has passed beyond the realm of advocacy and it has entered into the sphere of practical politics. It has become the subject of revolution and civil war, and so to-night I am not here to advocate woman suffrage. American suffragists can do that very well for themselves. I am here as a soldier who has temporarily left the field of battle in order to explain — it seems strange it should have to be explained — what civil war is like when civil war is waged by women. I am not only here as a soldier temporarily absent from the field of battle; I am here—and that, I think, is the strangest part of my coming—I am here as a person who, according to the law courts of my country, it has been decided, is of no value to the community at all; and I am adjudged because of my life to be a dangerous person, under sentence of penal servitude in a convict prison. So you see there is some special interest in hearing so unusual a person address you. I dare say, in the minds of many of you—you will perhaps forgive me this personal touch—that I do not look either very like a soldier or very like a convict, and yet I am both.

It would take too long to trace the course of militant methods as adopted by women, because it is about eight years since the word militant was first used to describe what we were doing; it is about eight years since the first militant action was taken by women. It was not militant at all, except that it provoked militancy on the part of those who were opposed to it. When women asked questions in political meetings and failed to get answers, they were not doing anything militant. To ask questions at political meetings is an acknowledged right of all people who attend public meetings; certainly in my country, men have always done it, and I hope they do it in America, because it seems to me that if you allow people to enter your legislatures without asking them any questions as to what they are going to do when they get there you are not exercising your citizen rights and your citizen duties as you ought. At any rate in Great Britain it is a custom, a time-honored one, to ask questions of candidates for Parliament and ask questions of members of the government. No man was ever put out of a public meeting for asking a question until Votes for Women came onto the political horizon. The first people who were put out of a political meeting for asking questions, were women; they were brutally ill-used; they found themselves in jail before twenty-four hours had expired. But instead of the newspapers, which are largely inspired by the politicians, putting militancy and the reproach of militancy, if reproach there is, on the people who had assaulted the women, they actually said it was the women who were militant and very much to blame.

It was not the speakers on the platform who would not answer them, who were to blame, or the ushers at the meeting; it was the poor women who had had their bruises and their knocks and scratches, and who were put into prison for doing precisely nothing but holding a protest meeting in the street after it was all over. However, we were called militant for doing that, and we were quite willing to accept the name, because militancy for us is time-honored; you have the church militant and in the sense of spiritual militancy we were very militant indeed. We were determined to press this question of the enfranchisement of the women to the point where we were no longer to be ignored by the politicians as had been the case for about fifty years, during which time women had patiently used every means open to them to win their political enfranchisement.

Experience will show you that if you really want to get anything done, it is not so much a matter of whether you alienate sympathy; sympathy is a very unsatisfactory thing if it is not practical sympathy. It does not matter to the practical suffragist whether she alienates sympathy that was never of any use to her. What she wants is to get something practical done, and whether it is done out of sympathy or whether it is done out of fear, or whether it is done because you want to be comfortable again and not be worried in this way, doesn't particularly matter so long as you get it. We had enough of sympathy for fifty years; it never brought us anything; and we would rather have an angry man going to the government and saying, my business is interfered with and I won't submit to its being interfered with any longer because you won't give women the vote, than to have a gentleman come onto our platforms year in and year out and talk about his ardent sympathy with woman suffrage.

"Put them in prison," they said, "that will stop it." But it didn't stop it. They put women in prison for long terms of imprisonment, for making a nuisance of themselves — that was the expression when they took petitions in their hands to the door of the House of Commons; and they thought that by sending them to prison, giving them a day's imprisonment, would cause them to all settle down again and there would be no further trouble. But it didn't happen so at all: instead of the women giving it up, more women did it, and more and more and more women did it until there were three hundred women at a time, who had not broken a single law, only "made a nuisance of themselves" as the politicians say.

The whole argument with the anti-suffragists, or even the critical suffragist man, is this: that you can govern human beings without their consent. They have said to us, "Government rests upon force; the women haven't force, so they must submit." Well, we are showing them that government does not rest upon force at all; it rests upon consent. As long as women consent to be unjustly governed, they can be; but directly women say: "We withhold our consent, we will not be governed any longer so long as that government is unjust," not by the forces of civil war can you govern the very weakest woman. You can kill that woman, but she escapes you then; you cannot govern her. And that is, I think, a most valuable demonstration we have been making to the world.

Now, I want to say to you who think women cannot succeed, we have brought the government of England to this position, that it has to face this alternative; either women are to be killed or women are to have the vote. I ask American men in this meeting, what would you say if in your State you were faced with that alternative, that you must either kill them or give them their citizenship, — women, many of whom you respect, women whom you know have lived useful lives, women whom you know, even if you do not know them personally, are animated with the highest motives, women who are in pursuit of liberty and the power to do useful public service? Well, there is only one answer to that alternative; there is only one way out of it, unless you are prepared to put back civilization two or three generations; you must give those women the vote. Now that is the outcome of our civil war.

You won your freedom in America when you had the Revolution, by bloodshed, by sacrificing human life. You won the Civil War by the sacrifice of human life when you decided to emancipate the negro. You have left it to the women in your land, the men of all civilized countries have left it to women, to work out their own salvation. That is the way in which we women of England are doing. Human life for us is sacred, but we say if any life is to be sacrificed it shall be ours; we won't do it ourselves, but we will put the enemy in the position where they will have to choose between giving us freedom or giving us death.

Why Are Americans Afraid of Dragons?

URSULA K. LE GUIN

This was to be a talk about fantasy. But I have not been feeling very fanciful lately, and could not decide what to say; so I have been going about picking people's brains for ideas. "What about fantasy? Tell me something about fantasy." And one friend of mine said, "All right, I'll tell you something fantastic. Ten yeas ago, I went to the children's room of the library of such-and-such a city, and asked for *The Hobbit*; and the librarian told me, 'Oh, we keep that only in the adult collection; we don't feel that escapism is good for children.' "

My friend and I had a good laugh and shudder over that, and we agreed that things have changed a great deal in these past ten years. That kind of moralistic censorship of works of fantasy is very uncommon now, in the children's libraries. But the fact that the children's libraries have become oases in the desert doesn't mean that there isn't still a desert. The point of view from which that librarian spoke still exists. She was merely reflecting, in perfect good faith, something that goes very deep in the American character: a moral disapproval of fantasy, a disapproval so intense, and often so aggressive, that I cannot help but see it as arising, fundamentally, from fear.

So: Why are Americans afraid of dragons?

Before I try to answer my question, let me say that it isn't only Americans who are afraid of dragons. I suspect that almost all very highly technological peoples are more or less antifantasy. There are several national literatures which, like ours, have had no tradition of adult fantasy, for the past several hundred years: the French, for instance. But then you have the Germans, who have a good deal; and the English, who have it, and love it, and do it better than anyone else. So this fear of dragons is not merely a Western, or a technological, phenomenon. But I do not want to get into these vast historical questions; I will speak of modern Americans, the only people I know well enough to talk about.

In wondering why Americans are afraid of dragons, I began to realize that a great many Americans are not only antifantasy, but altogether antifiction. We tend, as a people, to look upon all works of the imagination either as suspect, or as contemptible.

"My wife reads novels. I haven't got the time."

"I used to read that science fiction stuff when I was a teenager, but of course I don't now."

"Fairy stories are for kids. I live in the real world."

Who speaks so? Who is it that dismisses *War and Peace, The Time Machine,* and *A Midsummer Night's Dream* with this perfect self-assurance? It is, I fear, the man in the street — the hardworking, over-thirty American male — the men who run this country.

Such a rejection of the entire art of fiction is related to several American characteristics: our Puritanism, our work ethic, our profit-mindedness, and even our sexual mores.

To read *War and Peace* or *The Lord of the Rings* plainly is not "work" — you do it for pleasure. And if it cannot be justified as "educational" or as "self-improvement," then, in the Puritan value system, it can only be self-indulgence or escapism. For pleasure is not a value, to the Puritan; on the contrary, it is a sin.

Equally, in the businessman's value system, if an act does not bring in an immediate, tangible profit, it has no justification at all. Thus the only person who has an excuse to read Tolstoy or Tolkien is the English teacher, because he gets paid for it. But our businessman might allow himself to read a best-seller now and then: not because it is a good book, but because it is a best-seller — it is a success, it has made money. To the strangely mystical mind of the money-changer, this justifies its existence; and by reading it he may participate, a little, in the power and manna of its success. If this is not magic, by the way, I don't know what is.

The last element, the sexual one, is more complex. I hope I will not be understood as being sexist if I say that, within our culture, I believe that this antifiction attitude is basically a male one. The American boy and man is very commonly forced to define his maleness by rejecting certain traits, certain human gifts and potentialities, which our culture defines as "womanish" or "childish." And one of these traits or potentialities is, in cold sober fact, the absolutely essential human faculty of imagination.

Having got this far, I went quickly to the dictionary.

The *Shorter Oxford Dictionary* says; "Imagination. 1. The action of imagining, or forming a mental concept of what is not actually present to the senses; 2. The mental consideration of actions or events not yet in existence."

Very well; I certainly can let "absolutely essential human faculty" stand. But I must narrow the definition to fit our present subject. By "imagination," then, I personally mean the free play of the mind, both intellectual and sensory. By "play" I mean recreation, re-creation, the recombination of what is known into what is new. By "free" I mean that the action is done without an immediate object of profit — spontaneously. That does not mean, however, that there may not be a purpose behind the free play of the mind, a goal; and the goal may be a very serious object indeed. Children's imaginative play is clearly a practicing at the acts and emotions of adulthood; a child who did not play would not become mature. As for the free play of an adult mind, its result may be *War and Peace,* or the theory of relativity.

To be free, after all, is not to be undisciplined. I should say that the discipline of the imagination may in fact be the essential method or technique of both art and science. It is our Puritanism, insisting that discipline means repression or punishment, which confuses the subject. To discipline something, in the proper sense of the word, does not mean to repress it, but to train it — to encourage it to grow, and act, and be fruitful, whether it is a peach tree or a human mind.

I think that a great many American men have been taught just the opposite. They have learned to repress their imagination, to reject it as something childish or effeminate, unprofitable, and probably sinful.

They have learned to fear it. But they have never learned to discipline it at all.

Now, I doubt that the imagination can be suppressed. If you truly eradicated it in a child, he would grow up to be an eggplant. Like all our evil propensities, the imagination will out. But if it is rejected and despised, it will grow into wild and weedy shapes; it will be deformed. At its best, it will be mere ego-centered daydreaming; at its worst, it will be wishful thinking, which is a very dangerous occupation when it is taken seriously. Where literature is concerned, in the old, truly Puritan days, the only permitted reading was the Bible. Nowadays, with our secular Puritanism, the man who refuses to read novels because it's unmanly to do so, or because they aren't true, will most likely end up watching bloody detective thrillers on the television, or reading hack Westerns or sports stories, or going in for pornography, from *Playboy* on down. It is his starved imagination, craving nourishment, that forces him to do so. But he can rationalize such entertainment by saying that it is realistic — after all, sex exists, and there are criminals, and there are baseball players, and there used to be cowboys — and also by saying that it is virile, by which he means that it doesn't interest most women.

That all these genres are sterile, hopelessly sterile, is a reassurance to him, rather than a defect. If they were genuinely realistic, which is to say genuinely imagined and imaginative, he would be afraid of them. Fake realism is the escapist literature of our time. And probably the ultimate escapist reading is that masterpiece of total unreality, the daily stock market report.

Now what about our man's wife? She probably wasn't required to squelch her private imagination in order to play her expected role in life, but she hasn't been trained to discipline it, either. She is allowed to read novels, and even fantasies. But, lacking training and encouragement, her fancy is likely to glom on to very sickly fodder, such things as soap operas, and "true romances," and nursy novels, and historico-sentimental novels, and all the rest of the baloney ground out to replace genuine imaginative works by the artistic sweatshops of a society that is profoundly distrustful of the uses of the imagination.

What, then, are the uses of the imagination?

You see, I think we have a terrible thing here: a hardworking, upright, responsible citizen, a full-grown, educated person, who is afraid of dragons, and afraid of hobbits, and scared to death of fairies. It's funny, but it's also terrible. Something has gone very wrong. I don't know what to do about it but to try and give an honest answer to that person's question, even though he often asks it in an aggressive and contemptuous tone of voice. "What's the good of it all?" he says. "Dragons and hobbits and little green men — what's the *use* of it?"

The truest answer, unfortunately, he won't even listen to. He won't hear it. The truest answer is, "The use of it is to give you pleasure and delight."

"I haven't got the time," he snaps, swallowing a Maalox pill for his ulcer and rushing off to the golf course.

So we try the next-to-truest answer. It probably won't go down much better, but it must be said: "The use of imaginative fiction is to deepen your understanding of your world, and your fellow men, and your own feelings, and your destiny."

To which I fear he will retort, "Look, I got a raise last year, and I'm giving my family the best of everything, we've got two cars and a color TV. I understand enough of the world!"

And he is right, unanswerably right, if that is what he wants, and all he wants.

The kind of thing you learn from reading about the problems of a hobbit who is trying to drop a magic ring into an imaginary volcano has very little to do with your social status, or material success, or income. Indeed, if there is any relationship, it is a negative one. There is an inverse correlation between fantasy and money. That is a law, known to economists as Le Guin's Law. If you want a striking example of Le Guin's Law, just give a lift to one of those people along the roads who own nothing but a backpack, a guitar, a fine head of hair, a smile, and a thumb. Time and again, you will find that these waifs have read *The Lord of the Rings* — some of them can practically recite it. But now take Aristotle Onassis, or J. Paul Getty: could you believe that those men ever had anything to do, at any age, under any circumstances, with a hobbit?

But, to carry my example a little further, and out of the realm of economics, did you ever notice how very gloomy Mr. Onassis and Mr. Getty and all those billionaires look in their photographs? They have this strange, pinched look, as if they were hungry. As if they were hungry for something, as if they had lost something and were trying to think where it could be, or perhaps what it could be, what it was they've lost.

Could it be their childhood?

So I arrive at my personal defense of the uses of the imagination, especially in fiction, and most especially in fairy tale, legend, fantasy, science fiction, and the rest of the lunatic fringe. I believe that maturity is not an outgrowing, but a growing up; that an adult is not a dead child, but a child who survived. I believe that all the best faculties of a mature human being exist in the child, and that if these faculties are encouraged in youth they will act well and wisely in the adult, but if they are repressed and denied in the child they will stunt and cripple the adult personality. And finally, I believe that one of the most deeply human, and humane, of these faculties is the power of imagination: so that it is our pleasant duty, as librarians, or teachers, or parents, or writers, or simply as grownups, to encourage that faculty of imagination in our children, to encourage it to grow freely, to flourish like the green bay tree, by giving it the best, absolutely the best and purest, nourishment that it can absorb. And never, under any circumstances, to squelch it, or sneer at it, or imply that it is childish, or unmanly, or untrue.

For fantasy is true, of course. It isn't factual, but it is true. Children know that. Adults know it too, and that is precisely why many of them are afraid of fantasy. They know that its truth challenges, even threatens, all that is false, all that is phony, unnecessary, and trivial in the life they have let themselves be forced into living. They are afraid of dragons, because they are afraid of freedom.

So I believe that we should trust our children. Normal children do not confuse reality and fantasy — they confuse them much less often than we adults do (as a certain great fantasist pointed out in a story called "The Emperor's New Clothes"). Children know perfectly well that unicorns aren't real, but they also know that books about unicorns, if they are good books, are true books. All too often, that's more than Mummy and Daddy know; for, in denying their childhood, the adults have denied half their knowledge, and are left with the sad, sterile little fact: "Unicorns aren't real." And that fact is one that never got anybody anywhere (except in the story "The Unicorn in the Garden," by another great fantasist, in which it is shown that a devotion to the unreality of unicorns may get you straight into the loony bin). It is by such statements as, "Once upon a time there was a dragon," or "In a hole in the ground there lived a hobbit" — it is by such beautiful non-facts that we fantastic human beings may arrive, in our peculiar fashion, at the truth.

I Have a Dream

MARTIN LUTHER KING, JR.

I am happy to join with you today in what will go down in history as the greatest demonstration for freedom in the history of our nation.

Five score years ago, a great American, in whose symbolic shadow we stand today, signed the Emancipation Proclamation. This momentous decree came as the great beacon light of hope for millions of Negro slaves who had been seared in the flames of withering injustice. It came as the joyous daybreak to end the long night of their captivity.

But 100 years later the Negro still is not free. One hundred years later, the life of the Negro is still badly crippled by the manacles of segregation and the chains of discrimination. One hundred years later, the Negro lives on a lonely island of poverty in the midst of a vast ocean of material prosperity. One hundred years later, the Negro is still languished in the corners of American society and finds himself an exile in his own land. So we have come here today to dramatize the shameful condition.

In a sense we've come to our Nation's Capital to cash a check. When the architects of our republic wrote the magnificent words of the Constitution and the Declaration of Independence, they were signing a promissory note to which every American was to fall heir. This note was a promise that all men, yes, black men as well as white men, should be guaranteed the unalienable rights of life, liberty, and the pursuit of happiness.

It is obvious today that America has defaulted on this promissory note insofar as her citizens of color are concerned. Instead of honoring this sacred obligation, America has given the Negro people a bad check, a check which has come back marked "Insufficient Funds." But we refuse to believe the bank of justice is bankrupt. We refuse to believe that there are insufficient funds in the great vaults of opportunity of this nation. So we have come to cash this check, a check that will give us open demand, the riches of freedom and the security of justice. We have also come to this hallowed spot to remind America of the fierce urgency of now.

This is no time to engage in the luxury of cooling off or to take the tranquilizing drug of gradualism. Now is the time to make real the promises of democracy. Now is the time to rise from the dark and desolate valley of segregation to the sunlit path of racial justice. Now is the time to lift our nation from the quicksand of racial injustice to the solid rock of brotherhood. Now is the time to make justice a reality for all God's children.

It would be fatal for the nation to overlook the urgency of the moment. This sweltering summer of the Negro's legitimate discontent will not pass until there is an invigorating autumn of freedom and equality. Nineteen sixty-three is not an end but a beginning. Those who hoped that the Negro needed to blow off steam and will now be content will have a rude awakening if the nation returns to business as usual. There will be neither rest nor tranquility in America until the Negro is guaranteed his citizenship rights. The whirlwinds of revolt will continue to shake the foundations of our nation until the bright day of justice emerges.

But there is something I must say to my people who stand on the warm threshold which leads them to the palace of justice. In the process of gaining our rightful place we must not be guilty of wrongful deeds. Let us not seek to satisfy our thirst for freedom by drinking from the cup of bitterness and hatred. We must forever conduct our struggle on the high plane of dignity and discipline. We must not allow our creative protest to degenerate into physical violence. Again and again we must rise to the majestic heights of meeting physical force with soul force.

The marvelous new militancy which has engulfed the Negro community must not lead us to a distrust of all white people, for many of our white brothers, as evidenced by their presence here today, have come to realize that their destiny is tied up with our destiny. They have come to realize that their freedom is inextricably bound to our freedom. We cannot walk alone.

And as we walk we must make the pledge that we shall always march ahead. We cannot turn back. There are those who are asking the devotees of civil rights: "When will you be satisfied?" We can never be satisfied as long as the Negro is the victim of the unspeakable horrors of police brutality. We can never be satisfied as long as our bodies, heavy with the fatigue of travel, cannot gain lodging in the motels of the highways and the hotels of the cities. We cannot be satisfied as long as the Negro's basic mobility is from a smaller ghetto to a larger one. We can never be satisfied as long as our children are stripped of their selfhood and robbed of their dignity by signs stating: "For Whites Only." We cannot be satisfied as long as the Negro in Mississippi cannot vote and the Negro in New York believes he has nothing for which to vote. No, no, we are not satisfied and we will not be satisfied until justice rolls down like waters and righteousness like a mighty stream.

I am not unmindful that some of you have come here out of great trials and tribulations, some of you have come fresh from narrow jail cells, some of you have come from areas where your quest for freedom left you battered by the storms of persecution and staggered by the winds of police brutality. You have been the veterans of creative suffering. Continue to work with the faith that unearned suffering is redemptive.

Go back to Mississippi, go back to Alabama, go back to South Carolina, go back to Georgia, go back to Louisiana, go back to the slums and ghettos of our northern cities, knowing that somehow this situation can and will be changed. Let us not wallow in the valley of despair.

I say to you today, my friends, even though we face the difficulties of today and tomorrow, I still have a dream. It is a dream deeply rooted in the American dream. I have a dream that one day this nation will rise up and live out the true meaning of its creed: "We hold these truths to be self-evident: that all men are created equal."

I have a dream that one day on the red hills of Georgia the sons of former slaves and the sons of former slaveowners will be able to sit down together at the table of brotherhood.

I have a dream that one day even the State of Mississippi, a state sweltering with the heat of injustice, sweltering with the heat of oppression, will be transformed into an oasis of freedom and justice. I have a dream that my four little children will one day live in a nation where they will not be judged by the color of their skin but by the content of their character. I have a dream today.

I have a dream that one day down in Alabama with its vicious racists, with its Governor having his lips dripping with the words of interposition and nullification — one day right there in Alabama, little black boys and black girls will be able to join hands with little white boys and white girls as sisters and brothers.

I have a dream today.

I have a dream that one day every valley shall be exalted, every hill and mountain shall be made low, the rough places will be made plain and the crooked places will be made straight, and the glory of the Lord shall be revealed, and all flesh shall see it together.

This is our hope. This is the faith that I go back to the South with. With this faith we will be able to hew out of the mountain of despair a stone of hope. With this faith we will be able to transform the jangling discords of our nation into a beautiful symphony of brotherhood. With this faith we will be able to work together, to pray together, to struggle together, to go to jail together, to stand up for freedom together, knowing that we will be free one day.

This will be the day when all God's children will be able to sing with new meaning:

> My country 'tis of thee,
> Sweet land of liberty,
> Of thee I sing:
> Land where my fathers died,
> Land of the pilgrims' pride,
> From every mountain-side
> Let Freedom ring.

And if America is to be a great nation, this must become true. So, let freedom ring from the prodigious hill tops of New Hampshire. Let freedom ring from the mighty mountains of New York. Let freedom ring from heightening Alleghenies of Pennsylvania. Let freedom ring from the snowcapped Rockies of Colorado. Let freedom ring from the curvaceous slopes of California. But not only that, let freedom ring from Stone Mountain of Georgia.

Let freedom ring from Lookout Mountain of Tennessee.

Let freedom ring from every hill and molehill of Mississippi. From every mountainside, let freedom ring. And when we allow freedom to ring, when we let it ring from every village, from every hamlet, from every state and every city, we will be able to speed up that day when all of God's children, black men and white men, Jews and Gentiles, Protestants and Catholics, will be able to join hands and sing in the words of the old Negro spiritual: "Free at last! free at last! thank God almighty, we are free at last!"

Fiercely Canadian

JOHNNY LOMBARDI

Mr. Lombardi was invited to speak at a special session of the Court of Canadian Citizenship on April 15, 1987, by Presiding Judge, Maria Sgro. He was asked to speak to the new citizens and their families about "what it means to him to be a Canadian." His feelings ran deep as he celebrated with new Canadians the 40th anniversary of the first Canadian Citizenship Act.

"I am a Canadian by birth, born and raised here in Toronto. I know all about citizenship as it pertains to the early immigrant. My dad came here sometime at the turn of the century. He and all his early immigrant and pioneering buddies could hardly wait to become citizens. It had value in the early days, much more than today.

Being a Canadian means many things to many people. My mother and my father came from Italy with very little in the way of material possessions. They came because they wanted a better life. A better life for themselves, a better life for the children they knew they would one day bring into this world. Italians, like all others, are very family oriented. Children, family . . . these were important to my parents. The opportunity to raise a family in better circumstances than what they experienced in their homeland brought them to our beloved Canada.

My mom and dad came to Toronto at the turn of the century looking for the so-called streets paved with gold. They found the streets, but they weren't paved with gold. They worked hard together, as a team. They planned, they saved, they stretched, they made do, they persevered along with many other immigrants like them. I was born. My sister was born. Life was hard. Opportunities were all around however. You had but to reach out and make them happen because here in Canada anything can happen if you work. My mom used to say to me . . . "Gianni, never stop dreaming. Work hard, reach for the stars, Gianni, and you'll make it. If you don't, at least you will stand tall." It is with regret that I must stand before you and say to you that I didn't make it soon enough for my beloved mother to reap some of the benefits that I now am in a position to bestow upon her. She would have been proud of her Gianni, this I know.

As president of CHIN Radio/TV International, broadcasting in over thirty languages to over thirty different cultures, we try very hard to meet the needs of new Canadians.

Several years back I was appointed as a member of the Order of Canada. Why you ask? Well, for doing something that I love to do. Radio and television broadcasting and being community inspired.

Where but in my beloved country of Canada can I be recognized for doing something that I so love to do? Where else but in my beloved Canada can I be fiercely Canadian and so mighty proud of my Italian heritage? Where else but in my beloved Canada can I be whatever I choose to be and where I can stand tall and proud and free as I am standing here today saying to you, to all of you . . . welcome, welcome to *my* home, welcome to Canada.

The best advice I can give to you as new Canadians is to give to Canada your all and it will follow, as surely as night follows the day, that you, in turn, will receive all that this beloved country has to offer to you, and it has indeed so very, very much to offer and to give. Be good to Canada. It will be good to you."

The Task of the Poet

HENRIK IBSEN

. . . And what does it mean, then, to be a poet? It was a long time before I realized that to be a poet means essentially to see, but mark well, to see in such a way that whatever is seen is perceived by the audience just as the poet saw it. But only what has been lived through can be seen in that way and accepted in that way. And the secret of modern literature lies precisely in this matter of experiences that are lived through. All that I have written these last ten years, I have lived through spiritually. But no poet lives through anything in isolation. What he lives through all of his countrymen live through with him. If that were not so, what would bridge the gap between the producing and the receiving minds?

And what is it, then, that I have lived through and that has inspired me? The range has been large. In part I have been inspired by something which only rarely and only in my best moments has stirred vividly within me as something great and beautiful. I have been inspired by that which, so to speak, has stood higher than my everyday self, and I have been inspired by this because I wanted to confront it and make it part of myself.

But I have also been inspired by the opposite, by what appears on introspection as the dregs and sediment of one's own nature. Writing has in this case been to me like a bath from which I have risen feeling cleaner, healthier and freer. Yes, gentlemen, nobody can picture poetically anything for which he himself has not to a certain degree and at least at times served as a model. And who is the man among us who has not now and then felt and recognized within himself a contradiction between word and deed, between will and duty, between life and theory in general? Or who is there among us who has not, at least at times, been egotistically sufficient unto himself, and self unconsciously, half in good faith, sought to extenuate his conduct both to others and to himself?

I believe that in saying all this to you, to the students, my remarks have found exactly the right audience. You will understand them as they are meant to be understood. For a student has essentially the same task as the poet: to make clear to himself, and thereby to others, the temperal and eternal questions which are astir in the age and in the community to which he belongs.

In this respect I dare to say of myself that I have endeavored to be a good student during my stay abroad. A poet is by nature far-sighted. Never have I seen my homeland and the true life of my homeland so fully, so clearly, and at such close range, as I did in my absence when I was far away from it.

And now, my dear countrymen, in conclusion a few words which are also related to something I have lived through. When Emperor

Julian stands at the end of his career, and everything collapses around him, there is nothing which makes him so despondent as the thought that all he has gained was this: to be remembered by cool and clear heads with respectful appreciation, while his opponents live on, rich in the love of warm, living hearts. This thought was the result of much that I have lived through; it had its origin in a question that I had sometimes asked myself, down there in my solitude. Now the young people of Norway have come to me here tonight and given me my answer in word and song, have given me my answer more warmly and clearly than I had ever expected to hear it. I shall take this answer with me as the richest reward of my visit with my countrymen at home, and it is my hope and my belief that what I experience tonight will be an experience to "live through" which will sometime be reflected in a work of mine. And if this happens, if sometimes I shall send such a book home, then I ask that the students receive it as a handshake and a thanks for this meeting. I ask you to receive it as the ones who had a share in the making of it.

———

After an absence of ten years, Ibsen spent a couple of months in Norway during the summer of 1874. On September 10, Norwegian students marched in procession to Ibsen's home. This speech is Ibsen's reply to their greeting.

TIPS ON WRITING AND DELIVERING AN ORAL ESSAY

1. Review Orwell's six rules for language usage (p. 23).
   - As rule number 1 states, clichéd and tired language and images may slip by the eye, but not the ear. The medium truly is the message.
2. Focus on your specific purpose.
   - In a sentence or two, note specifically what it is you want your audience to take away with them. That will give you your focus.
   - Make sure every word counts, particularly the first few and the last few. It is in the first few minutes that you capture your audience's interest and attention and in the last few that you provide them with something to remember.
3. Know and respect your audience.
   - Consider the audience's point of view and prior knowledge. Notice how Tommy Douglas carefully built his argument in the face of a potentially hostile audience.

- Rigorously edit your speech so that you engage or entertain your audience. Add emotion where appropriate.

4. Use mental and physical signposts to help your reader follow your thinking.
   - Link your ideas with connective words and expressions and repetitions of key images, phrases, and words to assist your audience in following the logic and order of your presentation. Notice how effectively King, Jr. and Lombardi used these devices in their speeches.
   - Use rhetorical devices such as deliberate pauses, inflections in your voice, and gestures as visual and aural signposts. Make sure that these devices enhance what you are saying rather than detract from it. Avoid distracting or inappropriate gestures such as excessive hand movements.

5. Use memorable anecdotes and/or illustrations.
   - Audiences remember stories better than they remember disconnected ideas. Notice how effectively Ursula K. Le Guin used stories and anecdotes to illustrate her thesis.

6. Prepare carefully for the delivery or your speech.
   - Write your speech in large print or type, underlining words and passages that need emphasis, places where pauses would be appropriate, and other notes to yourself concerning your delivery.
   - Practise your speech with a friend or in front of a mirror with a tape recorder.
   - Stay calm. Concentrate on getting your message across.
   - Make eye contact with your audience. You should look around and speak to the audience in all parts of the room.
   - The speech should be so well-rehearsed that you are able to deliver it with a fresh and spontaneous manner.

10. The Social Science Essay

KEY WORK:

> "Violence against women" — Mary Labatt

ASSOCIATED READINGS:

> "It's a National Disgrace" — John Doe (student essay)
> "Authority and Socialization in a Primitive Society" —
>   Bronislaw Malinowski (adaptation)
> "Native Canadian Land Claims and Sovereignty" — Sarah
>   Neville (student essay)
> "Bizbuzz" — William Safire
> Tips on Writing a Social Science Essay

If you study subjects such as politics, economics, anthropology, sociology or, perhaps, law, you will be required to write social science essays, sometimes called thesis papers or simply "reports." (You will notice we deal with the report in a separate unit, although, as with most classifications, categories overlap.) Most often you will prepare a research paper in which you make a thesis statement, argue its validity, reconcile conflicting interpretations, and provide extensive referencing. Social science papers for university courses are formal, objective presentations built around facts. You will also notice that each discipline has its own specialized vocabulary — often called jargon — in which it couches its arguments. It is important that you become familiar with these specialized terms; however, good writers avoid obscuring their argument with jargon. For further discussion of this concept, see William Safire's "Bizbuzz" in the Associated Readings.

Today, popularized versions of social science essays appear as media articles. Magazines, such as *Psychology Today*, and newsletters and bulletins for professionals such as teachers and social workers also feature these essays. The Key Work, "Violence against women," first published in the Federation of Women Teachers' Associations of Ontario (FWTAO) Newsletter, is one such example. You will notice that Labatt uses less jargon and more judgemental (connotative) language than might be found in an academic work such as Neville's essay on native Canadian land claims. But extensive referencing justifies Labatt's statements. The adaptation of Malinowski's work demonstrates the format and specialized language you will encounter in anthropology and sociology courses.

Conventions of the Social Science Essay

Purpose	To educate, inform, argue a case
Audience	Specialized — academic or professional
Tone	Serious, objective
Voice	None to little
Response	Intellectual concern, curiosity
Language	LEVEL — Formal
	CHARACTERISTICS — Factual, mainly objective, denotative diction
Structure	Thesis statement most often in paragraph one; paragraphs dense, occasionally separated by subheadings as in a report

BEFORE READING

1. Invite a teacher-librarian or student services teacher to discuss inquiry methods used by the humanities, social sciences, and pure sciences.

2. In small groups, determine the extent to which you feel the media contribute to violence against children, women, and minority groups.

3. Review the conventions of the social science essay as outlined above, and compare them to the conventions of the report.

Violence against women

MARY LABATT

One year ago, on December 6, 1989, a lone gunman walked into École Polytechnique in Montreal and gunned down fourteen women engineering students. The victims were intelligent young women; they were killed on a bright morning in the last hour of term.

Their executioner, Marc Lepine screamed, *You're all a bunch of feminists. I hate feminists.* As he worked his way through the building, he systematically spared men and killed women. Marc Lepine was an abused child and the son of a battered wife.

In the days that followed, people tried to make sense of the murders. Few commentators wanted to listen to the murderer's statement. He said clearly that he was murdering feminists because he hated them.

VIOLENCE AGAINST WOMEN AND CHILDREN INCREASING

In Montreal, more women were killed by their partners in 1990 than were killed at the Polytechnique. But, nobody noticed these women because they were killed in their own homes. They were nameless and faceless victims.

In 1989, 119 women were murdered in domestic relationships. Most publications say that one in ten Canadian women is battered by her male partner, but research now indicates that one in four women is physically abused by her male partner (Smith, 1987). In the Smith study, an additional measure of abuse revealed an even higher incidence rate over 36 per cent. One study found that 80 per cent of the children witness their father's violence and it is known that this trauma can leave indelible scars on their developing personalities.

A Canadian woman is raped every seventeen minutes (Canadian Association of Sexual Assault Centres) and the incidence of rape is rising alarmingly. Eighty-four per cent of assaulted women are raped by someone they know and 57 per cent of the rapes occur on a date (Warshaw, 1988). And 60 per cent of rapes take place in private homes. Date rape is a new form of violence for women to fear.

The attitudes of young people towards date rape are unbelievable. One researcher found that fifty-four per cent of high school boys and forty-two per cent of the girls sampled said it was acceptable for a boy to hold a girl down and force her to have sexual relations with him if he had spent a lot of money on her, they had dated a long time, or she led him on (Giarruso, 1984). In another study, 65 per cent of the boys and 47 per cent of the girls thought a man could force a woman to have sex if they had been dating for more than six months (Toronto Star, May 3, 1988). A study at York University revealed that 31 per cent of the males and 22 per cent of the females thought the girl was to blame if her partner forced sexual relations on her (Check and LaCrosse, 1988).

A study in Toronto secondary schools found that 20 per cent of the girls had suffered sexual assault and eleven per cent reported physical violence while dating. Sixty per cent of the students had been exposed to dating violence, either as victims, perpetrators, witnesses or being told by friends. In all cases the girl continued the relationship after the first incident of violence. She did all the work in the relationship, adapted, watched his moods carefully and endured. Self-sacrifice featured strongly in the young woman's image of femininity (Litch Mercer, 1987). It is estimated that only 1 per cent of the date rapes are reported to the authorities (Russell, 1984).

Children are regular victims. One out of every four girls is sexually abused within the family or sexually assaulted by an outsider. One in nine little boys is sexually molested. One study found that one out of every two girls and one out of every three boys had suffered at least one unwanted sexual advance before the age of 21 years (Badgley Report, 1984). In Canada, the number of child abuse cases have increased by 500 to 1200 per cent in the past five years (Rogers, 1988).

The true extent of physical abuse and child neglect is unknown because only the most extreme cases come to the attention of the authorities. The Canadian Medical Association estimates that 8,000 children are badly injured by abuse every year, but that is only the tip of the iceberg (Health and Welfare, Canada, 1989). Emotional abuse often accompanies physical or sexual abuse and is part of the continuum of abusive behaviour which culminates in battering (Health and Welfare, 1989).

Statistics don't describe the scars that abusers leave on their victims' souls, the mistrust, alienation, delayed development, social and emotional maladjustment and isolation. Too many children are stunted before they have a chance to develop and it takes a lifetime to heal, if they ever do.

NEWSPAPER SHOWS SITUATION

A brief glance at the newspapers reveals the situation for women and children. As I write, the headlines in the Toronto Star tell us that an eleven year old girl has been gang raped by four, perhaps seven youths at a party while everyone watched. A spokesperson from the rape crisis centre said that party rape is common now. Every day, the rape crisis centre gets calls from parents seeking help for a daughter who has been raped at a party.

On the front page of the Toronto Sun, a woman's boyfriend threw her baby out of a moving car in Whitby. The infant was hit by a passing car and is at the moment clinging to life. On page five, perhaps because it's not unusual enough to merit the front page, a widow in Markham has been shot to death in her home by her nephew.

These are only the major stories in one twenty-four hour period. It is a completely random day, not a day selected for particular violence.

SOCIETY'S DENIAL OF THE PROBLEM

Most victims report that they are revictimized by the courts, police, friends and family by being made to share the blame. In cases of sexual assault, there is a great tendency to make the female victim part of the problem, by accusing her of being seductive, leading him on, giving false cues of consent. Blame is especially virulent in the cases of date rape where the victim is almost always accused of arousing her attacker. The whole notion that women somehow cause themselves to be raped, violated and battered is not only unjust, it prevents society from seeing the real issues.

Society must not get confused when an assailant claims his partner was enraging him or a woman aroused him. It is irrelevant that the child was affectionate or that he thought the child was sexually provocative. One of society's most vile traits is the way the victim is made to share the criminal's responsibility. The perpetrator of a violent act commits the act, not the victim. Until everyone agrees on that point, there can be no change. There will only be a continuation of sexism at its worst.

Language is another way we can lose a clear focus. Terms such as domestic violence, spousal assault and family violence make the violence sound like a mutual thing. Inappropriate language makes solutions more elusive because the problem is not clearly defined. Some writers are suggesting the term woman abuse because it includes the sexual, emotional and physical forms of violence (Randall, 1989). Terms such as wife battering and wife beating also clarify our thinking about who is the victim and who is the perpetrator.

There is also the tendency to focus on drugs, alcohol, stress levels and lack of anger control. If society is going to address male violence properly, we have to get rid of all these red herrings. Putting a violent husband in an alcohol treatment centre, only addresses one of his problems. A relationship between violence and alcohol exists, but evidence shows it as correlated, not causal (Kincaid, 1982).

Even helpful safety tips can miss the point. *Look in the back seat before you drive. Don't walk alone at night. You can't be raped if you aren't there*, is the message. No one would deny the usefulness of this advice, but when safety tips become the focus of rape prevention, society is denying the problem. Not being there does nothing for a man who has developed the mental, moral and emotional consent required to rape someone. He will find a victim.

Linda McLeod, author of *The City for Women — No Safe Place*, has concluded that there is no safe place for women. Women at home are open to violence, because most women are victimized at home. If women go out in the evening, their chances of attack increase, so they are caught in a constricting bind. They limit their behaviours so they won't attract violence. But they are usually attacked by relatives and friends anyway, so avoiding violence is impossible. The fear level women must endure is an equality issue (McLeod, 1989).

Every individual who commits violence has learned to accept violent behaviour. If we agree that it does not make sense to accept excuses for violence and it does not make sense to deny violence and it makes no sense to transfer responsibility to the victims, then we have to look at the roots of violence. Why is violence directed at women? Why did Marc Lepine scream, *You're a bunch of feminists?* What does feminism have to do with murder?

VIOLENCE IN THE HOME

Since the home is the crucible where individual character is shaped, the home is the starting point for serious inquiry. Wife battering has become a national epidemic with somewhere between 2.5 million and 6.25 million women assaulted by men they once loved (Randall, 1989). Wife battering affects everyone, women of all ages, all social class, racial, cultural, religious, economic, educational and professional backgrounds. People used to think it affected the lower socio-economic classes, not nice people. Not only is that assumption entirely wrong, it mitigates against the middle class woman who has had no experience with violence. She finds it very difficult to get out, because she is ashamed to admit it and she is bewildered by this unfamiliar and terrifying behaviour. In her classic study on wife abuse, *The Omitted Reality*, Pat Kincaid found that women who had experienced battering in their families of origin were the quickest to leave. Women with no experience of violence took up to 15 years to leave, compared to four years for the experienced group (Kincaid, 1982).

This has implications for an organization like FWTAO which serves 38,000 professional women. Calculations based on the Smith research indicate that there must be approximately 9,500 FWTAO members suffering violence from their male partners. If you teach with twelve women, the statistics indicate that three of them are being abused, by their boyfriend or husband. When we consider those numbers in light of the Kincaid research, we recognize that there are special barriers of pride and inexperience with violence that can make it hard for professional women to disclose, but disclose they must if they are ever to be free.

UNDERSTANDING THE WOMAN VICTIM

The victim suffers both physical and psychological trauma. The man tries to control where the woman goes and who she sees. This social isolation makes her more vulnerable because her home becomes more private. Immigrant women suffer terribly from isolation. They are prevented from seeking help by the controlling behaviour of their husbands and they are at a grave disadvantage due to language and lack of kinship networks in this country.

Sexual abuse, rape and coercion are often part of the pattern; the aggression is reinforced with verbal assaults, psychological denigration and intimidation. The aggressor needs to control every fibre of her being, even her self-image and her sense of hope. Women react predictably and become listless and develop a poor self-concept.

Violence escalates over time, so her task becomes more and more difficult as she tries to cling to some semblance of normal life and some mainstays within her own psyche. She restricts herself, adapts herself, teaches her children to adapt and molds herself to her powerless status in the vain hope that she will be spared further violence. She is like a small animal, sensing danger, watching for escape routes, coping with the children, hiding the problem from the neighbours and friends. Coping increases her isolation and her self-esteem plunges so much that many women seek refuge in drugs or alcohol.

The most frequently asked question is why didn't she leave? There are always inferences of masochism which demonstrate ignorance of the problem's etiology and psychology. Answers such as economic dependence and uncertainty about where to go are factors which can be relevant, but they are not the whole reason. In the research on date rape when a young woman can end the relationship any time, women stayed, because they didn't believe they had the right to govern their own lives and because their traditional view of femininity encouraged them to value self-sacrifice (Litch Mercer, 1987).

Answers lie in the nature of the trauma. The psychological trauma of a battered wife has been likened to the Stockholm Syndrome, the complex emotional dependency that has been observed in women who are kidnapped and abused by terrorists. It is not masochism. The Stockholm Syndrome is rooted in the experience of being battered, the near brush with death, the visceral knowledge that she could be killed so easily, the lack of control over her own body, her own fate. This kind of psychological terrorism comes from a hostage-type situation with intimidation over a period of time (Graham et al, 1988). The complex psychological phenomenon holds great promise for understanding the victims of wife assault.

UNDERSTANDING THE CHILD VICTIM

Men who batter consistently report that they witnessed their mothers being battered and received physical abuse themselves (Dutton, 1988). Violence is learned as a source of power and control in their first social group, the family.

The predicament of children who are captive in violent homes is terrible. Jaffe, Wolfe and Wilson in their study, *Children of Battered Women*, quote the work of L. Walker as the best description of a child's predicament. It is worth repeating: *Children who live in a battering relationship experience the most insidious form of child abuse. Whether or not they are physically abused by either parent is less important than the psychological scars they bear from watching their father beat their mother. They learn to become part of a dishonest conspiracy of silence. They learn to lie to prevent inappropriate behaviour and they learn to suspend the fulfillment of their needs rather than risk another confrontation. They expend a lot of energy avoiding problems* (Walker, 1979). There have to be serious psychological consequences for any child who is forced to live like that.

Wife battering strikes at the very heart of healthy child development. Mothers under stress are less able to respond to their infants so basic needs for attachment and routines of feeding and sleeping are disrupted. A mother who lives in fear may not be able to handle the stress of her infant's demands. Infants recognize their mother's lack of availability so they become cranky and fail to thrive (Hart and Brasard, 1987). Infants exhibit screaming and poor sleeping behaviours.

Preschoolers have been found to stutter, shake, yell, develop physical symptoms and hide from adults. Many authors have noted a significant overlap between wife assault and child abuse, so children are victimized directly and indirectly. Peak periods of woman abuse correspond to the peak periods of child abuse which are toddlerhood and the onset of the teen years (Jaffe, Wolfe and Wilson, 1990).

Children can internalize the conflict or externalize it in behaviour problems as they adapt to a roller coaster of emotion. Shame, fear, anxiety, guilt and intermittent rescue fantasies are common. At school, they are distracted and innattentive. At home, they are alert and tense as they lay in their beds waiting for the sounds of violence. They are condemned to grow up with very little peace and security in their lives (Jaffe et al, 1990).

Child and adolescent behaviours range from: psychosomatic complaints, absenteeism, delinquency, peer isolation or complete identification with peers, fears, loneliness, running away, poor impulse control, low self-esteem, depression, poor social skills, deceptiveness, lying, stealing, cheating, accepting blame or projecting blame, battering animals or siblings, alcohol/drug addiction, suicidal tendencies, carelessness (Boyd et al, 1984 in Jaffe et al, 1990).

Like their mothers, the children have been victimized by a type of post-traumatic stress disorder which can show itself at any age after trauma. Children's reactions to the violence are trauma responses, outbursts of anger, aggression, fixation on the trauma, emotional and somatic complaints, and the reduction of normal activities (Jaffe et al, 1990). The normal development of children is inextricably tied to safety and nurturance in their family, something that is not available to a child in a violent home (Van der Kolk, 1987). The post-traumatic stress symptoms can erupt later in unexpected ways such as juvenile violence, running away and extreme oppositional behaviour (Jaffe et al, 1990).

In general, younger children are the most sympathetic towards their mothers (Alessi and Hearn, 1984), but this sympathy seems to wane as children grow. As children get older, they often display anger and hostility towards their mother. Sometimes adolescents blame their mother for the family problems and batter her themselves to gain their own ends (Straus et al, 1980).

Parents usually deny that their children have witnessed violence, but studies have shown that almost all children can describe the minute details of the episode even when their parents think they have not seen it.

Latency-age children are looking to their parents as role models and begin to see violence as an acceptable form of conflict resolution. Hughes, 1982, noted that many latency-aged boys identified with their fathers and missed their fathers when they were taken to a shelter. McLeod (1987) in *Battered not Beaten* said it was extremely discouraging to see the daughters of battered wives coming back ten years later as battered wives.

Not every child exposed to wife battering becomes violent. In general, the more risk factors a child has at one time, the more likely he or she is to develop a psychiatric disturbance (Rutter, 1979; Rae-Grant, 1984). Additional risk factors are, poverty, alcoholic parent, parental deviance etc. For these unfortunate children, violence just continues in the next generation.

Violence radiates from a violent home. Not only does it spawn the next generation of abusers, it causes its teenagers to escape to the streets where they become homeless. Homeless adolescents not only become victims of street violence, they have to perpetuate violence in order to survive.

Wife battering is a problem with so many implications that it can be seen as the invisible core of violence within society. But, people want to avoid the issue. As Pat Kincaid said in her study, it's an *Omitted Reality*.

THE EFFECT OF MEDIA VIOLENCE

The media supports the culture of violence that the child sees in the home. In 1982, 3 to 11 year olds were getting 15 hours a week of violent cartoons. By 1986, it was up to 42 hours a week (Molnar, 1988) and by 1987, it had escalated to 43 hours a week (Carlsson-Paige and Levin, 1988). The average child spends the equivalent of 22 school days a year watching violence on television (Molnar, 1988).

Television is teaching children a world-view which includes violence as an acceptable solution, authoritarian power relationships, sex-role stereotyping and conflict as fun. And children do imitate what they watch and replicate it in play (Carlsson-Paige and Levin, 1988). A major review of research has concluded that television violence definitely affects aggression (Friedrich-Cofer and Huston, 1986). It should not be too surprising that dating violence has become such a problem. Young people from 12 to 17 years of age are the primary consumers of pornography in Canada. Thirty-five per cent reported watching rape, torture and bondage (Check, and LaCrosse, 1988).

Children from violent homes are especially susceptible to media violence. When inmates who were convicted of violent crimes were compared with a nonviolent control group who had not committed any offense, childhood television viewing habits alone were not predictive of adult violence. What was predictive was the interaction of large amounts of violent television and witnessing marital violence (Heath et al, 1986). Clearly, media violence contributes to the development of violent behaviour for a young person who has grown up with violence in significant adult role models.

SEXISM: THE ROOT OF THE PROBLEM

Sexism runs deep in western civilization. A little boy in this culture soon learns that he is heir to the status, authority, rights and privileges of being male. Conversely, little girls learn to subordinate themselves. This western notion of male dominance has some very serious implications for violence (Dobash and Dobash, 1979; Eichler, 1980; Kincaid, 1982).

In thousands of subtle little ways, girls learn to denigrate themselves while boys learn to speak out, be adventurous and suppress emotions adults consider feminine. Little girls learn they have a duty to men and little boys learn they have the right to dominate women (Eichler, 1980). People of conscience and intelligence are working to eradicate sexism, but change that goes against the whole history of a culture is profoundly difficult. Sexism is everywhere—advertising, entertainment, media, industry, magazines, business, law courts. Research found school readers filled with sexism (FWTAO, 1989), so if educational materials are inculcating sex role stereotyping, we shudder to think what the larger society is teaching children.

A patriarchy like ours places men in the position of power, privilege and leadership while conferring lesser status on women and children. For a patriarchy to work, everyone in the hierarchy has to be conditioned to accept their status, so a whole ideology has evolved to legitimize inequality among people (Dobash and Dobash, 1979). Although people don't like to see our society in these terms, the process is not much different than socializing people to accept serfdom, slavery or the divine right of kings. Those injustices have disappeared into history, but the patriarchy remains intact, supported by the awesome power of social conditioning, ideologies and the full structure of political and economic institutions.

In her research, *Not a Pretty Picture*, Shirley Litch Mercer demonstrates how adolescent dating violence illustrates this conditioning. Adolescents are experimenting with the gender roles they have learned and in their attitudes towards date rape, they express the male's right to do as he pleases with a woman of lesser status. It is not surprising that she found significant numbers of girls supporting male dominance. They are also echoing what they have been taught. The early childhood game of *playing house* gives way to the deadly adolescent game of *playing spouse* as children try on the adult roles they have been taught (Litch Mercer, 1987). In the words of one researcher; *Adolescents may seem wild and alienated . . . but their values are highly derivative of their parents' own* (Check and Lacrosse). Adolescents provide a mirror in which we can see the deadly consequences of providing children with role models of male dominance.

Systemic inequality is expressed in inadequate day care, sexual harassment at work, poverty, poorly enforced child support, lower pay, lack of promotions and sex discrimination. These injustices are forms of abuse that women suffer every day.

Violence is a natural outcome in a society that institutionalizes misogyny. Whenever a society devalues some of its members, it can expect that individual pathology will take up where institutionalized abuse stops. Like child beating, violence is the culmination of emotional and sexual domination that find its final expression in outright battering and even death.

Men growing up in a patriarchy learn that the natural order of things is for them to have superior status over women. It is not a status they have to earn, it is a birthright, a prescribed status. If their actual status in real life situations doesn't correspond to their prescribed status, the gap causes uncomfortable tension. This difference between real and prescribed status has been called a *lack of fit*. This lack of fit between actual status and prescribed status has been called a major cause of violence against women (Eichler, 1980; Allen and Straus, 1979).

Pat Kincaid (1982) says we systematically teach both girls and boys *a prescription of male dominance as if it had a biological basis*. The degree to which individuals believe the sexist promise of a prescribed status, is seen as the major variable in wife battering (Kincaid, 1982).

Some theorists argue that if actual and prescribed status were congruent, there would be less violence (Allan and Strauss, 1979). Mercifully, the terrible sexism of that theory has been spotted because it *supports a pattern of male dominance by emphasizing problems that arise with its maintenance* (Kincaid, 1982). Exactly. Instead of questioning sexism with all our intellect and all our wills, people take it as a given. They think it's a fact. The earth is round and men were created to be superior.

BACKLASH AGAINST FEMINISM

What does feminism have to do with murder? The answer is everything. Marc Lepine, beaten by a violent father and witness to his mother's battering, learned early that violence was the way to cope with frustration and he also learned to target women for that violence.

Women seeking equality have learned to expect backlash, but what is horrifying about the Montreal massacre is that it was the ultimate backlash. Those murders were not the usual misogyny that women struggle with all their lives. The murders point to a new and virulent backlash against women who dare break the stereotypes and get ahead educationally and economically (Lakeman, 1990).

In Marc Lepine's pocket, he had a hit list of successful women, all non-traditional and successful in their careers. He expressed his rage at the engineering students before he shot them. Society had broken its promise that he was superior to women.

Our society betrayed Marc Lepine just as surely as it betrayed his victims. He was raised on the belief in male domination and it fuelled his hate. When the 1970 Royal Commission on the Status of Women released its report, it didn't discuss violence. Now, twenty years later, violence against women has become untenable. FWTAO has gathered representatives from major women's groups to seek a Royal Commission on violence against women. It's time.

We know the roots of violence. We know that every generation of children is being conditioned to hold values that will wreck their lives. We know that sexism lies at the root of the problem. And we know that sexism is so deep that most people continue to deny it.

Sexism seeps into every area of our lives. Like a lethal, silent fog, it clouds perceptions, relationships, aspirations and goals. Sexism is a limitation placed on everyone and all humanity is diminished by it.

Violence is sexism's hideous offspring. It threatens everyone, but women and children most of all.

Isn't it time we did something about it?

SELECTED REFERENCES

Carlsson-Paige, Nancy and Diane Levin. *Children and Violence—Young Children and War Play. Educational Leadership, Dec. 1987/Jan. 1988.*

Check, James, and LaCrosse, Victoria. *Attitudes and Behaviour Regarding Pornography, Sexual Coercion and Violence in Metro Toronto Highschool Students.* **Toronto: The LaMarsh Research Programme Reports on Violence and Conflict Resolution, 1988.**

Dobash, Emerson and Dobash, Russell. *Violence Against Wives: A Case Against the Patriarchy.* **New York: The Free Press, 1979.**

Fantuzzo, J. and Lindquist, C. *The Effects of Observing Conjugal Violence on Children.* **Journal of Family Violence. Vol. 4, 1989.**

Friedrich-Cofer, L. and Huston, A. *Television Violence and Aggression: The Debate Continues.* **Psychological Bulletin, 3, 1986.**

Giarusso et al, cited in Adams, Caren et al. *No is Not Enough.* **California: Impact Publishers, 1984.**

Graham, S., Rawlings, E. and Rimini, N. *Survivors of Terror: Battered Women, Hostages and the Stockholm Syndrome* in *Feminist Perspectives on Wife Abuse.* **Beverly Hills: Sage, 1988.**

Hart, S. and Brassard, M. *A Major Threat to a Child's Mental Health: Psychological Maltreatment.* **American Psychologist, Vol. 42, 1987.**

Health and Welfare, Canada. *Family Violence: A Review of Theoretical and Clinical Literature.* **Health and Welfare, Canada, Mar., 1989.**

Heath, C., Kruttschnitt, C. and Ward, D. *Television and Violent Criminal Behaviour: Beyond the Bobo Doll.* **Violence and Victims, Vol. 1, 1986.**

Kincaid, Pat. *The Omitted Reality: Husband-Wife Violence in Ontario and Policy Implications for Education.* **Concord, Ont.: Belsten Publishing Ltd., 1982.**

Lakeman, Lee. *The Backlash Against Feminism: Women, Violence and the Montreal Massacre.* **This Magazine, Vol. 23, No. 7, Mar., 1990.**

Litch Mercer, Shirley. *Not a Pretty Picture: An Exploratory Study of Violence against Women in Highschool Dating Relationships.* **Toronto: Education Wife Assault, 1987.**

McLeod, Linda. *Battered but not Beaten.* **Ottawa: Canadian Advisory Council on the Status of Women, 1987.**

McLeod, Linda. *The City for Women: No Safe Place.* **Canadian Secretary of State, Sept., 1989.**

Molnar, Alex. *Children and Violence — Selling Our Souls.* **Educational Leadership, Dec. 1987/ Jan. 1988.**

Randall, Melanie. *The Politics of Woman Abuse: Understanding the Issues.* **Education Wife Assault, Nov. 1989.**

Rogers, Rix. *Reaching for Solutions. The Summary Report on Child Sexual Abuse in Canada.* **Health and Welfare, Canada, 1990.**

Russell, Diana. *Sexual Exploitation: Rape, Child Abuse and Workplace Harassment.* **Beverly Hills: Sage, 1984.**

Smith, Michael. *The Incidence and Prevalence of Woman Abuse in Toronto.* **Violence and Victims, No. 2, 1987.**

Sweet, Ellen. *Date Rape: The Story of an Epidemic and Those Who Deny It.* **MS Magazine, Oct. 1985.**

EXPLORING THE ESSAY

1. To what extent does Labatt appear to adapt the conventions of the social science essay for its intended audience and publication? Give specific examples to support your assessment.

2. Determine whether Labatt's writing style would be appropriate if the essay were written for an academic audience. Tip: You may wish to consult a teacher of law, politics, or sociology.

3. a. Labatt uses the American Psychological Association's style of referencing. Assess the strengths and weaknesses of this style as opposed to footnotes or endnotes.

   b. What impact does her extensive referencing have on the reader?

4. a. In small groups, research many definitions of the words "sexist" and "sexism." Tip: Your teacher-librarian may be able to suggest sources to get you started.

   b. Is one definition most helpful in determining whether or not Labatt's article is sexist?

5. a. Determine the balance between fact and opinion presented, citing specific examples of each. How might a reader verify one or more of Labatt's facts?

   b. To what extent does Labatt's argument persuade you to accept her thesis?

EXTENSIVE STUDY

1. Debate an issue which Labatt's essay raises. You might derive a resolution from one of the following quotations:

   "The most frequently asked question is why didn't she leave?"

"A spokesperson from the rape crisis centre said that party rape is common now."

2. Compare Neville's "Native Canadian Land Claims and Sovereignty" (p. 287) with Labatt's article, accounting for similarities and differences in:
   a. tone, and the level and type of diction
   b. structure and organization
   c. style and voice or author intrusion
   d. referencing
   e. types of evidence
   f. effective argumentation

3. With a partner, recast the introduction to Labatt's article for a scholarly audience and Neville's for a professional newsletter. Compare your work with that of another pair of students.

4. Read Malinowski's "Authority and Socialization in a Primitive Society" (p. 283) and consider what light his theory sheds on contemporary North American pop culture's choice of heroes and myths. You also may want to refer to Lippman's "How television is reshaping world's culture" (p. 115) and "Why Talk Shows Won't Shut Up" (p. 231).

5. a. Read Safire's "Bizbuzz" (p. 291) and determine what assessment he would make of the language in Labatt's, Neville's, and Malinowski's styles of writing. Do you agree?
   b. Referring to Labatt's and Malinowski's works, determine what role language plays in social violence and sexual stereotyping. (You may wish to refer to Orwell's "Politics and the English Language," page 12, to support your position.)

THE WRITING FOLDER

1. Respond in a form of your choice to an idea or issue raised in one or more of the essays in this unit.

2. Write a different conclusion for Neville's essay.

3. Draft a speech, lecture, editorial, or report on an issue raised in the essays in this unit.

INDEPENDENT STUDY

1. Develop a project around the media's depiction of violence and/ or sexual stereotypes, considering such sources as cartoons,

comics, rock videos, popular films, magazines, and newspapers. In consultation with your teacher, teacher-librarian, and/or a media teacher locate research that has already been done in this area and incorporate it into your project.

2. Compare the depiction of violence against women and/or children in two contemporary literary works or in literature published in different eras. You might select one male and one female author. Works to consider include: Pat Conroy, *Prince of Tides*; Thomas Hardy, *Tess of the D'Urbervilles*; Alison Lurie, *The Truth About Lorin Jones*; William Shakespeare, *The Taming of the Shrew*; Thomas Harris, *Silence of the Lambs*; Gail Godwin, *A Southern Family*.

   Note: Discuss with your teacher or teacher-librarian which titles are most appropriate for your tastes and needs.

3. Develop a project around literary works that depict the plight of Canada's Native people or another minority group. Authors to consider include: Neil Bissoondath, Joy Kogawa, Amy Tan, David Suzuki, Rohinton Mistry, V.S. Naipaul, Mordecai Richler, Tomson Highway, Bernard Malamud, Beatrice Culleton, Gabrielle Roy, and Ralph Ellison. Your teacher or teacher-librarian may suggest additional Canadian writers.

TIMED READING AND/OR WRITING

1. After reading Safire's "Bizbuzz" (p. 291), prepare an outline for a debate on the place of jargon in business language.

2. Write a letter to the editor of a specific newspaper or magazine stating your views on violence against women.

3. Read a social science essay written by a classmate. In a commentary, comment on strengths and suggest improvements.

It's a National Disgrace

JOHN DOE *(student essay)*

Reading Mary Labatt's essay, "Violence against women," poignantly reminded me of the woman who changed my life.

No, it's not what you think, guys. The woman's name is Laura Robinson and she's an ex-member of the Ontario and national cycling team. She'd come to our Physical Education class to talk about the inequalities facing women in sports. But what really disturbed me was the data she shared about the difficulties women face living in a male-dominated world.

I'll admit I was skeptical at first. I've never considered myself a feminist, nor have I been any more interested in the plight of women than most of my male contemporaries. I've spent my adolescence committed to athletics and calculus. But I'm a numbers man and Robinson supported her argument with statistics. Those statistics about the number of women and children who are raped, abused, or murdered each hour in Canada in their own homes establish the magnitude of what Labatt terms our "national disgrace." Ironically, the bride walks down the aisle, dressed in submissive white, into the arms of her alleged protector. But there's no safe haven, nowhere to go after the wedding.

These statistics brought a lump to my throat and I was forced to confront my past complacency. I'd dismissed these issues with a haughty, male "so what?" But I could no longer convince myself that the trouble was simply fabricated by a bunch of whining, man-hating radicals. For the first time, I actually *thought* about the fact that my mother or my sister could be one of the victims the statistics represent. I don't like to admit it, but the pig-headed refusal of guys like me to confront these issues simply perpetuates them.

Facing uncomfortable emotional issues is not something I excel at. Guys don't get much training in sorting out their feelings. In the past, when abused women and children appeared on "Geraldo" or "Oprah", I tended to scoff. Now, I have trouble holding back the tears (why do I still hold them back?) as a young woman tells of being raped by six star players of a college football team. She was treated like the person on trial, trying to prove she was not "easy". It seemed the courts were more concerned about her sexual history than her allegations. And the men? The men got off scot-free.

Shows like this, and women such as Robinson and Labatt, are several of the reasons I got to thinking and reading about this issue and what we could do about it. It wasn't easy. I had to reevaluate some of my basic thinking. Mike Tyson, whom I'd worshipped since the age of 13, could no longer be my idol — the person I wanted to be. His behaviour outside the ring, it turned out, epitomizes everything I now know is inexcusably wrong. "Rambo" can no longer be part of my personal mythology. Neither I nor other guys can continue to scoff at everything that "feminists" have to say. We may feel threatened by individuals and movements who try to bash stereotypes, but we can't turn our backs any longer. Change can only happen if we are willing to confront our fears and change our thinking. Teaching girls to be cautious — to "call if you need a ride", to carry rape whistles, and never work alone at the office at night — is not the answer. Changing our thinking about power and sexuality, sex roles and stereotypes is the only way to change the devastating statistics.

But there's another deeply personal reason that I got to thinking about this issue, that I care about change. It's perhaps why I found it so difficult to let down my macho self-image and admit I cared. Now that I *let* myself, I can identify with the abuse of women and children because I, too, was a victim. My uncle beat me up and a baby-sitter molested me. My reaction — typical of victims — was to feel guilty and ashamed, as if I had done something to deserve this abuse. My parents never knew, but I carried the pain with me and it's shaped a lot of my behaviour.

The problems of violence against *people* won't just vanish. We've got to deal with it openly. And one of the best places to do that is in classrooms — now.

Authority and Socialization in a Primitive Society

BRONISLAW MALINOWSKI *(adaptation)*

FREUD'S THEORY. According to Freudian psychoanalytic theory, the family universally gives rise to a typical constellation of feelings called the "Oedipus complex," in which the male child feels hostility toward his father because the child desires exclusive access to his mother. This hostility must be suppressed, but it manifests itself in later life as antagonism toward male authority figures. Freud held that the source of hostility to the father was sexual feeling on the part of the child for the mother. He believed that the Oedipus complex appears in disguised form in fairy tales, legends, and myths. For example, in the Greek mythical drama for which Freud named the complex, Oedipus unknowingly but inevitably killed his father and married his mother. Freud regarded the myth as evidence for the existence of the complex. The myth was a symbolic and socially acceptable form for expressing the repressed desire to return to a warm and intimate relation with the mother.

MALINOWSKI'S THEORY. Malinowski approached the study of the Oedipus complex from the standpoint of anthropological studies, which show wide variation in family structure. He held that the pattern of "conflicts, passions, and attachments" within the family varied according to the structure. Malinowski's hypothesis was that the hostility of the male child was directed against the father not in his role as husband of the mother, but in his role as authority over the child, and that the source of the Oedipus complex was not sexual jealousy but resentment of the father's power to dominate. He reasoned that if his hypothesis were correct, the Oedipus complex was not universal but a product of the middle-class family in Western society. This family is patriarchal, and the father has the dominant power within it. Other societies, however, distribute power differently, and the father has power in varying degrees. There are some societies in which he has very little power. Malinowski tested his hypothesis in the light of his extensive knowledge of the Trobriand Islanders (east of New Guinea), who vest authority over the child in the mother's brother rather than in the father.

THE FATHER. The Trobriand Islanders are matrilineal, that is, kinship is reckoned through the mother only, succession and inheritance descend in the female line, and children belong to the mother's family, clan, and community. A boy inherits the social position and the possessions, not of his father but of his maternal uncle.

Matrimony is monogamous except for chiefs. The Trobrianders are ignorant of conception and do not regard the husband as the father of the children. He gives the children loving care and tender companionship in early childhood, but his authority over them is only by virtue of his personal relations with them. The mother's brother is the socially recognized source of authority.

Marriage in the Trobriand Islands is patrilocal: the wife goes to live with her husband in a house in his community. The children *live* with the father in childhood, but they *belong* to the mother's community. Their real home is where their maternal uncle lives.

THE MATERNAL UNCLE. The child is integrated into the life of the community and learns his role and obligations in society from his mother's brother. This maternal uncle, not the father, directs the boy's occupations, teaches him tribal laws and prohibitions, and requires certain services of him. The work he does with his uncle contributes to his own community in which he will eventually take his place. Although he continues to work with his father, he does so out of good will and friendship, for this work contributes to his father's community of people who are legally strangers to him. The uncle holds the key to the boy's social status, wealth, power, and family pride. Therefore, to the Trobriand boy, the uncle is idealized as the model of right behavior and is the person to please and emulate.

During adolescence the young boy learns his duties, is instructed in traditions and magic, in arts and crafts. At this time relations between the boy and his uncle are most intimate and satisfactory, and the father suffers a temporary eclipse in the child's life.

The authority and discipline exercised by the uncle inevitably prove irksome to the child, and the ideal of behavior provided by him, a burden. Although the education received from his uncle is the road to mature status in the community, it requires from him the renunciation of childhood pleasures and the repression of childhood impulses. The child reveres his uncle, but he also resents him, and this hostility must be repressed and denied.

Unlike the father in our society, the Trobriand father escapes these feelings of hostility. Without authority and the power to discipline, he invokes no dislike on the part of the child. On the contrary, he provides a haven and a refuge when friction between the child and his uncle develops.

MYTH AND REALITY. Following Freud's suggestion that repressed feelings find outlet in myth and legend, Malinowski examined Trobriand stories. He found that the father is not mentioned in their mythology. Myths are based upon the matrilineal family pattern, and the central male role is usually taken by the maternal uncle, who is typically the villain. He abandons the nephew or withholds the art of magic from him and is murdered by the nephew. These myths are double-edged. They may mean that the uncle finds his duties to his nephew irksome or that the nephew would be glad to be rid of his debt of gratitude to his uncle.

The mutual hostility and suspicion between uncle and nephew in myths have their parallel in reality. While it is the duty of the uncle to pass on to his nephew the family possessions, the nephew is in fact bound to make a substantial payment for inheritance. When a father gives gifts to his son, he always does so out of sheer affection, and magic is as often received from the father as a gift as it is inherited from the uncle. However, when magic is inherited from the uncle, there may be a suspicion in the nephew's mind that he has been cheated of his full share. Suspicion does not arise when the magic is a gift from the father.

CONCLUSION. Malinowski disagreed with Freud on two counts. He concluded (1) that the Oedipus complex, as Freud described it, is not universal but a product of the patriarchal family in Western society, and (2) that the hostility found in the Oedipus complex is directed against the father, not because of his sexual relation to the mother, but because of his social relation to the child. This social relation is an *authority* relation, and hostility will center around whoever has dominant authority within the family.

The authority problem of the maternal uncle in Trobriand society lies in the divided loyalties of the uncle-father and the dilemma of authority and intimacy.

1. The family system of the Trobriand Islanders is subject to *divided loyalties*. The uncle is father to his own children and bound to them by ties of affection, and he may resent his obligation to his nephew — obligations which must have preference over his personal relations with his children and his wife. The nephew's fear of abandonment, hostility, and suspicion may, therefore, be not so much the result of rebellion against the uncle's authority as a recognition of the uncle's divided loyalties. By the standards of Trobriand culture, the uncle ought to be wholly committed to the nephew, but the nephew knows he is not.

2. The uncle is not only an authority figure for the nephew but his educator as well. Education must involve him in intimate relations with his nephew. When authority is combined with intimacy, it is likely to generate hostility. The intimacy leads to expectations that the person will be treated with affection and leniency, while the authority relation leads to a measure of impersonal judgment. In other words, it is not authority alone that engenders hostility, but authority combined with a personal or primary relationship.

CAUTION. While Malinowski's study is an interesting attempt to test psychological hypotheses by anthropological investigation, it should not be concluded that the specific issue treated here is definitely settled.

Native Canadian Land Claims and Sovereignty

SARAH NEVILLE *(student essay)*

Christopher Columbus is a celebrated hero in western culture, signifying the discovery of the New World, its space, wealth and freedom. But to North America's Native people, Columbus signifies the beginning of the end of their culture. Only recently have Native Canadians begun to agitate successfully for change. After a three hundred year legacy of mistreatment and neglect, Native Canadians should be granted fair land settlements and control over their own lands with minimal government intervention. These settlements would provide Native people with security from government policies, financial freedom, pride in their community and, finally, retribution for ancient wrongs.

Currently, Native Canadians can make no claims to security over their lands as Native lands are Crown lands controlled by the federal and provincial governments.[1] Governments' marginal concern with the rights of Native Canadians is seen in situations such as the James Bay Project. The Quebec government was prepared to flood 3516 square kilometres of Hydro-owned land — part of the Cree's traditional land — without conducting crucial environmental tests. This type of disregard for the land and its people has focused attention on Native rights.

Another point of concern is the government's readiness to override treaty promises to satisfy administrative difficulties. One prominent example is the Natives' right to unlimited hunting and fishing. Legislation such as the Migratory Birds Convention Act[2] which limits hunting seasons curtails their traditional practices. Although the Supreme Court struck down the law, other Acts and legislation have slowly diminished the Natives' land and their privileges over that land.[3]

That red tape often effectively invalidates legal guarantees is seen in regard to Section 25 of the Canadian Charter of Rights and Freedoms. It states:

> The guarantee in this Charter of rights and freedoms shall not be construed so as to abrogate or derogate from any aboriginal, treaty or other rights or freedoms that pertain to the Aboriginal peoples of Canada including. . . .
> b) any rights or freedoms that now exist by way of land claims agreements or may be so acquired.[4]

This statement appears to grant the Native community its right to the land and respect for the treaties. However, the phrase "existing rights" means they are, in fact, left with no changes because there are few accepted agreements and undisputed treaties. There are really no precedented, carved-in-stone "existing rights".[5]

The governments contend that the land is sovereign and not controlled by the Natives. In a 1991 Supreme Court of British Columbia decision, Chief Justice Allen McEachern denied the Gitksan and Wet'suwet'en tribes' claim to a huge territory in northwest British Columbia, arguing that Native Canadians have no right to self-determination due to provincial and federal sovereignty. His assertion that self-government can be achieved only by constitutional changes and that court cases on the issue cannot grant land ownership[6] further heightened Native Canadians' frustration. This type of decision simply tosses the ball into another court and inhibits change. Since they lack the power base to create sufficient political support for constitutional reforms or amendments, Native claims are effectively blockaded.

But Native activists such as Ovide Mercredi, the leader of the Assembly of First Nations and a national chief representing most of Canada's 500 000 status Indians, has pushed their concerns into the limelight during the current round of Constitutional talks.[7] Since the Federal Government cannot afford to ignore Native interests if it wishes talks to succeed, certain individual and defined rights and boundaries may be entrenched under the current heading of "existing rights". If change occurs, the current government practice of explaining away disturbances the legislation causes by arguing that laws must be based on the best interests of all Canadians may no longer be politically viable.[8]

Currently, the Inuit are trying to right the government's failure both to consult Natives about land use and allow them to benefit from land distribution.[9] If they win their claim to a large portion of Arctic land, Lorraine Turchansky of the Associated Press says:

> It will give the Inuit some say in how the resources are developed, how wildlife is managed, and how their language and culture are promoted.[10]

The Nunavit Inuit would become the largest private land owners in North America. However, squabbling between the Inuit and the Dene-Metis over cultural rights to the land has stalled final negotiations.

At the heart of this land claim and protests such as the 1990 Oka blockade lies a more important issue — Native Canadians' desire to reclaim pride and respect for their culture and assure rights for future generations. Frustrated by the governments' failure to act, Native Canadians are growing increasingly militant. As *The Ottawa Citizen* reported on April 13, 1991, "At a recent national native leaders' conference, chiefs spoke openly of forming a native army to protect their lands".[11] And the Cree are also legally stalling the James Bay Project expansion until their rights and titles have been addressed. The Cree do not deem the $225 million dollar compensation package for the use of land a reason to keep silent about the absence of environmental tests.[12]

Yet, all disputes must be resolved legally as Comprehensive Claims or Specific Disputes. The former deals with Natives who did not sign away their land, or rights to that land. To date, three such claims have been settled, six are being negotiated, nineteen have been accepted for future negotiation, three have been rejected and six are being reviewed — all at a cost of over 100 million dollars, not including the three settlements. Specific Claims deal with individual disputes in which Natives feel the government has withheld promised goods, funds or services, or has mismanaged interests and reserves. At this writing, of the over 587 Specific Claims which have been submitted, Ottawa has made only forty-five "deals."[13] Given the financial and psychological stakes and the fact that neither party is certain which papers, treaties and charters are binding, the claims will not easily be resolved.

Now, however, is a politically appropriate time to right ancient wrongs. A majority of Canadians polled by Angus Reid-Southam News support the concept of Native self-government, provided Natives are subject to the Canadian Charter and Criminal Code. And over eighty percent feel that they have the constitutional right to govern themselves and that constitutional rights should be entrenched.[14] By initiating positive change now the government would be adopting a popular stand and benefit from national and international recognition. The Natives, of course, would finally be compensated for old wounds.

Although the government is making progress by negotiating claims and grievances, the process must become more cost and time efficient. One approach would be to hold a series of conferences in which all bands and tribes outlined individual and communal claims. These claims would be heard by a panel of Native and non-native justices, and if deemed legitimate in whole or in part, be decided upon by those justices.

But before claims can be decided, the law must be clarified and guidelines for Native land use and ownership must be established. Entrenchment of specific clauses regarding issues such as self-government and land claims would help resolve Native problems regarding their rights and identity. Further, it would provide the government with a set of guidelines to follow in resolving disputes. With regard to compensation, the government might suggest a profit-sharing scheme whereby the tribes agree to a percentage of any profit obtained from government activities on their land, instead of a lump-sum payment.

Canada's Native people deserve an apology, the right to cultural pride through government recognition, and freedom from government policies and financial dependence. The Canadian government should grant fair land settlements and Native control over those settlements. This process will require honest communication by all parties and a willingness to entrench specific rights and privileges in the Constitution, and a fair and lasting compensation. Failure to act may accelerate the demise of Canada. Native Canadians are not going to fade away as previous governments seem to have hoped. Nor will they quietly integrate themselves into "white" society. The massive resurgence of cultural pride will not rest until their culture has been respectfully restored to its owners.

---

[1]R.P. Bowles, J.L. Hanley, and G.A. Rawlyk, *The Indian: Assimilation, Integration or Separation.* (Scarborough, 1972), p. 65.
[2]*Ibid.,* p. 67.
[3]*Ibid.,* p. 67.
[4]Canadian Charter of Rights and Freedoms, Section 25 preamble and part B, (Ottawa, 1982).
[5]James S. Frideres, *Native Peoples in Canada: Contemporary Conflicts* (Scarborough, 1988), p. 330.
[6]Larry Still, "Death of a Dream," *The Vancouver Sun,* March 9, 1991, no page reference available.
[7]Antonia Zerbisias, "Indian leader called a 'sell-out'," *The Toronto Star,* April 5, 1992, p. A8.

[8]Bowles and Hanely and Rawlyk, *Op. cit.*, p. 66.
[9]Sarah Scott, "Land Claims, Here's how they work and what's at stake," *The Montreal Gazette*, October 6, 1990, p. B4.
[10]Lorraine Turchansky, "Nunavit: Inuit stand on verge of becoming continent's biggest private landowners," *The Chronicle Herald*, April 7, 1990, p. C1.
[11]Jack Aubrey, "Another Oka," *The Ottawa Citizen*, April 13, 1991, p. B2.
[12]*Ibid.*, p. B2.
[13]Sarah Scott, *Loc. cit.*
[14]"Views on Natives Are Mixed, Poll Finds," *The Toronto Star*, March 1, 1992, p. A12.

Bizbuzz

WILLIAM SAFIRE

Nobody can apply for a job these days — or interface with a personnel recruiter in the hopes of impacting on his bottom line — without a degree in "bizbuzz," the jargon that prioritizes the career path of the rising young ballpark figurer.

I have already flunked. The figures of speech used in the preceding paragraph are already business archaisms that might as well have been the patois of Commodore Vanderbilt or Andrew Carnegie.

"The biggest 'bad' corporate word," opines Walter Kiechel 3d, associate editor of *Fortune* magazine, "is *impact* as a verb." The former noun has been used so often in its verb form in board rooms that *impact* on has lost its punch, and rising executives are now testing the effect of *affect*.

"*Interface* is a dying word in management," adds John F. Lubin, professor of management at the University of Pennsylvania's Wharton School. "It was taken from systems engineering, where it meant the juncture between two pieces. For a while, *system* was taking over the language of management, but this, too, is dying."

Bottom line is still kicking around, but too many outsiders have been using it, and in jargon, freshness is all. "The *bottom line* originally referred to earnings figures," reports Timothy B. Blodgett of the *Harvard Business Review*. "Bottom-line responsibility is responsibility for the economic welfare of a division or subsidiary that is supposed to turn a profit. However, the phrase has expanded to include more than just earnings and profits; it can mean, 'The onus is on us' for just about anything." Mr. Blodgett is a senior editor; he has a *straight-line responsibility* to the editor in chief, and a *dotted-line responsibility* to a bunch of other editors. Life follows chart. While we're entangled in lines, Professor Michael Porter at the Harvard Business School defines *dotted-line responsibility* as "when two people consult with or interact with each other, but one does not report to the other." In olden times, the "dotted line" was where the customer signed; now it is where the responsibility is diffused, and even that expression is fading fast.

Ballpark figure is developing a paunch, too. This derivation of "in the ballpark," an indication of proximity (in contrast to a ball hit clear out of the stadium), is being replaced by one of the new triple hyphenations that make up adjectival phrases dear to bizbuzz: *back-of-the-envelope*. There is a quickly figured difference in meaning, however: "A *ballpark figure* is a rough estimate," explains lexicographer Sol Steinmetz, "while a *back-of-the-envelope sum* is one simply or easily arrived at without the need of a pocket calculator."

Another example of the triple hyphenator is *top-of-the-line*, a compound adjective launched in the late 1960's by auto manufacturers to describe their most expensive models. The British equivalent is *top-of-the-market*, and the phrase is not considered run-down or ramshackle by bizbuzz linguists on top of the state of the art, which is the bottom line on *top-of-the-line*.

Now that we know what is out, what is in?

If you are sad about the loss of *impact on*, try the new *abstract away*. "This means to dwindle into nothing," says the *H.B.R.*'s Blodgett. "If something *abstracts away*, it has ceased to be definable." Nice phrase; to move from the concrete to the abstract and then to vanish, like the Cheshire cat, leaving only the grin.

Hands-on, a compound adjective with one measly hyphen, has a stranglehold on the throats of businesspeople today. (I almost wrote "businessmen." Somebody must be getting to me.) The original meaning was "vocational," and the first citation in the Barnhart files is "hands-on instruction" for vocational schools, and was a play on "hands off," or so theoretical that it abstracted away. Now it means "practical"; nobody with hands-on experience, in a job interview, would claim anything as outdated as "practical experience." A synonym is *line* experience; this time, the metaphor is probably not from accounting, as in *bottom line*, but from the military, which contrasts *line* (from "front line") and *staff* (or headquarters) experience.

When in need of a modern mystifier, and tired of systems and the same old interfaces, reach for the favorite new management noun: *matrix*. "This came out of organizational behavior," says Professor

Lubin, "and was used to describe orthogonal relationships." Asked to put that on a dotted-line basis, Professor Lubin explained: "That's when you have two bosses, or when responsibility is shared between divisions. Came from mathematics, and it's overused." He can hands-on that again. In the Wharton 1980 catalogue, a course in matrix management is advertised in this way: "The unique problem of changing, implementing and fine-tuning matrix forms will be highlighted." According to J.M. Rosenberg's *Dictionary of Business and Management*, "a matrix organization exists when organizational members have a dual allegiance — to a particular assignment or task and also to their department." O.K.: two bosses, a matrix and (soon to come) a patrix.

Students of bizbuzz (not to be confused with jargon scholars, who are in buzzbiz) search for optical combining forms. For a generation, combination-oriented linguists were studying the use of *-wise*, while formwise lexicographers were collecting the usages of *-oriented*. You could be *job-oriented*, *leisure-oriented*, or even *Occident-oriented*; similarly, languagewise, you could be *advertisingwise*, *careerwise*, or even *smartwise*.

Forget all that. The new combining forms are *-wide* and *-intensive*. According to Judy Uhl, senior editor of the division of research for the Harvard Business School, about whose dotted-line responsibilities I have not inquired: "A very common thing is to add *-wide* at the end of things to mean 'a totality,' such as *corporate-wide, industry-wide*. This can also be done without a hyphen, as in *personnelwide*."

On the *-intensive* front, the earliest entries were *labor-intensive* and *capital-intensive*, but Steinmetz has pockets bulging with citations for *profit-intensive, energy-intensive, people-intensive, assets-intensive*, and *technology-intensive*. His work is neologism-intensive, and applies dictionarywide.

Vision is a hot word in executive aeries, usually defined as "the ability to see around corners," rather than off into the distance. *Style* is equally sought after, and what *manager style* a corporation prefers determines its character. *Fortune's* Kiechel points to the popular *earthquake style*, "which is when a manager comes in and shakes everything up."

Bailout has replaced *rescue* in bizbuzz: A dispute is raging among etymologists about its derivation. One school holds that it is from the act of a pilot donning a parachute and leaping out of a falling airplane; another points to the frenzied activity of a fisherman bailing out a boat that is taking in water.

If a bailout fails, a company no longer goes bankrupt; it goes *belly up*, also a fishing metaphor, perhaps influenced by "belly up to the bar." At *Forbes* magazine, such a term is frowned upon. Geoffrey Smith, an assistant managing editor, who has a wavy-line responsibility to Malcolm Forbes, points to a memo directing writers to stay away from such bizbuzz as *clobber, plummet,* and *soar* (trite descriptions of earnings, gains or losses), along with *on stream, game plan, shortfall,* and *upscale.*

My top-of-the-line model has just intersected with my bottom-line judgment, forming a dotted-line responsibility to all those who want to bellow at bizbuzz and outplace all its speakers. That's earthquake style.

TIPS ON WRITING A SOCIAL SCIENCE ESSAY

Since the social science essay and the literary essay have much in common, you will notice that the following tips are similar to the tips on writing a literary essay.

1. Base your essay on a specific and significant question that you feel needs to be answered about the topic in question. For example, in "Violence against women" (p. 266) Labatt's focus question is "What are the causes and effects of society's violence against women?"
2. Once you have such a question brainstorm many answers to that question. Think specifically about the topic — for example, the scope, availability of information, resources, possible perspectives or biases.
3. Research the topic, meticulously recording sources and full bibliographical data. Make sure your research is up-to-date and covers the necessary range of material and perspectives.
4. With a working thesis statement — essentially your answer to the question — you may want to jot down a linear outline. If possible, you should discuss your thesis with your teacher or a knowledgeable classmate. If an outline does not take shape easily, you may want to push forward with your first draft. If you are using a computer, you can easily rearrange this rough draft later, or you can cut and paste your typed or handwritten draft.
5. Make sure the topic sentence for each paragraph deals with an aspect of your thesis. You may find it helpful to highlight crucial words in the thesis statement and the topic sentences. You may

need to revise your thesis and rework the topic sentences as you think through your writing process.

6. Once you have assembled your paragraphs, start revising, fleshing out details, cutting and rearranging ideas, and writing quotations in full with page numbers.

7. Be sure to check footnotes or endnotes for accuracy, ensuring that you have used the documentation system preferred by your teacher (MLA style sheet, Turabian, APA style). Remember that quotations of more than four lines in the original are indented eight spaces, single spaced, and appear without quotation marks.

8. Revise, edit, and polish, using the conventions of the social science essay as criteria.

For more help see the Suggested Supplementary Resources in Tips for Students, page 332, and in Tips on Your Writing Process, page 326.

11. Essays About University Life

KEY WORK:

> "Claiming an Education" — Adrienne Rich

ASSOCIATED READINGS:

> "Getting the Most Out of University Lectures" — Talin Arzumanian (student essay)
> "How to Choose the Right University" — Linda Frum
> "Life After Class" — Diane Brady
> "Transitions: An Interview with High School and University Students"
> "Ethics and Engineering" — John Aitken

Sooner than you think, you will begin a new phase in your life cycle — your postsecondary education. The essays in this final thematic unit have been selected to help you successfully complete this year and prepare for the big change.

The Key Work is a form of the university lecture, a convocation address by Adrienne Rich, professor of English and feminist studies at Stanford University. However, The Associated Readings are not lectures; rather, they invite you to explore philosophical as well as practical aspects of completing high school and moving on to university life. "Transitions" and the articles by Frum and Brady raise important issues you may wish to discuss with your Student Services counsellor early in the course. Aitken focusses on developing appropriate skills and thinking processes. Student Talin Arzumanian offers perhaps the most important tips of all on how to get the most out of the university lecture, the heart of the university experience.

Conventions of the University Lecture

Purpose	To educate, inform, argue a point of view
Audience	Specialized, educated
Tone	Most often scholarly and serious
Voice	Varies from neutral to strongly interpretive
Response	Informed, appreciative of learning

Language   LEVEL — Standard, formal
             CHARACTERISTICS — Blend of connotative and denota-
                tive but latter predominates
Structure   May resemble a formal essay or speech

BEFORE READING

1. List concerns you and your classmates share about the university
   world and explore practical strategies to deal with them.

2. Have someone deliver Rich's lecture and practise taking notes
   while you listen.

3. Review the conventions of the university lecture and consider in
   what ways it differs from a formal speech (see the conventions
   for the formal speech, p. 238).

Claiming an Education

ADRIENNE RICH

For this convocation, I planned to separate my remark into two
parts: some thoughts about you, the women students here, and
some thoughts about us who teach in a women's college. But ultimately, those two parts are indivisible. If university education
means anything beyond the processing of human beings into
expected roles, through credit hours, tests, and grades (and I believe
that in a woman's college especially it *might* mean much more), it
implies an ethical and intellectual contract between teacher and student. This contract must remain intuitive, dynamic, unwritten; but
we must turn to it again and again if learning is to be reclaimed from
the depersonalizing and cheapening pressures of the present-day
academic scene.

The first thing I want to say to you who are students, is that you
cannot afford to think of being here to *receive* an education; you will
do much better to think of yourselves as being here to *claim* one. One
of the dictionary definitions of the verb "to claim" is: *to take as the
rightful owner; to assert in the face of possible contradiction.* "To receive"
is *to come into possession of; to act as receptacle or container for; to accept*

as authoritative or true. The difference is that between acting and being acted-upon, and for women it can literally mean the difference between life and death.

One of the devastating weaknesses of university learning, of the store of knowledge and opinion that has been handed down through academic training, has been its almost total erasure of women's experience and thought from the curriculum, and its exclusion of women as members of the academic community. Today, with increasing numbers of women students in nearly every branch of higher learning, we still see very few women in the upper levels of faculty and administration in most institutions. Douglass College itself is a women's college in a university administered overwhelmingly by men, who in turn are answerable to the state legislature, again composed predominantly of men. But the most significant fact for you is that what you learn here, the very texts you read, the lectures you hear, the way your studies are divided into categories and fragmented one from the other — all of this reflects, to a very large degree, neither objective reality, nor an accurate picture of the past, nor a group of rigorously tested observations about human behavior. What you can learn here (and I mean not only at Douglass but any college in any university) is how *men* have perceived and organized their experience, their history, their ideas of social relationships, good and evil, sickness and health, etc. When you read or hear about "great issues," "major texts," "the mainstream of Western thought," you are hearing about what men, above all white men, in their male subjectivity, have decided is important.

Black and other minority peoples have for some time recognized that their racial and ethnic experience was not accounted for in the studies broadly labeled human; and that even the sciences can be racist. For many reasons, it has been more difficult for women to comprehend our exclusion, and to realize that even the sciences can be sexist. For one thing, it is only within the last hundred years that higher education has grudgingly been opened up to women at all, even to white, middle-class women. And many of us have found ourselves poring eagerly over books with titles like: *The Descent of Man; Man and His Symbols; Irrational Man; The Phenomenon of Man; The Future of Man; Man and the Machine; From Man to Man; May Man Prevail?; Man, Science and Society;* or *One-Dimensional Man* — books pretending to describe a "human" reality that does not include over one-half the human species.

Less than a decade ago, with the rebirth of a feminist movement in this country, women students and teachers in a number of universities began to demand and set up women's studies courses — to claim a woman-directed education. And, despite the inevitable accusations of "unscholarly," "group therapy," "faddism," etc., despite backlash and budget cuts, women's studies are still growing, offering to more and more women a new intellectual grasp on their lives, new understanding of our history, a fresh vision of the human experience, and also a critical basis for evaluating what they hear and read in other courses, and in the society at large.

But my talk is not really about women's studies, much as I believe in their scholarly, scientific, and human necessity. While I think that any Douglass student has everything to gain by investigating and enrolling in women's studies courses, I want to suggest that there is a more essential experience that you owe yourselves, one which courses in women's studies can greatly enrich, but which finally depends on you, in all your interactions with yourself and your world. This is the experience of *taking responsibility toward yourselves.* Our upbringing as women has so often told us that this should come second to our relationships and responsibilities to other people. We have been offered ethical models of the "self-denying wife and mother"; intellectual models of the brilliant but slapdash dilettante who never commits herself to anything the whole way, or the intelligent woman who denies her intelligence in order to seem more "feminine," or who sits in passive silence even when she disagrees inwardly with everything that is being said around her.

Responsibility to yourself means refusing to let others do your thinking, talking, and naming for you; it means learning to respect and use your own brains and instincts; hence, grappling with hard work. It means that you do not treat your body as a commodity with which to purchase superficial intimacy or economic security; for our bodies and minds are inseparable in this life, and when we allow our bodies to be treated as objects, our minds are in mortal danger. It means insisting that those to whom you give your friendship and love are able to respect your mind. It means being able to say, with Charlotte Bronte's *Jane Eyre*: "I have an inward treasure born with me, which can keep me alive if all the extraneous delights should be withheld or offered only at a price I cannot afford to give."

Responsibility to yourself means that you don't fall for shallow and easy solutions — predigested books and ideas, weekend encounters guaranteed to change your life, taking "gut" courses instead of ones you know will challenge you, bluffing at school and life instead of doing solid work, marrying early as an escape from real decisions, getting pregnant as an evasion of already existing problems. It means that you refuse to sell your talents and aspirations short, simply to avoid conflict and confrontation. And this, in turn, means resisting the forces in society which say that women should be nice, play safe, have low professional expectations, drown in love and forget about work, live through others, and stay in the places assigned to us. It means that we insist on a life of meaningful work, insist that work be as meaningful as love and friendship in our lives. It means, therefore, the courage to be "different"; not to be continuously available to others when we need time for ourselves and our work; to be able to demand of others — parents, friends, roommates, teachers, lovers, husbands, children — that they respect our sense of purpose and our integrity as persons. Women everywhere are finding the courage to do this, more and more, and we are finding that courage both in our study of women in the past who possessed it, and in each other as we look to other women for comradeship, community, and challenge. The difference between a life lived actively, and a life of passive drifting and dispersal of energies, is an immense difference. Once we begin to feel committed to our lives, responsible to ourselves, we can never again be satisfied with the old, passive way.

Now comes the second part of the contract. I believe that in a women's college you have the right to expect your faculty to take you seriously. The education of women has been a matter of debate for centuries, and old, negative attitudes about women's role, women's ability to think and take leadership, are still rife both in and outside the university. Many male professors (and I don't mean only at Douglass) still feel that teaching in a women's college is a second-rate career. Many tend to eroticize their women students — to treat them as sexual objects — instead of demanding the best of their minds. (At Yale a legal suit [*Alexander v. Yale*] has been brought against the university by a group of women students demanding a stated policy against sexual advances toward female students by male professors.) Many teachers, both men and women, trained in the male-centered tradition, are still handing the ideas and texts of that tradition on to students without teaching them to criticize its antiwoman attitudes, its omission of women as part of the species. Too often, all of us fail to teach the most important thing, which is that clear thinking, active discussion, and excellent writing are all necessary for intellectual freedom, and that these require *hard work*. Sometimes, perhaps in discouragement with a culture which is both antiintellectual and antiwoman, we may resign ourselves to low expectations for our students before we have given them half a chance to become more thoughtful, expressive human beings. We need to take to heart the words of Elizabeth Barrett Browning, a poet, a thinking woman, and a feminist, who wrote in 1845 of her impatience with studies which cultivate a "passive recipiency" in the mind, and asserted that "women want to be made to *think actively*: their apprehension is quicker than that of men, but their defect lies for the most part in the logical faculty and in the higher mental activities." Note that she implies a defect which can be remedied by intellectual training; *not* an inborn lack of ability.

I have said that the contract on the student's part involves that you demand to be taken seriously so that you can also go on taking yourself seriously. This means seeking out criticism, recognizing that the most affirming thing anyone can do for you is demand that you push yourself further, show you the range of what you *can* do. It means rejecting attitudes of "take-it-easy," "why-be-so-serious," "why-worry-you'll-probably-get-married-anyway." It means assuming your share of responsibility for what happens in the classroom, because that affects the quality of your daily life here. It means that the student sees herself engaged *with* her teachers in an active, ongoing struggle for a real education. But for her to do this, her teachers must be committed to the belief that women's minds and experience are intrinsically valuable and indispensable to any civilization worth the name; that there is no more exhilarating and intellectually fertile place in the academic world today than a women's college — if both students and teachers in large enough numbers are trying to fulfill this contract. The contract is really a pledge of mutual seriousness about women, about language, ideas, methods, and values. It is our shared commitment toward a world in which the inborn potentialities of so many women's minds will no longer be wasted, raveled-away, paralyzed, or denied.

EXPLORING THE LECTURE

1. Determine the extent to which Rich has followed the conventions of the university lecture by examining each component. Cite specific textual references.

2. How does Rich's opening sentence help the reader interpret her thesis, follow the main steps in the development of her argument, and feel intellectually satisfied with her conclusion?

3. Assess the success with which Rich argues her case for "claiming an education."

4. Identify several specific problems and issues Rich claims face female students and determine the extent to which each also applies to male students.

5. Compare your lecture notes with a partner's (see Before Reading). Using criteria developed by the class, determine whose notes would be more helpful for study and why.

EXTENSIVE STUDY

1. a. In approximately 50 words, summarize your sense of what Rich says about "taking responsibility toward yourself."
   b. Suggest other examples or techniques she might have used to illustrate her point.

2. a. With a partner, discuss what you understand Rich to mean when she says: "The difference between a life lived actively, and a life of passive drifting and dispersal of energies, is an immense difference." Prepare and present a mime or role-play which dramatizes this distinction.
   b. If you have read Thoreau's "Excerpt from *Walden*" (p. 174), Hughes' portrait of Tubman (p. 164), or Patterson's essay on Bethune (p. 182), consider how each *subject* might have responded to the above quotation.

3. Debate these statements. Resolved that:
   - Both males and females learn best in a sexually segregated environment. (You might first read Frum's "How to Choose the Right University" (p. 308) and consider why she does not list this factor in her "basic questions" list.)
   - Initiation is a significant rite of passage in a university student's life.

4. Judging from the information in "Ethics and Engineering" (p. 319), would Rich feel that Professor Friedman fulfiled his part in the academic contract? Justify.

5. a. With a partner, brainstorm a list of what you expect from a university education.
   b. Does Frum's "How to Choose the Right University" (p. 308) provide you with appropriate information to assist your choice? Justify.

c. Reread "Northrop Frye Talks About the Role of Humanities" (p. 5) and consider what implications, if any, his views about the humanities have for your university experience.

d. Read "Transitions" (p. 314) and consider specific steps you can take now to complete this year successfully and move on to university.

THE WRITING FOLDER

1. You are a would-be university student trying to decide which university to attend or whether to take a year to travel abroad or to work. Present your reasoning in one of the following forms:
   - interior monologue or stream of consciousness
   - a conversation with a teacher, peer, or parent
   - a statement of the place of formal education in your credo

   The final product should demonstrate that you understand the relevant points in Rich's argument and the Associated Readings in this unit.

2. Rewrite Rich's lecture for a co-educational or male university audience.

3. Respond in a form of your choosing to one or more ideas Rich and/or the authors of the Associated Readings advances.

INDEPENDENT STUDY

1. After reading or listening to many samples, research, write, and deliver a lecture for your peers on a stimulating intellectual issue. Consider sample work by intellectuals such as Northrop Frye, Margaret Atwood, C.D. MacPherson, or George Woodcock.

2. Investigate a feminist issue Rich raises in her lecture as it is reflected in nineteenth and/or twentieth century literature. Consider Leo Tolstoy, *Anna Karenina*, Gustave Flaubert, *Madame Bovary*, and most titles by contemporary female writers such as Katherine Govier, Edna O'Brien, Gail Godwin, Alison Lurie, Ellen Currie, A.S. Byatt, Anita Brookner, Mary Gordon, Margaret Laurence and Margaret Atwood. Prepare and present a lecture on your findings.

3. Ideas for projects may arise from reading authors who write in the field of educational philosophy such as Neil Postman, John Holt, Jean Jacques Rousseau, Ivan Illich, and John Dewey or in the area of feminist issues such as Naomi Wolf (*The Beauty Myth*), Betty Friedan, Kate Millet, Letty Pogrebin, Gloria Steinem, Susan Brownmiller (*Femininity*), Francis Lear, and Camille Paglia.

   You may wish to develop a comparative analysis of the same issue in two or more works.

TIMED READING AND WRITING

1. Using Arzumanian's essay, develop a one-page, point-form set of Tips for Getting the Most Out of a University Lecture.

2. Read or reread one of the Oral Essays that sounds like a university lecture, such as Douglas's "Capital Punishment," and make an outline or summary.

3. In your writer's notebook, reflect on the emotional changes university requires and speculate about your adaptability quotient.

Getting the Most Out of University Lectures

TALIN ARZUMANIAN (*student essay*)

Face it, frosh are inexperienced. Now that I've survived that big First Year, I feel qualified to help demystify one aspect of university life. No, this isn't about partying; those skills are probably pretty well developed, right? My topic is the university lecture.

When I was in your Nikes or Converse or Doc Martins, I didn't once speculate about this beast. And let me tell you, I got off on the wrong foot by adopting a passive, disorganized stance. Picture me, clad in my grotty jeans and T — not what I'd planned to wear, but I sort of overslept, you see. Out of breath, I plop myself into a deep corner of the amphitheatre, trying to affect a suitably nonchalant air to impress the blond dude beside me. He looks older . . . probably not a frosh. The prof eyes me maliciously as I fumble for a pen and paper. Darn. I must have left them on the bus. The Dude comes to my rescue, but the pencil is dull and the paper — well — it's the back of a crumpled envelope. Breathing deeply, I try to click into the prof's train of thought. What? It's a foreign language — something about "deconstruction of the feminine mystique". Forty minutes later, I'm depressed, half-asleep and the owner of an envelope inscribed, "Help!" The Dude, looking cool, smiles benignly as he sprints out the back door. "Don't worry — it gets better. It really does."

And you know, he was right. Let me share some strategies you can practise *now* to master the art of the university lecture. I've culled them from friends, my older brother, and even the professors themselves. Let me walk you through a series of steps in which you take charge of your life.

First things first. Your mother was right; it's easier to concentrate with a full stomach and well-rested mind. The latent heat of time fusion won't mesmerize your intellect if your growling gut sends the professor into catatonic shock or your eye lids are propped open with the proverbial matchsticks. As you may have discovered in senior high school, a gallon of black coffee provides temporary relief, but its assault on the nervous system is brutal.

The next essential is tools — paper, a pen or two, and perhaps a clipboard and some kleenex. University lecture halls are not equipped with the comforts of a high school classroom. You'll sometimes find a rickety arm rest to write on, but forget about posters, plants, pencil sharpeners, three-hole punches, or tissues. You'll find that spiral-bound notebooks — one for each course — are the best way to keep organized. Unlike high school, you're not likely to receive scads of handouts. And if you prefer a tape recorder or lap-top computer, just keep in mind that tapes must still be edited for main points and lap-tops may cry for recharging when all the outlets are engaged.

What to do if you miss a lecture? Of course, you have the best intentions of making every class, but sometimes, well, things get in the way. You're down with the flu or miss the bus or get stuck in the library check-out line. Plan ahead for such emergencies by sitting in the same general area for each lecture and jotting down names and phone numbers of those nearby. That way you'll make friends and have someone to fill you in about missed work. And don't let your green edges show by querying the prof as you did your high school teachers, "Did we do anything important while I was away?"

Now that we've worked through the basics, let's review some of the lecture's Big Secrets. Lectures are somewhat like speeches. But since their main purpose is to instruct — to transmit information and argue a point in great detail — they generally lack the rhetorical language which makes speeches easy on the ears. Your job is to listen to and record main ideas and appropriate supporting detail. Large classes afford little opportunity for the interaction you're accustomed to in high school. Since discussion is generally held until the end of the lecture or takes place entirely in your tutorials, your job is largely a reflective one. But remember that reflection is not a passive activity; you're in a silent dialogue with the lecturer as you listen and write.

So you're going to take notes. But how do you decide what to write? Be an active listener — someone who thinks, listens, and writes simultaneously. Good professors offer active listeners clues, but there'll be none of that familiar "take out your books and write this down." You'll need to think about the lecture's title and its implications; what directions does it suggest? What do you already know about the subject? How do ideas link with material in other courses? What contradictions or inconsistencies come to mind? Professors often begin by stating one or more key questions for exploration. Or sometimes they'll outline the three or four main points or issues for that lecture. Since these clues are generally tossed out in the first five minutes, you have another reason to get to class on time.

Let's say you've been given a title and four main points. Begin by printing the title in block capitals so it stands out. Then number and record the four main points beneath an underlined heading, "Key Points." As the lecture progresses, record each main point beside its number and underline or highlight it for visual clarity. You'll notice that the professor usually elaborates on one main point at a time. Record examples and illustrations, listening carefully for repetition of key phrases and concepts, and vocal intonation to help you sort main ideas from subpoints. You'll probably want to develop a personal short-hand — short forms such as leaving out most vowels and substituting symbols (lvng out x vwls). But don't make the mistake of trying to scribble down everything you hear. Discriminate.

These skills develop with practice, after you've grown accustomed to the professor's "style". There'll be the usual "ahems" and "ahas", throat-clearing, digressions, and even some wry attempts at levity. But within a few weeks you'll sort out the heart of the matter.

If you've unluckily met an undecipherable teaching style, you may want to discuss the problem with the professor or your teaching assistant, or even change courses.

That brings me to my next point — when in doubt, ASK. Chances are, if you're confused, so are others. Asking relieves that preoccupied, distracted feeling that anxiety creates. I know you're afraid of looking stupid, but it's time to forget about that hangup. But *when* do you ask?

That depends. If you're in a hall with 300 others and asked to hold remarks, put a large question mark beside your query. When it's time for discussion, find the symbol(s). Or, approach the professor at break time, after class or during office hours. The rumour that professors are intimidating is largely untrue. In fact, I was blessed with several thoughtful professors: one ushered me into his office and offered me hot tea and bibliographical references; another seemed happy to spend two hours chatting informally about a philosophical issue. But keep in mind that even professors who give out their home phone numbers, prefer not to be called at 1 a.m. Most of them are, after all, over thirty and prone to keeping the hours your working parents do.

If you're afraid you'll flounder in a large university lecture course, keep in mind that there are small group forums available. Most courses are supplemented by tutorials led by teaching assistants — generally graduate students — which offer you the opportunity to ask questions, debate issues, and sometimes deliver and critique papers. Or inquire about a skills lab to help you with essays, lecture notes or other remediation. Consider setting up a peer learning group composed of half a dozen interested classmates.

Finally, the single most important key to success is possessing an enthusiastic, open mind. In university lectures, you'll be exposed to a myriad of new ideas, some of which will attract you more than others. Approach it all with a healthy, curious skepticism, reflect on its significance for you and your world, and you'll feel your hours in the university lecture halls are well-spent. And that's crucial when you consider that getting the most out of a university lecture goes a long way toward getting the most out of the whole university experience.

How to Choose the Right University

LINDA FRUM

Most Canadian students choose a university automatically; they pick the closest school, or the one their parents attended. There is no excuse for this. The number of universities in Canada has doubled since your parents' college days, and the differences between schools can be enormous.

To have the college career of your dreams, I recommend that you go far, far away. You've lived at home long enough. Yes, Mom and Dad are swell. Yes, your old room is vastly nicer than anyplace else you're likely to live in. But it's time to grow up.

You grow up a lot faster when Mom isn't doing your laundry any more.

Going away doesn't just build character; it also sharpens your mind by plopping you down among people who talk funny, believe radically different things, hate your province, eat disgusting foods, and yet are still your fellow countrymen. Sadly, the second-biggest country on earth is a narrow and parochial place. Local chauvinism is as fierce as it is ignorant. But there's a simple way to overcome your ignorant stereotypes about Newfoundland, the Maritimes, Quebec, Ontario, the prairies, or BC — live there. You'll be a better and more sophisticated person for it. It's going to impress your friends in Sackville that you know the best disco in Vancouver. And wouldn't it be great to be the only person in Moose Jaw to have tasted genuine Newfoundland cod tongues?

Of course, going to school away from home costs money — money your parents may not want to give you. The solution to this problem is to do something you probably should do in any case: take a year off between high school and college, and work.

Universities in Canada often resemble high schools precisely because they're full of slightly older high-school students. Why not give yourself a year to think about what you hope to get from university? As Robertson Davies says: "Students need some contact with the outside world if they are to recognize the value of the education that a university can give them. Certainly they should not regard it simply as a continuation of high school."

Okay! Now that I've convinced you to leave home, you still have the task of figuring out which far-flung Canadian university will be blessed with your company. Here are some basic questions you must ask yourself before you arrive at a decision.

- *Do I want a big (20,000 or more), medium (5,000 to 20,000), or small (fewer than 5,000 students) school?* The most appealing schools — McGill, Queen's, Simon Fraser, Dalhousie — fall into the intermediate zone. Big schools, with the exception of Western, usually remind me of the sort of places that George Orwell and Franz Kafka so disliked. Small schools are the happiest, but are too often stifling and unintellectual.

- *Do I want a prestigious school?* If so, the University of Toronto is the most; UPEI probably is the least. A university that began as a private school — Bishop's, Dalhousie, McGill, Acadia — will often have more prestige than it deserves. Newer schools — Waterloo, for example — will often have less. Remember: prestige usually reflects what a university was like 20 years ago, and it usually depends upon grossly exaggerated differences in academic performance. Prestige is rarely an accurate guide to present conditions.

- *Do I want to be around people who like to read and talk about what they've read?* Intellectuals congregate at Toronto, above all. They may also be found — though in smaller numbers — at McGill and UBC. Subscribers to *The Idler* will feel ill-at-east at Saint Mary's and Lakehead.

- *Do I want to live in a city or a small town?* Do you need movie theatres, fashionable clothes, and bookstores? The hopelessly urban will consider only McGill, Concordia, the University of Toronto, or UBC. If you like to wake up to the chirping of birds, try Mount Allison, Acadia, St. FX, Victoria, Trent, or Bishop's. If the great outdoors is your life, you'll love Lakehead, Laurentian, or UNB.

- *How much do I care about beauty?* Canada has a surprising number of beautiful campuses, most of which are in the Maritimes. Acadia, UNB, St. FX, Dalhousie, King's, and — depending on your taste — Simon Fraser are all magnificent. The University of Saskatchewan, the University of Manitoba, Toronto, Guelph, McMaster, and Western used to be lovely, but have been vandalized by disciples of Mr. Freyssinet. If you can close your eyes when you're near the nasty bits, though, there remains plenty to enjoy.

- *What do I want to study?* I have put this question last deliberately: it's unreasonable to expect a first-year student to know what he wants to do with his life. As a character in a Philip Roth novel unhappily wonders: "What right did that eighteen-year-old have to decide that I would be a dentist?" Delay specialization as long as possible. If you really aspire to becoming a civilized human being, give some thought to the great-books courses at King's and Brock.

The answer to all these questions may depend on the answer to one big question: *How much can I afford to spend on university?* Cost depends not so much on how far away from home you go, but how expensive a city you choose to go to. It can be cheaper to go 3,000 miles to St. John's than 75 miles to Toronto. Many schools that don't look expensive can be ruinous if you want to keep up with the Joneses. Tuition at Western, after all, is only $1,585, and London is a relatively inexpensive city; but the cost of a Mustang convertible (not to mention fraternity dues) can make even the richest father wince. Some cheap-but-fun cities: Winnipeg (really), Montreal, and St. John's. Halifax and Ottawa are surprisingly expensive, but Ottawa is probably the easiest city in Canada in which to get a part-time job.

Warning: Most provincial governments will not lend you money to study outside the province. One exception is Quebec, which will lend money to students going to Glendon College in Toronto.

Above all, instead of trusting hearsay and the memory of your guidance counsellor, be sure to visit any school you're considering. You don't want to end up like the Calgarian who, having in mind the great night-life, applied to U of T and spent the summer looking forward to four years in swinging Etobicoke. Deciding on a school is a deeply intuitive and subjective business. Read this book. Gather all the information you can. Sleep on it, and trust your instincts.

Life After Class

DIANE BRADY

Before Cory Kuepfer even stepped into a classroom at McMaster University this fall, he found himself face-down in the mud during gruelling tryouts for the school's varsity football team. But for the 19-year-old first-year student from Stoney Creek, Ont., the struggle to win a position as wide receiver on the McMaster Marauders paled in comparison with passing the daunting trial of team initiation. With about 35 new recruits, Kuepfer spent the so-called rookie night running around the Hamilton campus doing stride jumps in student pubs and outside women's residences — sporting only running shoes and a jockstrap lined with heat balm. The evening was capped off by drinking an odious nonalcoholic concoction that Kuepfer likens to "cottage cheese and sardines." Then, reeling from nausea, he braced himself while senior teammates shaved a circle on his head. "I freaked out at first," says Kuepfer, now wearing a hat to cover his bald spot. "It sure leaves a lasting impression of your first week in university."

For many students, the most lasting lessons of campus life are learned outside the classroom walls — in an array of activities ranging from the passion of campus politics and social activism to the nervous exhilaration of collegiate sports and fraternity parties. It is where tomorrow's leaders in every field first test their ideas and discover their skills. Until recently, university officials have had little involvement in after-class activities, leaving campus groups to organize clubs, first-year orientation and a host of student services. But growing concern over alcohol abuse and sexual discrimination, coupled with increasing demands to accommodate students of diverse backgrounds, has raised the profile of extracurricular life. Says Dima Utgoff, director of student services at Acadia University in Wolfville, N.S., and president of the Canadian Association of College and University Student Services: "We are now being held accountable for everything that goes on."

Of all campus activities, the chief target for reform is first-year orientation, usually a week-long ritual that includes activities ranging from wearing bizarre outfits while screaming offensive chants to participating in alcohol-related tests of endurance. Says Louis Gliksman, a research psychologist with Ontario's Addiction Research Foundation who studied university students' drinking patterns, "The first year is the binge year and it usually starts with orientation." But some critics say that the rituals themselves, not the alcohol, are the problem. While Kuepfer emerged from the Marauders' rites of passage with some amusing anecdotes and a bad haircut, one of his fellow McMaster students was much less fortunate. During a Sept. 6 residence orientation organized by students, Mark Woitzik of Whitby, Ont., became paralysed from the chest down after slipping and hitting his neck on the ground while trying to do a headstand in the mud. Says Woitzik, now in rehabilitation for this spinal injury in Toronto's Lyndhurst hospital: "We were supposed to do pushups, but everyone got carried away."

Meanwhile, at Queen's University in Kingston, Ont., past controversy over sexist slogans and alcohol abuse led to a complete overhaul this year of its week-long orientation program. In addition to a ban on "hazing" — initiation rituals such as forcing first-year male and female students into an exercise where the men do pushups with women lying underneath them — the school's student council required each orientation leader to sign a pledge not to drink, lead offensive cheers or indulge in sexual activities with first-year participants. Says third-year student Colleen Kennedy, 20, the campus activities commissioner: "It might not be as fun, but it's not *their* frosh week."

The changing composition of the postsecondary student populace is challenging the status quo in other areas of campus activity. In particular the strong presence of older female students is giving a higher profile to day care, campus security and women's studies, as well as expanding the choice of after-class activities. Says Bernice Edward, a 32-year-old third-year education student at Saskatchewan Indian Federated College, which is affiliated with the University of Regina: "We hold family-oriented events instead of beer bashes or ladies' nights." But access is the issue for part-time students such as Paula Gauthier, 47, who is taking a social sciences course at the University of Prince Edward Island. Says Gauthier: "Services should not just shut down at night." Indeed, an executive at the Women's Legal Education and Action Fund told the University of Toronto student newspaper *The Varsity* that under the Canadian Charter of Rights and Freedoms' guarantee of "life, liberty and security of the person," university administrators could be held responsible for any untoward incidents unless they improve campus safety, especially after dark.

Still, despite the evolving complexity of academic life, many students look to conventional after-class pursuits to improve their employment opportunities after graduation. Faced with soaring numbers of university-trained competitors for fewer jobs, students say that an undergraduate degree alone has become common currency with most employers. As such, some campus leaders and administrators complain that extracurricular involvement is characterized by greed or apathy. "There's a real 'what's in it for me' attitude," says Kelly Lamrock, full-time national chairman of the

Canadian Federation of Students, an Ottawa-based service and lobby group that represents 400,000 university students.

Indeed, in a study of Canadian university presidents' perceptions of campus-life issues released in May, 1991, Queen's University professors Thomas Williams and Martin Schiralli found that the respondents' chief concern was student preoccupation with career goals. That serious tone also has touched extracurricular activities. "A lot of students are more concerned with recycling than partying," says Mary Jean O'Donnell, 25, a second-year women's studies student and co-ordinator of the Student Environment Centre at the University of British Columbia in Vancouver. Adds Terry Robinson, 21, a second-year physical education student at Lakehead University in Thunder Bay, Ont.: "You're trying to make contacts who might help out later on."

Despite academic and career pressures, the more traditional life around campus pubs, parties and sporting events still plays an important role in student activities. When University of New Brunswick officials in Fredericton announced in February that they would extend quiet hours during residence orientation, 300 students marched in protest. "People exploded all at once," says 22-year-old Jonathan Keith, a business student in his final year. "The social aspect of this university is too important." Even at schools that pride themselves on academic excellence, athletics remains a vital part of campus life. When the board of governors at St. Francis Xavier University in Antigonish, N.S., stopped funding the university's football program last November to cut costs, the school's alumni immediately protested and started a special fund to keep the team alive and safeguard future athletic programs.

Indeed, academic officials are becoming increasingly aware that extracurricular activities set the tone for entire universities. For some, the desire to create a more positive campus atmosphere is rooted in pragmatism. Says Robert Sproule, business manager for the University of Calgary's students union: "Students need to leave with a warm, fuzzy feeling if they are going to respond as alumni to university fund-raising efforts." And Tracy Lyn Lettner, a first-year student at Ottawa's Carleton University, says that she plans to become involved with peer counselling, sports and other activities in order to enjoy the university experience. "You're putting down $10,000 for a degree, not the courses," says Lettner. "So I might as well be silly for the next four years and have fun."

Transitions: An Interview with High School and University Students

If you're looking for tips to help you cope successfully with the transition from high school to university, you may find some useful perspectives in Brenda Chow's interview with Frank Calnan, Head of Student Services at Sir Oliver Mowat Collegiate Institute, Scarborough, and former students. The following four students, interviewed in June of their graduating year at Mowat, are identified below according to the university and program in which they subsequently enrolled: Peter Attia, Engineering, Queen's University; Ross Holder, Computer Science/Music, University of Toronto; Kathryn Hakomaki, Business, Wilfrid Laurier University; Mike Riettie, Chemistry, Dalhousie University; Genevieve Tan, Health Sciences, Queen's University, and Talin Arzumanian, Political Science, University of Toronto, had just completed first-year university at the time of their interview. Brenda Chow is currently enrolled in a sciences program at McGill University.

BRENDA: First, let's talk about goals. To what extent did you accomplish your goals for your graduating year?

ROSS: Well, I know I could've done better. But my only real goal was getting through the courses and I did.

KATHRYN: I wanted to maintain my Honours average. Picking the right courses — things I'm genuinely interested in — helped. No Physics!

PETER: I set goals and then revised them upward. At first I targeted a 90 average but I was doing better than I had anticipated, so I changed my aim to a 97.7 average. You have to keep challenging yourself to grow. I'm a little disappointed with my 97.3, but I guess I should be pleased.

MIKE: I set a lower goal than Pete's — an 85 average. But I surprised myself with a 92. I probably could've done better now that I see what's possible.

BRENDA: Hindsight is a great teacher. Looking back, what might you have done differently?

ROSS: I spent too much time with my extra-curricular music, drama, and variety shows. But I'd do it again.

MIKE: As I said, I could've worked harder.

BRENDA: Okay, so how did you cope with problems that arose during this very important year?

PETER: My biggest problem was the psychological change of being someone who did very little homework but worked out for hours every day to just the opposite. This year I turned my sports training discipline into working for academic success. I learned to put full effort into school work.

ROSS: I can't say that, but talking through tough assignments with friends really helped. I didn't have major problems with specific tasks — it was really a lack of focus and a time-management problem. There were days when I was really sort of one-foot-in-front of the other dead. But I knew it'd end.

MIKE: At the beginning of the year, I was stressed and made my family miserable. But by the spring, I'd learned there's a point of no return. You're going to do what you're gonna do.

BRENDA: What did you discover about yourself as a learner and an individual as you worked through this demanding year?

KATHRYN: This year being the SAC Representative reminded me it's important to be a well-rounded person. I want to maintain that balance next year at Laurier.

ROSS: I just realized that whatever had to be done had to be done. I didn't set long-term goals. I'm a more day-to-day person and that presents a problem because of a lack of focus.

PETER: I learned more about something I already sort of knew. I'm not the "innately brilliant" person that my marks might lead you to believe. So I take pride in the fact that I can work harder than anyone else, not that I'm better than anybody else. I learned there's no shame in admitting that you don't understand everything. Asking questions is never a bad move.

MIKE: I discovered that I learn best by myself. I can teach myself.

BRENDA: What tips would you offer graduating students in general? What especially could you recommend for English?

ROSS: Time-management is the biggie. In English, try not to get uptight about the work-load. It'll happen if you believe you can do it. If you get stressed out, you'll have a lot of problems.

TALIN: Okay, but keep in mind that university's going to ask a lot more of you. I went from doing well in high school without a whole lot of effort to being someone who did lots of work. Things move really fast. In high school English, for example, we spent perhaps 10 hours of class time on *Oedipus the King* and *Streetcar Named Desire*. In University, we dealt with these plays in a total of about three one-hour lectures.

KATHRYN: That's why it's important to focus on school work during school hours. Try to spread out the due dates for assignments. Don't be like me and leave revisions until the last minute; when I've left enough time, I do a whole lot better. Use a daily planner. Focus on the work so you get into the program you really want.

PETER: And that's why I say, be a goal setter. Write down specific numbers and put them under your nose. It doesn't have to consume you. Set realistic goals, work toward them, and revise them. Second, balance your life, but don't overdo the partying to relax — it's counterproductive. Exercise is a far better means of relaxation and stress release. Third, don't be afraid to ask questions. I set a world record this year for mine. I expanded my horizons and got more enthusiastic. Now about English — it's not my best subject, but I changed this year. I kept an open mind about Shakespeare. When your attitude improves, the marks come with it.

MIKE: Try. I never thought I could do what I did. All of a sudden everyone was trying this year. You get all gung-ho on school so you can get into university. English, well, that was probably the biggest mistake in my life. I was too young, too much of a joker to take it in grade 12. I didn't hand in three essays at the end so now I have five 92s and a 75 in English. Dumb, plain dumb.

BRENDA: Mr. Calnan, you've watched students struggle through their graduating year and try to make a successful transition to university. What are the characteristics of students who are successful in post-secondary school?

MR. CALNAN: Successful students are problem solvers, resilient, not easily thrown off, students who are focused on what they want to accomplish. They're people who have realistic personal objectives, who understand that they themselves are in charge of what happens. If all these characteristics are in line, then it doesn't so much matter whether their numbers are in the 60s or 92 when they graduate. They'll be successful in the terms that really matter.

BRENDA: What would you suggest to help students like Ross who know they aren't focused?

MR. CALNAN: Well, that's easy to talk about but harder to implement. Strategies like Pete used help some people. If you can't do it yourself, though, get help. Sit down with a counsellor and set immediate, practical goals based on personal values, not global ones. Spending a lot of time worrying about a profession way down the road — looking only at being that doctor or lawyer — no wonder students become immobilized. It impedes your day-to-day progress. So the implications for not doing well on a Calculus test on September 17th are blown out of proportion. We need to get rid of these global concerns and focus on immediate performance. It's not so seemingly unmanageable then.

BRENDA: But how does one learn to manage and focus?

MR. CALNAN: Being focused doesn't come naturally. You have to become problem-solvers. Then the benefits become very strong and personal and less to do with cut-off points at university. Avoid quick-fix solutions and all-or-nothing goals. That's what our society encourages, but it's unhealthy. Then you think if you don't achieve that one goal, you're a total failure. No. I like strategies and goals that have priorities to them.

BRENDA: How does time-management fit into the picture?

MR. CALNAN: It's crucial. One of my main objectives is to encourage graduating students to raise their performance level four or five notches. Not because of university cut-offs but for what it does for them personally. Once we've set our personal goals and strategies, we can better deal with the tremendous free-floating anxiety that students often encounter in first year university. You need to have your feet on the ground and feel good about yourself. Then we'll be people who are seeking challenges.

BRENDA: Genevieve, you've just finished first year Health Sciences at Queen's. How well did your graduating year courses — especially English — prepare you for the demands of this program?

GENEVIEVE: The English Independent Study project taught me to set out a step-by-step process instead of leaving everything until the last minute. I wish there'd been more emphasis on spelling and taking lecture notes, though. In university, it's really hard to pick out main points. Shorthand isn't really the solution — it's about synthesis. When we did précis work in high school, I thought it was dumb, but now I can see the values of those skills.

BRENDA: How did you find university demands different than high school?

TALIN: The biggest adjustment is to the work load; there's probably four times as much reading in courses like Politics, Philosophy, and English. You have to be a self-starter. Locate and learn to use the resources like the various libraries, tutorials and dons. And do lots of the extra-curricular stuff; that's really a big part of university life — speakers, and rallies and clubs. It really opens your mind to a whole new world.

GENEVIEVE: Yeah, it's about being a self-starter. In high school, I felt pressured by the teachers to do my work on time. But the profs handed out a reading list in September and left it to me to complete. The only test was the exam, and if I'd left it all to read at the last minute, I'd be sunk. It takes first-year students a while to pick up on the fact that you have to motivate yourself. The profs aren't interested in pushing you like some of the teachers did. You have to demand things of yourself. If you can't keep up with the work now, you'd better think about the implications for university.

BRENDA: Any final tips for graduating students?

TALIN: Work hard on developing essay-writing skills in high school. Every Arts course requires you to write papers in which you take a position and argue it with *evidence*. That's the profs' favourite word: what's your evidence? And stuff like "why?" and "how do you know that's valid?" are right up there, too. It's all about learning to think with words — in real depth — about complex, abstract issues.

GENEVIEVE: I'd say, keep up. Push yourself. Consider going away from home because you have to learn to take care of yourself. You learn practical stuff like how to do the laundry and dishes and . . . really be an adult. I'm responsible for myself and it means a lot to me to feel free and use my freedom well.

Ethics and Engineering

JOHN AITKEN

Zev Friedman, tense, shoulders scrunched, listens to the questions coming from students who have surrounded him. They are asking about determinism and freedom and want to bounce their ideas off him. He is drawn back to the blackboard where he scribbles some points and repeats a portion of what he has been trying to get across for the past hour: that while science depends upon determinism — events and actions are caused by preceding events and actions — determinism is inadequate for an understanding of humanity. There is freedom in humanity: the freedom to make moral judgements and choices. Where determinism absolves us, freedom holds us responsible for our actions.

Friedman, an associate professor of philosophy, has been lecturing on philosophical concepts of right and wrong, of *rights,* to 300 first year engineering students. It is the first time he has taught engineering students, although he has been teaching at U of T ever since he received his doctorate here 15 years ago.

"It's murder in there," he says later. "There is hostility to you and what you're trying to say." But what of the students, questioning, demanding more, interested? Surely that's encouraging? He shrugs. "There's no contact. You're not a person at all."

Derek Allen, associate professor of philosophy, teaches the first part of the course and Friedman the second. Allen has been at it for four years. "I'm more relaxed now," he says, "less formal. But it's hard work. These students have a different cast of mind. They're technically oriented toward quantitative issues and they're used to the idea that a problem can be solved according to a definite procedure. They're not used to dealing with questions that don't lend themselves to that sort of treatment. The anti-arts credo runs very deep, or at least voluble lip service is paid to it."

W.H. Vanderburg comes to engineering students as one of them (his Ph.D. thesis was in fluid mechanics). He went to France for four and a half years to study the social sciences "to see what they knew that would be useful to me." He found a contradiction: that while science dominates and shapes our culture, our lives, it was not regarded as a serious phenomenon in the social sciences. As he pursued his studies he became convinced that there is a whole sociology of science, and he approaches students as a sociologist with a solid engineering background. This year he has been nominated for a teaching award and course evaluations from his students are high.

He tells his students that to be a good engineer means more than improving the responsiveness of a transistor or the strength of a bridge, that engineers must have a sense of the impact of what they do, that "many of these moral and ethical dilemmas become invisible when you subdivide a particular job or project down to its metallurgical aspect, or its chemical engineering aspect."

By dealing with cases involving transportation of technology to hypothetical but specific situations where the people and their institutions are not prepared for them, he forces students to deal with them "not in a naive way but by looking at the constraints the system has and asking what can be done within them, what the options may be.

"It's sort of applied social science," he says, "within an engineering context. The most common tools I use I borrow from sociology."

We are talking of acid rain and disposal of hazardous wastes, of toasters with faulty wiring and automobiles with defective gas tanks, of urban development and environmental protection, of computers and privacy. There is little in our lives that is unaffected by scientific and technological advances often accompanied by the threat or reality of disaster and disruption. What the students are being asked to consider is the extent to which they must assume responsibility for the mischief that may be inflicted on society when things go wrong.

The students are, many of them, single-minded and uninterested rather than reluctant to consider the moral and social implications of what they do.

Engineering students, says Jack Stevenson, a philosopher who has taken up the cause with almost missionary zeal, are self-selected for strength in maths and science, further culled by the University which demands a 90 per cent high school average for admission. It isn't surprising that they have little interest in the arts and humanities, that they have little skill in writing, in expressing themselves outside their fields.

Deans of engineering had seen the changes occurring in society and in the profession. U of T has included ethics and other non-technical electives in its curriculum for almost 20 years, but these courses have now become mandatory and engineering students will spend one-eighth of their time here in them. That's new. Also new is the revised Professional Engineers Act, which came into being on Sept. 1, 1984, and for the first time spells out clearly and unequivocally that the essential purpose of the profession is to serve the public, that safety and health are paramount.

Dean Gordon Slemon had already moved. In 1980 he established a task force headed by Morris Wayman, a professor in the Department of Chemical Engineering and Applied Chemistry, to look into "what we should be doing in courses that link engineering with society." Such courses were already being tried but, as Wayman noted in an article in the *Bulletin*, the campus fortnightly newspaper, there were problems. One professor of philosophy spent an entire term discussing the pros and cons of capital punishment. "He was," wrote Wayman, "trying to teach them how to approach moral problems. But the students have moral problems far more relevant to engineers than capital punishment."

In the same article Wayman wrote of the roots of engineering, which "did not arise from science but from the practical arts, from military engineering and from agricultural engineering, from construction and surveying and the building of cathedrals, pyramids or Stonehenge, or to go farther back, from the making of bread and wine, from metallurgy and the many other non-scientific ways in which people feed, clothe, house, transport and protect themselves."

But there is little sense among engineering students today that arts and science professors have anything relevant to teach them. I caught something of this as I left Friedman's lecture and heard one student muttering to another: "Man, you can get a heavy if you think about this kind of thing too much." And another: "What does Plato matter anyway? I mean he's *dead*, isn't he?"

Early in 1981 Peter M. Wright, a professor of civil engineering who was a member of the Wayman committee and is now associate dean of engineering and acting dean of architecture, observed in another *Bulletin* article that "Marshall McLuhan, in *The Gutenberg Galaxy*, stated 'any technology tends to create a new human environment'." Was study of these changes not central to much of the humanities? "Engineers," observed Wright, "over the years have not been fully aware of the impact of their works and of the technology with which they are associated . . . The question for the rest of the University is, what role will it play in developing in engineers a better sense of perspective of their impact on the human environment. And conversely what place will engineering have in the university of the future."

There was much debate about importing philosophers, sociologists and historians. Not even all engineering faculty members were fully responsive, let alone the students. So much to be taught within the discipline, so much pressure on the students, was it reasonable to require them to spend a substantial part of their time studying such irrelevancies?

It certainly was and is, and the way had been prepared by, among others, Harold Innis and Marcus Long. "Innis," wrote Wayman, "was above all concerned from the beginning with the social impact of technology." Long, whom Slemon describes as "the famous raconteur of philosophy", was attracting interest which cut across disciplinary boundaries. "It's a long tradition," says Slemon. The result today is a cluster of courses designed to help engineering students understand professional ethics and comprehend the greater issues of social responsibility and moral awareness. They are also taught the complexities and confusions of whistle blowing and the heresy of the uncertainty principle.

Slemon is candid and pragmatic. Most engineers, he says, are employees. If their company is working on a design they know may be disadvantageous (not necessarily unsafe) to the public, what should they, as professionals, do about it? Blow the whistle? Talk to their supervisor? Call a press conference? He doesn't attempt to provide answers but feels strongly that nothing can be achieved without risk, and that the proper role of a professional engineer is to provide reliable information to both sides, especially in cases — the use of nuclear power for generating electricity is a good example — where neither side is right or wrong, simply polarized. "It is the most difficult position of all," says Slemon, "for the engineers will be castigated, they'll be thought of as traitors to both sides."

It is arrogance, says Slemon, for an engineer to say that something has been designed so that accidents cannot happen again. "There's hardly anything we can do without creating some difficulty, some danger for somebody else. And conversely if we don't do something, that will cause difficulty or danger to somebody else. The best we can do is to come to the best judgement of the best answer under existing circumstances, and that may not be the best answer next year. The only truth in many instances is that there is a part of it that we don't know."

Another thing that worries Slemon and Stevenson both is the misconception many engineering students seem to have about the work they'll be doing. Increasingly, says Slemon, "the engineer has to communicate, in a factory for example, with upper management, with the men on the floor, with union officials across a bargaining table, with the local city council or a protest group of concerned citizens — many different audiences. The same message has to go out in almost different languages and few engineers are prepared for that."

It was Jack Stevenson who developed the course in ethics and engineering. He studied the engineering code of ethics, and went on from there.

"One of the things I do," says Stevenson, "is put what I call a plate of spaghetti on the blackboard, a look at engineering as an activity under constraints of various kinds. It's not just the code of ethics, there are regulations under many acts, there's common law, civil actions, and by the time I put this up — all the various boxes, laws, regulations, moral obligations, rights — they get some sense that it's a very complex situation. Then I try to show the sources of all these restraints, a host of regulatory agencies they have to deal with. It's a concept they have to get hold of eventually. An engineer walking into a job situation can be very naive about this. I feel that my job is to inject a little realism into them."

It's one thing to say an engineer's duty to the public is paramount, but what does he do when his supervisor tells him to come in to the plant early Sunday morning and turn a valve that will release a 45-gallon barrel of dioxins into the lake? If he obeys he is ignoring the code and breaking the law. If he disobeys it's very likely that he'll be fired. "What's the welfare of the world?" asks Stevenson. "How do you measure it? You have to immerse the students in something close to reality and still be able to abstract from it to make it manageable. It's a process that involves finding some middle ground that's realistic on the one hand and yet simplified enough to see the issues and how to balance things off. You have to knock that simple-minded view out of their heads."

Stevenson does not teach philosophy by itself, out of context. "I'll discuss an ethical theory like utilitarianism but we only have 13 weeks so there's very little you can do and the students are very overworked. I have a kind intellectual ballast that I carry around with me that I can draw on. I don't pull Plato out of my back pocket, but he's in there, in what I'm saying."

He concentrates on cases drawn from reports or created hypothetically from his own knowledge and explores with the students their responsibilities, moral and legal obligations and options. Whistle blowing, for example. But again, he can't tell them how to react in a given situation. "That's cookbook science," he scoffs.

"There are methods that work a good deal of the time but they're not infallible. The students have to learn to recognize and deal with the relation between the known and the unknown; they have to understand the role of luck and serendipity, and that you can only improve your judgement with practice."

Is this ethics, philosophy or survival?

Part B

Tips for Students

INTRODUCTION

The material in this section offers strategies to help you improve your scholastic performance. It will help you complete the assignments in this text and prepare you for postsecondary endeavours. The tips include:

1. Tips on Your Writing Process
2. Tips on Conducting an Independent Study Project
3. Tips on Preparing a Seminar
4. Tips on Writing Examinations

You should skim through the material and use it as the need arises. You may wish to cross-reference this material with the conventions and tips for specific essay forms provided in the various units of the text itself.

TIPS ON YOUR WRITING PROCESS

If you have compared your composing process with peers, you may have discovered that people go about the process of writing in different ways. Your learning preferences, along with the temperament, attitudes, and feelings you bring to the task of writing, influence your success almost as much as your skill level.

Although there is no magic formula to meet the challenge of becoming a strong writer, the suggestions in this section will point you in the right direction.

Eight Steps to Thinking Through Your Writing Process

As a senior student, you are probably familiar with the phases of the writing process:

- prewriting — exploring and planning
- writing and revising — drafting, rethinking, redrafting, editing, polishing, proofreading
- postwriting — publishing and assessing

These phases are presented sequentially as steps for instructional purposes. In fact, they intersect just like a seed that simultaneously sprouts vertical and horizontal roots. You will not necessarily nurture each piece of writing through all the phases; you may decide to "bail out" after the first draft. You might distinguish the steps by visualizing yourself playing the following roles.

1. **The Explorer** In this creative thinking phase, your ideas brew just under the conscious surface. To encourage the creative flow, engage in activities which require repeated motions such as doodling.
2. **The Planner** In this architectural phase, you juggle and sift ideas. As you jot down ideas, your analytical and creative faculties organize and search for connections, patterns, and relationships until you identify a working blueprint. A word processor may enhance this process.
3. **The Builder** Next, you are the person who erects a scaffold. Dive right in and get the main ideas and connections on paper without regard for the niceties of spelling and grammar. Try to silence your internal critic — that part of your mind which nags, criticizes, and belittles. Keep these tips in mind.
   - Write regardless of whether it seems "good."
   - You do not have to begin at the beginning and work through to the end. Start with whatever idea is most comfortable. Rearranging comes later.
   - Avoid revising as you go. Turning off the computer screen or writing with a pen on paper underlaid with carbon may help you resist this temptation.
   - Take a break only when things are going well; that way, you will have the next thought ready to transcribe when you get back to work.

4. **The Reviewer** In this self- and peer-editing stage, you and your partner strive to resee, rehear, reshape — that is, to spot avenues for revision. Your goal is to wrest order out of chaos: to shape and pare and sculpt. Reading the piece aloud to yourself or in a conference with your partner can help you spot inconsistencies and redundancies. Try to listen to your words with an objective, open mind. As professor Lucy Calkins says, the conference is an opportunity to "interact" with your own work.

5. **The Reconstructor** Next, tap your critical faculties to reshape, delete, refine. You will probably need to delete or rearrange paragraphs. The real beginning may be buried in the middle of your essay. True revising is more like open-heart surgery than a facelift.

6. **The Editor** Now you get to the fine-tuning. Working with a partner, scour your work for grammar and spelling errors, stylistic inelegances, and so on. Focus on conciseness, word choice, and effective use of rhetorical devices — those all-important small touches which give your work flair and naturalness. You may also wish to complete a self-evaluation before moving on to the next step.

7. **The Publisher** At last it is time to enjoy the pleasures of sharing your polished work with your peers and teacher. Encourage others to give you feedback and offer them constructive responses, if asked.

8. **The Evaluator** Although it may be tempting to ignore comments from teachers and peers about polished work, it is wise to reflect on your own feelings and others' responses to your writing. If you are objective enough to examine strengths and weaknesses in a post-writing conference, you will be in a stronger position to improve your writing.

TIPS ON CONDUCTING AN INDEPENDENT STUDY PROJECT

As a senior student, you have probably tackled at least one independent study project — a self-directed project completed in cooperation with your teacher and, perhaps, a mentor or learning partner. Regardless of the particular focus or approach, the project is most likely to be evaluated for both process and product and have a written and oral component to it. The written part is usually an essay or report and the oral component is usually a seminar.

You are required to take charge of your own learning experiences, just as you will be expected to do in your postsecondary career.

Every project has four overlapping phases, as set out below. That is, the steps or phases are not mutually exclusive. You will need to revise your thinking as you go along.

Phase One   Investigating and Organizing Your Material

- With the help of your teacher, define your topic, working from the general to the specific. Only as you read and respond to the topic will a working thesis begin to form. It is important that you spend time exploring your subject of interest from all angles and letting your mind be open to all possibilities before narrowing your focus and determining your thesis. The example below demonstrates this process for developing a thesis based on a literary independent study project.

Subject of Interest: the research for self-realization

Focus Statement: barriers to women's quest for self-realization as depicted in the fiction of contemporary Canadian women

Focus Question: What barriers hamper the protagonists of Atwood's *The Edible Woman* and Laurence's *The Diviners* in their quests for self-realization?

Thesis Statement: In order for the female protagonists — Marian McAlpin and Morag Gunn — to achieve self-realization, they must come to terms with three repressive factors: the restrictive needs of the men in their lives, their sexual relationships, and society's expectations of the female role.

- Keep work logs and response journals which detail your day-to-day thinking, noting with each entry what you *learned* about your topic.
- Consult a mentor or peer learning partner about helpful resources within and outside the school library.
- Keep meticulous notes, recording all pertinent data for referencing quotations and paraphrases. You may wish to develop a form of personal shorthand which employs symbols for commonly used words such as "the" (x) and omits vowels (vwls).

Phase Two   The Composing Process

- Draft and revise your writing until it represents your best work. You will want to discuss the steps along the way with your teacher and, perhaps, your mentor or partner. If you are writing an essay, you may wish to refer to the text's relevant model essays (e.g., report, literary essay, review).

Phase Three   Sharing

- Present an imaginative reflection of your learning to the class. Be sure to include approaches that appeal to all types of learners and stimulate whole-brain thinking. For example, begin with a brief role-play which employs audio-visual aids.

Tip: Read "Whole Brain Learning" (p. 103) and Tips on Preparing a Seminar.

Phase Four   Reflecting and Assessing

- As you work through your project, reflect in writing on the growth of your work. Invite your mentor or partner to comment on the material as it evolves.
- Your teacher will likely evaluate the quality of thought and expression in your finished work, as well as such issues as:
  - punctuality and preparedness for interviews
  - evidence of goal-setting, initiative, problem-solving, curiosity, and thoughtfulness when dealing with others
  - your process of writing and thinking

Tip: You may wish to read Mannes's "How Do You Know It's Good?" (p. 195) and apply it to your own work.
See the Tips on Preparing a Seminar for the oral component.

TIPS ON PREPARING A SEMINAR

A seminar is an oral presentation. Its purpose is similar to the essay, but the format is somewhat different:
- The audience participates in the learning experience through discussion encouraged by the seminar leader.
- The leader learns from the audience. Seminar assignments help participants to develop and refine skills useful in postsecondary institutions and professional life.

1. Gather your material
   - Since preparing for a seminar is a form of independent study, follow the steps outlined in the tips on independent study. Refine the process according to the nature of your project.

2. Organize to deliver your seminar
   - Transfer your main points to a series of index cards; write one main idea in coloured ink across the top of each card.
   - For emphasis, underline the main idea or use block capitals.
   - In point form, list the subheadings and details (proof).

   Tip: If your presentation includes quotations from texts, do not write them out; attach small pieces of paper with paper clips to the relevant pages.

   - If your seminar involves audio-visual aids (slides, charts, photographs, films), prepare them carefully. Always check machinery to ensure it is in working order. When using transparencies, make sure that the audience can read them, and do not overwhelm your audience with too many transparencies or try to include too much information on each one.
   - Provide students with a written overview of your seminar, giving only the thesis, main headings, and page references.
   - You might want to practise before presentation day in front of a friend, or you could use a tape recorder. It is important to appear poised and confident.
   - Prepare your audience with some preliminary information before the seminar date (e.g., assign specific reading or thinking exercises).

3. Deliver your seminar
   - Be on time.
   - Indicate when questions should be posed.
   - Speak slowly and clearly, using your index cards for guidelines; do not simply read your notes or you may put people to sleep.
   - Ensure you make eye contact with your audience. Look around and speak to the audience in all parts of the room.
   - Keep an eye open for reactions: puzzled looks, questions, and signs of boredom.
   - Make sure you leave enough time for discussion. If necessary, help break the ice by asking specific people questions you have prepared in advance.
   - Listen carefully and respond in a reasoned manner to questions, comments, and criticisms.
   - See the Tips on Writing and Delivering an Oral Essay (p. 263) as well.

4. The final steps
   - Revise your material to incorporate valid points raised in discussion.
   - Write and submit the final draft of your essay or report.

TIPS ON WRITING EXAMINATIONS

Working under time limitations strains people's critical abilities. But time constraints are a fact of life. Therefore, a major objective of the senior English examination is to determine your ability to think, read, and write effectively under pressure. The following suggestions should improve your performance.

1. Practise working under time limitations
   - The suggested timed readings and writing assignments in this text offer practice that develops your response to working under pressure.
2. Anticipate the questions
   There are three general types of questions to prepare for:
   - Questions on reading which usually involve thesis identification, methods of development, evaluating effective use of rhetorical devices, summarizing and assessing ideas and opinions expressed.
   - General topic questions which may call upon you to offer and support your views about social and political issues in an essay; you should rely upon well-known methods of orderly argument such as cause and effect, pro and con, and analogy.
   - Literature-based questions which require an essay response. Such questions demand that you decide upon your thesis and set up your plan as quickly as possible, again by relying upon the well-known patterns of orderly development mentioned in the above point. Study for literature questions by forming possible hypotheses that synthesize the key ideas in each work and then try to formulate generalizations that link the ideas in various works. Finally, look for evidence to support these generalizations and consider how you would organize your proof in a written answer. (Many people find that annotating their notebooks helps them to identify the key ideas which run through the material.)

3. Interpreting an examination question

   As you read an examination question, note that most have three key parts: a key verb, an object, and a limiting factor.

   • Consider this example:

     "Writers create unique hero/heroines who depict the inner reality of humanity. They search out not only the sources of nobility and dignity, but also the elements of darkness and violence which form an integral part of humanity."

     Evaluate the validity of this generalization with reference to [name of character] in [name of work] and the protagonist of one other work studied.

     > key verb — the word "evaluate" tells you what to do
     > object — the phrase "the validity of this generalization" tells you the object on which you are to perform the task
     > limiting factor — the phrase "reference to the main characters in two works" suggests how you are to go about your task

4. Make sure you are familiar with the definition of key terms which may appear on the examination. For example, "discuss" means you should formulate an idea or thesis and then substantiate that thesis with examples; "compare" means you are to call attention to similarities and differences. You should clarify other key terms with your teacher.

SUGGESTED SUPPLEMENTARY RESOURCES

Students in any English course would find it useful to have these key reference and language texts in the Resource Centre:

M. Abram, *A Glossary of Literary Terms* (New York: Holt, Rinehart and Winston, 1966)

Judith Barker-Sandbrook, *Thinking Through Your Writing Process* (Toronto: McGraw-Hill Ryerson Limited, 1989)

E.M. Beck, ed., *Bartlett's Familiar Quotations*, 15th edition (Toronto: Little, Brown and Company, 1980)

W.R. Benét, *The Reader's Encyclopedia* (New York: Thomas Crowell, 1965)

T.M. Bernstein, *The Careful Writer: A Modern Guide to English Usage* (New York: Atheneum, 1983)

R. Burchfield, *The English Language* (New York: Oxford University Press, 1985)

D.J. Enright, ed., *Fair Speech: The Uses of Euphemism* (New York: Oxford University Press, 1985)

H.W. Fowler, *A Dictionary of Modern English Usage,* 2nd edition (New York: Oxford University Press, 1983)

C.O.S. Mawson and K. Whiting, eds., *Roget's Pocket Thesaurus* (Toronto: Simon and Schuster, 1976)

Kenneth McLeish, *Bloomsbury Good Reading Guide* (London: Bloomsbury Publishing, 1988)

M. Northey, *Making Sense: a student's guide to writing and style* (New York: Oxford University Press, 1983)

John Parker, *The Process of Writing,* 2nd edition (Toronto: Addison-Wesley, 1989)

Hugh Robertson, *The English Essay: A Guide to Essays and Papers* (Toronto: McGraw-Hill Ryerson Limited, 1993)

H. Shaw, *McGraw-Hill Handbook of English* (Toronto: McGraw-Hill Ryerson Limited, 1985)

W. Strunk, Jr. and E.B. White, *The Elements of Style* (Toronto: Macmillan of Canada, 1972)

Trent University Press, *Thinking It Through,* 2nd edition (Peterborough: Trent University Press, 1987)

F. Watkins and W. Dillingham, *The Practical English Handbook* (Boston: Houghton Mifflin, 1982)

GUIDE TO THEMES AND TOPICS

Although this text is not organized thematically, teachers and students may wish to pursue certain threads that are developed in more than one essay or unit. This list outlines *some* of these interconnecting ideas (with corresponding page numbers shown at right).

The Craft of Writing

	All of Unit 1
Ciardi	Robert Frost: The Way to the Poem (p. 85)
Glover	Her life entire (p. 204)

CREDITS

reprinted by permission of Nuage Editions from *Between Two Worlds: The Canadian Immigrant Experience,* copyright © 1988 by Milly Charon; **p. 152** *The Globe and Mail;* **p. 156** Reprinted by permission of the author. Copyright held by the author; **p. 164** Reprinted by permission of Harold Ober Associates Incorporated. Copyright © 1954 by Langston Hughes. Copyright renewed 1982 by George Houston Bass; **p. 174** Reprinted from *Our Literary Heritage,* published by McGraw-Hill Ryerson Limited; **p. 179** Reprinted from *Maclean's* Magazine, July 6, 1992; **p. 182** Reprinted by permission of Michelle Patterson. Copyright held by the author; **p. 188** Robertson Davies is the author of ten novels, numerous plays and works of criticism. His novels have been translated into seventeen languages; **p. 195** "How Do You Know It's Good?" by Marya Mannes, copyright © Marya Mannes, 1962, 1990; **p. 201** Reprinted with permission — The Toronto Star Syndicate; **p. 204** Reprinted by permission of the author; **p. 212** *The Globe and Mail;* **p. 218** Reprinted from *The Globe and Mail* by permission of the author; **p. 223** Reprinted courtesy of Professor Sandford Borins. Sandford Borins teaches public management at the University of Toronto. His most recent book is *Political Management in Canada,* co-authored with the Honourable Allan Blakeney, and published by McGraw-Hill Ryerson Limited in November 1992; **p. 225** John Riley for "Why dogs are the cat's pajamas" published by *The Globe and Mail,* February 25, 1992. © 1992, John Riley; **p. 227** Reprinted by permission of James Taylor; **p. 229** *The Globe and Mail;* **p. 231** This article was originally published in *Mademoiselle.* Reprinted by permission of Georges Borchardt, Inc. on behalf of the author. Copyright © 1992 by Barbara Grizzuti Harrison; **p. 235** Copyright 1985 Time Inc. Reprinted by permission; **p. 251** Copyright © 1974 by Ursula K. Le Guin; first appeared in *PNLA Quarterly.* Reprinted by permission of the author and the author's agent, Virginia Kidd; **p. 256** Copyright © 1963 by Martin Luther King, Jr. Reprinted by permission of Joan Daves Agency; **p. 260** Johnny Lombardi, President and C.E.O. CHIN Radio/TV International; **p. 266** Federation of Women Teachers' Associations of Ontario, *FWTAO Newsletter,* December 1990/January 1991. By Mary Labatt, editor of the *FWTAO Newsletter;* **p. 281** Reprinted by permission of the author. John Doe is the pseudonym of a student. Copyright held by the author; **p. 283** Copyright © 1927 by Bronislaw Malinowski. Reprinted by permission of John Hawkins & Associates, Inc.; **p. 287** Reprinted by permission of Sarah Neville. Copyright held